JAWAHARLAL NEHRU

A Biography

VOLUME TWO
1947–1956

Sarvepalli Gopal

JAWAHARLAL NEHRU

A Biography

VOLUME TWO
1947-1956

HARVARD UNIVERSITY PRESS
CAMBRIDGE, MASSACHUSETTS
1979

LIBRARY OF CONGRESS CATALOGING IN PUBLICATION DATA

GOPAL, SARVEPALLI.

JAWAHARLAL NEHRU: A BIOGRAPHY

INCLUDES BIBLIOGRAPHIES AND INDEXES.

CONTENTS: V.I. 1889–1947. V. 2. 1947–1956.

I. NEHRU, JAWAHARLAL, 1889–1964. 2. INDIA—POLITICS

AND GOVERNMENT—20TH CENTURY. 3. PRIME MINISTERS—

INDIA—BIOGRAPHY.

DS481.N35G66 1976   954.04′092′4 [B]   75-33411

ISBN 0–674–47310–8 (V. I)

ISBN 0–674–47311–6 (V. 2)

PRINTED IN GREAT BRITAIN

Preface

This second volume of the biography of Jawaharlal Nehru covers the first nine years of the prime ministership, from August 1947 to November 1956. I have chosen the latter date as a convenient point at which to end this volume not only because, chronologically, it falls approximately half-way in Nehru's term of office, but also because, in domestic affairs, economic planning, foreign policy and almost every other sphere of his public activity it marks, curiously, the end of one phase and the beginning of a second, and more sombre, period.

As in the first volume, this is more than the personal story of an individual. The analysis, of course, throughout takes as its starting-point the hopes and efforts of the Prime Minister. More is said about matters in which Nehru was keenly interested, while those problems in which his involvement or responsibility was marginal have received correspondingly less attention. But the book spreads out to become, in a sense, the history of the first years of free India.

I am grateful to Shrimati Indira Gandhi for access to the private papers of Jawaharlal Nehru for the period after 1947. All letters and other documents to which no references are given are from these papers. The only official records which I have been able to consult are some files of the Prime Minister's secretariat.

Mr Christopher Hill most kindly read the manuscript and made many suggestions for its improvement. I have been sustained, during the making of this book, by the support of my colleagues at the Centre for Historical Studies in the Jawaharlal Nehru University.

Preface

Contents

Abbreviations

AICC	All-India Congress Committee
B.B.C.	British Broadcasting Corporation
C.P.I.	Communist Party of India
MEDO	Middle East Defence Organization
N.A.I.	National Archives of India
NATO	North Atlantic Treaty Organization
N.M.M.L.	Nehru Memorial Museum and Library
R.S.S.	Rashtriya Swayamsevak Sangh
SEATO	South East Asian Treaty Organization
U.P.	United Provinces, later Uttar Pradesh
U.P.P.C.C.	Uttar Pradesh Provincial Congress Committee

Illustrations

Picture credits

The author and publishers would like to thank the following for
permission to reproduce copyright material in the illustrations:

Central Press Photos Ltd: Plate 1
Jawaharlal Nehru Memorial Fund: Plates 2-12, 14-29; illustrations in the
   text on pp. 237 and 314
R. K. Laxman: cartoon reproduced on p. 163
Cartoon by David Low by arrangement with the Trustees and the London
Evening Standard: reproduced on p. 172
Radio Times Hulton Picture Library: Plate 13
K. Shankar Pillai (Shankar): cartoon reproduced on p. 160

1

Sad Morning

The mood of elation evoked by the achievement of freedom was wiped out almost within hours. The immediate developments in India and Pakistan set a dazzling cast of characters in a context of primitive action and of the mingled frenzy of violence, idealism, triumph, passion and intrigue. The presence of Gandhi in Bengal helped to cool tempers in that area, but a 'human earthquake'[1] engulfed the divided Punjab. As early as March 1947 communal rioting in what was to be West Pakistan had led to migrations of non-Muslims; and the collapse of the non-League government and the administration of the province by officials had added to communal tensions. Yet no one, neither the Government of India nor the leaders of the Congress and the League, had paid much attention to this gathering potential of tragedy. So when, on 14 August, trouble started on a large scale almost simultaneously in Lahore and Amritsar, large towns lying just within the new border on either side, and spread out to West and East Punjab and even to Delhi, the reaction was one of surprise and helplessness. In the following weeks, a great number of people were killed,[2] and there were migrations, with attendant murders and abductions, of at least five to six millions each way. The boundary force of about 23,000 men not only proved inadequate to control the situation but was itself weakening in morale, and some of its members were believed to have participated in these massacres on both sides.[3] 'People have lost their reason completely and are behaving worse than brutes. There is madness about in its worst form.'[4]

This was both a psychological and an administrative crisis. All calculations had gone wrong. Partition, which had been accepted by the

[1] Nehru's speech at Lahore, 8 December, *Hindustan Times*, 9 December 1947.

[2] Estimates vary. Moon (with whom Mountbatten agrees) reckoned the figure to be about 200,000 (*Divide and Quit*, London, 1961, p. 283); G. D. Khosla believed that it was about 400 to 500,000 (*Stern Reckoning*, Delhi n.d., p. 299); Ian Stephens places the figure at 500,000 (*Pakistan*, London, 1963, p. 80) and M. Edwardes at 600,000 (*Last Years of British India*, London, 1963, p. 223).

[3] R. Jeffrey, 'The Punjab Boundary Force and the Problem of Order, August 1947', *Modern Asian Studies* (1974), pp. 491-520; Kirpal Singh, *The Partition of the Punjab* (Patiala, 1972), p. 108.

[4] Nehru to Lady Ismay, 4 September 1947.

Congress as a drastic way out of communal hatred, had only multiplied it; and as Nehru acknowledged, had the leaders of the Congress anticipated this, they might well have preferred to keep India united and distraught. Nehru made no secret of his discomfiture at events, and was honest enough to acknowledge his own errors of judgment.

> Late in 1946, I was about to leave India, where I had been based for quite a long time, and I went to see Nehru to say goodbye and also for a last interview . . . We — mostly Nehru — talked for over two hours. As I was going, he walked with me to the door, put a gentle hand on my arm and said: 'Marcuse, there are three things I want you to remember. One, India will never be a Dominion. Two, there will never be a Pakistan. Three, when the British go, there will be no more communal trouble in India.'
>
> I was back in Delhi after 15 August 1947 . . . I hadn't the heart, of course, to remind Nehru of his three predictions. At the same time, I couldn't put them out of my mind and, as I asked the usual questions, I felt acutely embarrassed. Not he, though. For, after a while, he gave me one of his charming smiles and abruptly said: 'You remember, Marcuse, what I told you? No Dominion, No Pakistan, No . . .'
>
> He broke off there and we were both silent for several seconds. You could have heard a fly fly, as the French say. And then he added, 'Wasn't I wrong?'
>
> There was, I thought, more than a touch of greatness there.[5]

The first news of the murders and atrocities in West Punjab left Nehru numb. 'I feel peculiarly helpless. In action one can always overcome this feeling whatever the result of the action might be. But as I cannot take immediate action that can have any effect, the burden becomes heavy.' But he pulled himself together.

> I cannot and do not wish to shed my responsibility for my people. If I cannot discharge that responsibility effectively, then I begin to doubt whether I have any business to be where I am. And even if I don't doubt it myself, other people certainly will. I am not an escapist or quitter and it is not from that point of view that I am writing. The mere fact that the situation is difficult is a challenge which must be accepted and I certainly accept it.[6]

There were only two ways: to go under or overcome, 'and we are not going under.'[7] With the reaction in India to the atrocities in Pakistan, Nehru's main task was to harry his own people back to sanity.

[5] See article by Jacques Marcuse in Richard Hughes, *Foreign Devil* (London, 1972), pp. 289-92.

[6] Nehru to Mountbatten, 27 August 1947.

[7] Nehru's remark to Sri Prakasa at Jullundur, September 1947. See Sri Prakasa's article in *Nehru Abhinandan Granth* (Delhi, 1949), p. 225.

Life here continues to be nightmarish. Everything seems to have gone awry although superficially we seem to be improving. But our foundations have been shaken and all our standards seem to have disappeared. Only a certain pride and a sense of duty keeps one going . . . We have to build anew and that building must begin with the foundations at home. If the roots dry up, how long will the leaves and flowers continue?[8]

Nothing was to be gained by delving for the initial responsibility; horror had, whatever its origin, gained such momentum that it was futile to suggest at this stage that one side was worse than the other. Nehru moved tirelessly round Delhi, extending the protection of his personal interest to frightened Muslim families, and frequently jumped into mobs of fanatic rioters to scold and even to smite in order to quell. But more important than the maintenance of the public peace was the necessity to exorcize the madness, born of fear, which had seized the Indian people. Nehru addressed meetings throughout northern India and broadcast repeatedly that they should build an India where no citizen felt insecure because of his religion. Secularism, always a principle of the Congress, was now rendered more urgent by the compulsion of events. Everyone seemed to be thinking in terms of retaliation, but the Government would not adopt that as a policy.[9] If the people of India had not retaliated, the Indian army, instead of being occupied with subduing mob violence and guarding hospitals in India itself, could have marched into Pakistan for the protection of the minorities there. Butchering Muslims was not just a matter of personal degradation and communal fanaticism; it destroyed the dignity of India and the prestige of her government, betrayed the philosophy of Gandhi which had inspired the struggle for freedom, and threatened democracy and liberty by strengthening the forces of fascism. 'The battle of our political freedom is fought and won. But another battle, no less important than what we have won, still faces us. It is a battle with no outside enemy . . . It is a battle with our own selves.'[10]

In performing this duty, his first as the leader of a free people, Nehru could not rely on the unqualified support of his Cabinet. Some of the members, such as Azad, John Matthai, Kidwai and Amrit Kaur, were with him; but they carried little influence with the masses. The old stalwarts of the Congress, however, such as Patel and Rajendra Prasad, with the backing of the leader of the Hindu Mahasabha, Syama Prasad Mookerjee, believed not so much in a theocratic state as in a state which symbolized the interests of the Hindu majority. Patel assumed that Muslim officials, even if

[8] Nehru to K. P. S. Menon, 12 October 1947.

[9] Speech on 29 November 1947, Constituent Assembly (Legislative) Debates 1947, Vol. II, pp. 917-22.

[10] Speech at Allahabad, 14 December, *National Herald*, 16 December 1947.

they had opted for India, were bound to be disloyal and should be dismissed; and to him the Muslims in India were hostages to be held as security for the fair treatment of Hindus in Pakistan. He, therefore, resisted Nehru's efforts to reserve certain residential areas in Delhi for Muslims and to employ Muslims to deal with Muslim refugees. Even more non-secular in outlook than Patel was Rajendra Prasad, the meek follower of Gandhi but untouched in any real sense by the spirit of Gandhi's teachings. One-sided action, he wrote to his Prime Minister, could not bring the desired results but would in fact lead to most undesirable and unexpected consequences. There was no use in bringing in the army to protect the Muslim citizens of Delhi if the Hindus and Sikhs were expelled from the cities of Pakistan. 'Our action today is driving the people away from us.' Nehru's exhortations to his countrymen to behave in a civilized manner only seemed to Prasad to convince world opinion of India's guilt.[11]

Nehru, therefore, had not merely to goad the rioters into reason; he had also to persuade the most influential of his colleagues. It was not, he reminded them, what he said but what foreigners reported that had brought India's name into the mud and made him ashamed even to meet members of the diplomatic corps.

These events taken as a whole have shown a picture of all Muslims, irrespective of their position or standing or residence, being hunted down and killed wherever possible. Every Ambassador's house has been visited by gangs in search of Muslim servants . . . there is a limit to killing and brutality and that limit has been passed during these days in north India. A people who indulge in this kind of thing not only brutalize themselves but poison the environment . . . The future appears to be dark not so much because 50,000 or 100,000 people have been murdered, but because of the mentality that has accom-panied this and that perhaps might continue. I quite realize that I am out of tune with this environment and not a fit representative of it. Yet I am entirely convinced that if we surrender to this mentality, then indeed we are doomed as a nation.

There was a time when under Bapu's guidance and insistence we used to condemn terroristic acts even when by normal standards they might have been justified in the cause of national freedom. Now open murder committed in the most brutal way stalks everywhere and we hesitate to say much about it lest we may lose our hold on the people. I must confess that I have no stomach for this leadership. Unless we keep to some standards, freedom has little meaning, and certainly India will not become the great nation we have dreamt of for so long . . . We have faced and are facing the gravest crisis that any

[11] Rajendra Prasad to Nehru, 17 September 1947.

Government can have to face, more especially a new Government. The consequences of each step that we might take are bound to be far-reaching. The world is watching us also and the world's opinion counts. But above all we are watching ourselves and if we fail in our own estimation, who will rescue us?[12]

Gandhi approved of this letter; and in fact Nehru, functioning in the eye of the storm as a man inspired,[13] drew close once again to Gandhi and relied more heavily upon him than he had done in the two years prior to the transfer of power.

How many of you realize what it has meant to India to have the presence of Mahatma Gandhi these months? We all know of his magnificent services to India and to freedom during the past half-century and more. But no service could have been greater than what he has performed during the past four months when in a dissolving world he has been like a rock of purpose and a lighthouse of truth, and his firm low voice has risen above the clamours of the multitude pointing out the path of rightful endeavour.[14]

Gandhi, back in Delhi on 7 September, supported Nehru's efforts to protect the minorities, shun vengeance, abide by the old ideals and resist the narrow outlook that appeared to be gaining strength at every level of Indian opinion. But Gandhi could lend no power to the Prime Minister in his role as head of the administration; and in this sphere Nehru recruited the services of Mountbatten, even though he was a constitutional head of state. Mountbatten's sharing of authority in handling the disintegrating situation was common knowledge even at the time. Indeed, Mountbatten was present at the press conference when Nehru announced that the emergency committee of the Cabinet, which was attended by the heads of departments concerned, was being presided over by Mountbatten.[15] This involvement of Mountbatten in the government of the country has enabled him, in recent years after the death of Nehru, to make extravagant claims

[12] Nehru to Rajendra Prasad, 19 September 1947; see also report of his speech at a public meeting in Delhi 30 September, *The Hindu*, 1 October 1947.
[13] ' . . . to see Nehru at close range during this ordeal is an inspiring experience. He vindicates one's faith in the humanist and the civilised intellect. Almost alone in the turmoil of communalism, with all its variations, from individual intrigue to mass madness, he speaks with the voice of reason and clarity. The negotiations for the transfer of power between March and August did not seem to me to evoke his full powers. A certain moodiness and outbursts of exasperation were the visible signs of overstrain; but now somehow he has renewed himself, and in this deeper crisis he is shown at his full stature — passionate and courageous, yet objective and serene; one of the enlightened elect of our time.' A. Campbell-Johnson's diary entry, 13 September 1947, *Mission with Mountbatten* (London, 1951), p. 189.
[14] Address to the Allahabad University jubilee convocation, 13 December, *National Herald*, 14 December 1947.
[15] The *Statesman*, 14 September 1947.

for his own role.[16] 'From March 1947 to April 1948 I gave him [Nehru] a course in administration, and he had enough confidence in me and liking for me to let me do it.'[17] But we need not go further than what has been said, on the basis of Mountbatten's papers, that he had been asked to assist in governing.[18]

The problem of administration extended rapidly from preventing murders and organizing refugee camps and hospitals to the broader issue of relations with the new state of Pakistan. Nehru believed that the division of India was a short-term political solution which could not override cultural affinities and economic compulsions. So the Government of India disavowed any intention of harming Pakistan or treating it as an enemy and expressed their continuing hope that, when the current turmoil ended, the two states might unite by the free will of their peoples.[19] But events did not help to restore this goodwill and balance. Just as the fury in the two Punjabs was beginning to abate, a crisis emerged in Kashmir. On the eve of the transfer of power, the Maharaja's Government, unable to decide between accession to India or to Pakistan, proposed to sign standstill agreements with both countries. The Government of Pakistan agreed, but from the Government of India there was no response, because the Maharaja's proposal reached them only long after the trouble started.[20] In fact, the official Indian attitude was indifference as to the Maharaja's decision. Though Nehru was aware that Pakistan was seeking to force events[21] and believed that the Pakistan Government intended to raise capital in the United States in return for leases and special privileges in Kashmir, his advice to the Kashmir authorities was merely to invite Sheikh Abdullah, who had been released by the end of September, to form a provisional government and to announce fresh elections; nothing should be done about accession until then.[22] Abdullah too campaigned for democratic rights and did not publicly concern himself with accession.

More than Kashmir, the Government of India were at this time concerned with Junagadh, a small State with dispersed territory on the west coast. On 15 August 1947 its Muslim ruler, despite the fact that over

[16] Mountbatten's version is that Nehru and Patel jointly appealed to him to handle the situation for them, and that he agreed, provided his active role was kept secret for the time being and, while he would go through the motions of consulting his ministers, in fact what he decided would be final. These conditions were accepted. Interview with the author, 28 May 1970. Since then, Mountbatten has asserted that Nehru and Patel asked him, in so many words, to take over the country. Interview reported in the *Listener*, 30 October 1975.

[17] Mountbatten's interview with the author, 28 May 1970.

[18] H. V. Hodson, *The Great Divide* (London, 1969), p. 413.

[19] See Nehru's statement to the press 16 September, *Times of India*, 17 September 1947.

[20] It has been said (with what justification it is difficult to be sure) that the letter to the Government of India was held up in Lahore, the Kashmir postal system having been within the Punjab circle before partition.

[21] See his letter to Patel, 27 September 1947, *Sardar Patel's Correspondence*, Vol. 1 (Ahmedabad, 1971), p. 45.

[22] Nehru to M. C. Mahajan, Prime Minister of Kashmir, 21 October 1947.

80 per cent of the population was of a different religion, declared the accession of his State to Pakistan. What happened to Junagadh would be important, as both the Governments of India and Pakistan recognized, not only in itself but because it would serve as a precedent in the larger issues, which were still pending, of Kashmir and Hyderabad. Mountbatten, though Governor-General of India alone and not of both dominions, inhibited his Government's options. Concerned about his own position, he threw his weight against military action.[23] The three British officers who commanded India's armed services followed suit; and when the Government of India objected to their assumption of political authority Mountbatten took on the chairmanship of the Defence Committee of the Indian Cabinet and thus ensured that no military decision was taken without his knowledge. His suggestion of arbitration in the case of two bits of territory whose incorporation in Junagadh State was doubtful was vetoed by Patel.[24] But Mountbatten was more successful in persuading Nehru to rule out war and commit himself to a plebiscite in Junagadh.

> I emphasized the importance of Pandit Nehru's statement to Mr Liaqat Ali Khan, and assured him that the Government of India would abide by it, and that Pandit Nehru would agree that this policy would apply to any other State, since India would never be a party to trying to force a State to join their Dominion against the wishes of the majority of the people. Pandit Nehru nodded his head sadly. Mr Liaqat Ali Khan's eyes sparkled. There is no doubt that both of them were thinking of Kashmir.[25]

Pakistan, therefore, had gained considerable vantage on the question of Kashmir even before the crisis broke. On the night of 24 October, news reached Delhi that well-organized tribesmen had entered Kashmir from Pakistan and were marching on Srinagar. The Defence Committee, meeting the next morning, decided to send arms to the Kashmir Government. Mountbatten was in favour of at least a temporary accession to India, but neither Nehru nor Patel attached any importance to this. Nehru was more concerned that the Maharaja should associate Abdullah with the resistance.[26] The next day, when the Prime Minister of Kashmir saw Nehru and requested that Indian troops be flown into Kashmir, Nehru declined and was only persuaded by Patel and Abdullah to agree.[27] Clearly, therefore, whatever Nehru's romantic attachment to the mountains of

[23] See his report to the King cited in Hodson, op. cit., pp. 430-1.
[24] Mountbatten to Patel, 29 September, and Patel's reply, 1 October 1947, *Sardar Patel's Correspondence* Vol. 1, pp. 388-9.
[25] Mountbatten's report to the King, Hodson, op. cit., p. 436.
[26] Hodson, op. cit., pp. 449-50.
[27] M. C. Mahajan, *Looking Back* (Bombay, 1963), pp. 151-2.

Kashmir, it did not influence his policy, and the decisions on Kashmir were not, as has been frequently suggested, being taken by him alone in an overwhelming mood of sentiment.

At the meeting of the Defence Committee on 26 October, Mountbatten and the Chiefs of Staff advised against flying troops to Kashmir; but when Mountbatten saw that his ministers were determined to do so, he gave in. He was wise enough to discern that on this issue Nehru and the Cabinet might have ignored his views, especially as Gandhi felt as strongly as they did and terminated what Nehru later termed 'a difficulty of the spirit'[28] by telling Nehru that there could be no peace by submission to evil in Kashmir. But Mountbatten succeeded in persuading Nehru and Patel to link military assistance to immediate accession and the offer of a plebiscite after law and order had been restored. The accession of Kashmir was accepted and Indian troops were flown out on the morning of 27 October, just in time to prevent the sack of Srinagar and to thwart what was believed to be the plan of Pakistan to proclaim accession after the city had been captured so that Jinnah could make a triumphal entry.[29]

Once these decisions had been taken, for Nehru the main task was to drive out the raiders.

> We have taken on a tough job. But I am dead sure that we shall pull through. Ever since the decision was taken yesterday and I heard today that our troops had reached Srinagar I have felt much lighter in heart. We have taken the plunge and we shall swim across to the other shore. It has become a test of our future.[30]

To be fighting side by side with the people of Kashmir against fanatic hordes was a heartening experience which set aside for the moment the memories of communal strife and partition; and the fact that Hindu communal elements in India were opposed to the accession of Kashmir because it had a Muslim majority added to the thrill of the adventure.

> I trust in this defence we shall give a demonstration to all India and to the world how we can function unitedly and in a non-communal way in Kashmir. In this way this terrible crisis in Kashmir may well lead to a healing of the deep wounds which India has suffered in recent months.[31]

Faced with the presence of Indian troops in Kashmir, Jinnah, as was

[28] Speech in Parliament, 8 March 1949, Constituent Assembly of India (Legislative) Debates, 1949, Vol. II, Part II, pp. 1225-36.
[29] Campbell-Johnson, op. cit., p. 224; Hodson, op. cit., pp. 452-4; Nehru to Sir T. B. Sapru, 1 November 1947.
[30] Nehru to Sheikh Abdullah, 27 October 1947.
[31] Nehru to the Maharaja of Kashmir, 27 October 1947.

usual with him, secured concessions by threatening the British with the possibility of a full-scale war with India. This time it was Ismay and Auchinleck who were subjected to this blackmail, and they persuaded Mountbatten that he should conduct Nehru to Lahore for talks. Nehru agreed to go on what Patel regarded as a mission of appeasement; but an official statement issued by Pakistan accusing India of 'fraud and violence' in Kashmir caused Nehru to cancel his visit. So Mountbatten went alone to hear Jinnah denounce India, accept implicit responsibility for the tribal raiders by offering to 'call the whole thing off' if India agreed to withdraw her troops, and reject a plebiscite conducted by the United Nations – a proposal to which Nehru had already been won over by Mountbatten.[32] Nothing material came of this meeting, and the fighting in Kashmir continued. Nehru turned down Abdullah's suggestion that an ultimatum be given to Pakistan and war declared at the end of it;[33] but though he was not willing to launch into an all-out war with Pakistan, there was no slackening in the efforts to clear Kashmir of the invaders. Mountbatten still rather naïvely believed that Nehru and Liaqat Ali Khan could patch up a settlement and assiduously sought to leave them alone in a room; he could never see that the differences were too deep and the conflict of interests too great for any personal negotiations. The only result was interminable talk, with both sides holding to their positions and Nehru now and then losing his temper and making such statements as that he would 'throw up his prime ministership and take a rifle himself, and lead the men of India against the invasion.'[34]

Gandhi, more realistic than Mountbatten, believed that a solution could be imposed by the British if they took a hard line;[35] but Attlee was unwilling to do this, and paid no heed to Mountbatten's prompting that he fly out and meet Nehru and Liaqat Ali Khan. Nehru had no thought of compromise. Kashmir had become to him a symbol of the basic conflict in India and on the decision there 'one might almost say, depends not only the future of Kashmir but the future of Pakistan and to a considerable extent the future in India. Thus we are playing for much higher stakes than might appear on the surface.'[36] However, Mountbatten succeeded in persuading him to refer the Kashmir problem to the United Nations by arguing that the only alternative was a full-scale war. Mountbatten would have preferred a general reference to the United Nations to stop the fighting and conduct a plebiscite; but the Government of India would do no more than make a specific reference with regard to Pakistan's aggression. Though India was committed to allow the people of Kashmir to decide their own

[32] See Nehru to M. C. Mahajan, 31 October 1947.
[33] Nehru to Sheikh Abdullah, 4 November 1947.
[34] Cited by Mountbatten, Hodson, op. cit., p. 465.
[35] See Ismay's record of his interview with Gandhi, 20 November 1947, R. Wingate, *Lord Ismay* (London, 1970), p. 174.
[36] Nehru to Sheikh Abdullah, 3 December 1947.

future, Nehru was unwilling now to tie this up with the reference to the United Nations. Nehru also made this clear to Liaqat Ali Khan when they met on 21 December. He added that if Pakistan continued its aggression, India might have to extend the minor war, which it had been waging so far, in order to strike at the base of operations, which was in Pakistan, as well as at the lines of communications. Liaqat Ali Khan said he would welcome the intervention of the United Nations, but did not raise two issues which had dominated so much of the earlier discussions, the internal administration of Kashmir and the Indian troops that might be left in Kashmir after the fighting was over. When Mountbatten suggested that Liaqat Ali Khan might be shown the draft of India's reference to the United Nations, Nehru refused; and Liaqat Ali Khan, who was in a strangely subdued mood, said he did not think it necessary to see the draft.[37]

So the limited reference was made to the United Nations. Patel had not been in favour even of this;[38] and Gandhi too, whom Nehru consulted, consented to it with some reluctance. He saw the draft and revised it to remove the suggestion of an independent Kashmir as a possible alternative to accession to either State. It was unfortunate — and Nehru was later deeply to regret it — that Mountbatten, who had no clear understanding of international affairs, had succeeded in persuading Nehru to bring the United Nations into the picture. Having achieved this, he now set himself to prevent any extension of the war. Nehru, however, was determined to 'see this Kashmir business through. We do not believe in leaving things half-done.'[39] He insisted to Mountbatten, even after the decision to refer the matter to the United Nations had been taken, that expulsion of the raiders was still the first priority:

> on no account would we submit to this barbarity whatever the cost . . . I am convinced that any surrender on our part to this kind of aggression would lead to continuing aggression elsewhere, and whether we want it or not war would become inevitable between India and Pakistan. We are dealing with a State carrying on an informal war. The present objective is Kashmir. The next declared objective is Patiala, East Punjab, and Delhi . . . we must not carry on our own operations in a weak defensive way which can produce no effective impression on the enemy. We have refrained from crossing into Pakistani territory because of our desire to avoid complications leading to open war. Thereby we have increased our own peril and not brought peace any nearer . . . To surrender to this invasion will involve a complete degradation of India which I could not possibly

[37] Nehru's note on conversations with Mountbatten and Liaqat Ali Khan, 21 December 1947.
[38] See his letter to Arthur Henderson, 3 July 1948, *Sardar Patel's Correspondence*, Vol. 6 (Ahmedabad, 1973), pp. 386-7.
[39] Speech at Jammu, 6 December, *Statesman*, 7 December 1947.

tolerate . . . There is an imminent danger of an invasion of India
proper. Can we afford to sit and look on? We would deserve to be
sacked immediately. We have taken enough risks already, we dare not
take any more . . .[40]

The reference to the United Nations of Pakistan's aggression was,
therefore, expressly coupled with full military preparations to move the
war, if necessary, into Pakistan. The British Government claimed to fear
that India would attack Pakistan simultaneously with the filing of the
complaint with the Security Council.[41] But, in fact, Mountbatten made sure
that Nehru would permit no such action not merely by arguing that the
matter had become *sub judice* but also by threatening that, in any such
contingency, he would vacate the governor-generalship.[42] It was agreed
that the Defence Committee need not consider for the time being the
possibility of Indian troops entering Pakistan. No more was done than to
keep a plan ready in case the defence of India should require an attack on
bases in Pakistan.[43]

By the reference to the Security Council India stood to suffer in every
way. To the Indian request on 31 December 1947 that Pakistan be directed
not to participate or assist in any way in the invasion of Kashmir, Pakistan
replied not only with a denial but with general allegations against India of
hostility to Pakistan, 'genocide' against Muslims and securing the accession
of Kashmir by fraud and violence. The Security Council, under the
guidance of the British delegate, Philip Noel-Baker, ignored the specific
complaint of India and made clear its preference for Pakistan. It was
assumed that India and Pakistan had an equal interest in Kashmir and
therefore whatever was done should seem fair to the Government of
Pakistan and the tribesmen as well as to the Government of India. Further,
in virtual acceptance of Pakistan's general charges against India and
ignoring the fact that the United Nations had been approached on a limited
issue, the 'Kashmir question' was replaced on the agenda by the 'India-
Pakistan question'.

In Kashmir itself, while India was inhibited from a full-scale effort to
drive out the invaders, there was no abatement in Pakistan's offensive. It
was in this context that the Indian Cabinet decided in January 1948 to
withhold payment of Rs 55 crores (about £ 40 million), due to Pakistan as
part of the assets of partition, until a settlement had been reached in
Kashmir, for it was clear to them that this amount would be used for the
purchase of arms to sustain the fighting against India. Patel took the lead in

[40] Nehru to Mountbatten, 26 December 1947.
[41] See report of United States chargé d'affaires in London, 29 December 1947. *Foreign Relations of the
United States 1947*, Vol. 3 (Washington, 1972), p. 185.
[42] Campbell-Johnson, op. cit., p. 259.
[43] Nehru to Baldev Singh, 24 January 1948.

this matter, — 'not a pie' he had said at the Cabinet meeting[44] — but Nehru had been in full agreement. Yet Mountbatten, acting unconstitutionally, criticized the decision of his Cabinet when Gandhi raised the matter and described it as both unstatesmanlike and unwise and the 'first dishonourable act' of the free Government of India.[45] On Kashmir, Gandhi had no doubt that the troops of Pakistan would have to be driven out. He would not accept the premise that Muslims should, by the mere fact of their religion, be regarded as not Indian. When, at what turned out to be their last interview, Mountbatten spoke of partition of the state as a possible compromise, he and Gandhi parted, in Mountbatten's naval phrase, 'brass rags'.[46] But the withholding of payment of money to which the Government of India were committed appeared to Gandhi to be on a different footing. This was one of the chief causes which impelled Gandhi to commence, on 13 January, a fast to quicken the conscience of the Indian people and improve relations between Hindus and Muslims. So the Cabinet reopened the question and, while convinced that their decision had been right on merits, decided to make immediate payment if Gandhi wished it. When all the facts were placed before Gandhi he advised full payment and the Cabinet announced a reversal of their decision.

The fast itself, which lasted five days, seemed to Nehru to have had generally a good effect even in Pakistan. He himself had fasted in sympathy for one or two days, eliciting from Gandhi, when he heard of it, affectionate concern. 'Give up your fast . . . May you live long and continue to be the jewel of India.'[47] But the good effect wore out soon enough in both countries, the evil of religious hatred being too deep-set to be cured easily, and on the evening of 30 January 1948 Gandhi was assassinated. Death in the cause of human harmony was the perfect end to Gandhi's life, the last line of the sonnet. He himself would have seen it as the final accomplishment. As long back as 1926, when informed that Swami Shradhanand had been murdered by a religious fanatic, Gandhi had remarked, 'Unbearable as it is, my heart refuses to grieve; it rather prays that all of us may be granted such a death.'[48] In Delhi, a few weeks before his own death, he had asked a crowd of refugees from Pakistan: 'Which is better — to die for the sake of one's faith with the name of God on one's lips, or to die a lingering death of sickness, paralysis or old age? I for one would infinitely prefer the former.'[49] As Nehru observed in one of his superb flights of English prose,

[44] C. D. Deshmukh's interview with the author, 21 January 1969.

[45] Campbell-Johnson, op. cit., p. 265; Pyarelal, *Mahatma Gandhi: The Last Phase*, Vol. 2 (Ahmedabad, 1958), p. 700.

[46] Kingsley Martin's oral testimony, N.M.M.L.

[47] J. Nehru, *A Bunch of Old Letters* (Bombay, 1958), p. 499. Original in Hindi. The phrase 'jewel of India' is a reference to the name Jawahar, which means jewel.

[48] Speech at the AICC, 24 December 1926, *Collected Works of Mahatma Gandhi*, Vol. 32 (New Delhi, 1969), p. 452.

[49] Pyarelal, op. cit., p. 449.

Gandhi had unconsciously become the perfect artist in the art of living, and even in his death there was a complete artistry.

As he grew older his body seemed to be just a vehicle for the mighty spirit within him. Almost one forgot the body as one listened to him or looked at him, and so where he sat became a temple and where he trod was hallowed ground . . . Why, then, should we grieve for him? Our memories of him will be of the Master, whose step was light to the end, whose smile was infectious and whose eyes were full of laughter. We shall associate no failing powers with him of body or mind. He lived and he died at the top of his strength and powers, leaving a picture in our minds and in the mind of the age that we live in that can never fade away.[50]

This was written a fortnight after Gandhi's death; but Nehru's immediate reaction was almost identical. The personal blow was, of course, overwhelming. Rushing to Birla House on hearing the news, he 'bent his head down and began to sob like a child.'[51] But within a few hours of the murder, pushed by Mountbatten in front of the microphone, his voice was again contained, and he mingled his heavy sense of loss with thanksgiving and a fresh call to duty.

Friends and comrades, the light has gone out of our lives and there is darkness everywhere . . . The light has gone out, I said, and yet I was wrong. For the light that shone in this country was no ordinary light . . . that light represented something more than the immediate present, it represented the living, the eternal truths, reminding us of the right path, drawing us from error, taking this ancient country to freedom . . . A great disaster is a symbol to us to remember all the big things of life and forget the small things of which we have thought too much. In his death he has reminded us of the big things of life, the living truth, and if we remember that, then it will be well with India . . .[52]

[50] *Harijan*, 15 February 1948.
[51] D. G. Tendulkar, *Mahatma*, Vol. 8 (Bombay revised edition, 1963), p. 288. Nehru approved this sentence, letter to Tendulkar, 12 October 1952.
[52] Broadcast, 30 January 1948. *Speeches*, Vol. 1, 1946-49 (New Delhi, 1949), pp. 42-4.

2

Kashmir and Hyderabad

The witness of Gandhi and his own commitment to what he regarded as the essential values held Nehru together in these first months of shock. Gandhi's last efforts and the circumstances of his death reinforced Nehru's awareness of Gandhi's superhuman eminence. He was not ashamed to admit that, rationalist as he was, he bowed his head every time he passed the scene of the crime.[1] Daily, when confronted with a problem, his first thought was to run up to Gandhi for advice, and only then to remember that now he stood alone. There was the solace of Lady Mountbatten, gentle and companionable, seeking to brush away the worry and the sorrow. But it was not easy to carry on and often it seemed to Nehru that he was condemned to walk in darkness for the rest of his days.

> I do not myself see any peaceful or safe anchorage for my mind anywhere. I have to wander through life, pulled in various directions, often doubting as to what I should do and what I should avoid . . . the only satisfaction I have is in working. Perhaps that is mere escapism, for much of my work is undoubtedly trivial. Isn't life itself mostly trivial? We live for the high moments which seldom come and when they come they pass too soon.[2]

In these early months of 1948 there was in India as much tension and suspicion as sorrow in the air and Nehru was enclosed in a tight ring of security which he found irksome and unnatural. In matters of policy, too, on all sides Nehru encountered disillusion and bafflement. Developments in New York on Kashmir continued to be upsetting. Noel-Baker informed the Indian delegation that from his own sources he was satisfied that Pakistan had provided no assistance to the raiders.[3] This could only mean that the British High Commissioners in Delhi and Karachi and British officers serving in Pakistan had persuaded Noel-Baker to reject India's case

---

[1] Nehru to G. D. Birla, 22 May 1948.
[2] Nehru to Clare Booth Luce, 1 July 1948.
[3] N. G. Ayyangar's telegram to Nehru, 7 February 1948.

even without considering her delegation's arguments at New York. In fact, the British delegation took the view that the crisis in Kashmir had started with a massacre of Muslims instigated by the Maharaja, and sought to persuade the United States to insist on military policing of the state by Pakistan and refusal to recognize Abdullah's government.[4] The British attitude was generally regarded in India as a hangover from pre-independence days and a conversion of British support for the Muslim League into support of Pakistan, as well as a reflection of the desire of Britain and the United States to win back the support of the Islamic world, lost by their policy in Palestine.[5] Some of the propositions put forward by these countries in the Security Council seemed to Nehru monstrous, and rather than 'surrender either to the gangster tactics of Pakistan and the raiders or to the attempts at bullying by Britain and the United States', Nehru was willing to consider defiance of the United Nations[6] – the organization to which he had taken the initiative in appealing. Nehru felt deeply about this, especially as the decision to refer the case to the United Nations had been so much a personal one. Had he let his people down?

> The world seems a very dark, dismal and dreary place, full of people with wrong urges or no urge at all, living their lives trivially and without any significance . . . I feel overwhelmed, not so much by the great problems facing us but rather by the affection and comradeship of friends who expect so much from me. A sense of utter humility seizes me in the face of this faith and trust.[7]

In the same strain he wrote to Mountbatten that he contemplated resignation. 'I think I should tell you that, subject to developments, I might have to consider my position in Government. I have made statements and have given pledges to the people of Kashmir and I do not propose to go against them.'[8]

The hostility of Britain and the United States showed itself not only in the debates in the Security Council but also in the difficulty India experienced in securing arms and petrol. Nehru made it clear that India would react.

> I must say that prepared as I was for untoward happenings, I could not imagine that the Security Council could possibly behave in the trivial and partisan manner in which it functioned. These people are supposed to keep the world in order. It is not surprising that the world

[4] See Warren Austin's dispatches from New York to State Department, 8 and 16 January 1948, *Foreign Relations of the United States 1948* Vol. 5 Part I (Washington, 1975), pp. 275 and 283.
[5] To Krishna Menon, 20 February 1948.
[6] Ibid.
[7] To Zakir Hussain, 16 February 1948.
[8] To Mountbatten, 13 February 1948.

is going to pieces. The United States and Britain have played a dirty role, Britain probably being the chief actor behind the scenes. I have expressed myself strongly to Attlee about it and I propose to make it perfectly clear to the British Government what we think about it. The time for soft and meaningless talk has passed.[9]

No doubt Mountbatten informed Attlee that this would affect India's relations with Britain, and both Attlee and Cripps assured Nehru that the British representative at the United Nations would cease to be so partisan. Mountbatten's own characteristic suggestion was that Nehru should have a heart-to-heart talk with Liaqat Ali Khan; and this was repeated by Attlee. But any chance there might have been of a bilateral settlement was destroyed by the unexpected support Pakistan had received in the Security Council; and despite the assurance of the British Government, there was no real change in the British delegation's attitude. The Nationalist Chinese delegate introduced a resolution which the Indian Government accepted. The British Government promised Nehru that they would permit no material change in this; but their delegate suggested considerable alterations. The resolution as revised did not recognize the sovereignty of India over Kashmir, asked India to agree to a coalition government in Kashmir, toned down Pakistan's obligations to secure the withdrawal of her troops and the tribesmen and vested the plebiscite administrator, to be appointed by the United Nations, with powers which implied that India and Pakistan had equal status in Kashmir. Attlee then, to Nehru's astonishment, pressed him to accept the modified resolution.

I can only say I am amazed after all that has happened and the assurances that have been given to us. Quite apart from any differences of opinion, one has an uncomfortable feeling that an attempt has been made to lull us into a feeling of security when developments were taking place which were considered by us to be entirely objectionable.[10]

Nehru's reaction was to ignore the Security Council and to press ahead with quick and effective military action in Kashmir, while being generous on other matters such as the flow of the Indus canal waters to Pakistan.[11] Attention now centred on the Commission set up by the United Nations and to which India had considered nominating Belgium or Sweden but ultimately, because of her distrust of the Western bloc, had chosen Czechoslovakia. Mountbatten repeatedly hinted at the advantages of

[9] To Vijayalakshmi, 16 February 1948.
[10] To Mountbatten, 17 April 1948.
[11] Nehru to Baldev Singh, 16 and 22 April 1948; Nehru to G. C. Bhargava, Chief Minister of East Punjab, 28 April 1948.

partition, while Nehru was urged at private conferences to push out Sheikh
Abdullah for some time at least from the Kashmir administration. On the
latter point Nehru refused to yield. The Security Council then extended the
scope of the Commission to include Junagadh, 'genocide' and other matters
raised by Pakistan and irrelevant to Kashmir. This was a deliberate affront
to India, yet Nehru did not refuse to cooperate with the Commission; the
Government of India would state their objections before it and reiterate
their position on Kashmir.[12]

As soon as the Commission arrived in Pakistan in July, it was informed
by the Pakistan Government that three brigades of regular Pakistani troops
had been fighting in Kashmir since May. Mountbatten, who had laid down
office a few weeks earlier, was as full as ever of bouncing optimism, and
assured Nehru that with such evidence before it, the Commission would
come up with a reasonably favourable report which would enable the
United Nations to resolve the tangle in a way acceptable to India.[13] But to
Nehru the situation appeared fantastic and 'Gilbertian'. An undeclared war
was being waged between the two countries and British officers were
planning and carrying out military operations against India in what was
legally Indian territory. Such a situation could obviously not continue
indefinitely and would, if not brought under control, extend into a regular,
general war. Nehru braced himself for either alternative, and the British
Government were informed that India was prepared for a withdrawal of
British officers from both sides.[14] With Pakistan reported to be getting
ready for an all-out offensive in Kashmir and developments in Hyderabad
coming to a boiling point, 'things are moving so rapidly that by the end of
this month there may be a bust-up.'[15] However, Attlee had warned Liaqat
Ali Khan that if Pakistan attacked Indian military aircraft on airfields in
Kashmir, all British officers in both India and Pakistan would be
withdrawn,[16] and a month later the United Nations Commission eased the
situation. Without commenting on the implication of Pakistan's admission
about the presence of its troops in Kashmir, the Commission took the fact
into account in its resolution of 13 August 1948. There should be a cease-
fire and a withdrawal of Pakistani troops, nationals and tribesmen; India
should begin to withdraw the bulk of her forces after Pakistan had
withdrawn her tribesmen and nationals and her troops were being
withdrawn; and the future status of the State would be determined by a
plebiscite.

Mountbatten urged Nehru to accept the cease-fire. A general war with
Pakistan would lead to communal massacres such as would make the

[12] To Chief Ministers, 4 June 1948.
[13] Mountbatten (from London) to Nehru, 15 July 1948.
[14] Nehru to Mountbatten, 1 August and to H. S. Suhrawardy, 3 August 1948; Bajpai's telegram to
Krishna Menon, 2 August 1948.
[15] Nehru to Vijayalakshmi, 12 August 1948.
[16] 8 July 1948.

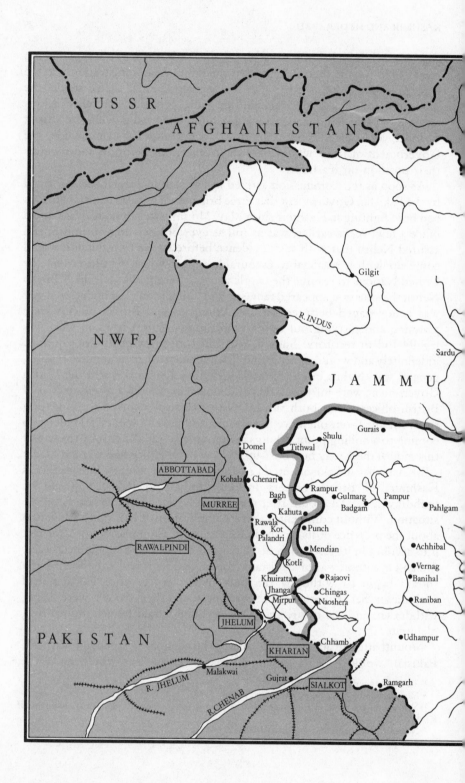

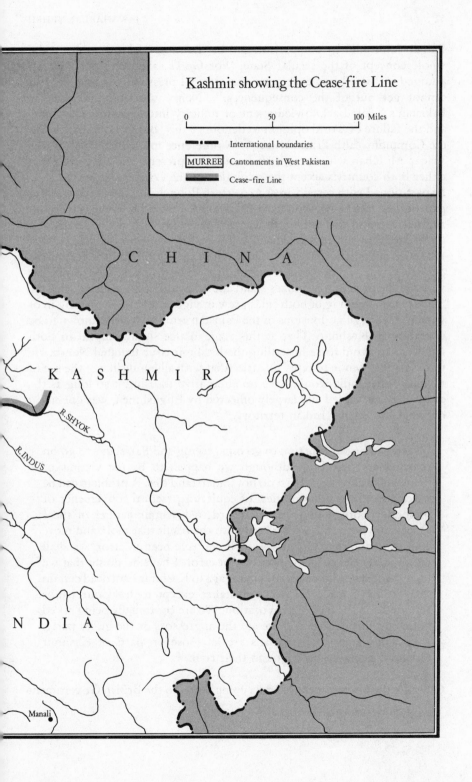

Kashmir showing the Cease-fire Line

| 0 | 50 | 100 Miles |

- ▬ ▬ · ▬ · International boundaries
- MURREE Cantonments in West Pakistan
- ▬▬▬ Cease-fire Line

C H I N A

K A S H M I R

R.SHYOK

R.INDUS

N D I A

Manali

Punjab look mild by comparison and be the most inglorious end to the whole concept of the secular State. 'For God's sake don't get yourself plunged in "war" however great the internal pressure, for once in you cannot get out of the consequences.'[17] Nehru was still indignant at Pakistan's belated acknowledgment of military intervention in Kashmir and the failure of world opinion to denounce this. But in London, during the Commonwealth Prime Ministers' Conference in October, Nehru met Liaqat Ali Khan with some British ministers present, and suggested that either both countries accept the resolution of the Commission or the State be partitioned with certain areas in western Poonch and the north-western part of the State being allotted to Pakistan. Liaqat Ali Khan rejected both alternatives, and was willing to accept a cease-fire only if the details of a plebiscite were settled immediately; and on his return to Karachi, Liaqat Ali Khan suggested that a vote be taken in the Valley and the rest of the State be divided on the basis of the religion of the majority. This manifestly violated the principle of India's stand and was summarily rejected; and the military campaigning of both sides grew in vigour despite the setting in of winter. Two regular divisions of the Pakistan army were now known to be operating in Kashmir. That at this stage Attlee should appeal to both countries to avoid force in settling the Kashmir issue irritated Nehru. He told Krishna Menon to reply to Attlee that with all her dislike of the use of military force India would have no alternative to using it so long as the army of Pakistan, led and largely officered by Englishmen, was operating on what was legally Indian territory.[18]

> It seems to be our function to go on agreeing and Pakistan's to go on refusing and rejecting, although we happen to be the victims of Pakistan's aggression. I just do not understand this. A problem can be tackled from the point of view of equity or practical convenience or preferably both. I find that in regard to Kashmir neither of these aspects has been fully considered with the result that more and more confusion and difficulty arises . . . if we have been in error, we shall gladly suffer the consequences of that error. I have no doubt that we have made many mistakes. But in regard to Kashmir I am dead certain that we have made no major mistakes except to hold our hands repeatedly in the face of provocation. We are continually being asked not to do this or that as if we are the aggressors or the guilty party. Meanwhile a set of barbarians are let loose on parts of Kashmir territory, bringing up havoc in their train.[19]

Officially the Government of India complained to the British Government

[17] Mountbatten to Nehru, 15 August 1948.
[18] Nehru to Krishna Menon, 18 November 1948.
[19] To Cripps, 17 December 1948.

1 Nehru in 1947

2   Mahatma Gandhi and Nehru at a refugee camp near Delhi, 1947

3   Announcing the death of Mahatma Gandhi, Birla House, Delhi, 30 January 1948

that the Kashmir problem would have been much nearer solution but for the encouragement given by British civil and military officers serving in Pakistan.[20] In fact, it was not a matter of a few odd individuals acting according to their prejudices. As had been suspected in India, Ernest Bevin, the Foreign Secretary, attached importance to Pakistan's role in his strategy of organizing the 'middle of the planet' and promoting cordial relations with the Arab states. He had asked Liaqat Ali Khan to take the lead in the matter.[21] This naturally influenced Britain's attitude on the Kashmir issue.

Yet, despite all provocation, Nehru, shying away from the prospect of a widening war with Pakistan, accepted the resolution of the United Nations Commission. It was a decision taken on general considerations rather than in India's special interests. His visit to London and Paris brought home to him how much India was being judged by her conduct in Kashmir and Hyderabad.[22] He was forced to recognize that his policies did not appear as impeccable to others as they did to him. But probably what weighed with Nehru more than anything else was the effect a cease-fire could have in lifting the fear and suspicion of India which obsessed the leaders of Pakistan. In London Liaqat Ali Khan's attitude had appeared to him 'a frightened man's approach and not a strong confident man's approach.'[23] Nehru's early hopes of a quick reunion with Pakistan had not lasted long, and even in January 1948 he had given a public assurance that the Government of India had no desire to reunite Pakistan with India 'for the present' and wished to devote attention to building up India.[24] Six months later he was even more categorical, and declared that any reunion was for the distant future; for the present, if Pakistan wished to join India, the latter would not agree.[25] A cease-fire in Kashmir, precluding any extension of the war, provided strong practical testimony to these assurances of Indian acceptance of Pakistan, and could help to eliminate any genuine fears of India which might still be lurking in that country.

Within India, once the immediate crisis of partition had been surmounted, freedom had to be translated into economic and social policy. It was in taking these first steps in dealing with the economic problem, which to his mind was more vital than anything else,[26] that Nehru recovered a little of his old enthusiasm. Even before independence, he had realized that prime attention should be given to the standards of living of the Indian people, and giving them some hope to live and work for; this would itself

[20] Nehru's letter to Krishna Menon, 18 December 1948, and telegram, 20 December 1948.
[21] Hugh Dalton's diary entry, 15 October 1948, quoted in P. S. Gupta, *Imperialism and the British Labour Movement 1914-1964* (London, 1975), p. 299.
[22] Nehru to Patel from Paris, 27 October 1948.
[23] Press conference, 12 November, *National Herald*, 14 November 1948.
[24] Speech at Delhi, 18 January, *Hindustan Times*, 19 January 1948.
[25] Speech at Madras, 25 July, *Hindu*, 26 July 1948.
[26] Nehru to Asaf Ali, 10 January 1948.

ease all other problems, social, economic and human. But the enthusiasm was now tempered by the responsibilities of office. Radical theories of distribution gave place to an emphasis on production, and he no longer regarded nationalization as a talismanic concept. A sub-committee of the Congress, of which Nehru was a member, still advocated, in January 1948, ceilings on incomes and profits and widespread nationalization along with an encouragement of village and cottage industries. But Nehru, as Prime Minister, spoke in more cautious tones and committed himself to nationalization only if it did not impede production or upset the existing structure. The Government could not speak in vague formulae but had to consider every aspect of the problem and more especially what could be done in the immediate present. It was no longer a question of adopting a certain outlook, but of timing, priorities and the manner of implementation. Progress should be gradual, with the greatest amount of goodwill and taking into account the availability of trained personnel; otherwise the result might be a period of semi-disaster.[27]

Nehru claimed that this approach did not contradict the report of the Congress sub-committee which had placed emphasis on nationalization of new industries without much affecting the existing ones. He also urged his Minister for Industry to ensure that the official statement on industrial policy was broadly in conformity with the party's proposals.[28] But in fact the Government restricted public ownership to munitions, atomic energy and railways, reserved to themselves the right to start new industries only in coal, iron and steel, aircraft manufactures, shipbuilding, telephone and telegraph materials and minerals, and promised that there would be no nationalization of existing industries for at least ten years.

This was not merely a new emphasis on production; the Government of India was clearly moving away even from what Nehru had termed as no more than 'a strong tendency towards socialism'. Nehru bravely defended this in public. There was never a clear slate with which to start afresh in life, and a sudden and completely new course had to be discarded because it was inconsistent with any intelligent approach.[29] 'If nationalization would increase our production, we will have it. If it does not, we shall not have it.' It was far better to spend money on setting up new industries than to use it in buying up existing ones.[30] Even in the areas of industrial expansion in which the Government did not retain a monopoly, it would participate alongside the private sector, especially in relation to certain basic industries such as fertilizers and drugs. But in private he did not dissemble his distress. 'There is so much that seems to me wrong that I do not know how

[27] Speech of 17 February 1948, Constituent Assembly (Legislative) Debates, 1948, Vol. II, pp. 825-34.
[28] To S. P. Mookerjee, 5 and 9 March 1948.
[29] Address to Central Advisory Council of Industries, 24 January, *Hindustan Times*, 25 January 1949.
[30] Statement at press conference, 5 August, *National Herald*, 6 August 1949.

and where to begin.'[31] The widespread communal outlook, aided by the violent hostility of the Communists and the 'quite astonishing folly of the Socialists was promoting a markedly reactionary trend. Whatever the reasons, the fact remains that we are looking in the wrong direction.'[32] The only hopeful development was the progress on the projects to harness the great rivers so as to provide a multitude of services. These appealed to Nehru's sense of scale, and the statute for setting up an authority to develop the Damodar valley, the first of these schemes, was to him 'in many ways the most notable piece of legislation that has ever been passed in this country.'[33] Soon after, he inaugurated work on the Hirakud dam in Orissa, and as he threw in some concrete 'a sense of adventure seized me and I forgot for a while the many troubles that beset us.'[34] When, the next year, an economic crisis necessitated curtailment of public expenditure, Nehru ordered retrenchment even in the defence services but would not allow a scaling down of these river valley projects.

The building of a new India on these lines was not, however, merely a matter of funds; even more important was the recruitment of trained personnel with a commitment to the job. Could socialism be planned and constructed by cadres trained in the service of empire? When the Congress took over the administration it was manned at all the higher levels by members of the Indian Civil Service. Before independence, none had been severer than Nehru in criticism of these officials; but he did not, when the chance came, promptly retire them. Their retention was, in a sense, a concession to his basic generosity. Even Englishmen who were willing to remain gained his support.[35] But perhaps also, in the pressure of post-partition events, there was no alternative to reliance on the Indian Civil Service if the administration was not to break down completely.

Nehru never, like Patel, became the unqualified champion of these officials, who were conservative by training and temperament. 'A Government should stand by its officers. But a Government's reputation should not be too closely attached to everything that an officer does.'[36] He was particularly concerned at the increasing resort to shooting by the police and the refusal of Patel and some Chief Ministers to order inquiries. But he gave loyal support to those civil servants who served him with efficiency. The most striking case was that of Sir Girija Shankar Bajpai, who had risen to the topmost ranks of the bureaucracy under the British and had, during the war, been posted as Indian Agent-General in Washington. He had then, as part of his job, been obliged to propagate the anti-Congress policy of the British Government, and this had aroused considerable resentment in

[31] Nehru to Patel, 27 April 1948.
[32] Nehru to Vijayalakshmi, 5 May 1948.
[33] Nehru to Chief Ministers, 20 February 1948.
[34] Nehru to Chief Ministers, 15 April 1948.
[35] H. Trevelyan, *The India We Left* (London, 1972), p. 242.
[36] Nehru to Patel, 3 March 1950.

India. But in 1947 Nehru, overcoming some initial reluctance and influenced by Krishna Menon's recommendation, appointed Bajpai Secretary-General in the Ministry of External Affairs. The appointment evoked surprise among many of Nehru's colleagues, and the surprise grew as Bajpai rapidly gained Nehru's confidence. But to those who recalled Nehru's conduct as Mayor of Allahabad over twenty years before, this would have been easily understandable. Nehru did not expect officials to be partners in ideology; no more could be expected of these conventional men in secure jobs than ability and hard work, and he was, with the attainment of freedom, prepared to abandon his earlier resentment of their seeming lack of patriotism. 'I am so tired of second rate work that sheer efficiency appeals to me.'[37]

As the years passed, however, it was not only loyal implementation, such as Nehru expected, that the officials provided; they gradually encroached on the making of policy. They were encouraged in this not only by Patel, who approved of their traditional attitudes, but also by Mountbatten, who though temperamentally close to Nehru, was in ideology akin to Patel. In his farewell memorandum to his Prime Minister he advised Nehru to proceed slowly with socialist measures so that foreign capital might not be frightened, and not to nationalize industries until there was an adequate supply of efficient managers. In the same conservative vein, he pleaded that the civil servants should be given every encouragement and the best of them posted on retirement as governors or ambassadors.[38] It was, in fact, Mountbatten's pressure which led Nehru to appoint V. P. Menon as Acting Governor of Orissa — a decision which nearly precipitated a Cabinet crisis. Rafi Kidwai and Sri Prakasa offered their resignations and Nehru had to persuade them not to insist. But Mountbatten found that even his influence was not strong enough to secure V. P. Menon's election to Parliament and appointment to the Cabinet.

With an increasing variety of problems pressing on ministers and their minds preoccupied with political rivalries, the opportunities for civil servants to take major decisions grew. Nehru realized and regretted this; but he also recognized that there seemed little he could do about it. 'It is true that the services are playing a very important role in our official life, both at the Centre and in the provinces. This is due to a large extent to the fact that our other human material, with a few exceptions, is very poor. The services realize that and therefore feel much more assured about themselves than they used to. Our internal conflicts and quarrels among public men give the services a certain vantage point.'[39] It would have been easier to have changed the over-bureaucratized system of government at the time of the transfer of power, but the nature and context of that occasion had

[37] To K. P. S. Menon, 12 October 1947.
[38] Mountbatten's memorandum, 19 June 1948.
[39] To Krishna Menon, 12 August 1949.

prevented it; and now the system, even though it lacked intrinsic strength, had succeeded in perpetuating itself.

On this issue, Patel had been helped by circumstances; but there were many other matters on which the Prime Minister and his deputy severely disagreed. It would, indeed, have been surprising if friction had not developed from the start between them. Their temperamental and ideological differences had been kept under control in earlier years by the transcendent leadership of Gandhi and by the common commitment to the cause of India's freedom. But now, with independence and the steady weakening of Gandhi's authority, it was difficult for these pre-eminent men, one with a massive hold on popular affection and the other with a sure grip on the Party, to work together in the unaccustomed field of administration. Matters came to a head within a few months of taking office, and on 23 December Patel was on the verge of formal resignation. The crunch came on the question of the authority of the Prime Minister. Nehru believed that he was, by virtue of his office, more responsible than anyone else for the general trends of policy and it was his prerogative to act as coordinator and supervisor with a certain liberty of direction. This meant that, if necessary, he should intervene in the functioning of every ministry, though this should be done with tact and with the knowledge of the minister concerned. It would be impossible for him to serve as Prime Minister if this overriding authority were challenged, or if any minister took important decisions without reference to the Prime Minister or the Cabinet.[40] But Patel's interpretation of the Prime Minister's role was very different. It was for each ministry to implement the decisions of the Cabinet; and the Prime Minister's responsibility was merely to see that there was no conflict between ministries. To the extent that Nehru was seeking to do more and was taking decisions in matters which fell within the purview of ministers, he was, in Patel's view, acting undemocratically.[41]

The dispute was referred to Gandhi, and each, as could be expected of them, offered to resign in favour of the other if this would help to resolve the situation. But Gandhi urged them to continue to pull together, and his death within minutes of giving this advice made it to both men a binding order. Patel still offered to resign, if only because the murder of Gandhi implied inefficiency on the part of the Home Ministry, but Nehru brushed the suggestion aside.

> Now, with Bapu's death, everything is changed and we have to face a different and more difficult world. The old controversies have ceased to have much significance and it seems to me that the urgent need of the hour is for all of us to function as closely and cooperatively as

[40] Nehru to Patel, 23 December 1947, and Nehru's note of 6 January 1948 sent to Gandhi and Patel.
[41] Patel's note to Gandhi and Nehru, 12 January 1948.

possible. Indeed, there is no other way . . . It is over a quarter of a century since we have been closely associated with one another and we have faced many storms and perils together. I can say with full honesty that during this period my affection and regard for you have grown, and I do not think anything can happen to lessen this. Even our differences have brought out the far greater points of agreement between us and the respect we bear to each other. We have even learnt to agree to differ and yet carry on together.

Anyway, in the crisis that we have to face now after Bapu's death I think it is my duty and, if I may venture to say, yours also for us to face it together as friends and colleagues. Not merely superficially, but in full loyalty to one another and with confidence in each other. I can assure you that you will have that from me. If I have any doubt or difficulty I shall put it frankly to you, and I hope you will do the same to me.[42]

Patel responded as warmly,[43] and for a time personal cordiality surmounted differences on policy. They aired, for example, healthily and in the open, their divergence of priorities on the communal issue. Nehru was concerned about the recrudescence of Hindu communalism in the form of the Rashtriya Swayamsevak Sangh, while Patel attached more importance to the failure to check the immigration of Muslims from Pakistan.[44] But other difficulties cropped up, wearing away at their decision to work together. Patel had suffered a heart attack and was away in Mussoorie. Though Nehru did his best to keep him informed, Patel resented the necessity of many decisions having to be taken without consulting him, while Nehru was irritated by the inevitable delay in action in the ministries under Patel's charge.

An even more crucial issue on which Nehru and Patel found themselves coming up against each other was the problem of Hyderabad. It was being dealt with by Patel as part of the work of the States Ministry; but Nehru was keenly concerned not only as Prime Minister but because the future of Hyderabad had an obvious bearing on India's policy on Kashmir, and both were, apart from the local issues involved, parts of the general question of relations with Pakistan. Hyderabad, with a Muslim ruler but a Muslim population of about only 11 per cent, had not acceded to either Dominion before 15 August 1947. The Nizam was known to be expanding his army and buying arms in Europe, and he had engaged the formidable legal talents of Sir Walter Monckton with a view, it was thought,[45] to

[42] Nehru to Patel, 3 February 1948, *Sardar Patel's Correspondence*, Vol. 6 (Ahmedabad, 1973), pp. 29-30. There is no copy of this presumably handwritten letter in the Nehru papers.

[43] Patel to Nehru, 5 February 1948.

[44] Nehru to Patel, 2 May 1948, and Patel's reply, 4 May 1948, *Sardar Patel's Correspondence*, Vol. 6, pp. 318-20.

[45] See letter from Hyderabad to N. G. Ayyangar, 31 August 1947, *Sardar Patel's Correspondence*, Vol. 7 (Ahmedabad, 1973), p.56.

prolonging negotiations with India until he was ready either to assert his sovereignty or to accede to Pakistan. Hyderabad was, in Monckton's phrase, land-locked in India's belly and could not avoid a treaty or agreement of association; but this was compatible with Hyderabad's sovereignty. In negotiations for such an agreement Monckton had the advantage that Mountbatten, who was a personal friend, had pledged that he would not be a party to any 'improper pressure' on Hyderabad.[46] Apparently Mountbatten and Monckton were agreed on nominal independence and de facto incorporation of Hyderabad in India[47] — a formula which could not be said to be in India's interest. As a result of Mountbatten's persuasion, the Government of India, though keen on accession, were induced to sign a standstill agreement for a year, with an understanding that within that period the problems of accession and responsible government would both be satisfactorily settled.

However, the increase of tension between India and Pakistan in the winter of 1947-8 encouraged the Nizam to stall further; and with the open sympathy of his government a fanatic Muslim organization, the Razackars, terrorized the State. Nehru desired an amicable settlement on Hyderabad, if only because he feared that any other course might lead to trouble and misery on a large scale. He did not wish to force or hasten accession. All that he sought immediately was that the standstill agreement should be fully honoured and there should be no disturbances within the state or on its borders. If Hyderabad ceased to be a feudal and autocratic State and its people decided on their own future, the Government of India would be willing to await their decision.[48] Hyderabad could not possibly run away from India or the Indian Union even though the bigoted men in power could do much mischief.

Such moderation of the Government of India was interpreted in Hyderabad as weakness and the negotiations were not taken seriously. The violent Razackar outbursts, at which the Hyderabad Government connived, destroyed all semblance of order in the State and threatened the peace of the whole of southern India; and it was becoming increasingly difficult for the Government of India to remain passive. 'I wish to avoid, as you must also do, any action on our part which might be construed as indicating aggression on Hyderabad State. Nevertheless we have to be prepared to protect the people.'[49] It was not now a question of accession or even of responsible government, although these issues were important by themselves; the real question was that a certain section of the people in Hyderabad was committing hostile acts against the Government of India,

[46] Monckton's note to the Nizam, 15 September 1947, Ibid., pp. 59-62.
[47] See Campbell-Johnson's diary entry, 20 September 1947, A. Campbell-Johnson, *Mission with Mountbatten* (London, 1951), p. 198.
[48] Nehru to Chief Ministers, 11 March 1948.
[49] Nehru to Baldev Singh, 16 April 1948.

and if the Hyderabad Government could not stop this, other measures would have to be adopted.[50] The movement of the armoured brigade and two infantry brigades to the south might in itself prevent any further deterioration of the situation. So Nehru ordered the Bombay Government not to obstruct the transit of non-military goods to Hyderabad. 'I am anxious that our hands should be as clean as possible in our dealings with Hyderabad and we should not give any valid excuse to our enemies and opponents.'[51] When, without his knowledge or that of the Government of India, the dispatch of salt to Hyderabad was stopped, Nehru pulled up the Bombay Government for this breach of his assurances.[52]

Mountbatten was now satisfied that Nehru would authorize no military action against Hyderabad save in dire emergency such as a large-scale massacre.[53] Monckton returned to India, despite a cable from Mountbatten advising him against it, and he and the Prime Minister of Hyderabad, Laik Ali, came again to Delhi. They resorted once more to delaying tactics, but Nehru did not think that a decision could now be postponed for long. 'Our position is a strong one and there are many ways of showing our strength.' It was of course possible that the Hyderabad Government or the Razackars might compel military action; but after the experience in Kashmir, Nehru preferred to avoid this or at least delay it by about two months. Immediate military action might weaken the campaign in Kashmir at a time when there was a possibility of these operations spreading and developing into a regular war with Pakistan; and 'it is easier to begin military operations than to end them.' The primary task was to weaken the morale of the anti-Indian elements in Hyderabad so that any action against India was precluded; if this were done, one need only await developments. The presence of strong contingents of the Indian army near the borders of Hyderabad might in itself be sufficient.[54]

In June an agreement, on the lines demanded by the Nizam, was imposed by Mountbatten on Nehru and Patel; but once again the Nizam wriggled out.[55] 'I have little doubt that Hyderabad has been hand in glove with Pakistan and it is Pakistan that has prevented them from coming into line with us.'[56] War material was being regularly flown from Karachi by British crews in four-engined bombers registered in Britain; it was known that the Nizam's government, on the advice of British armament firms, was maintaining air squadrons for use against India in East Bengal, West

[50] Nehru at Bombay, 26 April, *National Herald*, 27 April 1948.

[51] To B. G. Kher, Chief Minister of Bombay, 3 May 1948.

[52] Telegram to Kher, 24 May 1948.

[53] Campbell-Johnson's diary entry, 25 May 1948, Campbell-Johnson, op. cit., p. 342.

[54] Nehru to Patel, 30 May and 6 June, 1948.

[55] J. Terraine, *The Life and Times of Lord Mountbatten* (London, 1968), p. 164; Lord Birkenhead, *Walter Monckton* (London, 1969), p. 250; H. V. Hodson, *The Great Divide* (London, 1969), pp. 485-6.

[56] Nehru to Sri Prakasa, 16 June 1948. Laik Ali agrees that the Nizam's hope was not so much in the United Nations as in Jinnah. *The Tragedy of Hyderabad* (Karachi, 1962), p. 261.

Pakistan, Iraq and Iran; British secret service men were loaned to the Hyderabad Government; and a secret treaty was signed by Hyderabad with Portugal granting Hyderabad the use of Goa in return for her developing port and harbour facilities. Even Monckton took the line that if the Nizam was pushed too far, his advice would be to fight it out.[57] Patel was for firm and definite action,[58] but he was ill and absent from Delhi, and the Government of India, under Nehru's guidance, were still content to wait for wiser counsel to prevail in Hyderabad. There would be no independence for Hyderabad unless India disintegrated; but Nehru repeated that it was against India's policy to secure accession by compulsion.[59] All that was done, in face of known preparations for prolonged defiance, was to permit action and hot pursuit to repel minor raids from Hyderabad and to impose an economic blockade; only food, salt, medical stores and chlorine were to be allowed entry.

It may not be true, as Laik Ali has suggested, that Mountbatten had agreed to a plebiscite run by an outside body other than the United Nations.[60] But he enjoyed influence in Hyderabad and inhibited action in Delhi. His departure in June 1948 removed the last hope of any settlement. It was now clear that a conflict could not be avoided. Negotiations had ended, the blockade was tightened, there were daily reports of deteriorating conditions on the borders and within Hyderabad, and all preparations were made for large-scale military intervention. Yet the Government of India delayed action, 'in the faint hope that something might happen.'[61] But there were no signs of either a formation of a representative government or control of Razackar atrocities. On the other hand, gun-running, blood and thunder speeches, intrigues with Pakistan and preparations for war with India continued and even increased in momentum. There were reports that the Hyderabad authorities were eager to precipitate a conflict before the economic blockade weakened them further, and were planning to invade parts of the Indian Union. 'All this is sheer lunacy. But madmen are in charge of Hyderabad's destinies.'[62] Throughout India there was a widespread conviction that military action was inescapable, and that Nehru was the one person standing against it. However, even he was coming round.

I have tried my utmost, and not without success, to avoid and postpone any large-scale action against Hyderabad. The result of this has been that, in so far as this matter is concerned, I am completely

[57] Interview with Campbell-Johnson, 3 June 1948, Campbell-Johnson, op. cit., p. 346.
[58] See his letter to N. V. Gadgil, 21 June 1948, *Sardar Patel's Correspondence*, Vol. 7, p. 217.
[59] Nehru's speech at Naini Tal, 11 June, and statement at press conference in New Delhi, 17 June, *National Herald*, 12 and 18 June 1948 respectively.
[60] Laik Ali, op. cit., pp. 207-9.
[61] Nehru to Rajagopalachari, 3 July 1948.
[62] Nehru to Mountbatten, 3 July 1948.

distrusted by large numbers of people here. I do not worry much about this . . . I am quite convinced now that there can be no solution of the Hyderabad problem unless some effective punitive measures are taken; and if they have to be taken then there is not much point in indefinitely delaying them.[63]

Indeed there was some advantage, if action had to be taken, in taking it quickly; for delay endangered communal peace in India.

On 7 September, Nehru announced that a contingent of the Indian army would be sent to re-station itself in the old Indian cantonment in Hyderabad. This would be purely an action to maintain law and order, with no influence on accession; but 'when you indulge in a dynamic operation, numerous consequences follow, which you cannot foresee.'[64] Even at this stage the Governor-General, Rajagopalachari, appealed to Mountbatten to persuade the Nizam to control his officials so that it might not be necessary for the Government of India to take over the administration.[65] But it was too late to arrest the course of events.

The impact of the action in Hyderabad on the rest of India was unreservedly healthy. The problem of the States was finally settled and the central Government was recognized as paramount all over India. The Hindus lost their sense of fear and the Muslims had less reason to feel insecure. Pakistan talked less, for the time being at any rate, of war, and few in India, too, seemed to think in such terms. There was improvement in public morale and a general lowering of communal tension. The Muslims of India had made it clear — to those who required such testimony — by their attitude during the crisis that they were full citizens of the Indian Union who wished to fit themselves into the Indian structure. Secularism had come through its second test.

[63] Nehru to Mountbatten, 29 August 1948.
[64] Nehru at a press conference in New Delhi, 10 September, *National Herald*, 11 September 1948.
[65] Rajagopalachari to Mountbatten, 8 September 1948.

3

The Shaping of Foreign Policy

ONE

On joining the Interim Government in September 1946, Nehru made clear that India would develop an active concern in world affairs, pursuing an independent policy compatible with her own national interests[1] – a statement of objective which remained true throughout his years in office. But at the start, not surprisingly, there was little precision and definiteness about this objective. It appeared to consist primarily of vague and rather grandiose hopes of closer ties between the Asian countries and even the formation of two or three Asian federations. India, said Nehru, could play a positive role in the stretch from Australia and New Zealand to East Africa, and, as the first of the Asian and African countries to have gained freedom, would adopt an uncommitted and influential stand on international issues.[2] It was not easy to put all this into practice and, as Nehru recognized, India's views on world affairs were to some extent 'a continuation of British foreign policy; to some extent a reaction against it. For the rest they consist of benevolent intentions for all concerned.'[3] But the foreign policy of a newly independent nation does not emerge overnight, and with the general directions clear in his mind, Nehru set about building up the foreign policy of India brick by brick, in the process discarding the generalizations which had taken the place of rigorous thought.

For India, with much economic and diplomatic potential but little actual power, it was difficult to make any impact without at the same time arousing resentment in a world already riven by the cold war. The makers of policy in the United States were, despite their monopoly of nuclear weapons, not free of nervous tension, while Stalin and his colleagues were suspicious of every one who was not fully with them. Nehru's constant reiteration of the need to cast out fear and suspicion irritated both sides;

[1] Interview reported in *New York Times*, 1 September 1946.
[2] Interview reported in *National Herald*, 17 August 1946.
[3] Note, 18 January 1947.

43

and the reference of the Kashmir issue to the United Nations provided them with an occasion to display their displeasure. The United States, following Britain's lead, declined to come to grips with the facts of aggression. 'It is astonishing', complained an irritated Nehru, 'how naïve the Americans are in their foreign policy. It is only their money and their power that carries them through, not their intelligence or any other quality.'[4] As for the Russians, they denounced non-alignment as a policy of collaboration with British imperialism, held aloof on the Kashmir issue and threw out hints of the need for India to make up her mind and not to refrain from joining either side. But Nehru, despite the pressures of Kashmir, was in no mood to revise his policy. It was not that he was priggishly parading principles and was determined to develop, at whatever cost, a policy of independent judgment of each issue because that was ethically the right position. He emphasized from the outset the practical advantages to India of non-alignment and judged its efficacy on a pragmatic basis. It was firmly based on the current realities of the world. Though in later years he often expounded the moral virtues of non-alignment or annoyed other governments by seeming to claim a great deal for India, he did not lose sight of the utility of his policy. It was not so much a code of conduct as a technique to be tested by results. It was 'not a wise policy to put all our eggs in one basket . . . purely from the point of view of opportunism, if you like, a straightforward, honest policy, an independent policy is the best.'[5]

So, in these early years, Nehru saw no reason to be thrown off his course of equidistance by the hostility of the Great Powers. There being no immediate threat to India's security, she could afford to take a long-term view and build up her industry and defence in the context of non-alignment rather than seek immediate support by involvement in the cold war, for neither protagonist of which he had much intellectual respect.

> After all that has happened in India during the past year, I have little conceit left about my capacity to handle any difficult problem. Nevertheless it does surprise me how the Great Powers of the world behave to each other. Quite apart from the principles involved, there is an extraordinary crudity about their utterances and activities. I do not suppose that there will be any war because nobody is prepared for it. But anything may happen to this unhappy world when the men in charge of its destiny function in the way they have been doing.[6]

With the Soviet Union directing the Indian Communist Party to rebellion and condemning all the policies of the Government of India, relations between the two countries deteriorated further.

[4] To Vijayalakshmi, 25 March 1948.
[5] Speech in Constituent Assembly, 8 March 1948, J. Nehru, *India's Foreign Policy* (Delhi, 1961), p. 35.
[6] To Krishna Menon, 4 August 1948.

We want friendship and cooperation with Russia in many fields but we are a sensitive people and we react strongly to being cursed at and run down. The whole basis of Russian policy appears to be that no essential change has taken place in India and that we still continue to be camp-followers of the British. That of course is complete nonsense and if a policy is based on nonsensical premises it is apt to go wrong.[7]

It was obviously worth making an effort to clear the air, but one difficulty in doing this was the poor contacts the Indian Ambassador in Moscow, Vijayalakshmi, had with the Soviet Government.

There was a suggestion of a change of approach by the Soviet Union in September 1948 when its Ambassador informed a member of Nehru's Cabinet that his Government would be willing to help, particularly as regards Hyderabad and Kashmir, but India had not sought such help. However, nothing came of this. Mere lack of hostility and intent to be neutral in case of conflict still did not satisfy the Soviet Union; and Nehru was determined to go no further. The Soviet Government were not totally wrong in distrusting India; for it was clear that at this time Indian neutrality would be benevolent towards the Western Powers. Nehru himself recognized this and directed that Britain and the United States be informed that, in the world as it was, there was not the least chance of India lining up with the Soviet Union in war or peace.[8] At the Conference of Commonwealth Prime Ministers in October 1948, Nehru, while critical of the expansionism of the United States, particularly in economic matters, declared that Asian peoples had no sympathy for Soviet expansionism and recommended publicity being given to this aspect of Soviet policy rather than to communism as an economic doctrine or a way of life.[9] Non-alignment was, therefore, very much a hypothetical concept; Nehru was, thanks to some extent to the Soviet attitude, leaning heavily towards the Western Powers. The policy which Nehru was seeking to construct assumed a certain understanding on the part of the Great Powers. Stalin did not see this at this time, just as Dulles failed to grasp it later. The consequence at both times was a wavering of non-alignment.

TWO

This spiral, of Soviet antipathy and Indian reaction to it which in turn gave strength to Soviet criticism, provides an important element of the background to Nehru's decision to retain India in the Commonwealth. After 15 August 1947, Nehru had no intention of going back on the

[7] Nehru to Krishna Menon, 26 June 1948.
[8] Nehru's notes of 11 and 12 September 1948.
[9] Bajpai's note on Commonwealth Prime Ministers' Conference, October 1948.

resolution of the Constituent Assembly that India should be a free and sovereign republic. But the advantages of retaining a link with the Commonwealth were also becoming stronger. It was known that Jinnah was hoping to tease India out of that association, leaving Pakistan as the 'northern Ireland' of the sub-continent; and there was the continuous advocacy of Mountbatten and Krishna Menon at Nehru's elbow. Apart from the need to prevent the Commonwealth from becoming anti-Indian, the military weakness and economic dependence of India could not be ignored; and the Commonwealth, while not limiting India's independence and freedom of action, appeared likely to promote stability and peace, and ensure the continuance of 'the British connection' in a healthier context.[10] But the hostility of Stalin's Russia in the early years of India's freedom also weighed in Nehru's mind.

To Nehru it was the political advantage of a continuing link with the Commonwealth which at that time was primary, and he believed himself to be acting, to some extent, under 'a certain pressure of circumstances.'[11] He had, it is true, a sentimental attachment to Britain, but this did no more than tinge his policy. Nor did he, unlike some others at that time, see the Commonwealth as an effective entity in world affairs or as providing Britain with an opportunity to project her leadership. To him the Commonwealth was never anything more, in this respect, than a multi-racial association for exchange of views. He does not even seem to have expected the Commonwealth to play such a minor role effectively for long; for in reply to Jayaprakash Narayan's criticism that membership suggested a lack of self-confidence and an implicit commitment to one of the power blocs, he spoke of the great practical help that India's association would secure for at least two or three years, and at very slight cost.[12] The future was free as air and India could walk out of the Commonwealth at any time she wanted. But in these years the Soviet Union was still aloof and distant, and the conflict with the Communist Party in India created additional barriers. So, while maintaining a friendly posture towards the Soviet Union and seeking to develop contacts, India could do little more. This, along with the need for financial and technological assistance, compelled close relations with the United States; and Nehru was looking for means by which he could avoid an over-dependent bilateral connection with that country. The United Nations, after its stand on Kashmir, could not be relied upon; but the Commonwealth seemed to provide a grouping which not only would safeguard the stability of a newly integrated India but would enable her to resist any stifling embrace of the United States.

[10] M. Brecher, *India and World Politics* (London, 1968), p. 19; M. Brecher, 'India's Decision to remain in the Commonwealth', *Journal of Commonwealth and Comparative Politics*, March and July 1974, pp. 62-70.

[11] Nehru's report on the Commonwealth Conference, 7 May 1949.

[12] Jayaprakash Narayan to Nehru, 10 April, and Nehru's reply, 14 April 1949.

American diplomats themselves suspected that the British encouraged an anti-American attitude in India.[13]

As it was not clear on what basis India could retain her ties with the Commonwealth, Nehru, on whom the burden of this decision primarily lay, let the matter lie for the time being.[14] But on 11 March 1948 Attlee raised the question privately with Nehru, suggesting that India remain in the Commonwealth and accept common allegiance to the Crown. India did not, in Attlee's view, have a native tradition of republicanism, which was basically an importation from the West. There would be no political problem as long as the head of the state under India's new Constitution enjoyed no greater powers than the Governor-General, and there would be considerable advantage in having as the head of the state a person who was not only above but outside the political battle. Continuance in the Commonwealth would also help India's relations with Pakistan, Ceylon and Malaya and promote the unity of India and of the world. Following this up, Mountbatten advised Nehru to replace the word 'republic' in the Indian Constitution by either 'commonwealth' or 'state'. This was impractical as well as meaningless; for even if Nehru had agreed, it would have made no difference to the whole structure of the Constitution, which was republican. But on the general question of membership of the Commonwealth Nehru made, and indeed could make, no commitment. Public opinion in India was in favour of going out and at this time Nehru shared this opinion.[15] Certainly India could not remain a Dominion but would become a republic; whether the republic could have a closer relationship — 'some vague bond'[16] — with Britain than with other states was the only issue for consideration. Nehru and many of his colleagues favoured close and intimate friendship, which was more important than a formal link, primarily, said Nehru, because of the change in British policy and more particularly because the presence and activities of the Mountbattens had enabled Indians to forget the heavy legacy of British rule.[17] None the less, the attitude of British officials on Kashmir and of British interests in Hyderabad strengthened the dislike of any link with Britain. Krishna Menon wrote to Attlee stating his intention to resign the high commissionership in London as his mission had been a failure.

I left you on the last occasion for the first time with more than a

[13] 'On more than one occasion, Mountbatten has warned Nehru against dollar imperialism . . . I have waited patiently for a hand of cooperation from the British, but it has never come . . . The British are not happy about the strong position which we have in India, or about the weak position which they have.' Dr Grady, first United States Ambassador in Delhi, to State Department, 26 December 1947, *Foreign Relations of the United States 1947*, Vol. 3 (Washington, 1972) pp. 177-8.

[14] Nehru to B. C. Roy, 20 June 1947; Campbell-Johnson's note, 10 November 1947, Campbell-Johnson, *Mission with Mountbatten* (London, 1951), p. 242.

[15] See his letters to Krishna Menon, 6 and 16 April 1948.

[16] Note, 12 September 1948.

[17] Nehru to Attlee, 18 April 1948.

passing feeling that we were making no impression and that there
were barriers which appear almost unbreakable . . . I have the
uncomfortable feeling that I am letting my side down by not
recognizing that we are very much on the outside and will perhaps
remain so . . . We have the distressing feeling that decent behaviour is
penalized and ethical values at a discount, and that reasonableness lays
us open to being regarded as weak or even cowardly . . . at any rate by
lack of information, you should not find yourself against us on
Hyderabad, practically waging war on us in Kashmir, or, worse than
all this, treating Pakistan and us alike![18]

Even Rajagopalachari thought in these terms.

For it is the maintenance of peace as between the units in the
Commonwealth that justifies the connection and when this incidence
of Commonwealth connection is openly negatived, there is nothing
left to say on its behalf . . . You have achieved the impossible and
created tremendous goodwill when there was nothing but illwill and
distrust before. This is now being, I do not wish to say has been,
undone by the stupidity and shortsightedness of a few British
officers.[19]

The integration of Hyderabad had cleared the path to some extent by the
time Nehru went to London in October 1948 for the Prime Ministers'
Conference. Attlee and Cripps were friendly and recognized India's
potential as a power in Asia. The talks with Liaqat Ali Khan in the
presence of British ministers were fruitless; but Nehru had no reason to
object to the attitude of the British Government. Therefore, as Attlee
continued to press the desirability of India's association with the
Commonwealth, Nehru formulated his proposals. India would be a
republic, but a separate statute could be enacted providing for common
Commonwealth citizenship. This was an idea which probably owes much
in its breadth of vision to Churchill's offer to France in 1940 and, if taken
up, would have altered the nature of the Commonwealth far more than the
mere admission of a republic. 'The King as the first citizen of the
Commonwealth will be the fountain of honour so far as the
Commonwealth as a whole is concerned.' This would require no legislation
but only understandings and administrative arrangements. In any fresh
legislation or treaties Commonwealth countries would not be treated as
foreign states or their citizens as foreigners; and in any new commercial
treaties it would be made clear that for the purpose of the 'most favoured

[18] Krishna Menon's strictly personal and secret letter to Attlee, 1 September 1948. Attlee Papers
Box 6.
[19] Rajagopalachari to Mountbatten, 8 September 1948.

nation' clause the Commonwealth countries were in a special position and not regarded as foreign states. 'These proposals represent a sincere desire to continue the Commonwealth association and what is practicable and adequate at present. No doubt as the relationship is not a static arrangement further development by way of association may take place.'[20]

Although Nehru's proposals had been drafted after full discussion between his legal adviser, B. N. Rau, and British legal experts,[21] the British Government now thought that they were insufficient from the legal viewpoint. Attlee suggested, in addition to an Indian enactment adopting the British Nationality Act, a declaration by all members of the Commonwealth that they wished to be and regarded themselves as still bound in a special form of association within the Commonwealth. Nothing less than a formal acceptance of the Commonwealth as a continuing association of long standing would help to withstand any challenge in a court of law by other nations seeking the same 'most favoured nation' treatment as India.[22] The Australian, Canadian and New Zealand Governments also urged Nehru to give weight to the strength of sentiment in their Dominions in favour of the King as the symbol of Commonwealth association and as such exercising the authority to appoint ambassadors.[23]

Nehru, who was having difficulty in India in securing assent even to the concept of the King as the fountain of honour, thought that these new suggestions had no chance of acceptance. It was then suggested that the King be recognized as the Head of the Commonwealth with no allegiance owing to him from India.[24] Krishna Menon linked with this his own ingenious suggestion of 'dormant sovereignty', whereby India would not assert all her sovereign rights but permit the King to exercise some of them. But even these proposals seemed unlikely to be acceptable in India. There was, in fact, such opposition in the Congress Parliamentary Party to any hint of a subordinate status for India or her President that Nehru avoided a vote and merely sought and secured general agreement for a link with the Commonwealth. He discerned that although there was keen sensitivity about any formal diminution of India's status, there was little resistance to substantial inroads into Indian sovereign exclusiveness.

The real point is that there is a basic difference in approach between the United Kingdom people and our people. The very point the United Kingdom wishes to emphasize for legal or sentimental reasons

[20] Nehru to Attlee, 28 October 1948.
[21] Nehru to Mountbatten, 22 November 1948.
[22] Attlee to Nehru, 19 and 20 November 1948.
[23] Bajpai's telegram to Nehru forwarding the views of H. V. Evatt, Lester Pearson and Peter Fraser, 18 November 1948. The Canadian viewpoint at this stage seems in contrast with that of her Prime Minister, Mackenzie King, a few weeks earlier, when he had advised Nehru to lay stress on a Community of Free Nations rather than on the Crown. Brecher, op. cit. (1974), p. 72.
[24] Krishna Menon's telegram to Nehru, 27 November 1948.

is objected to here. Most people are prepared to accept the common citizenship idea plus a declaration that we are in the Commonwealth. If you go beyond this, there is difficulty . . . Our people want to make it perfectly clear that they are making a new start and that, as the Constitution will itself declare, sovereignty resides in the people and in no one else in any shape or form.[25]

So, while Attlee and some of the Dominion Prime Ministers desired a special stress on the role of the Crown, India preferred omission of any mention of the King. Krishna Menon, who was as anxious as any British statesman for a continuance of the Commonwealth association, suggested as a compromise that India need not undertake any overt act of recognizing the King, but he could continue to be the president, as it were, of the club in which India was remaining as a member.[26] Nehru agreed. India would neither recognize nor repudiate the King. There would be no mention of the King as the fountain of honour, and it would be specifically stated that the Commonwealth was not a super-state but an association of free and independent states which accepted the concept of Commonwealth citizenship. The Indian people and their representatives, including the President of the Republic, would exercise all functions of sovereignty.[27] But he once again at this time had doubts whether the Indian public would agree to remain in the Commonwealth in face of Britain's failure to treat India 'fairly or squarely'[28] on other matters. Her delegate openly supported Pakistan at the United Nations, her nationals helped Pakistan to plan a military offensive in Kashmir and her Government supported Dutch efforts to crush Indonesian nationalism.

> I am distressed that matters should take a wrong turn and come in the way of that close cooperation between India and the United Kingdom which I had looked forward to. I feel that British policy has not been very happy in Asia, in India and in Kashmir. Why it should have been so is more than I can understand, because I see no benefit to the United Kingdom in adopting this policy towards India. India counts even now and will count a great deal later.[29]

Nehru's formal complaints were rejected by Attlee[30] in his usual dry tone which Nehru found irritating. 'We can only conclude that this general unfriendly attitude towards India in regard to Kashmir has nothing to do

[25] Nehru to Krishna Menon, 28 November 1948.
[26] Krishna Menon's telegram to Nehru, 29 November 1948.
[27] Nehru's revised Commonwealth memorandum, 2 December 1948.
[28] Telegram to Krishna Menon, 31 December 1948.
[29] To Cripps, 17 December 1948.
[30] Attlee to Nehru, 28 December 1948.

with justice or equity, but is apparently based on some other reasons which we are unable to understand.'[31]

'You must', replied Cripps, 'be fair, Jawaharlal, and not take the attitude that any stick will do to beat the British with!'[32] But Britain could not just rest on her achievements in ending colonialism in South Asia, and the hostile reactions to her seeming anti-Indian prejudices surfaced again. Nehru, though he thought the reactions to be justified, had no intention of yielding to them, and he strengthened his hand by securing a resolution at the annual session of the Congress welcoming 'free association with the independent nations of the Commonwealth.'[33] But he was also firm that he would go no further than what he had agreed to in London, and was surprised by the British Government's inclination to treat India's adherence to the Commonwealth as a legal and technical rather than a political question. The relationship between a republic and a Commonwealth headed by a king, if desired by both sides, could not be settled by any formula delegating authority to the Governor-General. 'I have done my best in the matter. Somehow matters have come to a standstill. I do not quite know where we are.'[34]

Attlee and some Dominion Prime Ministers persisted in attaching importance mainly to the position of the King and talked in terms, if need be, of associate but not full membership for India.[35] Winston Churchill was more imaginative and found a precedent in Roman history for the presence of a republic in the Commonwealth;[36] but both he and the King seem to have thought in terms of the King becoming the President of India.[37] Attlee then wrote what Nehru justifiably termed 'a surprisingly naive'[38] letter, extolling the virtues not merely of the King but of the royal family, whom he saw as symbolizing in a very real sense the family nature of the Commonwealth. 'The family is the basic unit of society. It is something universal, transcending creeds and races.' Drawing Nehru's attention to the 'solid advantages' in retaining the King in the Indian Constitution, he suggested that a title might be found for him in India's heroic age.[39]

It seemed pointless to Nehru to carry on further discussions on this juvenile basis; and the position was not improved by Mr Gordon Walker's visit to India to suggest a Commonwealth Privy Council, a Commonwealth 'honour' and the recognition of the King's right to appoint arbitral tribunals or to delegate to the President of India powers of appointment of

[31] Nehru's telegram to Krishna Menon, 30 December 1948.
[32] 7 January 1949.
[33] At Jaipur, 18 December 1948.
[34] Nehru to Mountbatten, 20 February 1949.
[35] Nehru's note on interview with the British High Commissioner, 23 February 1949.
[36] Krishna Menon to Nehru, 11 March 1949.
[37] Attlee's letter to the King, 2 March 1949, cited in F. Williams, *A Prime Minister Remembers* (London, 1961), p. 218.
[38] Nehru to Patel, 26 March 1949.
[39] Attlee to Nehru, 20 March 1949.

certain dignitaries. But Mr Gordon Walker had one useful suggestion
—that the King might be recognized as the symbol of the unity of the
Commonwealth and designated as its 'Head' or 'Protector'.[40] Nehru,
while he rejected the idea of the King delegating powers to the President,
did not commit himself on the other suggestions; but it was clear that the
solution lay in finding some place for the King in the Commonwealth
relationship without giving the Crown a place in the Indian Constitution.
Attlee was told politely that, whatever the advantages of a hereditary
kingship, any attempt to revise the Constitution in its final stages would
lead to an uproar.[41] The Lord Chancellor, Jowitt and Cripps then drafted
formulae whereby India recognized the King 'as the (fountain) head of the
Commonwealth.'[42] Both the Indian Cabinet and the Congress Working
Committee considered this idea. Nehru himself disliked the phrase 'Head
of the Commonwealth' as it might create the impression that the
Commonwealth was some kind of a superstructure, and preferred the
language of the Statute of Westminster, 'symbol of the free association of
the members of the Commonwealth'. On the other hand, he was willing to
go further than Attlee and the Dominion Prime Ministers in substantive
matters and continued in vain to propose a common citizenship.[43]

At the Conference of Prime Ministers which opened in London on 22
April 1949, Nehru tabled his three-point formula of Commonwealth
citizenship, India's continued membership and acceptance by her of the
King as the symbol of the free association of Commonwealth countries.
Australia, New Zealand and Canada stressed that they could accept no
solution which modified their allegiance to the Crown, but Nehru was not
prepared to agree to any arrangement which gave India a lower status than
that of other countries. Surprisingly, Malan of South Africa supported
Nehru. He thought it natural that a general relaxation of the common
allegiance should accompany the growing consciousness of separate
nationhood. More realistic than Attlee, he recognized that the Crown could
not be a strong unifying factor in countries whose populations were not
wholly of British descent. It was the awareness of a common outlook and
way of life and a sense of community of interest which could give the new
Commonwealth strength and cohesion; and a fresh step in adaptation could
do it no harm.

The Prime Ministers authorized Attlee, Cripps and Nehru to draft a
formula which could keep India in the Commonwealth on these terms. The
idea of a common citizenship could have had far-reaching consequences;

[40] Bajpai's note on Mr Gordon Walker's interview with Nehru, 30 March 1949.
[41] Nehru to Attlee, 1 April 1949.
[42] B. N. Rau's telegrams from London to Bajpai, 2 and 5 April 1949.
[43] Nehru to Patel, 14 April 1949, *Sardar Patel's Correspondence*, Vol. 8, pp. 10-11; also Nehru to
Krishna Menon, 14 April 1949. For Attlee's indifference to the idea of common citizenship and the
objections of other Commonwealth countries, see H. Tinker, *Separate and Unequal* (London, 1976),
pp. 372-5.

one has only to consider the difference that would have been made by the peoples, say, of India, Pakistan and South Africa having common citizenship in the years after 1949. But this revolutionary idea was not taken up by the British side. On this point, the Conference was willing to go no further than record, in a separate, confidential minute, as a sop to Nehru, 'that nationals of other member countries are not [to be] treated as foreigners,'[44] without saying anything as to how this was to be done. The Prime Ministers concentrated their attention on the King's status and proposed the phrase 'Head of the Commonwealth and symbol of free association', which, under Nehru's pressure, was amended to 'Head of the Commonwealth as the symbol of free association.' It was originally decided to issue two declarations, one reaffirming the allegiance of the old members and the other defining India's adherence; but later the two declarations were merged and this had the advantage of not implying a different status for India. India accepted 'the King as the symbol of the free association of its independent member nations and as such the Head of the Commonwealth.'[45] Nehru still disliked the phrase 'Head of the Commonwealth' but did not think it worthwhile to insist on its deletion, especially as Malan had it placed on record that this designation did not imply that the King discharged any constitutional function by virtue of the headship. The declaration also made it clear that all members were 'free and equal', with no commitments in policy but 'freely cooperating in the pursuit of peace, liberty and progress.' The original draft spoke of 'peace, security and progress', but Nehru replaced 'security' with 'liberty', for neither India nor any other Commonwealth country could assume that it would be supported by all other members of the Commonwealth in all circumstances. Fraser, the Prime Minister of New Zealand, asked the conference, and Nehru in particular, what cooperation could mean in such circumstances. 'Nehru, who was put on the spot, made a brilliant reply, arguing that there could be no cooperation except for constructive and peaceful purposes, and that it was not enough to build up a Commonwealth defence bloc and hope to check communism in that way. I have seldom listened to a more impressive dialectical statement. Nehru certainly displayed a magnificent mind.'[46]

Though there was a wide consensus of support in India for Nehru's decision, the criticism of a few was severe. The Socialists in particular quoted Nehru's past speeches against Dominion Status and condemned his

[44] Tinker, op. cit., p. 387.

[45] King George VI himself seems to have been helpful in securing the acceptance of this formula and won the appreciation of a sentimental radical like Krishna Menon. 'He was a really good man', cabled Menon to Nehru on the King's death (6 February 1952), 'and a greater man than usually believed. He was very thoughtful of us and understood and respected us. An occasion may well not arise again for me to say this, but it is part of history that in the last few years he did far more than is known or need be said to help. I feel sad and distressed perhaps strangely so.'

[46] Lester Pearson's diary entry, April 1949, Memoirs, Vol. 2, 1948-57 (London, 1974), p. 105.

present action as 'an outrage on the national sentiments of the Indian people', while *Pravda* gave the lead to Communist opinion by regarding the arrangement as the creation of a new military-political basis for the British plan to keep India within the Empire.[47] On the other side, the *New York Times* talked in the same vein of 'a historic step, not only in the progress of the Commonwealth but in setting a limit to Communist conquest and opening the prospect of a wider defence system than the Atlantic Pact.'[48] Patel's statement, that association with the Commonwealth would inevitably have some influence on India's policy, strengthened the critics; and the execution of an Indian trade union leader in Malaya for possessing arms belied the hope that membership would make it easier for India to look after the interests of Indians overseas. But Nehru himself, in this case the prime decision-maker,[49] had no second thoughts. He was convinced that the London declaration was honourable to India in every way, and such as Gandhi would have approved. The Commonwealth was no super-state or arbitration tribunal, and without any compromise of her independence India had secured a 'family arrangement'[50] which shored up her stability, provided 'somewhat of an outer cordon,'[51] saved her from isolation and probably even gave her greater freedom of action. Even Asian countries, many of whom were by nature timid, felt more confident about consultation and closer relations with India merely because she was in the Commonwealth. 'We are apt', Nehru warned Jayaprakash Narayan,[52] 'to be too sure of our stability, internal and external. Taking that for granted we proceed to endeavour to remodel the world.'

The stand India continued to take on such questions as the status of Indians in South Africa made clear that Patel was wrong in suggesting even friendly pressure; but the mere fact that India had opted for membership had brought, in Nehru's phrase, 'a touch of healing'[53] to her relations with Britain. To Cripps in particular it was the moment of fulfilment.

> I have somehow looked upon this meeting as the climax of our mutual efforts over the last nine years and more! I am very happy and I do believe that you have done something really big in world history . . .

[47] 26 April 1949.

[48] 28 April 1949.

[49] 'I had able colleagues to advise me, but I was the sole representative of India and in a sense the future of India for the moment was in my keeping. I was alone in that sense and yet not quite alone, because, as I travelled through the air and as I sat there at the Conference table, the ghosts of many yesterdays of my life surrounded me and brought up picture after picture before me, sentinels and guardians keeping watch over me, telling me perhaps not to trip and not to forget them . . . I stand before you to say with all humility that I have fulfilled the mandate [of the Congress] to the letter.' Nehru in the Constituent Assembly, 16 May 1949, *India's Foreign Policy*, pp. 137-8.

[50] The phrase was Lady Mountbatten's; see Krishna Menon's undated note to Nehru, written sometime before Nehru's departure for London, October 1948.

[51] Krishna Menon's note, ibid.

[52] 14 May 1949.

[53] Speech in Constituent Assembly, 16 May 1949, *India's Foreign Policy*, pp. 145 and 146.

It is good that we have been given this chance to work together — not always seeing eye to eye — but always working heart to heart.[54]

THREE

Nehru's marked leaning towards the Western Powers, his ties with the Commonwealth and India's poor state of relations with the Soviet Union improved Nehru's standing in the United States. The acceptance of a cease-fire in Kashmir helped to establish his bonafides and his positive anti-colonial role was not resented. The Dutch swoop in Indonesia and arrest of the Republican Government had led him to convene in Delhi a conference of the States bordering on the Indian Ocean. They extended from Egypt and Ethiopia to the Philippines, Australia and New Zealand; but he refused to invite the United States and Britain, despite, in the case of the latter, the urgings of Krishna Menon. The presence of Australia and New Zealand was sufficient testimony that this was a regional conference and not the first step in the formation of an Asian bloc animated by hostility to the West. To talk of an Asian bloc had no great meaning when all the countries concerned were relatively weak and would only rouse hostility and add to the tension in the world. Yet at this time, when China was still split by war and was not yet a force in world politics, Nehru thought in terms of an Asian federation with India as its nerve-centre,[55] or at least an Asian regional organization on the lines of the Organization of American States, based on multi-racialism, anti-colonialism and mutual cooperation;[56] and he saw the conference on Indonesia as the first step in such a development.

> From the point of view of Asia, this conference has been a turning-point in history. It means new alignments and a new balance of power, if not now, then in the near future. We do not want to form a new bloc but inevitably the countries of Asia will come closer together and India will play a leading part in this.[57]

It was in line with this new role which he envisaged for India in Asia that Nehru gave paternal advice to U Nu, Sukarno, Hatta and Shahrir, volunteered to mediate between the Government of Burma and the Karen insurgents,[58] and sent invitations for another conference, this time to Britain, Australia, New Zealand, Pakistan, Ceylon and Burma.[59] U Nu was

[54] Cripps to Nehru, 28 April 1949.
[55] Speech at Congress session, 17 December, *Hindu*, 18 December 1948.
[56] See his speech at the inauguration of the conference of 18 nations on Indonesia, 20 January 1949. *Speeches*, Vol. 1, 1946-9 (Delhi, 1949), pp. 325-30.
[57] To Chief Ministers, 3 February 1949.
[58] Nehru's telegram to U Nu, 10 February 1949.
[59] Circular telegram, 21 February 1949.

unwilling to agree to mediation, but even so the representatives of these countries met informally and offered to send a conciliation commission.

All these efforts met with marked approval in the United States, and by the beginning of 1949 there was in that country general acclaim for Nehru. Walter Lippmann hailed him as 'the greatest figure in Asia' and advised the United States Government to begin intimate consultation with him on their policy in China and Indonesia.[60] The *Baltimore Sun* commented:

> He is in many ways the most impressive statesman to emerge on the post-war scene. His greatness is the greatness of a man who is neither exclusively oriental nor occidental, politician nor ascetic, highbrow nor dire poor. Pandit Nehru is in part all of these things, and he speaks as a man who has straddled two worlds, two philosophies and two standards of living. The key to Nehru's greatness as a statesman is his ability to leave past conflicts behind him as he enters new situations.[61]

Life wrote a long article on him,[62] and his was, in the same week, the cover portrait on *Time*.[63] The State Department was not far behind, and the Ambassador called on Nehru to stress the need for mutual understanding with a view to cooperation in as many fields as possible.

Nehru responded to all this with pardonably complacent warmth. The United States and India, he told the American Ambassador, had much to give each other, for they were both nations of actual or potential significance.

> Fate and circumstances have thrust a tremendous responsibility on the United States. Fate and circumstances have also placed India in a rather special position in Asia and, even though those of us who happen to control to some extent India's destiny today may not come up to the mark, there can be no doubt that the new India will go ahead. It may stumble often, but it has the capacity to stand up again and take some more steps forward.[64]

He was confident that India had turned a big corner in her domestic affairs and was now on the upgrade; so she could now play a more prominent role in the world. He told Parliament that India, having emerged again into the main trend of human affairs as a meeting-ground between the East and West, would now adopt a positive policy which was not neutral or sitting on the fence, or vaguely middle-of-the-road. Asia, unlike Europe, had no legacy of conflict and India could therefore keep aloof from power alignments and seek friendly cooperation with all. She would approach all

[60] *New York Herald Tribune*, 10 January 1949.
[61] 28 January 1949.
[62] 29 January 1949.
[63] 30 January 1949.
[64] Nehru to Loy Henderson, 8 January 1949.

problems in her own way and not be restricted by any ideology emanating from Europe.[65] There was now a growing emphasis in Nehru's outlook on Indian-ness rather than on pragmatism. It was as a part of this new approach that he selected for the Embassy in Moscow not a politician or professional diplomat but Radhakrishnan, who, more than anyone else, represented as well as defined Indian values to the world.

Such a positive policy demanded a clarity of relationship with both the United States and the Soviet Union. The United Nations was important, but not as important as Nehru had thought or hoped; so for the moment vital work lay elsewhere. Nehru was anxious, despite Soviet criticism of his government and support for the Indian Communist Party, to be as friendly as possible and develop contacts in such non-political matters as exchange of films and cultural delegations, to continue talks on a possible trade agreement and offer to buy petrol.[66] But the fact remained that, whatever the theoretical premises of non-alignment, India was much nearer to Britain and the United States than to the Soviet Union. It was to the Western Powers that India mainly looked for economic and technical assistance; and her political and trade connections were also mostly with them. So it was but logical that Nehru, strengthened by the Commonwealth connection, should be willing to explore the chance to develop direct relations with the United States. In Washington the Ambassador was his sister, Vijayalakshmi, but as she was unable to transform the cordiality into even a semblance of an entente Nehru decided to accept the invitation which Truman had been extending repeatedly for over a year.[67] Soon after, the attitude of the United States on Kashmir caused sharp disappointment. Though the fighting had stopped, the United Nations Commission had been unable to make any progress on the implementation of the resolution of the Security Council. So it came forward in May 1949 with proposals which Nehru found unacceptable. He felt that the Commission was trying step by step to pull India away from her moorings, and there were limits beyond which she could not go without endangering her political and military position in Kashmir.[68] The withdrawal of Indian forces depended on the total withdrawal of regular and irregular Pakistani troops and the disbandment of forces in 'Azad Kashmir', the area under Pakistani occupation, of which there were already thirty-five well-trained battalions. India could not allow her armies to be so weakened as to be unable to meet any internal or external danger, especially as Pakistan continued to be in an aggressive mood, and there was still a risk of war. This also made it essential for India to hold certain strategic areas in northern Kashmir.

[65] 8 March 1949, *Speeches*, Vol. 1, pp. 233-50.
[66] Nehru's note, 14 February 1949.
[67] Nehru to Bajpai, 10 April 1949.
[68] To Chief Ministers, 14 May, and to Krishna Menon, 14 May 1949.

Faced with an unbridgeable gap between the two sides, the Commission suggested arbitration by Admiral Nimitz on points of disagreement regarding the withdrawal of the forces of India and Pakistan. Truman and Attlee intervened to urge acceptance even before the terms of reference were laid down. 'All this barrage is, I suppose, meant to sweep us away.'[69] Nehru informed the American Ambassador that India would stick by what she considered right in Kashmir, whatever the cost. There were moral issues involved, and Pakistan's behaviour in Kashmir had been disgraceful from beginning to end. It was utterly wrong to balance India and Pakistan on the Kashmir question, and India was not going to surrender feebly to aggression.[70] He also, rejecting the advice of Mountbatten that India should make further concessions,[71] wrote to Attlee that India was not opposed to the principle of arbitration, but any arbitration would have to be on a precise and defined issue; neither was the disbandment of 'Azad Kashmir' forces a matter for arbitration. All that was required was an immediate and positive decision.[72]

'We want', cabled Nehru to Krishna Menon, 'to be friendly with the United Kingdom and the United States but neither pressure tactics nor lure of help will make us give up a position which we are convinced is right from every point of view.'[73] He also stated publicly that his government had rejected the proposal for arbitration which Truman and Attlee had pressed on him, and asserted that Indian troops would not be withdrawn from Kashmir unless the people of that State desired it and the Government of India were satisfied that the safety of Kashmir would not be endangered thereby.[74] The *Manchester Guardian*, usually friendly to India, commented that India seemed desirous of avoiding a plebiscite.[75] Such censure in turn encouraged Pakistan to increase her threats of recourse to war, and trade between the two countries came to a virtual standstill. When the Commission reported failure, the Security Council nominated its president, General McNaughton, to hold informal discussions with India and Pakistan. His proposals, providing for demilitarization by equating the forces of India and Pakistan in Kashmir as well as the troops of the Kashmir Government and the 'Azad Kashmir' forces, also seemed to India to be heavily weighted against her.

So the Kashmir problem 'remains as insoluble as ever and perhaps there is more tension now than ever before.'[76] For this Nehru attributed

[69] Nehru to Patel, 30 August 1949, *Sardar Patel's Correspondence*, Vol. 1 (Ahmedabad, 1971), pp. 294-5.
[70] Nehru to Vijayalakshmi, 24 August 1949.
[71] Letter to Nehru, 2 September 1949.
[72] Nehru to Attlee, 8 September 1949.
[73] Personal telegram, 11 September 1949.
[74] Speeches at Ferozepur, 17 September, and at Srinagar, 24 September, *National Herald*, 18 and 25 September 1949 respectively.
[75] 7 September 1949.
[76] Nehru to Mountbatten, 22 September 1949.

considerable responsibility to what appeared to him to be the lack of fairness shown by the United States. Yet he did not cancel or postpone his visit; rather, recognizing its enormous significance, he carefully prepared his mind for it. India needed the assistance of the United States, particularly in food, machinery and capital goods; 'why not', as Nehru asked Krishna Menon, 'align with the United States *somewhat* and build up our economic and military strength?'[77] The question was not wholly rhetorical. But he was not prepared to pay the price of subservience to the foreign policy of the United States, which Nehru believed was prone to be immature and cocksure. It was important too not to get tied up too much with American business interests, and the much-needed financial aid would have to be secured on terms such as deferred payment which would not be humiliating to India. For Nehru was certain that India in her own way was of some importance to the United States; there was not at that time another country in Asia which had anything near the strength of India. 'India has much to give, not in gold or silver or even in exportable commodities, but by virtue of her present position. It is well-recognized today all over the world that the future of Asia will be powerfully determined by the future of India. India becomes more and more the pivot of Asia.'[78]

Nehru, therefore, decided that, while in the United States, he would remain his natural self, be friendly and talk frankly about the need for American assistance, not in any pleading tone but with confidence, conscious of India's position in the world and with faith in her future.

I think often, whenever I have the time to think, of this coming American visit. In what mood shall I approach America? How shall I address people etc.? How shall I deal with the Government there and businessmen and others? Which facet of myself should I put before the American public — the Indian or the European, for after all I have that European or English aspect also. I shall have to meet some difficult situations. I want to be friendly with the Americans but always making it clear what we stand for. I want to make no commitments which come in the way of our basic policy. I am inclined to think that the best preparation for America is not to prepare and to trust to my native wit and the mood of the moment, the general approach being friendly and receptive. I go there to learn more than to teach. Indeed I have no desire to teach, unless of course people learn indirectly and rather casually. I have met a large number of Americans and read a good number of books on America. And yet I am not really acquainted, in the intimate way one should be acquainted, with the American atmosphere. I am receptive if I want to be and I propose to be receptive in the United States. I want to see their good points and

[77] See Krishna Menon's account of this conversation in his letter to Nehru, 7 August 1952.
[78] To Chief Ministers, 2 October 1949.

that is the best approach to a country. At the same time I do not propose to be swept away by them. I do not think there is much chance of that.[79]

The visit in October 1949, punctuated in the middle by a short stay in Canada, was not without its gaffes, giving point to the quip which Nehru had been fond of quoting that one should never go to America for the first time. The wealth and material prosperity were occasionally flaunted, as at a lunch of businessmen in New York, where he was informed that twenty billion dollars was collected round that table; and it is said that at the banquet in the White House most of the time was taken up in a debate between the President and the Chief Justice on the relative merits of Maryland and Missouri Bourbon whiskey.[80] The official discussions with Truman and Acheson also failed to develop any cordiality or understanding. Both sides adopted condescending attitudes.[81] Nehru hotly defended India's position on Kashmir and was critical of the equivocal attitude of the United States.[82] His hosts, on their part, disagreed with his assessment of events in China and resented the early recognition, which was clearly in the offing, by India of the new People's Government. As for economic assistance, Loy Henderson informed Deshmukh, Nehru's financial adviser, that Truman would give Nehru anything he asked for;[83] but Nehru refused to beg or to do more than to state India's requirements of food and commodities in general terms. The result was that at a time when there was a glut of wheat in the American market and it would have been easy to make (as was widely expected) a gift of a million tons, India was not offered even special terms.

So the official side of Nehru's visit was a disappointment to all. 'He was so important', wrote Acheson much later, 'to India and India's survival so important to all of us, that if he did not exist — as Voltaire said of God — he would have to be invented. Nevertheless, he was one of the most difficult men with whom I have ever had to deal.'[84] Nehru's own assessment at the time was that the United States Government had expected acquiescence from him on all issues, and were unwilling to assist India for anything less. 'They had gone all-out to welcome me and I am very grateful to them for it and expressed myself so. But they expected something more

[79] To Vijayalakshmi, 24 August 1949.

[80] C. L. Sulzberger, *The Last of the Giants* (London, 1970), p. 131.

[81] See the reports given to Marquis Childs by both Nehru and Acheson soon after the discussions. M. Childs, *Witness to Power* (New York, 1975), p. 134.

[82] Cf. 'It would be prejudical to American interests in the Middle East and Far East to develop an Indian policy without taking into account Pakistan's legitimate interests.' Memorandum of Stephen J. Springarn, Assistant to President Truman, 23 August 1949. Truman Papers. Reprinted by Dr M. Jha in *Mainstream* (New Delhi), 7 August 1971.

[83] Deshmukh's interview with the author, 21 January 1969.

[84] D. Acheson, *Present at the Creation* (London, 1969), p. 336.

than gratitude and goodwill and that more I could not supply them.'[85]

Yet the visit was not a failure, for more important than the hard bargainings in Washington were the impact of Nehru on the American public and the first-hand appreciation which he acquired of many of the attractive aspects of American life. Huge crowds turned out to receive him with demonstrative acclaim wherever he went, and an American remarked that he was surprised to find the *darshan* habit spreading in the United States. 'A World Titan', said the welcome editorial in the *Christian Science Monitor*. 'Only a tiny handful of men', said Adlai Stevenson, welcoming him to Chicago, 'have influenced the implacable forces of our time. To this small company of the truly great, our guest . . . belongs . . . Pandit Jawaharlal Nehru belongs to the even *smaller* company of historic figures who wore a halo in their own lifetimes.'[86] Elsie Morrow reported in the *St Louis Post Dispatch* that 'Nehru has departed from us, leaving behind clouds of misty-eyed women.' But there was more to Nehru's popularity than merely a captivating personality. To an American public that tended to view Asia in terms of the Kuomintang he brought fresh vistas of a continent striving once more towards the common goals of justice, liberty and peace. In particular he provided a striking image of the new, free India, eager to be friendly with the United States without becoming a tiresome supplicant, weak in material strength but willing to make its contribution to world affairs and, having shed every fear complex under the guidance of Gandhi, keen to help in removing any similar complex from international relations. He also repeatedly explained that India's detachment in the cold war did not imply isolation and indifference on basic issues. Non-alignment did not exclude commitment to principles. 'Where freedom is menaced or justice threatened or where aggression takes place, we cannot be and shall not be neutral.'[87] Total agreement with all that the United States said or did was not necessary in order to establish India's binding faith in the basic values and her unfailing endeavour to ensure them. 'When man's liberty or peace is in danger we cannot and shall not be neutral; neutrality would be a betrayal of what we have fought for and stand for.'[88]

Not alliance or agreement but understanding and, in Nehru's phrase, 'emotional awareness'[89] appeared to him important; and it was these that he sought to promote by his many speeches in the United States. He hoped for close ties with the United States; but the 'most intimate ties are ties which are not ties.'[90] He believed that, whatever the resistance in Washington, he had made some impact on the common folk; and indeed the harmony of

[85] To S. Radhakrishnan, 6 February 1950.
[86] 26 October 1949. W. Johnson (ed.), *The Papers of Adlai E. Stevenson*, Vol. 3 (Boston, 1973), p. 181.
[87] Speech to the Joint Session of Congress, 13 October, *National Herald*, 14 October 1949.
[88] Address at Columbia University, 17 October, *National Herald*, 19 October 1949.
[89] Broadcast from New York, 19 October, *National Herald*, 21 October 1949.
[90] Talk to journalists in New York, 15 October, *National Herald*, 16 October 1949.

outlook that appeared to have been established led the Soviet Government
to protest informally. They had been suspicious of his visit from the
start – the warning article in the *New Times*[91] had been entitled 'Chiang
Kai Shek's successor?'; and later the Indian Ambassador was summoned
for a pointed inquiry,[92] with reference to Nehru's statement that India
would not be neutral where aggression took place, into who the aggressor
was that Nehru had in mind.

The impact, however, was not solely one-sided. Nehru himself was
deeply influenced by what he saw, and the recognition of the specifically
distasteful was accommodated within a general appreciation. In the last
years of the freedom movement he had hoped for much from the United
States. In prison at Ahmadnagar he had secured a book list from Pearl
Buck, read Truslow Adams and Benjamin Franklin and, like any
schoolboy, copied in his notebook the full text of the Gettysburg Address.
Yet until 1947 the United States had not been to him more than a distant
beacon; and the first years of freedom had brought considerable disappointment in official relations. Now the direct exposure to the people of the
United States, and their intellectuals and scientists, altered his notions of
that country.

I found my visit to America not only interesting but rather exciting.
America is of course a strange mélange. We all know of its worship of
success and dollars. But I found something much more appealing to
me and much more enduring there. This made me feel almost at home.
In a sense America shows up the essential conflict that is present all
over the world, a conflict of the spirit of man. I have come back
therefore with a larger measure of confidence than I had when I
went.[93]

FOUR

On his return from the United States, relations with the Truman
administration became even worse than before. A message from Acheson
on Kashmir appeared to Nehru highly objectionable and in the nature of an
ultimatum. 'I am sick and tired of the attitude that the British and the
American Governments have been taking in this matter.'[94] He rejected the
suggestion of arbitration on Kashmir[95] and expressed strong resentment at
international pressure. 'The people who run the Government of India have
a record in the past of standing for what they consider to be right,

[91] 12 October 1949.
[92] S. Radhakrishnan's telegram from Moscow to Nehru, 29 October 1949.
[93] To Professor Harlow Shapley, 3 December 1949.
[94] Nehru to B. N. Rau, 17 January 1950.
[95] Statement at press conference 6 January, *Hindustan Times*, 7 January 1950.

regardless of the consequences, for the last thirty years and they propose to do that in regard to Kashmir or any other matter.'[96] Yet it did strike him that this critical attitude to India's case on Kashmir might be due not only to the general policies of Britain and the United States but also to an ambiguity in India's outlook and an increasingly communal approach to the Muslim minority in India.[97] So he sought to take the initiative in lessening tensions between India and Pakistan. Far from his efforts succeeding, by March 1950 the two countries moved to the brink of war; and Nehru continued to believe that this could be attributed mainly to the unbroken encouragement given by the United States, Britain and other countries to Pakistan in some of its policies.[98] The gilt was also taken off his memories of his stay in the United States by the effusive welcome given to Liaqat Ali Khan in Washington in May 1950 and the obvious attempt to build him up as a great Asian leader against Nehru, who was human enough to be piqued.

> I must say that the Americans are either very naïve or singularly lacking in intelligence. They go through the identical routine whether it is Nehru or the Shah of Iran or Liaqat Ali . . . All this lessens the value of their fervent protestations and the superlatives they use. A superlative used too often ceases to have any meaning. Having been trained in a school of more restrained language and action, I am afraid I do not appreciate this kind of thing.[99]

But it was not just the vulgarity which was worrying and his vanity which was hurt:

> It does appear that there is a concerted attempt to build up Pakistan and build down, if I may say so, India. It surprises me how immature in their political thinking the Americans are! They do not even learn from their own or other people's mistakes; more especially in their dealings with Asia, they show a lack of understanding which is surprising.[100]

Even so, Nehru took care to see that the stand-offishness of the United States Government did not push India nearer to the Soviet Union, and he avoided any step which might worsen relations with the Western Powers. For he was still wary of the Soviet Union.

[96] Statement at press conference 6 February, *Statesman*, 7 February 1950.
[97] Nehru's note for the Cabinet, 16 January 1950.
[98] Cf. Lester Pearson's account of Philip Noel-Baker's activities in Karachi at this time: 'He has certainly taken a very strong anti-India stand on this matter and is, I think, not doing much to help settle things by his activities.' *Memoirs*, Vol. 2, p. 115.
[99] Nehru to Vijayalakshmi, 10 May 1950.
[100] Nehru to Vijayalakshmi, 29 May 1950.

India does think that international communism is aggressive, partly because of communist philosophy and partly because communism today is very much Slavism. India does not charge the Soviet Union with responsibility for Communist activities in India, but we have little doubt that Russia has encouraged them and can certainly stop them if it so chose.[101]

When Radhakrishnan in Moscow suggested a friendship treaty and even Bajpai, the Secretary-General, who rarely approved of Radhakrishnan's ideas or style of functioning, was willing to consider it, the Prime Minister directed them to move cautiously, not to go too far, and to watch reaction (presumably of the United States) at every stage.[102]

If there is a world war, there is no possibility of India lining up with the Soviet Union whatever else she may do. It is obvious that our relations with the United States as with the United Kingdom in political and economic matters are far closer than with other countries. We have practically no such relations with the Soviet, nor is it likely that they will develop to any great extent for obvious reasons.[103]

With the developing crisis in East Bengal and poor relations with the Western Powers, he directed Radhakrishnan to go slowly in taking even obvious steps towards closer relations with the Soviet Union, as these might further disturb relations with Britain and the United States.[104]

This coolness towards the Soviet Government and concern about the expansionist tendencies of international communism also coloured Nehru's attitude to the new government in China. The acid criticism of him that poured continuously from Peking he charitably ascribed to the 'exuberance of a victorious revolution'.[105] In any event, this could not erase the need for a careful formulation of policy. The establishment of the new regime in China was obviously a world event of the first magnitude, and the reaction of other countries would determine the way in which this event would alter the balance of forces. At the start, China would generally support Soviet foreign policy, but she was too large and distinctive to function merely as a camp-follower. The new rulers had come to power in their own way, without Soviet assistance; and what could be of importance was not that this regime was communist but that it provided a strong central government. It had been welcomed by the Chinese people not for its ideology but because anything seemed better to them than the Kuomintang. There was little chance of any internal upheaval, and so the

101 Nehru's note on foreign policy, 7 February 1950.
102 Nehru's note to Bajpai, 6 February 1950.
103 Nehru's note on foreign policy, 7 February 1950.
104 Nehru to Radhakrishnan, 5 March 1950.
105 Nehru to President Sukarno, 22 December 1949.

4   With Lady Mountbatten, 1948   5   With the Mountbattens, Delhi, 1947

6   Nehru and Patel, 1948

7   Nehru and Mountbatten, Delhi University Convocation, March 1948

other nations would have to deal with the communist government. The coming years appeared to Nehru to be crucial in determining in which direction China would develop. If recognition were withheld, that in itself would lead to barriers and hostility between China and the rest of the world and a correspondingly closer association between the Soviet Union and China. But if China were befriended, she might be encouraged to take what seemed the more natural course of walking out of the Soviet ring. Apart from dissolving the uniformity of communist development, a divergence of foreign policy might also be expedited. Especially in South East Asia, the Soviet Union had adopted a wholly destructive line and seemed to be aiming solely at chaos in order to weaken the countries of the area and prevent them from serving as bases for the Western Powers; but China would probably be more inclined to prevention of conflict, at least until the People's Government had stabilized themselves at home and gained some measure of economic strength.

So Nehru advocated an attitude of 'cautious friendliness' towards China. It should be made manifestly a friendly approach, and there should be no support of the enemies of China or formation of any bloc which could be regarded as anti-Chinese or anti-communist. He promptly rejected U Nu's suggestions of a defence pact between India, Burma, Ceylon and Pakistan — which was anyway impractical — and of an extension of the Truman doctrine to South East Asia. But, although he saw at this time little danger of any Chinese aggression across the Indian borders, he intended to make it quite clear, when occasion arose, that the slightest attempt at such aggression, whether in India or Nepal, would be stoutly resisted. As for aggressive communism, it could be best resisted in South East Asia by removing every vestige of colonial control and strengthening the nationalist forces. The Commonwealth Foreign Ministers, meeting at Colombo in January 1950, agreed; and Nehru secured general acceptance that what was needed was not a Pacific pact on the lines of NATO but the raising, with the assistance of the Commonwealth countries, of the economic standards of the region.[106]

---

[106] Nehru to U Nu, 7 January 1950, his notes for speech at Colombo Conference, 9 January 1950, speeches at the Colombo Conference, 10 and 12 January 1950, and S. Dutt's report on the Colombo Conference, 21 January 1950.

4

Domestic Pressures

ONE

Kashmir and Hyderabad had spilt over into foreign affairs. But there were other problems as pressing, even if of a long-term nature, which were almost purely domestic. They caused a quick waning of Nehru's confidence that, after the strains of the first few months, the forces of democratic and secular progress seemed to be prevailing.[1] Under the first shock of Gandhi's murder, Hindu communal forces lay low and public opinion supported drastic action against them. 'These people have the blood of Mahatma Gandhi on their hands, and pious disclaimers and dissociation now have no meaning.'[2] The Muslim League showed sign of disintegrating, and Tara Singh's arrest in February 1949 decapitated the Akali movement. But there were other growing elements of dissension. Indeed, Nehru's own political position was becoming isolated. Gandhi's death had removed a primary support and there was both an increasing alienation of left-wing elements outside the Congress and a weakening of radical forces within the Party itself. The decision of the members of the Congress Socialist Party in 1948 to leave the Congress had been a blow for Nehru, who sympathized with their general viewpoint and liked many of their leaders. Until now, in the long history of the Congress Party, it had always been the more conservative elements that had been regularly shed; and it was not a pleasant reflection that for the first time there had been a major withdrawal of progressive forces. He was particularly sorry that Jayaprakash Narayan should have been lost to the Congress. To many in India Narayan appeared cross-grained, woolly-minded and exasperatingly self-righteous; but Nehru recognized his physical courage and moral integrity and even in 1946 had seen in him a future prime minister.[3] Their personal relations too were knit close by affection; and Narayan was one of the two

[1] Nehru to Chief Ministers, 20 February 1948.
[2] Nehru to G. C. Bhargava, 11 February 1948.
[3] See his remark cited by Louis Fischer in A. K. Azad, *India Wins Freedom* (American edition, 1960), p. 142 fn.

persons outside the family — the other being the scientist Homi Bhabha — who addressed Nehru as *bhai* (brother). So Nehru worried about the expanding breach between Narayan and himself. Narayan was

apt to go astray very often and act in an irresponsible manner. But he is one of the straightest and finest men I have known, and if character counts, as it does, he counts for a great deal. It seems to me a tragedy that a man like him should be thrust, by circumstances, into the wilderness.[4]

With the hope, therefore, of making the return of the Socialists easier he advised his colleagues to say and do nothing which might add to the rift.[5] He also, in an effort to win the Socialists back, wrote to Jayaprakash offering to consider how the gulf could be bridged and requesting him to do the same. 'I am greatly distressed at many things in India. But perhaps what distresses me most is the wide gap which is ever growing between many of us and the Socialist Party.' This was not good for the Socialists, who would find themselves either isolationists or cooperating with groups with whom they had little in common; it was not good for the Congress; and it was not good for the country.

I cannot, by sheer force of circumstance, do everything that I would like to do. We are all of us in some measure prisoners of fate and circumstance. But I am as keen as ever to go in a particular direction and carry the country with me and I do hope that in doing so I would have some help from you . . . It may be that we are not strong enough or wise enough to face these problems, but for the moment I do not see any other group that can do so more successfully. You will remember the least that the recent history of Europe has taught us, that an attempt at premature leftism may well lead to reaction and disruption.[6]

These approaches to the Socialists proved fruitless. Jayaprakash was severely critical of Nehru's general outlook. 'You want to go towards socialism, but you want the capitalists to help in that. You want to build socialism with the help of capitalism. You are bound to fail in that.'[7] He ignored an appeal not to launch a railway strike[8] and objected vehemently to the legislation outlawing strikes in the essential services, describing it as 'an ugly example of growing Indian fascism.'[9] There was also severe

[4] Nehru to G. B. Pant, 1 July 1948.
[5] Nehru to Chief Ministers, 1 April 1948.
[6] To Jayaprakash Narayan, 19 August 1948.
[7] Jayaprakash Narayan to Nehru, 10 December 1948, quoted in A. and W. Scarfe, *J. P. His Biography* (Delhi, 1975), p. 237.
[8] Nehru to Jayaprakash Narayan, 22 December 1948.
[9] Jayaprakash Narayan's telegram to Nehru, first week of March 1949.

criticism of the decision to maintain India's link with the Commonwealth. Criticism in itself was not unacceptable to Nehru. 'I am not afraid of the opposition in this country and I do not mind if opposition groups grow up on the basis of some theory, practice or constructive theme. I do not want India to be a country in which millions of people say "yes" to one man, I want a strong opposition.'[10] But leftism in India seemed to him an infantile phenomenon, a collection of odd elements united by frustration and a dislike of the Congress.[11] The Socialists had no positive alternative to offer and contented themselves by giving petty trouble on minor issues to the government. Nehru was not prepared to endow them with popular sympathy by keeping them in jail and ordered their immediate release whenever they were arrested for disorderly demonstrations. 'As for the Socialists, they continue to show an amazing lack of responsibility and constructive bent of mind. They seem to be all frustrated and going mentally to pieces.'[12] While office was corrupting the Congress, irresponsibility was corroding the opposition.

> Of course, there is nobody and no group that can take our place, and yet we grow stale and the mere fact that we appear immovable annoys and irritates many people. It would be a good thing if they were given a chance to have some other people. Whether they will take their chance or not, it is for them to decide. But anyhow this will clear up the atmosphere.[13]

The Socialists also sought to regard Nehru as standing apart from Patel and the other Congress leaders; but the Prime Minister, while pressing his colleagues in private to be more flexible and to agree to judicial inquiries in case of use of firearms by the police, presented a united front to the outside world. 'All I can do', Jayaprakash wrote to him, 'is to wonder how far apart we have travelled in looking at things. No doubt I am academic and doctrinaire.'[14] They drew even further apart when a crisis developed in Nepal. The King of Nepal, until then a figurehead, fell out with the powerful Ranas and took refuge in the Indian Embassy, from where he was flown out to Delhi. With China consolidating her position in Tibet, Nepal was obviously a sensitive area. Nehru had always intended to make it clear that India's strategic frontier lay on the northern side of Nepal, and any attack on Nepal would be regarded as aggression on India. Now an occasion had arisen which could be utilized to strengthen India's position in Nepal, but clearly the cards would have to be played carefully. China was

[10] Speech at Trivandrum, 2 June, *National Herald*, 3 June 1950.
[11] Nehru to Chief Ministers, 15 August 1949.
[12] To Patel, 30 June 1949.
[13] To Krishna Menon, 1 July 1949.
[14] 18 October 1950.

on the alert, while the British Ambassador, who exercised a powerful influence in Nepal, was in sympathy with the Ranas. Nehru's policy was to compel the Ranas to carry out political reforms which would reduce their autocracy and to receive the King back, and to effect this by pressure rather than by open support of the Nepal Congress. It was not that Nehru disapproved of the Congress, but he did not wish to promote a messy and drawn-out situation of fighting between popular elements and the loyal Nepal army. So, when the Nepal Congress started a revolt and B. P. Koirala came to Delhi seeking military support, Nehru declined to see him but kept Koirala informed of his attempts to prevent a civil war and establish constitutional government in Nepal. Such efforts at subtlety angered Jayaprakash.

So this is how you wish to treat a democratic revolution in a neighbouring state! . . . You are destroying yourself. One by one you are denying your noble ideals. You are compromising, you are yielding. You are estranging your friends and slipping into the parlour of your enemies . . . And please learn to discipline your temper.[15]

At least on this occasion Nehru did not lose his temper and explained carefully to Jayaprakash the elements of the situation as he saw them.

I am distressed at the lack of understanding that you have shown and I am more than distressed by the astonishing stupidity of some of the things that the leaders of the Nepal Congress have been responsible for . . . I quite agree with you that the opportunity of securing freedom for Nepal has come and that the trump cards are there. When I see this opportunity being almost lost and every kind of bungling being done by amateur politicians who know nothing about politics and less about insurrection, I have a right to be upset . . . Nothing can stop a revolution in Nepal except the folly of those who are supporting it . . . Widespread propaganda is being carried on by our opponents abroad to show that this is just an example of Indian imperialism and that we have engineered all this. This obviously can do a great deal of harm to the whole movement. We cannot ignore external forces at work against us. What Koirala suggested would have put an end to the idea of an indigenous movement and made it just an adventure of the Indian government.

That is just what I am afraid of. Adventurist tactics in politics or warfare seldom succeed. Daring does succeed and risks may be taken, but adventurism is infantile.[16]

[15] Jayaprakash Narayan to Nehru, 17 November 1950.
[16] Nehru to Jayaprakash Narayan, 20 November 1950.

Nehru's policy was successful. The British Government, informed by Nehru that it might become almost impossible for him to attend the Commonwealth Prime Ministers' Conference in January 1951 if they recognized the boy king, whom the Ranas had enthroned in place of his grandfather in exile,[17] modified their attitude; the Ranas agreed to a compromise, and the king returned in triumph to Kathmandu. But the Socialists continued to be aggrieved.

The Communists were even fiercer during these years in their opposition to Nehru's government. The escapist mood of the Socialists was as nothing compared with their disruptive tactics. For the first few months after the transfer of power, the Communist Party supported the new Government. Palme Dutt, still the mentor of Indian Communists, praised Nehru's opposition to foreign intervention in India and his efforts to seek a basis for cooperation with Pakistan;[18] and P. C. Joshi, the secretary of the Party, urged all progressives to rally round Nehru.[19] But the attitude of the Soviet Union was different, and this was soon reflected in the attitude of the Communists. Foreigners are thought, at a meeting of the Indian Communist Party, to have denounced the Government of India and secured a change of communist leadership.[20] Joshi was replaced in December 1947 by the more militant B. T. Ranadive, who first supported Nehru against what he described as the reactionary elements in the Congress,[21] but later criticized 'opportunist illusions about bourgeois leadership' and attacked the Government as a whole. 'In the absence of strong mass pressure from the left, Nehru's utterances remain mere words and Nehru becomes more and more the democratic mask for Patel.'[22] There should be violent opposition to the Government 'in all spheres and on all fronts', and by waging 'serious, very serious battles', power should be seized in a short time. 'The day of veiled imperialism under the form of slave-controlled "independence" will not last long.'[23]

The Communists then began, in March 1948, militant mass movements in various areas; and these appeared to Nehru to have developed into an anti-national campaign, worse than an open rebellion and aiming at total disruption which would result in widespread chaos, regardless of consequences.[24]

I have not the least feeling against communism or against communists

[17] Nehru's telegram to Krishna Menon, reporting conversation with British High Commissioner, 24 November 1950.

[18] *Daily Worker*, 8 October 1947.

[19] Public statement, 9 October 1947.

[20] See Nehru to Vijayalakshmi, 15 April 1948.

[21] See his article in *World News and Views*, 6 December 1947.

[22] C.P.I. Statement, 21 December 1947.

[23] R. Palme Dutt in February 1948.

[24] Speech on 5 March 1949, Constituent Assembly (Legislative) Debates, 1949, Vol. II, Part II, pp. 1164-7.

as such. As you know, the British Tory press often describes me as a pal of Stalin. But I must confess that the way the communists are carrying on in India in the shape of the most violent activity and writing is enough to disgust anyone. There is a complete lack of integrity and decency.[25]

This agitational activity lasted for nearly three and a half years and at its height seriously affected Telengana in Hyderabad, Travancore-Cochin, Tripura, Manipur, Malabar in Madras, Andhra and parts of west Bengal, Bihar, eastern Uttar Pradesh and Maharashtra. In Hyderabad the Communists seemed to be with the Razackars against the Indian army, denouncing the occupation of the State. 'Sardar Patel's army went to Hyderabad to stop the onward march of history, to save the Nizam and the oppressive feudal order, to save the bourgeois-feudal rule from the rising tide of the forces of the democratic revolution.'[26] It was then decided to organize an upheaval all over India, built round a railway strike, on 9 March 1949, and Nehru was fiercely condemned for a 'fascist offensive' against the working class 'at the dictates of Anglo-American capital' and for a 'policy of national treachery'.[27] But the strike proved a failure, and from then on the agitation moved downhill, with the emphasis shifting to rural guerilla warfare, not violent action in the cities. Conditions remained disturbed in Telengana, and there seemed no intention of calling off the struggle. India was said to be still 'a colonial and semi-feudal country', with a government that represented 'the anti-national big bourgeoisie and feudal classes.'[28]

Even with the Korean war and Nehru's support for People's China, there was no immediate shift in thinking. The Nehru Government was still condemned for 'compromise, collaboration and national betrayal.'[29] But Palme Dutt believed that Nehru's foreign policy showed indications of divergence — 'even though still hesitant and limited' — from the imperialist war policy;[30] and a few months later he advised the Indian Communist Party to move along an Indian path in relation to concrete Indian conditions.[31] In October 1951 the Telengana struggle was finally called off.

Nehru was firm in resisting such activity and sabotage while it lasted, but was anxious to do so by open tactics. Obviously action would have to be taken against persons subverting law and order, but he insisted that this should be in accordance with normal legal processes. Repeatedly he urged

[25] To Mountbatten, 4 August 1948.
[26] G. M. Adhikari, *What is Happening in Hyderabad?* (Delhi, 1949) pp. 7-8.
[27] C.P.I. statement, 2 March 1949.
[28] C.P.I. statement, 7 April 1950.
[29] Draft policy statement of C.P.I. Politbureau, 15 November 1950.
[30] *Cross Roads* (journal of the C.P.I.), 19 January 1951.
[31] *Cross Roads*, 29 June 1951.

the Chief Ministers to respect civil liberties.[32] 'We are getting very unpopular in other countries and our reputation now is that of a police state suppressing individual freedom.'[33] To ban the Communist Party, as proposed by some, would only intensify its underground activities and by implying condemnation of its ideology evoke a measure of public sympathy. The Party had adopted a wrong course even from its own viewpoint, caused division in its ranks and isolated itself; as he said later, the greatest enemy of communism in India was the Communist Party of India.[34] It was not for the Government to redress the balance at a time when momentous developments were taking place in China and the negotiations regarding the Commonwealth were at a delicate stage. There should not even be large-scale arrests, but individual members suspected of organizing trouble should be taken into custody.[35]

Only Bengal, under the determined but reactionary leadership of Bidhan Roy, ignored Nehru's directive, banned the Communist Party and took recourse to repressive action. Nehru warned Roy:

There is always the grave danger of this kind of thing becoming almost a normal routine for our police. It is a slippery slope and the police have to be continually kept in check. There is no doubt in my mind that ultimately the only way to check and suppress all these violent and objectionable tendencies is to have a positive programme of approach to the people and that pure repression will fail.[36]

Communist leadership in India was to Nehru's mind devoid of any moral standard or even any thought of India's good; and for once he saw little difference between communism and communalism.[37] But a distortion of leftist ideology, of which he thought the Communists guilty, could be defeated not at its own level but by a higher idealism. The real problem was something deeper than the killing and violence of the Communists; it was the need to deal with the economic distemper at a time when expectations had been aroused and a political consciousness had spread among vast masses of the people.

The point was driven home by a by-election in Calcutta, where the Congress candidate was routed. Everywhere the Congress, living on its

[32] E.g. to S. K. Sinha, Chief Minister of Bihar, 8 June and to O. P. R. Reddiar, Chief Minister of Madras, 10 August 1948.

[33] To G. Bardoloi, Chief Minister of Assam, 4 September 1948.

[34] Speech at Calcutta, 14 July, National Herald, 15 July 1949.

[35] To Chief Ministers, 1 April 1948 and 16 April 1949.

[36] Nehru to Roy, 13 May 1949.

[37] 'Question: Between communism and communalism, which is the lesser evil?
Nehru: An extraordinary question to ask. Which do you prefer, death by drowning or falling from a precipice?' Report of press conference, 5 August, Hindustan Times, 6 August 1949.

past prestige, was losing touch with the people, but nowhere more so than in Bengal; and old majorities in assemblies were to Nehru no solace for a general weakening of the moral fibre, and rule by repression. The Congress should be in office because the people wanted it and not merely because there was no other party worth mention. 'We as a government, whether at the Centre or in the Provinces, have no desire to continue governing people who do not want us. Ultimately, people should have the type of government they want, whether it is good or bad.'[38]

The first personal reaction was one of weariness and vexation of spirit. 'There is', he had written in the spring of 1949, 'gradually back in India an air of optimism in spite of everything. Whether that is justified or not I do not know. But I share it and in any event that does create a helpful atmosphere.'[39] This cheerfulness now slumped. 'Ever since I returned from England, I have had to face very heavy weather here. Somehow quite a number of difficult problems all collected together to bear down upon me. All this, added to the heat, has not made life very pleasant or agreeable. Here we carry on from day to day, thankful that that day is over and rather apprehensive of what the next day might bring.'[40] But he was soon bouncing back.

Oddly enough, after a long period of something approaching depression I feel revitalized now. Why? Because I suppose things are pretty bad in so many directions and all the spirit of defiance and rebellion in me rises up to meet this challenge on whatever front it might exist. I am not, repeat not, going into a monastery. I am just going to fight my hardest against all this sloth and inertia and corruption and self-interest and little-mindedness that we see around us. Whether I or you succeed or not is after all a little matter. The main thing is throwing off one's energy into a struggle for something one considers worthwhile.[41]

This even brought reward of a kind.

The world is a difficult place to live in wherever we might be, and life becomes more and more complicated with its unending problems. If we are fortunate, we can sometimes feel the fragrance of it and some glimpses of reality.[42]

The first round of this struggle was a visit to Calcutta. Bidhan Roy believed that repression was the only answer to opposition and thought

[38] To N. R. Sarkar, acting Chief Minister of Bengal, 2 July 1949.
[39] To Krishna Menon, 21 March 1949.
[40] To Mountbatten, 29 June 1949.
[41] To Asaf Ali, 2 July 1949.
[42] To Maria Lorenzini, 2 July 1949.

that Nehru was weakening his position by displaying no resistance to communism.[43] Roy, however, had to take leave on medical grounds and the ministers in charge could not prevent Nehru from coming to Calcutta and holding, despite their discouragement and a call from the opposition parties for a total boycott, a public meeting which was the largest even in Nehru's memory. Though the police were in a state of acute nervous tension, the large crowd remained generally inert and passive. But the atmosphere in Bengal was saturated with suspicion, violence and a feeling of martyrdom. 'The Bengali terrorist mentality of extreme emotionalism colours their so-called communist viewpoint and makes them look sometimes quite insane. There is a violence and an intense hatred looking out of their eyes.'[44] Nehru believed that his visit had, to some extent, exorcised their passions, helped towards restoring the general confidence and given the local Congress a healthy jolt. But Calcutta and Bengal were only part of the general problem of the decline of the Congress and of political standards.

Nehru's own disillusion with the job-hunting, factional struggles and money-making in the Congress ranks was intense. 'It is terrible to think that we may be losing all our values and sinking into the sordidness of opportunist politics.'[45] The Congress was converting itself from a party of broad principle to a narrow-minded caucus living on past capital. But resignation from office or abandonment of the Congress did not seem to him to be the answer. He had also persuaded Rafi Kidwai, who was closer to him than most others in the Cabinet, not to resign. Kidwai did not intend to join the Socialists, but he had been disappointed with the Congress and had wished to work from outside for its reform.[46] Nehru replied:

I am, I suppose, at least as much distressed by recent developments as you can possibly be. Indeed I shoulder a greater responsibility, so my distress is all the greater. I doubt myself if existing conditions can continue for long. Obviously I cannot run away from a difficult situation. So I have given the most intense thought to this matter. It will I think be very wrong and injurious for you either to resign immediately or to take part in the U.P. election campaign, or indeed to issue any statement. It is often better to be silent than to have one's say.[47]

The hostile postures of the Communists and the Socialists made it to Nehru all the more necessary to restore right direction to the Congress. For this reason he paid no heed to the advice of those such as Kingsley Martin[48]

[43] See his letter to Patel, 20 June 1949, *Sardar Patel's Correspondence*, Vol. 6, pp. 152-3.
[44] Nehru to Krishna Menon, 16 July 1949.
[45] Nehru to Krishna Menon, 14 April 1948.
[46] R. A. Kidwai to Nehru, 11 April 1948.
[47] Nehru to Kidwai, 11 April 1948.
[48] K. Martin to Nehru, 5 August 1948.

who wished him to divide the Congress and join forces with the Socialists. Though sometimes, in the depressed moods which regularly flitted across his quicksilver nature, he himself thought of taking the step against which he had advised Kidwai, he swiftly shook off these feelings of defeatism.

> If I chose according to my own inclination, I would like other people to carry on the business here and to be left free to do some other things that I consider very important. Yet with all modesty, I think that my leaving might well be in the nature of a disaster. No man is indispensable, but people do make a difference at a particular time.[49]

It was as part of this effort to rally round him those in the Congress who shared his viewpoint that Nehru brought Rajagopalachari to Delhi. Nehru had not forgotten Rajagopalachari's weakening of the Congress in the years from 1942 to 1945.[50] But he had been impressed by Rajagopalachari's balance and clarity of mind while holding office in the interim Government, and later as Governor of Bengal; and Rajagopalachari had officiated as Governor-General when Mountbatten was on leave for a fortnight, and had borne himself with unassuming dignity. Mountbatten too supported his name for the permanent vacancy.[51] So, in the spring of 1948, Nehru offered Rajagopalachari the governor-generalship.

> I have little doubt that we are rapidly deteriorating and becoming reactionary in our outlook and activities. Each step can often be justified by something else, but the net result is progressively bad. On account of all this sometimes I feel that it will be good for me as well as for India if I were out of the picture for a while.
>
> I have been anxious for you to come here because I feel that you might help me a little to get my bearings. You know that I have often disagreed with you and I suppose we shall continue to disagree about many matters. But somehow these disagreements seem rather trivial when we come up against some basic factors. It is in regard to these that I want to seek your help and guidance.[52]

Rajagopalachari indicated his unwillingness and suggested that Nehru should be Governor-General and Patel Prime Minister.

> This would be an arrangement of great international value besides being an efficient arrangement for internal affairs. Much preferable to my appointment. You are big enough to understand the spirit in

[49] Nehru to Krishna Menon, 24 August 1949.
[50] 'As for Rajagopalachari — is there a more dangerous person in all India'. Entry in Nehru's diary maintained in Ahmadnagar prison, 5 August 1944.
[51] See Nehru to Rajagopalachari, 30 March 1948.
[52] To Rajagopalachari, 6 May 1948.

which I suggest this. I feel your power will be greater in the set-up I propose which is what I want.[53]

For once in those years, it would seem, Rajagopalachari had not dissembled his thoughts and had stated clearly that he would have preferred Patel as Prime Minister. But Nehru, without doubting his intent, brushed aside the suggestion and insisted that he succeed Mountbatten. So Rajagopalachari came to Delhi and got on well with Nehru. They shared a common viewpoint, in contrast to Patel, on the need to deal gently with the minorities; and this support was helpful because Patel represented the viewpoint of a large majority of Congressmen. The Hindu communal outlook, whose rapid spread in India caused Nehru more concern than anything else,[54] had not been extinguished even in the higher levels of the Congress Party and was inspiring the decisions of the central and provincial governments. Both Bidhan Roy in Bengal and Patel had had to be snubbed for suggesting that the Pakistan Government be informed that if Hindus migrated from East Bengal, India would expel an equal number of Muslims from West Bengal.[55] Mohanlal Saxena, an old colleague of Nehru, was the Union Minister for Rehabilitation; and he ordered the sealing of Muslim shops in Delhi and the United Provinces. To Nehru this was much more than merely an erroneous administrative decision.

I suppose you know me well enough to realize that the personal equation does not interfere very much with my impersonal reactions to events and things. I do not very much care what happens to me. If something that I care for goes wrong, in the ultimate analysis it is not important where I am and where you are ... We deal and we have been dealing in the past two years with problems of tremendous psychological importance. People of little wit and no vision think of them in petty terms of rupees, annas and pies or of retaliation and the like, forgetting that we might thus be undermining our whole future and shattering such reputation as we may still have.

Personally I care little for what happens to me, but I do care a great deal for what I have stood for throughout my life. I have repeatedly failed and made a mess of things, but I hope I have not forgotten the major ideals which Gandhiji taught us. As I see things happening in India, in the Constituent Assembly, in the Congress, among young men and women, which take us away step by step from those ideals, unhappiness seizes me. Gandhiji's face comes up before me, gentle but reproaching. His words ring in my ears. Sometimes I read his writings

[53] Rajagopalachari's telegram to Nehru, 12 May 1948.

[54] 'I am not alarmed at anything in the world today, but at this narrow-mindedness in the human mind in India. This is a most terrible thing.' Speech to students of Allahabad University, 3 September, *National Herald*, 4 September 1949.

[55] Nehru to B. C. Roy, 25 August, and to Patel, 27 October 1948.

and how he asked us to stick to this or that to the death, whatever others said or did. And yet those very things we were asked to stick to slip away from our grasp. Is that to be the end of our lives' labour? . . . All of us seem to be getting infected with the refugee mentality or worse still, the R.S.S. mentality. That is a curious finale to our careers.[56]

It was in this context that Nehru relied heavily on Rajagopalachari. Moreover, Rajagopalachari's conversation was stimulating; he was not above attempts at ingratiation;[57] and he enjoyed the confidence of the Mountbattens. So Nehru favoured Rajagopalachari's continuance as President after the promulgation of the Republic. But Rajagopalachari's past vacillations had not been forgiven by the rank and file of the Congress; they preferred Rajendra Prasad, the President of the Constituent Assembly, a loyal party man but of inferior intellectual quality and with a social outlook which belonged to the eighteenth century. When this feeling in the Parliamentary Party in favour of Prasad surfaced, a surprised Nehru wrote to Prasad hinting that he should announce his lack of interest in the office and propose Rajagopalachari's name. Prasad declined to oblige, and said he left it to Nehru and Patel to edge him out if they so desired. What Nehru did not know was that Patel favoured Prasad, and had arranged for a widespread expression of opinion in Prasad's favour at an informal meeting of the Party. So Nehru had to accept defeat and let Rajagopalachari retire. But from the start relations between the new President and his Prime Minister were uneasy. Prasad's known dislike of the Hindu Code Bill, reforming the personal laws of the Hindus, to which Nehru was fully committed, was only one indication of the wholly different viewpoints of the two men. Prasad objected to 26 January 1950 as the date for inaugurating the Republic on astrological grounds and drew a withering reply from Nehru.

I am afraid I have no faith in astrology and certainly I should not like to fix up national programmes in accordance with the dictates of astrologers. The change of date 26th January for another date would require a great deal of explanation and would not redound to our credit in the world or, for the matter of that, with large numbers of people in India. Many indeed would resent it greatly and there would be a bitter controversy from which we would not emerge happily. I rather doubt if millions and millions of men and women are represented by the writer of the letter sent to you. If they are so

[56] Nehru to Mohanlal Saxena, 10 September 1949.
[57] E.g., 'I have pronounced the thousand names of God to bless you and your work.' Rajagopalachari to Nehru on the latter's birthday, 14 November 1948. 'Your generosity, your trust and your affection have made life worth living for me. My only sorrow is that I should not deserve it all even more than I do.' Rajagopalachari to Nehru, 25 May 1950.

represented, then we can either combat this delusion, if we consider it
so, or allow others, who believe in astrology, to take charge of the
destiny of the nation.[58]

TWO

There was also, throughout these years, the continuous work of framing
the Constitution. While Nehru served as chairman of the committee of
experts set up by the Congress in 1946 as well as of three special committees
instituted by the Constituent Assembly, his major contribution was in
settling the general lines on which the Constitution was to be drawn up. He
drafted and moved in December 1946 the objectives resolution, stipulating
that India would be an independent sovereign republic, free to draw up her
own constitution, which would provide to all social, economic and
political justice, equality of status and of opportunity and before the law
and personal and civil liberties; and adequate safeguards would be ensured
to the minorities and the tribal and backward areas. His interest thereafter
was to see that the Constitution created a parliamentary democracy which
would enable these objectives to be realized. The details he left to the
lawyers and the specialists, interfering only occasionally and even then not
insisting on acceptance of his viewpoint. He controlled the enthusiasts for
Hindi and secured the retention of English as one of the official languages
until at least 1965. 'Language ultimately grows from the people; it is
seldom that it can be imposed.'[59] He voiced the feeling of the majority in
securing the rejection of proportional representation. Apart from the fact
that in countries where it had been tried proportional representation had
usually led to unstable governments, it was impracticable in India, from
both the organizational viewpoint and that of the voter who would not
understand it. He also favoured amendment of the Constitution by a simple
majority in Parliament during the first five years, but did not feel strongly
enough to move an amendment to this effect.[60] He could not prevent the
mention of the banning of cow-slaughter among the directive principles of
state policy, although he, following Gandhi, regarded it as an aspect of
Hindu revivalism.[61]

On two more serious issues, the difference in outlook between Nehru
and Patel assumed prominence. Patel demanded that the privy purses
sanctioned to the Princes as the price for accession be guaranteed to them
by the Constitution for perpetuity. He felt so keenly about this that he was
prepared, despite his illness, to come up from Bombay to sponsor this

[58] 27 September 1949.
[59] Nehru's speech quoted in B. Shiva Rao, *The Framing of India's Constitution*, introductory vol.
(Delhi, 1968), p. 789.
[60] G. Austin, *The Indian Constitution: Cornerstone of a Nation* (Oxford, 1966), p. 260.
[61] See his letter to Rajendra Prasad, 7 August 1947. Prasad Papers, National Archives of India.

clause in the Constituent Assembly.[62] Nehru and the rest of the Cabinet thought it unrealistic to bind the country to pay these pensions, which amounted in 1949 to Rs 4·66 crores free of tax, for all time. 'I confess that I had not realized this fact of perpetuity before. I am not sure in my own mind if any government is capable of guaranteeing any payment in perpetuity.'[63] But it was decided to postpone the final decision until Patel's return to Delhi; and in fact the commitment was formally made in the summer of 1950, when Nehru was away in Indonesia.

These lavish privy purses irked Nehru; but he was not prepared to repudiate them unilaterally. 'There is such a thing as a Government's word and a Government's honour.'[64] What he hoped for was a voluntary surrender by the Princes of a large part of their privy purses.[65] This, coupled with a similar reduction in the President's salary, would have a healthy psychological effect. As there was obviously no hope of the Princes themselves taking the initiative, Nehru wrote to them in the autumn of 1953 a long, educative letter with no specific proposal but a general argument which could only lead to one conclusion. He pointed out that, while covenants could not be set aside lightly, the rapid pace of events and the urgent demands of the times could also not be ignored. The continuance of a functionless group and the payment to it of large sums of money could not be justified by any moral, political or social theory.Apart from theory, in a democracy where the masses were growing in awareness and struggling hard to better their wretched lot, privy purses were an anachronism. 'Should we wait till the people put an end to this? Political wisdom consists in anticipating events and guiding them.'[66]

Nehru's invitation to the Princes to make specific recommendations brought no response; so he wrote again the next year, making a 'minimum possible suggestion'[67] of a voluntary contribution to the public revenue of ten to fifteen per cent of the privy purse, depending on its size.[68] This again evoked no constructive reply, and during Nehru's term as Prime Minister, no way of even reducing this unproductive public expenditure could be found.

Property was the other controversial item. Nehru had opposed the listing of the right to property among the fundamental rights, but had to give in.[69] From this arose the question of the right to compensation in case of expropriation of private property. Patel sent from Bombay a note arguing that the right to fair and equitable compensation was a logical

[62] Patel to Nehru, 9 August 1949.
[63] Nehru to Patel, 11 August 1949.
[64] Nehru to B. Ramakrishna Rao, 14 March 1953.
[65] Nehru's note, 25 August 1952.
[66] Nehru's letter to 102 Princes, 10 September 1953.
[67] Nehru to Rajendra Prasad, 14 June 1954.
[68] Nehru to the Princes, 15 June 1954.
[69] K. M. Munshi, *Pilgrimage to Freedom*, Vol. 1 (Bombay, 1967), p. 395.

consequence of the right to property. To remove all stimulus to private enterprise at that juncture in the country's history was to sign the death-warrant of India.[70] Nehru stopped the circulation of this note, presumably more because of its strong wording in favour of private property than because of any objection to the principle of compensation. There was no difference in the Congress Party on the latter issue. But Nehru, Pant and others who were eager to press forward with the abolition of the *zamindari* system wished to make it clear that it was for the legislature and not the courts to lay down the principles on which compensation should be paid. So Article 31 stipulated that the law must specify the compensation or the principles on which it should be paid. The courts would have no say unless the compensation was so grossly inadequate as to amount to a fraud on the right to property.

Patel appears to have been satisfied with this, but Nehru found later that there was enough room for the courts to hold up the land reform statutes; and as a result a revolutionary situation was being created in some rural areas.[71] So in 1951 the Constitution was amended, enabling the acquisition of estates despite any inconsistency with fundamental rights. Even this did not fully shelter land legislation from judicial scrutiny. Nehru believed that there should be a ceiling on compensation.

My views about compensation for land are very definite. Beyond a certain figure, I do not think any compensation should be given. The whole social purpose of our land legislation is defeated if we give exorbitant compensation... We have got into strange ideas of thinking private property sacrosanct, and unfortunately our Constitution makes us partly succumb to these ideas. The only thing sacrosanct is the human being and other matters should be judged from the social point of view of human betterment.[72]

This view was not shared by the Supreme Court. It held that if state action withheld any property from the possession and enjoyment of the owner or materially reduced its value, this amounted to deprivation which neces-sitated compensation. The Court also defined property very widely to include contractual rights; and it held that whether the compensation paid was a just equivalent was a justiciable issue. In 1955, therefore, the Constitution was again amended, at Nehru's instance, debarring the courts from examining the adequacy of compensation; and it was also laid down that deprivation short of actual transfer of ownership could not be deemed to be compulsory acquisition entitling the owner to compensation.

[70] Patel's note, 3 August 1949.
[71] Nehru to G. Mavalankar, Speaker of Lok Sabha, 16 May 1951.
[72] Nehru to K. N. Katju, 28 August 1953.

THREE

The proclamation of the Republic on 26 January 1950 offered a new opportunity for fresh endeavour. For it fulfilled the pledge taken twenty years earlier, and Nehru's colleague John Matthai drew his attention to what seemed to Nehru a very apposite text in the Bible: 'And ye shall hallow the fiftieth year, and proclaim liberty throughout all the land unto all the inhabitants thereof, it shall be a jubilee unto you; and ye shall return every man unto his family.'[73] Of the messages of congratulation that came from abroad, the one which moved Nehru most was that from Malan:

> This happy outcome to many years of struggle is above all due to the wise statesmanship of Mr Gandhi and yourself and to the firm determination to seek a settlement of India's problems on a basis of negotiation and discussion rather than by other means. May the new Republic of India long continue to be inspired by this the example of her greatest sons.

Yet Nehru had no deep sense of exhilaration. Apart from the personal deprivation in the departure of Rajagopalachari, he sensed a reluctance in the country to confront the problems which were piling up on every side.

> I entirely agree with you that as a people we have lost the public sense of social justice. To put it differently, our standards have fallen greatly. Indeed, we have hardly any standards left except not to be found out . . . We drift along calmly accepting things as they are. We see the mote in other people's eyes and not the beam in our own or our friends' eyes. We are strong in condemnation of those who are our opponents, but we try not to see the obvious faults of our friends. What are we to do? I confess my mind is not clear, although I have thought of this a great deal.[74]

The inauguration of the Republic was an appropriate occasion for at least new resolves, for starting afresh with open minds and with open hearts even for those who differed from India, for deciding to function rightly and with integrity of mind.[75] But even the desire to do well seemed to Nehru to be lacking.

> On the eve of a new phase in our history, what is most necessary is a flaming enthusiasm for the tasks in hand — faith, confidence, energy and the spirit of concerted effort. Do we find any of these today in

[73] Leviticus, xxv, 10.
[74] Nehru to B. G. Kher, 26 July 1949.
[75] To Chief Ministers, 18 January 1950.

India? Certainly in some measure in some people. But, certainly also, a lack of all of them in most people most of the time. Disruptive forces grow and people's minds are full of doubt as to what they should do and so they turn to criticism of others without doing much themselves. The tone of our public life goes down. We take the name of Gandhi, as we did before and as no doubt we shall continue to do in the future, and yet I often wonder what he would say if he saw us now and looked at the picture of India.

The Communists had practically become terrorists, the communalists had the same mental attitude as the Nazis and fascists, and the capitalists and landowning classes were singularly lacking in a social outlook. 'We talk of capitalism and socialism and communism, and yet we lack the social content of all of these.'[76]
This disappointment with the general mood gradually extended into a sense of his own isolation from the rank and file of the party. To Nehru the issue of secularism was always one on which no compromise was possible.

> So far as I am concerned, my own mind is perfectly clear in these matters and I have viewed with dismay and sorrow the narrow and communal outlook that has progressively grown in this country and which shows itself in a variety of ways. I shall cease to be Prime Minister the moment I realize that this outlook has come to stay and that I cannot do my duty as I conceive it.[77]

Such a moment now seemed to have been reached. A rapid increase in February 1950 of migration of Hindus from East Bengal was followed by a panic among Muslims in Calcutta and a mounting war fever in Pakistan. But Nehru, while fully prepared for every possible development, was keen that India should not be dragged into the vicious circle of mutual recrimination. 'India-Pakistan relations are certainly pretty bad. I suppose we have to go through this business and live down our past *karma* in regard to it.'[78] But here was a chance for the new Republic to demonstrate its desire to make a fresh start. Rather than pay attention to the Security Council, which refused to come to grips with the basic facts of the Kashmir dispute, he made direct approaches to Pakistan and sought to secure a no-war declaration.[79] He also telegraphed to Liaqat Ali Khan suggesting that the two Prime Ministers should together tour the two Bengals. It was not a matter of arranging for the smooth transfer of populations, for, apart from

[76] To Chief Ministers, 2 February 1950.
[77] Nehru to Mehr Chand Khanna, 6 June 1949.
[78] Nehru to Sri Prakasa, 4 January 1950.
[79] Nehru's note to Cabinet, 16 January, letter to B. N. Rau, 17 January, and telegram to B. N. Rau, 19 January 1950.

everything else, it seemed quite impossible for India once again to absorb and rehabilitate a few millions. The real necessity was to provide the Hindus of East Bengal with a sense of security so that they would remain where they were, and for this Nehru would have to don the mantle of Gandhi. Any such striking act was, however, in total discord with the views of a substantial section of the Congress Parliamentary Party which, even on such a subordinate issue as evacuee property, adopted an attitude which seemed to Nehru communal. So, acting on an idea which had been in his mind for sometime,[80] Nehru offered to resign the prime ministership for at least a few months and visit East Bengal in a private capacity.

> The Party has repeatedly made it clear by their [sic] speeches that they disapprove of much that we have done in regard to Pakistan. Now this is a very vital matter and I entirely disagree with many of the criticisms made by the Party. The difference is basic. If that is so then it is improper for me to continue guiding some policy which does not meet with the approval of members of the Party. On the other hand, I could not possibly act against my own convictions on vital issues . . . That is a negative approach to the problem. The positive approach is a strong and earnest desire on my part to spend some time in the Bengals. This is apart from that joint tour with Liaqat Ali Khan that I suggested. I think I could make a difference there and it is of the highest importance that we should not allow ourselves to be submerged by the Bengal problem. Hence I come to the conclusion that I should get out of office and concentrate on one or two matters in which I think I can be helpful. The principal matters would be the Bengal problem and Kashmir. I cannot do this as Prime Minister, more especially because the views of the Party are not in line with my own . . . I have considered all the arguments for and against and I suddenly realized that whatever I might do would bring a certain amount of confusion. In the balance, however, I am quite convinced that I would serve the cause of our country much better today in a private capacity than in the public office that I hold . . . I wish to repeat that, constituted as I am, I find it more and more difficult not to take some such action.[81]

Patel sought to dissuade him with little effect.

> I have no illusions about my ability to stop the course of fate, if fate it is, or break the chain of action and circumstances. Yet I have, at the same time, some faith in myself, if I throw myself into a task with all the strength and energy that I possess. There is this positive feeling in

[80] See Nehru to John Matthai, 29 December 1949.
[81] Nehru to Patel, 20 February 1950, with a copy to the President, Dr Prasad.

me that I must devote myself to this Bengal problem and do so on the spot. The problem itself demands that. But in addition to that, the memory of Bapu and all he did in Bengal comes back to me and I grow restless and unhappy . . . it is time we all shook ourselves up. We grow too complacent and smug. We want a little fire in our minds and in our activity.[82]

But the personal crisis was postponed by Liaqat Ali Khan's rejection of the proposal for a joint visit and there was no hope of Pakistan permitting Nehru to wander about on his own in East Bengal.

The exodus of Hindus from that State continued and Nehru, instead of being a messenger of peace, was forced to think in terms of even war being better than a tame submission to fate and tragedy.[83] In his first draft of a statement to be made in Parliament he had hinted at resignation: 'It may be that I can serve these causes better by some other method than is open to me at present or in some other capacity than I occupy. I am deeply troubled by recent events and my mind is constantly trying to find out how best I can discharge my duty and my obligation to my people.' Patel requested him to revise this paragraph as it would cause bewilderment and, even from Nehru's own point of view, weaken the shock therapy by providing advance information. So Nehru reworded these sentences, but in a manner which hinted at not merely resignation but war as well:

If the methods we have suggested are not agreed to, it may be that we shall have to adopt other methods. I am deeply troubled by recent events and my mind is constantly trying to find out how best I can serve these causes and discharge my duty and my obligation to my people.[84]

So Nehru was ready to face war and to let this be known. The Government of India redeployed the army in fresh dispositions which did not long remain a secret from Pakistan. The British Government were also informed, with the obvious intention of the message reaching Pakistan, that if confidence were not restored expeditiously and effectively among the minorities in Pakistan, Parliament and public opinion would force the Government of India to undertake the protection of the minority in East Bengal.[85] Yet Nehru strove not to be driven into war on what was basically a communal issue. The Hindus continued to leave East Bengal and the situation in West Bengal, as well as in some other parts of northern India,

---

[82] Nehru to Patel, 21 February 1950.

[83] To C. Rajagopalachari, 21 February 1950.

[84] Nehru's first draft of statement, 23 February, Patel to Nehru, 23 February, and Nehru's statement in Parliament, 23 February 1950, Constituent Assembly (Legislative) Debates, 1950, Vol. 1, Part II, pp. 749-55.

[85] Bajpai's telegram to Krishna Menon, 25 February 1950.

deteriorated. Muslims in India began to lose their sense of security and mass hysteria spread among the general population. Nehru, because of his efforts to break the spiral of inhumanity, was the recipient of a large mail of abusive letters and even threats of assassination. 'An evil fate seems to pursue us, reducing many of us to the level of brutes.'[86]

The answer obviously lay in some common effort by India and Pakistan to create confidence in the minorities in each State. Nehru, despite the rebuff of his first proposal by Liaqat Ali Khan and considerable opposition from some members of his Cabinet,[87] proposed a joint declaration by the two governments. There being again no constructive response from Pakistan, Nehru wrote to Attlee, hoping that the British Government would help him out. What he wanted was not their mediation, and he rejected Krishna Menon's suggestion that Lord Addison come out and be present at any talks between India and Pakistan. But he hoped that Britain would bring pressure to bear on Pakistan to negotiate with India. To Nehru Attlee sent only a general disapproval of theocratic states;[88] but on Liaqat Ali Khan he seems to have urged negotiations.

Baffled, and nostalgic for the days when he was a popular leader unloaded with office, Nehru once again acted on his hunch and wrote formally to the President indicating his resolve to resign.

I feel that I have practically exhausted my utility in my present high office and that I can serve my country and my people better in other ways. My heart is elsewhere and I long to go to the people and to tell them how I feel. If they accept what I say, well and good. If not, then also I shall have done what I felt like doing . . . It is my intention, soon after the Budget is passed, to offer you my resignation, and together with it, the resignation of the present Cabinet. Thereupon a new Council of Ministers will have to be formed. I would beg of you then not to charge me with this responsibility.[89]

That the intention to resign was serious is substantiated by Nehru's letters to Vijayalakshmi, Krishna Menon and Bajpai directing them not to resign their posts along with him.[90] Though the immediate purpose of resignation had been thwarted in February by Liaqat Ali Khan, perhaps there might be some advantage in administering a 'psychological shock' to the people. Something had to be done, and functioning on a different plane seemed a gamble worth taking, if only for lack of any other remedy.[91]

[86] To Aruna Asaf Ali, 12 March 1950.
[87] See Nehru to G. S. Bajpai, 13 March 1950.
[88] Nehru to Attlee, 20 March, Krishna Menon's telegram to Nehru, 27 March, and Nehru's telegram to Krishna Menon, 28 March, and letter, 30 March 1950; Attlee to Nehru, 29 March 1950.
[89] Nehru to President Rajendra Prasad, 20 March 1950.
[90] To Vijayalakshmi and Krishna Menon, 20 March, and Bajpai, 21 March 1950.
[91] See his letters to Sri Prakasa, 5 March, and to Rajagopalachari, 10 March 1950.

Thinking of this Bengal problem, as well as all that has gone before it and might possibly follow after it, I am filled with deep distress and a sense of failure. All the ideals we have stood for in the past seem gradually to fade away and new urges and emotions fill the people. Circumstance drives us onward from one position to another, each further away from what we used to consider our anchor. We cannot run away from the task that history sets us. But a cruel destiny seems to pursue us and nullify all our efforts.[92]

Nehru, however, changed his mind about resignation when he discovered that intrigues were afoot to push him out of office. Patel, though he accepted the secular ideal, attached more blame to Pakistan than Nehru did; and he also believed that the Muslims in India should be obliged to assert and give proof of their loyalty. But to Nehru it was patently wrong to seek guarantees of loyalty; that could not be produced to order or by fear but could come only as a natural product of circumstances, and it was for the majority, in India or in Pakistan, to create such circumstances. This difference of approach was not merely voiced in the Cabinet but reflected in discussions in the Party and in the conduct of senior officials. It was reported that Patel had convened a meeting of Congressmen in his house at which he had been strongly critical of Nehru's policy and disclaimed any responsibility for it. The officials of Patel's line of thinking took their cue from this, and V. P. Menon was said to have spoken to the British and American envoys of the near prospect of war.[93] So Nehru now wrote to Patel not of resigning but of referring the whole issue to the Working Committee and an emergency meeting of the AICC or even a full session of the Congress. They had pulled together, despite differences of temperament and viewpoint, in the larger interest and because of Gandhi's wishes; but now

new developments have taken place which have made me doubt seriously whether this attempt at joint working serves a useful purpose or whether it merely hinders the proper functioning of Government . . . As a Government we seem to be fading out of the picture and people publicly say that our Government has contradictory policies and, as a result, no policy at all. The belief that retaliation is a suitable method to deal with Pakistan or what happens in Pakistan is growing. That is the surest way to ruin in India and Pakistan . . . In these circumstances, the fact that you and I pull in different directions, and in any event the belief that we do so, is exceedingly harmful . . . The matter is far too important for a decision by individuals. It involves national policy. The Party of course must have a say in the matter.

92 Nehru to Chief Ministers, 19 March 1950.
93 See Nehru to V. P. Menon, 29 March 1950.

When Patel protested his loyalty, Nehru replied that he was troubled by something more basic and fundamental.

> The personal aspect is that in spite of our affection and respect for each other, we do things differently and therefore tend to pull differently in regard to many matters . . . The second, impersonal aspect is the drift in the country, whether it is governmental, Congress or other . . . I see every ideal that I have held fading away and conditions emerging in India which not only distress me but indicate to me that my life's work has been a failure . . .[94]

However, the mood of abdication had given way to a determination to stop the rot and give a different direction to events. Authorizing strong action and even, if necessary, the imposition of martial law in parts of West Bengal,[95] Nehru invited Liaqat Ali Khan to Delhi.[96] The only choices open were war, a massive exchange of populations, international intervention or negotiation. War, even a successful one, would result in no gain and would be regarded in the world as initiated by India; a transfer of minorities was neither feasible nor desirable; intervention by other powers was unwelcome; so it only remained to negotiate with Pakistan and devise a machinery for implementing whatever assurances could be secured. But if India was to negotiate with any confidence, the internal situation had first to be toned up. A proclamation of emergency was kept ready for West Bengal, and the governments of other provinces were ordered to control communal pressures and request those officials who did not accept this policy to leave the service. 'For my part, my mind is clear in this matter and, so long as I am Prime Minister, I shall not allow communalism to shape our policy, nor am I prepared to tolerate barbarous and uncivilized behaviour.'[97] The Government of India themselves, both ministers and officials, were divided in counsel and action. 'Things here', reported Nehru from Delhi to Rajagopalachari, 'are in a perfect jam or, to put it differently, they seem to be moving in various directions at their sweet will. The outlook is none too hopeful.'[98] But, fortunately, Liaqat Ali Khan accepted the invitation and arrived in Delhi; and Nehru got the chance to seek an understanding.

What made this easier was that Liaqat Ali Khan too seemed to shy away from the brink of war and was as keen on a settlement as Nehru. The talks lasted a week and eleven drafts were produced before an agreement was finally signed. Liaqat Ali Khan was at pains to contend that Pakistan was a democratic state and all that was meant by an Islamic state was that

[94] Nehru to Patel, 26 March, Patel to Nehru, 28 March, and Nehru to Patel, 29 March 1950.
[95] Telegram to B. C. Roy, 26 March, and letter, 29 March 1950.
[96] Telegram to Liaqat Ali Khan, 26 March 1950.
[97] To Chief Ministers, 1 April 1950.
[98] 1 April 1950.

Muslims would have their personal laws, but no special privileges. Azad asked him to affirm this in public and Liaqat Ali Khan replied that he was prepared to make this perfectly clear at any time, though he could not denounce the concept of an Islamic state. The Indian side pressed for a joint commission for East Bengal, West Bengal and Assam to secure fair treatment of minorities, but Liaqat Ali Khan was willing to go no further than joint meetings of two separate commissions, his fear being that a joint commission might create the impression that this was the first step to the unification of Bengal.[99] Azad proposed that there should be ministers for minority affairs in the two Bengals. Liaqat's response was that the principle should be accepted for the two countries and not just for the two Bengals; but the idea of a minister for minority affairs in the central Government met with vehement opposition in the Indian Cabinet. 'I am quite sure that the party will *not* accept it and the country will *not* swallow this bitter pill. We have conceded one Pakistan; that is more than enough. We cannot promote any further such mentality, let alone do anything which will perpetuate it.'[100]

The agreement signed on 8 April reiterated the policy of both governments to ensure complete equality of citizenship to minorities. Migrants would be given all facilities and not deprived of their immovable property. Commissions of inquiry would be established to report on the disturbances and, to prevent their continuance, each government would depute a minister to the affected areas. Representatives of the minority communities would be included in the cabinets of East Bengal, West Bengal and Assam and minority commissions constituted.

Nehru was aware of the imperfections in the agreement, but he believed that it expressed the desire of the large majority in India, which was eager for peace and better relations with Pakistan. So his despondency vanished. 'Do not give up hope about me so easily. I have still enough energy and strength left in me to face many storms and I have every intention of overcoming and controlling the present storm.'[101] The agreement should be implemented without reserve as it afforded the first chance since 1947 to set relations with Pakistan on a new road. 'We have to go full steam ahead. We have taken a turn in life's journey, so far as our nation is concerned, and it would be foolish for us now to loiter or linger on the way or to hesitate.'[102] He tried to persuade Syama Prasad Mookerjee and, even more, K. C. Neogy, the members of the Cabinet who disapproved of the talks with Liaqat, not to resign, but to accept the agreement, however unsatisfactory, and work it.[103]

[99] Nehru to B. C. Roy, 4 April 1950.
[100] Patel to N. G. Ayyangar, 6 April 1950.
[101] To Sri Prakasa, 6 April 1950.
[102] To Gopinath Bardoloi, Chief Minister of Assam, 8 April 1950.
[103] To K. C. Neogy, 7 April and to S. P. Mookerjee, 12 April 1950.

At this moment, however, it was Patel who stole the scene. He had earlier been in favour of a military occupation of East Bengal but had given up the idea on hearing of terrorization of Muslims in West Bengal, for this to him deprived India of any moral authority to take action against Pakistan.[104] Once an agreement had been reached, he appealed at the meeting of the Party, though without success, to the two Bengali ministers to remain in office, for both honour and self-interest demanded that India should fully implement the agreement; not to do so would bring not only discredit but harm, and to do so half-heartedly would bring discredit and no benefit. Then, in contrast to Rajagopalachari who declined Nehru's suggestion that he visit the two Bengals unless he was given 'an independent and higher position' than that of a mere minister,[105] Patel visited Calcutta, calmed Bengali opinion, and secured support for the agreement from quarters which refused to listen to Nehru. 'Vallabhbhai', remarked Nehru, 'has been a brick during these days.'[106] Patel proved that, whatever his personal prejudices, he would abide by his last promise to Gandhi to support Nehru, and was equal to the demands of circumstance. It was at this time that he stood forth in the full stature of his greatness.

At the start, the agreement worked well, particularly on the Pakistan side. *Dawn*, the leading newspaper of Karachi, 'has undergone a sea change for the better'[107] and dropped its vituperative tone. A meeting of Indian and Pakistani editors in Delhi ended in much fraternizing. 'Literally these fire-eaters wept on each other's shoulders and became quite soppy. How extraordinarily emotional our people are.'[108] The migrations from both sides diminished in number, and Nehru urged some prominent Congressmen from East Bengal to go back.[109] A temporary trade agreement was also concluded. 'There is no doubt', reported Nehru, 'that the Agreement and what has followed it have changed the whole atmosphere of India and Pakistan. It has brought immediate relief to millions and a certain glimmering hope for the future.'[110]

The first setback to the new understanding between the two countries came soon after, when Liaqat Ali Khan visited the United States and he and his wife made speeches which Patel regarded as a 'diabolical breach' of the Delhi agreement.[111] Nehru sent Liaqat Ali Khan a telegram of protest, but the Indian Ambassador, Vijayalakshmi, did not deliver it as the speeches were being revised for publication.

---

[104] H. V. R. Iengar (then Home Secretary), 'Bangladesh', *Swarajya* (Madras) annual number, 1972.
[105] Rajagopalachari to Nehru, 14 April 1950.
[106] To Rajagopalachari, 14 April 1950.
[107] Nehru to Sri Prakasa, 16 April 1950.
[108] Nehru to Krishna Menon, 8 May 1950.
[109] See his letter to P. C. Ghosh, 19 April 1950.
[110] Nehru to Chief Ministers, 2 May 1950.
[111] Nehru to Rajagopalachari, 11 May 1950.

FOUR

The Kashmir issue had also got bogged down; but this being a national conflict, which had nothing to do with the communal aspect of the problem between the two Bengals, there was to Nehru no question of a compromise. Secularism demanded both the retention of Kashmir and the avoidance of war in the east. Nehru had hoped, in place of McNaughton, for a single mediator rather than an arbitrator.[112] Sir Owen Dixon, an Australian jurist, was appointed by the United Nations to mediate. Dixon's impartiality was beyond doubt, but his approach was legalistic without regard to the principles or the practical difficulties involved. Agreement on the pre-liminaries for an overall plebiscite proving impossible because of his inclination, despite recognition that Pakistan's actions in Kashmir were contrary to international law, to permit Pakistan to retain some of the advantages of her presence in Kashmir, Dixon sought to arrange zonal plebiscites. India's willingness to consider this was quickly dissolved by Dixon's proposal, which Nehru promptly rejected, to replace the regular government of Kashmir by an administrative body consisting of officers of the United Nations. In fact, Pakistan virtually ceased to think in terms of any settlement. Liaqat informed Dixon that public opinion in Pakistan would never permit him to concede the Valley to India, and there was nothing Pakistan could offer to India to induce her to give up the Valley.[113] Nehru's reaction was 'to go back to where we started from' and, instead of the 'Alice in Wonderland business' of vague proposals for replacing the existing government in Kashmir, consider the 'fundamental realities' of the situation.[114]

Dixon himself confessed that he could think of no solution.[115] But his report was, on the whole, unjust to India. He acknowledged that Pakistan had been guilty of aggression in Kashmir, but concluded that no fair plebiscite could be held unless the government in Kashmir was changed. He did not take note of India's offer that no arrests or detentions, even in the normal course of maintaining law and order, would be effected before and during the period of plebiscite without the approval of the plebiscite commission, and refused to see that a change of government would in itself influence the voting and be regarded as the beginning of Pakistan's final victory. Dixon's 'astonishing' formula amounted to converting the Valley and other parts of Kashmir into 'a kind of half Pakistan' even before the plebiscite.[116]

So Nehru rejected outright the suggestion to replace the Kashmir

[112] Nehru's telegram to Bajpai in New York, 7 January 1950.
[113] Nehru's telegram to Dixon, 16 August 1950 and Bajpai's note on conversation with Dixon, 19 August 1950.
[114] Press conference in Delhi, 24 August, *National Herald*, 25 August 1950.
[115] See Rau's telegram to Bajpai, 13 September 1950.
[116] Nehru to Chief Ministers, 1 November 1950.

Government. His faith in the United Nations was rapidly evaporating.

I am a little tired of the intrigues and various moves of Britain, the United States etc. in Kashmir and have lost interest in them. It should be made perfectly clear to Britain that we are not prepared to change our position in the slightest degree . . . This Kashmir question would have been settled long ago but for the pro-Pakistan attitude and activities of Britain and some other countries.[117]

If a solution could not be attained by agreement between the parties concerned, the alternative was a continuing stalemate; for India had ruled out war, and though Pakistan declined to sign a no-war declaration, Liaqat Ali Khan had declared that Pakistan would not attack India. Nehru's general policy now was to try and improve relations between the two countries in every way without giving in on any important or vital issue. Looking at a world where every problem got mixed up with others, it seemed to Nehru an achievement just to hold on and prevent a worsening of the situation.

FIVE

Nehru also utilized the crisis in East Bengal to carry through a cleansing and toning up of the Congress Party. The decay in the character and discipline of the Party was particularly noticeable in the United Provinces, where the organization was, from the start, riven by cliques and individual ambition. He had urged Kidwai and Purushottam Das Tandon not to pit themselves against each other publicly and, while his sympathy lay with Kidwai, he had appealed to Tandon to show a greater spirit of accommodation.

We should at least try to understand each other as we have done in the past, even though we might not wholly agree. I hope that however we might differ in our views, we have respect and affection for each other and that after all is the fundamental thing in human relationships. All of us have to carry our burden ourselves and decide what course we have to pursue in this dense jungle that is called public life and public affairs.[118]

But such advice was little heeded by any of the groups. Worse, when the mass migration of Hindus from East Bengal began in the spring of 1950, a narrow, bigoted outlook invaded the U.P. Congress. Even the State

[117] To B. N. Rau, 17 November 1950.
[118] Nehru to Tandon, 7 June 1948.

Government was not immune; despite repeated directives from Nehru, it took little action to curb Hindu communalism and, as a result, over 200,000 Muslims began to migrate from the province. Tandon, now President of the provincial Congress, called upon Muslims, even after the signing of the agreement with Liaqat Ali Khan, to adopt 'Hindu culture'.

> People die and the fact of killing, though painful, does not upset me. But what does upset one is the complete degradation of human nature and even more, the attempt to find justification for this . . . Indeed the U.P. is becoming almost a foreign land for me. I do not fit in there. The U.P. Congress Committee, with which I have been associated for thirty-five years, now functions in a manner which amazes me. Its voice is not the voice of the Congress I have known, but something which I have opposed for the greater part of my life. Purushottam Das Tandon, for whom I have the greatest affection and respect, is continually delivering speeches which seem to me to be opposed to the basic principles of the Congress . . . communalism has invaded the minds and hearts of those who were pillars of the Congress in the past. It is a creeping paralysis and the patient does not even realize it . . . The fact of the matter is that for all our boasts, we have shown ourselves a backward people, totally lacking in the elements of culture, as any country understands them. It is only those who lack all understanding of culture, who talk so much about it.[119]

Such protests and exhortations had little, if any, impact, and the deterioration in the spirit of the Congress in the U.P. and elsewhere continued. Pant, though personally close to Nehru, was not as firmly opposed to communalism as Nehru would have liked, and the Prime Minister planned to move him from the U.P. and bring him to the central Cabinet. Muslims who had been given personal assurances by Nehru were harassed by officials of the central Ministry of Rehabilitation. 'Human beings are more important than property and the word of a prime minister ought to have some importance in this country.'[120] Patel himself, after his splendid showing in the East Bengal crisis, was relapsing into his old attitude of suspecting the loyalty of Muslims in India.[121] It seemed to Nehru that, whether because of the inherent weakness of the people or the self-complacency of the leaders, the country generally and the Congress Party in particular were going to pieces. 'We have lost something, the spirit that moves and unless we recapture that spirit, all our labour will yield little profit.'[122]

[119] Nehru to Pant, 17 April 1950.
[120] Nehru to Mohanlal Saxena, 18 April 1950.
[121] See his letter to Nehru, 28 May 1950, *Sardar Patel's Correspondence*, Vol. 9 (Ahmedabad, 1974), pp. 478-9.
[122] Nehru to B. C. Roy, 8 July 1950.

Matters came to a head in August 1950 with manoeuvres for the election of the president for the annual session of the Congress. None of the candidates, Tandon, Kripalani and Shankarrao Deo, inspired any enthusiasm; but Nehru believed that it would be Tandon's election which would be the most harmful. So he took the honest course of writing directly to Tandon.

> The Congress is in a bad way and, unless some steps to rejuvenate it are taken, is likely to fade away. As it is, it seems to have lost such inner strength that it possessed and we are concerned chiefly with faction fights and manoeuvring for position and place. It is sad to see this great organization function in this petty way . . . It has been our misfortune during the past two or three years or so to have drifted apart to some extent . . . Probably you think that much that I say or do is wrong. For my part, I have often read your speeches with surprise and distress and have felt that you were encouraging the very forces in India which, I think, are harmful . . . I think the major issue in this country today, if it is to progress and to remain united, is to solve satisfactorily our own minority problems. Instead of that, we become more intolerant towards our minorities and give as our excuse that Pakistan behaves badly . . . Unfortunately, you have become, to large numbers of people in India, some kind of a symbol of this communal and revivalist outlook and the question rises in my mind: Is the Congress going that way also? If so, where do I come into the picture, whether it is the Congress or whether it is the Government run by the Congress? Thus this larger question becomes related to my own activities.

It became, therefore, as he saw it, his public duty to give expression to his opinion about Tandon's unsuitability for the presidency.[123]

Tandon, however, had the support of Pant and the U.P. ministry as well as of Patel, who wrote to Nehru not to oppose Tandon but to talk to him about their differences. But Nehru refused to weaken, this being to him not a personal matter but the major issue of stopping the inner rot in the Congress.[124] He informed Patel that if Tandon were elected he might find it difficult to continue as a member of the Working Committee or even of the Government and issued a public statement which made clear where his sympathies lay. 'I have committed myself so far that I cannot possibly continue as I am if Tandon is elected. If I did so, I would be completely helpless and no one would attach much value to me or to what I said or did.'[125]

[123] Nehru to Tandon, 8 August 1950.
[124] Patel to Nehru, 9 August, and Nehru's reply of the same date.
[125] To Krishna Menon, 25 August 1950.

The election was now generally interpreted not solely as a clash between individual viewpoints but as a tussle for supremacy between Nehru and Patel.[126] So, with Tandon's victory, all seemed set for the kill. Nehru himself was willing to give in.

> I cannot possibly continue to function as I have done when I receive a public slap on my face and an expression of Congress disapproval of what I stand for . . . There is no point in my being Prime Minister in these circumstances. I shall be frustrated and disheartened and totally ineffective.[127]

But, even if he continued in office, his opponents were confident that they could diminish his effective authority. Indeed, this would have suited them better than Nehru's total withdrawal, and there is a strong hint of a ganging up against Nehru for this purpose. Patel, believing that Nehru, as in Gandhi's time, would adjust himself to the new situation, offered to make defeat less galling by issuing with Nehru a joint statement to the press that no personal issues were involved in Tandon's election.[128] Rajendra Prasad, as President, delayed assent to the Bihar Land Bill which had been strongly recommended to him by the Cabinet meeting without Patel, and Nehru had to force the President's hand, despite a protest from Patel, by threatening the resignation of himself and the Government.[129] Rajagopalachari, whom Nehru had brought back in the summer as minister without portfolio because he seemed the one senior leader who supported Nehru's secular policy and enjoyed the friendship of the Mountbattens and of Sir Archibald Nye, the British High Commissioner,[130] and Lady Nye, was now characteristically playing both sides. Nehru had objected to the Home Ministry's proposal that Muslim officials who wished to visit Pakistan should secure permission because this would suggest a general lack of confidence in those officials. Rajagopalachari informed Nehru that he wholly agreed with him, but wrote to Patel that he thought the proposal was reasonable but should not be pressed in view of the Prime Minister's strong views on the subject.[131] Patel forwarded Rajagopalachari's letter to

---

[126] Cf. K. Hanumanthaiya, then Chief Minister of Mysore, to Tandon, 22 August 1950: 'So far as Mysore votes are concerned, almost to a man, they will stand by you and by the policies you have publicly propounded. I had also [a] discussion with Sardar Patel. I expect you and the Sardar to work unitedly in all matters affecting the destinies of our country and lead us all out of the chaos and confusion that Pandit Nehru's leadership has landed us in.' Tandon Papers, N.A.I.

[127] Nehru to Patel, 26 August 1950, *Sardar Patel's Correspondence*, Vol. 10 (Ahmedabad, 1974), p. 217.

[128] Nehru to Patel, 25 and 26 August, Patel to Nehru, 27 August, Nehru to Patel, 28 August, and Patel to Rajagopalachari, 27 August 1950, *Sardar Patel's Correspondence*, Vol. 10, pp. 215-24.

[129] Nehru to Rajendra Prasad, 11 September and Rajendra Prasad's reply of the same date, Patel to Nehru, 11 September, and Nehru to Patel, 12 September 1950.

[130] Sir Archibald Nye had earlier been Governor of Madras.

[131] Patel to Nehru, 11 September, Nehru to Patel, 12 September, Patel to Nehru, 13 September, Nehru to Patel, 14 September, and Patel to Nehru, with two enclosures, 16 September 1950.

Nehru, and this gave Nehru the first clear indication that Rajagopalachari's personal loyalty to him was not cast-iron.

When he became aware that he was being pushed into surrender or continuance in office without power, Nehru accepted battle and conducted the fight with a political skill which was not generally associated with him. He had both a relish for conflict and a killer instinct. He did not meekly hand over his resignation or agree to remain on the terms hinted at by his antagonists.[132] Rather, with a series of hard-hitting speeches,[133] he secured acceptance by the Congress bodies of resolutions which all expressed his own viewpoint. Then, fortified by this, he declined to serve on the Working Committee formed by the new President. He also seriously considered depriving Patel of the States Ministry. He drafted a letter drawing Patel's attention to the reports that pressure had been applied on governments in the erstwhile States to secure votes for Tandon. The States Ministry functioned as a general overlord over the State governments, assuming authority in matters which properly pertained to other ministries, and referred matters to the Cabinet only very rarely. Hyderabad, in particular, was being administered as an estate by a local government set up by the States Ministry and acting under its orders.

> We have developed in these States a peculiar form of government which is certainly not democratic and is at the same time not directly under the Government of India . . . Then there is the fact that all this tremendous burden, and together with it the other great burden of the Home Ministry, rests on you. Your shoulders are broad enough, but it is inevitable that you cannot have the time or energy to pay special attention to the many important matters that arise. The result is likely to be that much is disposed of without your knowledge or with only a brief reference to you. I should like you to give thought to these matters so that we can discuss them at a later stage.[134]

The letter was not sent, probably because Nehru knew that Patel was by now a dying man; but he let it be known through Rajagopalachari that he was dissatisfied with the conduct of the States Ministry, particularly in Hyderabad.[135] He also wrote directly to Patel on the same lines, but without

[132] Later, Nehru stated that he had decided to continue in office principally because of his interest in foreign affairs: 'I think that I can do something in the international field.' Speech at Lucknow, 3 October, *National Herald*, 4 October 1950. This was for him to underrate his own political vitality and instinct for resistance.

[133] E.g., 'If democracy means surrendering one's judgement to the crowd, then let this democracy go to hell. I will fight such mentality wherever it raises its head. Yes, democracy can ask me to quit the prime ministership. I will obey this order. If Congressmen think of giving up their ideal simply for the consideration of a few votes in the coming elections, then the Congress will become lifeless. I do not need such a corpse.' Speech at the Congress session at Nasik, 21 September, *National Herald*, 22 September 1950.

[134] Draft letter to Patel, 28 September 1950.

[135] To Rajagopalachari, 13 October 1950.

any suggestion of divesting him of the States portfolio.[136] He agreed to serve on the Working Committee but made known his disapproval of the selection of many other members by Tandon, and claimed the right to raise basic issues at the first meeting of the new committee. 'Having acted against my own logic and inner urge as well as my intuitive feeling in the matter, I feel as if I had done something wrong, that I had indulged in something approaching disloyalty to myself.' He could only continue as a member if he felt that the situation in the Congress would be grasped in the way he wanted and a new turn given to the organization.[137]

SIX

Over all these personal and political confrontations lay the need to work out a plan to ensure economic progress. If this was started satisfactorily, other issues would gradually fall into what were really minor places. In the early years, with crises seeming to threaten India's existence, the struggle for national survival pushed all else to the background. 'All I can do is to hope and work and pray.'[138] But even then, Nehru did not forget the crucial significance of planning.

We have many important preoccupations, but the fundamental and basic problem still continues to be the economic problem. This may well break us if we cannot deal with it satisfactorily. We have at present no method of dealing with it properly. Our effort to have a Cabinet committee on the subject has been a complete failure. It is no one's responsibility to look on the broad economic picture and to suggest ways and means of tackling our economic problems as a whole.[139]

The Government were doing no more than watch passively the continuous rise of the cost of living index.[140] He suggested to the Cabinet that it approve the appointment of a minister for social and economic affairs, with no administrative functions and solely to give continuous consideration to economic problems. He would be assisted by a council of economic advisers who would collect and coordinate data and statistics and look at the picture as a whole.[141] Nehru saw this as a prelude to the establishment of suitable machinery for the consideration of economic problems, but the

[136] Two letters to Patel on 19 October 1950 and again on 29 October 1950.
[137] To Tandon, 16 October 1950.
[138] Nehru's remark in 1950, quoted in Y. Menuhin, *Unfinished Journey* (London, 1977), p. 254.
[139] Nehru to Patel, 6 June 1948.
[140] Nehru's note to Cabinet, 26 June 1948.
[141] Nehru's note for Cabinet, 4 August 1948, Prime Minister's Secretariat File 37(114)/54-PMS Vol. II, Serial 1A.

8   Nehru, Patel and Pant, Congress session, December 1948

9   Nehru and Eden, Delhi, 22 March 1949

10 Commonwealth prime ministers at Downing Street, London, April 1949

11 Nehru and Churchill, April 1949

proposal was not accepted by the Cabinet and the economic situation continued to deteriorate with little effort at general understanding or control. 'Indeed, I have almost come to the conclusion that it would be a good thing if we stopped all other work and concentrated on our economic and food policy and how to implement it with the greatest rapidity.'[142] A firm decision should be taken to make India self-sufficient in food and stop all import of grains within two years, the provinces should be geared to cooperate with the central Government in this task and overall planning and agrarian reforms should be given concrete shape.

> The unprecedented and in many quarters unexpected success of your Government in taking over so smoothly the control of the country is a tremendous achievement; but the great ideals for which India has fought will disappear like burst soap bubbles unless the next step is taken without delay. That step must be the rapid increase of agricultural production for food, clothing and housing.[143]

This warning came as no surprise to Nehru. Even to secure the newly won political freedom, it seemed essential to him that the people of India should feel that they were heading towards prosperity; and agrarian reforms, which had made some progress and alone gave the Government stability and the Congress backing among the peasantry, had to be carried much further. Particularly in face of the communist successes in China and South East Asia, the vital issue was an improvement in the standards of the masses. The *Manchester Guardian* summed up the problem in words of which Nehru approved:

> The underlying social and economic problems need more radical treatment than the new government has yet been able to give them . . . If the economic stagnation continues India will not be able to bring into play the power and influence which it should exercise internationally. However impressive its outside, it will be what the Chinese call a 'paper tiger'. It will also be very vulnerable to Communist propaganda. The remedy is social and economic reorganization on the largest scale . . . By looking northwards, at their neighbour China, the two Dominions can draw constant warning of what happens when a country has too much politics and does not solve the basic problems of the agrarian system.[144]

Any effort at advance, however, was impeded at the source itself once more by a problem of personalities. Those in charge of economic policy 'cannot get out of the old ruts of their thinking and are frightened at the

---

[142] To J. Daulatram, Food Minister, 7 January 1949.
[143] Lord Boyd Orr to Nehru, 2 May 1949.
[144] 13 January 1949. For Nehru's approval, see his letter to Matthai, 23 January 1949.

prospect of any marked change. Yet, if change does not come on our initiative, it will come without it and in a much worse way.'[145] Jairamdas Daulatram, the Food Minister, was unequal to his job, and John Matthai, the Finance Minister, did not believe in planning. Daulatram was quietly replaced in the summer of 1950, but Matthai proved more difficult to handle. Nehru had respect for Matthai's integrity and polished mind and therefore tried, over a period of weeks, to persuade him of the virtues, and in fact the necessity, of planning. It was not a matter of greater expenditure than India could afford, but a clearer vision of the objectives and a definite notion of the approach to these objectives. There was plenty of money available in the country and the problem was to secure it for public purposes by a definite overall plan and a raging campaign to secure popular support and participation. The capitalist classes had 'proved totally inadequate to face things as they are today in the country. They have no vision, no grit, no capacity to do anything big. The only alternative is to try to put forward some big thing ourselves and rope in not only these classes but the people as a whole. Otherwise we remain stagnant and at the most ward off catastrophe.'[146] Dealing with specific problems separately left the major problem of general economic progress unsolved; and for this both a more effective machinery and a more far-reaching outlook were required. Each province too was functioning more and more as a separate unit, not thinking of the rest of India or sometimes even of its own coordinated development. 'The more I think of it, and I have given it a great deal of thought during the past few months especially, the less I understand myself what we are aiming at. If I do not understand this clearly, how much less can we expect the intelligent or unintelligent public to understand it.' A negative policy could never be sufficient, especially when it had been a failure. The changes required were not easy to determine, but changes there had to be.

> We may make mistakes and pay for them, but surely the greatest mistake is not to view the whole scheme of things in its entirety, realistically and objectively, and to decide on clear objectives and plans. If once this is done, the next step of complete coordination follows much more easily and only by coordinated effort can real results be achieved.[147]

Finding that the approach of Matthai, with his long association with private industrialists, was different and not likely to be revised, Nehru, without pressing the issue, suggested full discussions in Cabinet and directed senior officials to examine all aspects of national planning. His intention was to appoint a planning commission with Prasad as chairman;

[145] Nehru to Krishna Menon, 24 August 1949.
[146] To John Matthai, 13 September 1949.
[147] To John Matthai, 29 September 1949.

when Prasad preferred the presidency of the Union he first offered the post
to Rajagopalachari and then finally, and wisely, decided to retain direct
control. No one else in the Congress leadership could be expected to guide
planning on the right lines, for no one else had so clear an understanding or
strong a faith in planning as Nehru himself.

The creation of the planning commission early in 1950 brought the
differences with Matthai to a head. He knew that Nehru was less inclined
than before to stress production rather than distribution and was keener on
industrial development in the public sector. Matthai saw the planning
commission as a tool of Nehru to reduce the importance of the industrial and commercial classes, whom Nehru now openly criticized, and to:
'balance the various social forces at work in India, and pay more attention
to what might be called the vital forces which will ultimately lead to
progress.'[148] Matthai was certain that the planning commission and the
Cabinet Economic Committee (of which Nehru at this time was not a
member) would be in conflict with the Finance Ministry, particularly as the
Government still was, in its general policy, friendly to the industrialists and
seeking to win their support.

The difference of opinion between Nehru and his Finance Minister on
this specific issue of the planning commission soon spread to other areas
and even affected their personal relations. In the Cabinet Matthai supported
Syama Prasad Mookerjee in opposing the talks with Liaqat Ali Khan, not
from any communal viewpoint but on the grounds that the Government
had not sufficiently utilized the many levers it possessed to force Pakistan
into more moderate behaviour. Nehru, on the other hand, did not fail to
point out that he was somewhat of a political missionary responsive to the
masses and ready for action in their interest, in contrast to men such as
Matthai, who had spent their lives in offices irrespective of whether the
government was British or Indian. 'I owe something to the people who
have trusted me and to the leader under whose sheltering care I grew up.'[149]

In these circumstances, both men were pained at what each regarded as
the other's discourteous attitude; and early in June, when Nehru was on the
high seas on his way to Indonesia, Matthai announced his resignation with
a bitterly worded statement, accusing Nehru of wasteful expenditure,
appeasement and the surrender of vital national interests. But some even of
the ministers who remained had no liking for the planning commission and
failed to cooperate with it and facilitate its working.[150] Nor was there much
progress in planning itself. 'We seem to have lost all capacity to consider
anything from the point of view of a new approach. We go round and
round in circles and cannot get out of our grooves.'[151]

[148] Nehru to Matthai, 16 February 1950.
[149] Nehru to Matthai, 4 May 1950.
[150] See Nehru to Munshi, 2 September, and to H. K. Mahtab, 7 October 1950.
[151] Nehru to Rajagopalachari, 15 April 1951.

5

Korea and Tibet

War broke out in Korea on 25 June 1950, and the same day a resolution was brought forward in the Security Council blaming North Korea for an armed attack and calling on all members of the United Nations to render every assistance to the organization in securing the cessation of hostilities and the withdrawal of North Korean forces to the 38th parallel. B. N. Rau had no time to consult his government and voted for this resolution on his own initiative. Delhi believed that Rau had been justified in considering North Korea an aggressor; but he was directed not to commit India further without prior consultation, and he abstained from voting on the resolution of 27 June directing member states to furnish such assistance as might be required to South Korea to repel the armed attack. However the Cabinet, after two meetings held without Patel, issued a statement accepting this resolution too. The reshuffle in May had given the right wing of the Congress greater weight in the Cabinet, and Patel's presence was not necessary to make sure that no decision savouring of support for communism would be taken. 'U.S.S.R.', wrote Munshi, a new entrant, to the Prime Minister, 'never has been a friend and never will be. Why should we lose the goodwill of friends without whom we cannot face Russian expansion? If they fall, we go under.'[1] But, although Nehru accepted the two resolutions without the least enthusiasm, it was not as if he was acting against his better judgment. He was convinced of the rightness of the decision; well-planned aggression had taken place and to surrender to it was wrong and would have meant the collapse of the United Nations structure as well as leading to other dangerous consequences. Having accepted the first resolution, the second followed. 'I think that logically and practically there was no other course open to us.'[2] But he thought that the Government's statement, while satisfying the United States and Britain, yet maintained the balance and left India with freedom of action.[3] In fact, it was

[1] 29 June 1950.
[2] To Chief Ministers, 2 July 1950. Nehru also stated this publicly at a press conference on 7 July, *National Herald*, 8 July 1950.
[3] To Patel, 29 June 1950.

reiterated, almost, as Patel complained,[4] in a defensive tone, that the support of the United Nations resolution did not involve any modification of India's foreign policy, which would continue to be an independent one based on the development of friendly relations with all countries. 'No country can be hundred per cent independent in such matters because every act or policy flows from other acts done before and other things happening in the world. But within those limitations one can be more or less independent. We have preferred to be more independent.'[5]

This reassertion of non-alignment was meant to indicate India's refusal to accept the United States Government's effort to link up the Korean issue with Formosa and Indo-China. Nor was military assistance provided in Korea; India's armed services were intended solely for defence at home, financial stringency did not allow any expansive gestures, and it was embarrassing to put Indian troops in the charge of MacArthur, who was in command not only in Korea but over the whole area. 'Our moral help is a big enough thing, which out-balances the petty military help of some other countries.'[6] Such help, of course, annoyed Russia and China, and Nehru realized that India's acceptance of the two resolutions of the Security Council had weakened even the little influence which she had with the Communist Powers. 'Still we have not quite lost our old position and there is some hope that we might be able to play a useful role in preventing the conflict from spreading or in bringing the warring factions nearer to one another.'[7]

Having, in fact, supported the American side of the argument in the first instance, Nehru disliked the hustling which was then attempted and which hindered his effort to persuade Russia and China to help in localizing the conflict in Korea.

> I must say that the Americans, for all their great achievements, impress me less and less, so far as their human quality is concerned. They are apt to be more hysterical as a people than almost any others except perhaps the Bengalis. The Russians follow wrong courses often enough, but they remain calm and collected about it and do not show excitement.[8]

His unease was doubtless increased by Krishna Menon's rejection of the Government's Korean policy and his offer to resign on that issue,[9] Radhakrishnan's dislike of the policy, and the widespread criticism of it in India.

[4] To Nehru, 3 July 1950.
[5] To Chief Ministers, 15 July 1950.
[6] Nehru to B. N. Rau, 1 July 1950.
[7] Ibid.
[8] To C. Rajagopalachari, 3 July 1950.
[9] Krishna Menon to Nehru, 2 July 1950.

Not being swept away by passion, not possessing a single-track mind, trying to judge of events as objectively as possible, and at the same time having to consider all kinds of forces at work in India and outside, it is no easy matter to come to a decision . . . It is always a frightfully difficult matter to try to balance oneself on the edge of a sword. Whether India's policy will turn out to be right or wrong, the future will show. Meanwhile, we have of course displeased very much many people and countries and not pleased anybody.[10]

His suspicions of the Soviet Union were unchanged, but he was worried about the implications of the American position.

We face today a vast and powerful Soviet group of nations, which tends to become a monolithic bloc, not only pursuing a similar internal economic policy but a common foreign policy. That policy is an expansionist one and thus there is a tendency for it to come into conflict with others. It is expansionist not only in the normal political sense but also in encouraging internal trouble in other countries . . . On the other hand, the approach of the rival group, though democratic in theory, tends more and more to encourage reactionary and military elements in various countries, especially of Asia. By the logic of events it supports the relics of colonial rule.[11]

It was all the more necessary, therefore, to follow a policy which was not only expedient but in keeping with the temper of Asia. To fall blindly into line with anybody was to walk into a trap.

The war hysteria and the drift to a world conflict gathered pace, and at this moment Nehru found his cluster of powerful ambassadors almost an embarrassment, for they began to display the disadvantages of their eminence. Each pursued an almost independent foreign policy. Vijayalakshmi was eager to talk to President Truman, Krishna Menon met Attlee repeatedly, Panikkar saw himself as China's line of communication to the world, Radhakrishnan, with his formidable personal prestige, conducted his own private negotiations for peace with the Soviet Foreign Office and the American Ambassador in Moscow, and B. N. Rau at Lake Success assumed all too willingly, without awaiting the approval of Delhi, the leadership of the non-permanent members of the Security Council. But guiding this team with a much lighter rein than was approved by his officials at headquarters, Nehru sent personal messages to Stalin and Acheson stressing the need to admit People's China to the United Nations and bring back the Soviet Union to the Security Council.[12] Nothing came

[10] To Vijayalakshmi, 8 July 1950.
[11] To Chief Ministers, 15 July 1950.
[12] 13 July 1950.

of the messages beyond indicating India's desire to arrest a drift to war and perhaps weakening the general feeling of fatality that nothing more was possible except to jump into the abyss; 'we have made everybody sit up a little and think, and that is some small achievement, when passion and prejudice govern people's minds.'[13] It also improved relations with the Communist Powers. The Soviet Union appeared more appreciative of India's attitude and China expressed her gratification at India's support for her entry into the United Nations. Nehru had legitimized China's interest in the Korean war and may have fortified the Soviet Union in its decision to lift its boycott of the Security Council.[14] Even the United States took advantage of this *rapport* by requesting Nehru to convince China that her own interests required that she should avoid intervention in Korea or an attack on Formosa.[15] Nehru agreed to forward this message[16] but grew increasingly concerned by the bellicosity which seemed to underlie such acts of United States policy as the widespread and indiscriminate bombing of North Korea and MacArthur's visit to Formosa.[17] There was no clear realization by the Western Powers of the mood in Asia, and a too facile impression that military strength and economic resources would win the battle. If, in pushing back aggression, the spirit of vengeance led to the destruction of the whole of Korea, then the effort of the United Nations would have resulted in total failure. 'They may win a war. But how can they possibly deal with any part of Asia afterwards? They will have fewer and fewer friends here, if they behave as they have been doing.'[18] The future of Asia depended to a large extent on what happened in China. Isolation from the rest of the world would subdue the powerful national characteristics of the Chinese people and strengthen Soviet influence; and the United States was achieving just that. 'The United States policy is the one policy which will make China do what the United States least wants. That is the tragedy or comedy of the situation.'[19] He did not expect the United States to call off the military operations or even to desist from crossing the 38th parallel, though in September Britain and the United States assured him that their forces would not cross the parallel without a directive from the United Nations. Soon after, the United States requested India to represent to Peking not to react sharply to the success of the American forces in South Korea. Panikkar did not act on this suggestion, but reported back that direct participation by China in the fighting in Korea seemed 'beyond range of possibility' unless Russia intervened and a world war resulted. While the

[13] To S. Radhakrishnan, 6 August 1950.
[14] A. S. Whiting, *China Crosses the Yalu* (New York, 1960), pp. 61-2.
[15] Acheson to Nehru, 26 July 1950.
[16] Nehru to Acheson, 29 July 1950.
[17] The visit, as we now know, was not authorized by the United States Government. D. S. Mclellan, *Dean Acheson The State Department Years* (New York, 1976), p. 279.
[18] To B. N. Rau, 10 August 1950.
[19] To Vijayalakshmi, 30 August 1950.

Chinese saw Korea as the cover for a general Western effort to recover lost authority throughout Asia, they would not move even under provocation as they knew they were not ready. This feeling of assurance, passed on to the United States, may have encouraged the United States to adopt a more rigid line and veto the admission of China to the United Nations, a step which seemed to Nehru foolish and 'the policy of a destructive nation.'[20]

China's reaction was also bitter, and on 21 September Chou En-lai for the first time repeatedly warned Panikkar that 'if America extends her aggression China will have to resist', for it would endager China's security. Nehru sent Chou a personal message urging patience.

New China is strong enough to face the future with dignity and calm. The countries of Asia more especially look to China as a friendly neighbour with respect . . . By waiting a little longer China will, I feel sure, achieve all that she desires, peacefully and thus earn the gratitude of mankind.[21]

But this effort was stultified by the Western Powers who, believing that Russia and not China was the main opponent, decided to cross the 38th parallel. Nehru pressed on Bevin the vital need to act with circumspection and secured the omission from a United Nations resolution of the possibility of crossing the parallel; but he could not alter the decision to move into North Korea. Possibly the doubts cast by officials in New Delhi on the accuracy of Panikkar's reporting[22] weakened the force of Nehru's warnings. Chou reiterated to Panikkar that if MacArthur's troops continued to advance, China would be compelled to take immediate steps. Again Nehru appealed to Chou to hold his hand; but in face of the continued progress of MacArthur's troops beyond the 38th parallel and the call to North Korea to surrender, Chinese 'volunteers' began to cross the Manchurian border.

The phase of the Korean crisis when all sides turned to Nehru and sought the support of his influence,[23] when, as Nehru proudly phrased it, 'the world looks upon us as representing the centre of Asian feelings',[24] now seemed past. No heed was paid to his urging that military methods need not be pursued 'to the utmost and the last', and the proper psychological moment, when North Korean forces had been defeated,

[20] To B. V. Keskar, 9 October 1950.

[21] 27 September 1950.

[22] D. Stair, *The Diplomacy of Constraint* (Toronto, 1974), p. 127. Stair quotes confidential Canadian sources for this statement.

[23] The struggle for Asia 'conceivably could be won or lost in the mind of one man — Jawaharlal Nehru . . . To have Pandit Nehru as an ally in the struggle for Asiatic support is to have many divisions; to have him as an opponent or even a critic could jeopardize the position of Western democracy throughout Asia.' *New York Times*, 30 August 1950.

[24] Speech at the Congress session at Nasik, 18 September, *National Herald*, 19 September 1950.

should be seized to rebuild a united Korea.[25] All that such unpalatable advice secured Nehru was severe censure in the United States. Both the Government and the press were critical of India, and in particular of her Prime Minister, for mobilizing support for China's admission to the United Nations.[26] Nehru's public replies were cool and unyielding,[27] and he ordered his representatives in the United States to continue to repeat India's views politely but forcibly.[28] 'It really is amazing how great nations are governed by very small people.'[29]

The Korean situation was now complicated by developments in Tibet. Nehru had never taken seriously suggestions, made even by Panikkar during the civil war in China, of establishing an independent Tibet,[30] and he realized at the time the Communists came to power that Tibet was likely to be soon invaded. 'The result of all this is that we may have the Chinese or Tibetan Communists right up on our Asian, Bhutan and Sikkim border. That fact by itself does not frighten me.'[31] But later he thought the Chinese might prefer to send trained Tibetans from China to weaken or even upset the Dalai Lama's administration.[32] So, on hearing in the autumn of 1950 that a military invasion of Tibet was imminent, the Government of India were surprised and decided to represent to China the advantage of desisting from any such action. Probably Nehru was encouraged into taking this indiscreet step by Panikkar's assurance that People's China was desirous of maintaining the friendliest relations with India.[33] Anything in the nature of pressure tactics was ruled out, because ultimately India had no effective sanction and to take up an attitude of resistance without the strength to follow it up would have been, as Nehru later observed, 'political folly of the first magnitude'.[34] But Nehru felt that India, while recognizing China's suzerainty over Tibet, had a right to express her interest in the maintenance of Tibetan autonomy; and a friendly caution might not be misunderstood.

[25] Press conference at Delhi, 30 September, *National Herald*, 1 October 1950.

[26] 'India's title to leadership in the new Asia is unquestioned. But an ineluctable condition of leadership is that one should lead. A mere wringing of the hands over all the obvious difficulties and perils of a situation is not leadership; and until the Indian statesmen can show a more precise power of decision they will inevitably find themselves swept along upon a current of events which they cannot hope to control.' 'India's position', editorial in *New York Herald Tribune*, 5 October 1950. 'Pandit Nehru purports to speak for Asia, but it is the voice of abnegation; his criticism now turns out to have been obstructive, his policy is appeasement. Worst of all, one fails to find a valid moral judgement in his attitude. One can feel certain that history will condemn the Nehru policy as well-intentioned but timid, shortsighted and irresponsible.' 'Plain words to Indians', editorial in the *New York Times*, 12 October 1950.

[27] Statements at press conference, 16 October, *National Herald*, 17 October 1950; interview with Sefton Delmer, reprinted in *Tribune* (Ambala), 24 October 1950.

[28] Telegrams to Vijayalakshmi and Rau, 25 October 1950.

[29] To K. M. Panikkar, 25 October 1950.

[30] Panikkar's note from Nanking, 20 November 1948.

[31] Nehru to John Matthai, 10 September 1949.

[32] Nehru's notes for speech at conference of foreign ministers at Colombo, 9 January 1950.

[33] Panikkar to Nehru, 2 August 1950.

[34] Note, 5 March 1953.

However, in reply to India's suggestion, made 'without any political or territorial ambition', that a peaceful settlement be worked out,[35] China asserted that Tibet was Chinese territory which it was China's sacred duty to liberate, even though this problem should be solved by peaceful and friendly means.[36] This satisfied Nehru, though, as he later said,[37] it was not quite clear from whom Tibet was to be liberated, and it seemed to him that China was showing, at least at that time, a desire to be friendly to India. 'I attach great importance to India and China being friends. I think the future of Asia and to some extent of the world depends on this.'[38] But the official reply expressing appreciation of China's assurance misled the Chinese about India's understanding of the status of Tibet by stating the hope 'that the forthcoming negotiations will result in a harmonious adjustment of legitimate Tibetan claims to autonomy within the framework of Chinese sovereignty.' By an oversight the word 'sovereignty' had been used instead of 'suzerainty' and, though it was later decided to correct this error, the Chinese were never formally informed of this correction. Panikkar had a nimble, reactive and uncommitted mind, and while he shrewdly projected China's views to the world, he was not as successful in making China aware of the weight and force of India's attitude on various questions.

Nehru's assessment of China's attitude to India was also naïve.

The change in relations between India and China during the past few weeks has been rather remarkable. I think this began slowly after my visit to America last year when they realized that I was not exactly anybody's stooge, as they had imagined. Our championing China's case in the United Nations has gone a long way also. Panikkar has done a good job and gets on very well with the Chinese Government. I have no doubt that the friendly influence we have exercised on China during the past few months has helped the cause of peace. They listen to us, even though they might not agree, because they feel that our advice is disinterested.[39]

So when, in October, there were reports of military action without waiting for a Tibetan delegation to reach Peking, the Government of India unhesitatingly expressed their surprise and regret and pointed out that this would give a handle to those who were opposing China's admission to the United Nations. The problem of Tibet was not urgent or serious, and a delay would not have affected Chinese interests or a suitable final

[35] Interview of Indian Ambassador at Peking with Chinese Vice-Foreign Minister, 13 August 1950.
[36] Note of the Foreign Minister of China, 21 August 1950.
[37] 6 December 1950. Lok Sabha Debates, 1950, Vol. VI, Part II, pp. 1257-71.
[38] To Panikkar, 2 September 1950.
[39] To Vijayalakshmi, 14 September 1950.

solution.[40] Because of the shortcomings of Indian diplomacy in Peking, the Chinese reacted to the Indian protest with a surprise which was not wholly feigned. There had been a failure to convey, between August and October, India's deep interest in this matter. Nehru's concern at the end of August at possible Chinese intervention in Formosa and Tibet had not been communicated to the Chinese Government; and later Panikkar was content with Chou's public reference to peace negotiations in Tibet. He now explained to his own Government what he described as a sudden change of Chinese policy in Tibet by their expectation of a general war, in which case Tibet might also be stirred up by unfriendly countries; he did not add that the use now, without explanation, by India of the word 'suzerainty' perhaps seemed to them a shift in policy as the result of foreign influence. As Bajpai observed, Panikkar's protests on Tibet compared closely with Neville Henderson's protests in Nazi Germany on behalf of Czechoslovakia.

> What interest the Ambassador thinks he may be serving by showing so much solicitude for the Chinese Government's policy of false excuses and wanton high-handedness towards Tibet passes my understanding . . . I feel it my duty to observe that, in handling the Tibetan issue with the Chinese Government, our Ambassador has allowed himself to be influenced more by the Chinese point of view, by Chinese claims, by Chinese maps and by regard for Chinese susceptibilities than by his instructions or by India's interests.[41]

It is not surprising, therefore, that the Chinese reply was sharp. Tibet, asserted the Chinese Government, was an integral part of Chinese territory and they were resolved on a military occupation of Tibet in order to liberate the Tibetan people and defend the frontiers of China. This was entirely a domestic problem in which no foreign interference would be tolerated, and it had nothing to do with the admission of China to the United Nations. As for India's protest, China 'cannot but consider it as having been affected by foreign influences hostile to China in Tibet . . .'[42]

Resentful of such accusations, Nehru thought that China was not playing fair with India.

> If the Chinese Government distrust India and think that we are intriguing against it with the Western Powers, then all I can say is that they are less intelligent than I thought them to be. The whole corner-stone of our policy during the past few months has been friendly

---

[40] Unofficial and unsigned note handed by Indian Ambassador to Chinese Foreign Office, 21 October 1950.

[41] Bajpai's notes to Prime Minister, 27 and 31 October 1950.

[42] Note of the Government of China, 30 October 1950.

relations with China and we have almost fallen out with other countries because of this policy that we have pursued.[43]

He repudiated the insinuation of foreign influence, pointed out that the military action had affected not only friendly relations between India and China but also the interest of world peace, and stressed that it was with no desire for advantage that India had recommended a peaceful adjustment.[44] But he refused, as advised by Patel and Rajagopalachari, to push matters to an open breach, and ignored a vague hint from Loy Henderson, the United States Ambassador, that the State Department would be glad to help if asked.[45] Chinese action in Tibet was to him not a demonstration of general unfriendliness or studied deception but an act of extreme discourtesy, explicable to some extent by misunderstanding, reliance on Soviet sources of information and a belief that a general war was imminent and Tibet was part of the overall strategy of the United States. So, even as the flow of Chinese troops into Korea grew in volume, China had strengthened her position in Tibet.

Nehru did not reply directly to Patel's letter charging the Chinese with 'little short of perfidy' and calling for urgent preparations against 'a potential enemy'. But in letters to others, of which copies were sent to Patel, he stressed the importance of understanding the new China.

Chinese psychology, with its background of prolonged suffering, struggle against Japan, and successful communist revolution, is an understandable mixture of bitterness, elation and vaulting confidence to which the traditional xenophobia and present-day isolation from outside contacts have added fear and suspicion of the motives of other powers. For inducing a more balanced and cooperative mentality in Peking, it is essential to understand those psychological factors.[46]

Whether it was possible for India to have friendly relations with China was not clear, but the attempt had to be made, because anything else would be bad in the long run not only for the two countries but for Asia as a whole. Friendship between India and China would be a very powerful force for peace in the world; conflict or fear of conflict between them would render a vast area of the world a prey to constant fear and apprehension and impede India's efforts at progress. The invasion of Tibet had been a blow to these efforts and had therefore pleased the Western Powers and, to some extent, even the Soviet Union; but this was all the more reason to persevere and not be swept away by the fears and passions of the moment.[47] China should

[43] To Panikkar, 25 October 1950.
[44] Note of the Government of India, 31 October 1950.
[45] See Nehru to Vijayalakshmi, 1 November 1950.
[46] Nehru to Ernest Bevin, 20 November 1950.
[47] Nehru to Chief Ministers, 17 November, and note, 18 November 1950.

be in no doubt that India would defend the Himalayan borders. 'Whether India had the necessary military resources or not, I would fight aggression whether it came from the mountain or the sea . . . I am not thinking in terms of blocs. I am on my side and on nobody else's side. I am on my country's side.'[48] But this need not mean an open breach with China. The best way to help Tibet retain a large measure of autonomy was not by breaking with China but by retaining some influence with her. For the same reasons, he discouraged the Dalai Lama from fleeing to India.[49]

Nor was the issue of Tibet allowed to cloud the Korean problem. On 9 November India suggested that some territory in North Korea, in which China had a direct interest, might be demilitarized in order to avoid open confrontation; and the idea was taken up by Bevin, whose general policy was not to 'create a situation' even while Britain acted in close cooperation with the United States. But regular Chinese army units had entered the war, President Truman talked about the possible use of the atom bomb and both sides prepared for a general conflict. Power, thought Nehru, had clearly gone to the heads of both the United States and China and the chances of preventing war appeared slender. 'So far as we are concerned, we shall try to keep out of it. We may be benevolently neutral. Whether we can succeed ultimately in keeping out, it is impossible to say.'[50]

In this context, Nehru regarded as impractical the proposal of Lester Pearson, the Foreign Minister of Canada, that he make a public appeal for an immediate cease-fire in Korea and the cessation of Chinese armed intervention as a preliminary to exploring the possibility of a settlement in which China could participate. But India did, along with ten other Asian states, appeal to China and North Korea to declare their intention not to cross into South Korea. Nehru also urged on Attlee, who was on his way to Washington, to work for a cease-fire and demilitarization, to be followed by negotiations, with China participating, to settle the future of Korea and Formosa. The same formula was put to Chou En-lai, who showed interest but would not commit himself without knowing the attitude of the United States. Truman's Government, however, were firm in refusing to discuss Formosa, and would not even consider the other items in Nehru's formula until the fighting in Korea stabilized; and then, when the military situation improved in their favour, their attitude further stiffened. The corollary of this, as usual, was criticism of India. 'Nehru', Truman was reported to have told a Congressman, 'has sold us down the Hudson. His attitude has been responsible for our losing the war in Korea.'[51] On the verge once more of semi-famine in various parts of the country, the Government of India were obliged again to request the United States to ship 1·5 to 2 million tons of

[48] Speech in Parliament, 7 December, *Hindustan Times*, 8 December 1950.
[49] Nehru's telegram to Indian Consul-General at Lhasa, 2 December 1950.
[50] To C. D. Deshmukh, 30 November 1950.
[51] Vijayalakshmi to Nehru, 18 December 1950.

foodgrains; but the response was not encouraging.[52] Krishna Menon suggested that Nehru visit Peking before coming to London for the Commonwealth Prime Ministers' Conference and then go on to Washington to meet Truman. 'On America its effect would be that of an ice bag on a delirious patient with high temperature. It would give time and receptivity for further treatment.' For lack of a definite and energetic initiative India was in effect becoming a passive accomplice to war and allowing the gathering of prime ministers to assume the shape of a pre-war rally. 'I am bound to say that you are *not* allowing the importance of the role you play to have its due weight.'[53] But Nehru was not to be flattered into empty, dramatic moves. It was foolish for any individual to expect at this stage to thaw the seemingly frozen attitudes of China and the United States. There was a growing appreciation in other countries of China's case.

> I am afraid however that the belief of the Chinese government and people in the inevitability of war is making any attempt at peace more and more difficult. China's position is strong in every way. They need take no risks and yet they can be a little more accommodating in smaller matters and in approach.[54]

Nor was there any purpose in flying to Peking unless he had something definite to offer, and this was only possible if the United States took a less rigid attitude on Formosa. So all that Nehru did was to urge on Attlee again to press this viewpoint on the United States.

Neither in Korea nor on Tibet did Nehru, by the end of 1950, have any tangible results to show. The Western Powers involved in Korea had not listened to him; General Wu, the special delegate of China to the United Nations, had told the Secretary-General that India's views did not count for much since, among other things, India had no soldiers in Korea;[55] and on the issue of Tibetan autonomy Nehru had been snubbed by China. So the depression that clouded his spirit on his birthday is understandable.

> Somehow I have felt very dispirited today because of all kinds of happenings in India and the world. This world and this country of ours seem to go awry and I feel more and more that I am doing little that I want to do. I work hard, but doubts come to me as to the results of that work. So many things happen which depress me. One can only work with energy and a measure of enthusiasm if one has certain

[52] Nehru's telegram and letter to Vijayalakshmi, 13 December, and Vijayalakshmi's letter communicating Acheson's reply, 18 December 1950.
[53] Krishna Menon's personal telegrams to Nehru, 18 and 20 December 1950.
[54] Nehru's cable to Panikkar, 30 December 1950.
[55] Trygve Lie, *In the Cause of Peace* (New York, 1954), pp. 354-5.

definite ideals and objectives. If the ideals fade, then that energy and enthusiasm also fade.[56]

Yet it was generally recognized that Nehru, more than any other individual, had done what little he could to stave off a general war, and had struck a note of sanity among the loud, shrill voices pressing for a conflict. James Cameron, who met him in Delhi on the day the United Nations forces crossed the 38th parallel, recollected what they had always said, that Jawaharlal Nehru could take the curse off moral platitudes by the curious method of believing in them; he reminded one momentarily of what one had almost forgotten, that somewhere between the excesses and threats that hemmed the world round there was a point of view that put a higher value on principle than on expediency.[57] By the end of 1950 Nehru had become a world figure whose stature had little relation to his country's strength and whose constituency extended far beyond India. He was the spokesman of all those, everywhere, who were sick of war and chauvinist passion and hoped for the dominance of reason, justice and tolerance in world affairs. While sensitive to India's interests as he saw them, he strove to reconcile them with civilized values in the highest public sense — civil liberties, the modernization and development of the countries of Asia and Africa, and the strengthening of peace everywhere. The slight, trim figure in the buttoned-up tunic and with a red rose in the button-hole, the tense, impatient face usually crowned with a Gandhi cap concealing the baldness, became the chief symbol in the world's eyes of national freedom and progress and international goodwill.

Nothing made this clearer than the election to the chancellorship of Cambridge University at the end of 1950. The death of Field-Marshal Smuts earlier in the year had rendered the office vacant, and a large number of the younger dons decided to put up the name of Nehru. They soon derived support from some of the most distinguished figures on the rolls of the University — Bertrand Russell, E. M. Forster, R. A. Butler, Pethick-Lawrence, Mountbatten — and eighty-nine members of the Senate formally nominated Nehru. A fly-sheet, signed by six of his most eminent supporters, was circulated among the voters.

The Prime Minister of India is, among Cambridge men available for the office of Chancellor, incontestably the most eminent . . . Pandit Nehru, as Prime Minister of India, has it in his power to offer to a world distracted by hatred and prejudice services incomparably more valuable and more pacific than lie within the grasp of any other Cambridge man at this time. We ask members of the University to

[56] Nehru to Patel, 14 November 1950, *Sardar Patel's Correspondence*, Vol. 9 (Ahmedabad, 1974), pp. 290-91.
[57] J. Cameron, *Point of Departure* (London, 1969 edition), pp. 143-5.

offer to Pandit Nehru, who is a scholar as well as a statesman, the office of Chancellor as a mark of admiration of his qualities of character and of intellect, and as a sign of our hope for and trust in the peaceful reconciliation of the different races and creeds of mankind.

The other candidate was Lord Tedder, an airman of distinguished service; but his name did not evoke anything like the same excitement as that of Nehru, and it was generally recognized that in any election Nehru would carry the majority. But the forces of reaction were not routed yet. Even though the statutes did not require acceptance of the nomination, the Vice-Chancellor wrote formally wishing to know if Nehru agreed to his name going forward. This immediately raised political and international issues. If Nehru accepted the nomination and then lost the election, Indian opinion would be deeply upset; even if he won, the fact that a number had voted against him might well be resented. Only a unanimous election could be considered; and this was not feasible. So Nehru informed his supporters that his name should be withdrawn. He set aside the gratifying prospect of the most honourable office which his old University could bestow because he could not risk endangering Indo-British relations at a time when he was effecting a transformation of the nature of the Commonwealth. But many would have agreed with E. M. Forster: 'I wish he had risked it.'[58]

[58] To Kingsley Martin, 6 November 1950. Kingsley Martin Papers.

6

Kashmir 1951-1953

Rejecting U Nu's offer in December 1950 to mediate on Kashmir, Nehru observed that no other country could help in this matter. 'The only way to solve it is for India and Pakistan to know that the burden is upon them and on no one else'.[1] But in January 1951 Pakistan demanded that Kashmir be discussed by the prime ministers of the Commonwealth meeting in London. Nehru would have been well within his rights in objecting to it, but he willingly agreed to some of the other prime ministers joining Liaqat and himself in informal talks on the Kashmir question. At these talks Nehru's line was that nothing should be done to upset the somewhat unstable equilibrium that had been slowly reached in the relations between the two countries; nor could India agree to Pakistan's claim to Kashmir on the basis of the two-nation theory. This brought the discussion back to a plebiscite and the status of the Abdullah Government. Liaqat rejected any partial plebiscite and insisted that it should cover the whole State. On the question of the Kashmir Government, Menzies proposed as a compromise that that Government need be deprived only of functions relating to the plebiscite and the Commonwealth countries could provide a security force for Kashmir. Nehru rejected the last suggestion on the grounds that the return of British or Dominion troops to India would be highly provocative; nor could a joint Indo-Pakistan force be tolerated as India could never allow the aggressor to send troops to any part of the State. But he was willing to consider the mustering of a local force by the Plebiscite Administrator, even though this raised complicated issues involving India's responsibility for the defence of Kashmir.[2]

Nehru's spirit of accommodation was soon stifled by the attitude of Britain and the United States at the Security Council. Their draft resolution on Kashmir went against India's position on every issue. It objected to the convening of a constituent assembly in Kashmir and provided for the

[1] U Nu to Nehru, 5 December, and Nehru's reply, 10 December 1950.
[2] Nehru's note, 9 January, and telegram to Indian Ambassador in Ankara, 26 January 1951; statement in Parliament, 12 February 1951. Parliamentary Debates 1951, Vol. VIII, Part II, Cols. 2697-2706.

supersession of the Kashmir Government and the possible entry of foreign troops. A United Nations representative should effect demilitarization and raise a neutral or local force and, in the event of the parties failing to agree, there should be arbitration under the auspices of the International Court of Justice. The United States was at this time angry with India and its hostility was expected; but Nehru had hoped that at least now Britain would be less partisan.[3] Rau suggested acceptance of the Anglo-American resolution with reservations, particularly after Britain abandoned the idea of a United Nations force: but Nehru ordered total rejection, whatever the consequences. The resolution amounted to a treatment of India such as no self-respecting country could tolerate. 'It appears to us to be a deliberate attempt to injure us in Kashmir and to discredit our wider policies.'[4] Such a severe reaction, reinforced perhaps in London by Mountbatten, who claimed to have warned Gordon Walker that if Britain questioned the legality of Kashmir's accession he might have to speak out,[5] led the British Government to tone down. They now argued that they had proposed arbitration, not on the general issue of Kashmir but on specific points of varying interpretation of the agreement between India and Pakistan. But the resolution as passed with British support, and the criticism in the British press of India's Kashmir policy, convinced Nehru that no fair play could be expected from Britain on this issue. It seemed to him that, from Attlee downwards, they had convinced themselves from the start that Kashmir, being predominantly Muslim, should go to Pakistan, and they consistently followed a policy to that end. 'They tried to cover this up by a seeming impartiality. But that veil grew thinner and thinner till it was worn away completely.'[6] The speeches of the British and American representatives at the Security Council might have been, in Nehru's view, delivered by the Pakistani delegate. The British Foreign Office appeared to be still relying on Pakistan as a means of retaining British influence in West Asia. Britain and the United States could not grasp that to India Kashmir was not merely a matter of a patch of territory but a basic question of policy.

> If Pakistan's communal approach and policy prevail in Kashmir, it would not only be a tragedy for Kashmir, but it would upset the whole scheme of things in India, and of course in Pakistan. We would enter a phase of trying to exterminate each other. These are terrible thoughts which come to me, and I find the American and British people skating merrily on this very thin ice over the deep ocean, and accusing us of intransigence.[7]

[3] Telegram to Krishna Menon, 24 February 1951.
[4] Telegram to Rau, 26 February 1951.
[5] Mountbatten to Nehru, 25 April 1951.
[6] Nehru's note, 26 May 1951.
[7] Nehru to Vijayalakshmi, 2 and 25 June 1951.

India, therefore, refused to accept or implement the resolution. Dr Frank Graham, the new United Nations representative, would be received with courtesy and any points raised by him would be explained; but beyond that India would not go, and the constituent assembly for Kashmir would meet as scheduled.

These pressures on India strengthened the belligerent elements in Pakistan. Zafrullah, the Foreign Minister, threatened war, and it seemed possible that Pakistan might attempt to occupy the Valley by a swift military action. Troops were concentrated on the Kashmir border, new divisions raised, reserves called up, leave cancelled and raids and sabotage in Kashmir stepped up. Nehru decided that the best way to prevent escalation was to take counter-measures and let it be known that this was being done. The armoured division was moved up to the Punjab border and no great secrecy was maintained about the fact. It was also stated clearly that if Pakistan took any aggressive action India would carry the war into West Pakistan.[8] These steps had their desired effect soon enough. Liaqat Ali Khan protested both publicly and in a telegram to Nehru about Indian army movements, and there was a diminution of Pakistan's bluster as well as of preparation. To Graham, the story told was one of fear of India and of her intent to put an end to the partition and to Pakistan. To Nehru it always seemed that the Pakistan authorities kept up the tension and propaganda not just because of their Kashmir policy but for their own domestic reasons. 'The Government of Pakistan is like someone riding a bicycle. They feel that the moment they return to normalcy, the bicycle stops and they fall down.'[9]

Nehru assured Graham that, apart from Pakistan's fear being baseless, India was eager to have a speedy settlement in Kashmir by holding a plebiscite. Not just the bulk of Indian troops, but three-quarters or even more, would be brought back if Pakistan troops were withdrawn and the 'Azad Kashmir' forces disbanded. The massive victory of the National Conference in the elections to the constituent assembly made Nehru more optimistic than ever about the result of a plebiscite, and he discussed with Abdullah the possibility of a plebiscite in the State, excluding 'Azad Kashmir'. The United Nations authorities could check the electoral rolls which had been prepared and then hold the plebiscite. Indian troops would be moved to the cease-fire line to prevent incursions, but Abdullah was prepared to permit a few well-known persons from Pakistan or 'Azad Kashmir' to come and canvass, provided the same facilities were given to him when a plebiscite was held in 'Azad Kashmir'.[10]

Graham's report was mainly a factual one, though he made some new suggestions which were not in line with the decisions of the United Nations

[8] Nehru at press conference, 13 March, *National Herald*, 14 March 1951.
[9] Nehru's note for Sheikh Abdullah, 25 August 1952.
[10] Note of Nehru, 9 September 1951.

Commission or what had been agreed to earlier.[11] Liaqat Ali Khan proposed that the Security Council should now impose a solution, but Nehru replied that no imposed formula would be acceptable to India. Once more Pakistan prepared for a quick war which she thought she would win.[12] At the Security Council, for the first time the Soviet Union adopted a positive attitude and criticized the policies of Britain and the United States. To Nehru this was an embarrassment for it made Kashmir a part of cold war rivalry and stiffened the stance of the other powers. The British and American Governments were therefore informed that India had not sought Soviet support. But when Britain responded by advising further concessions by India, particularly as regards the quantum of forces maintained by her, Nehru reacted sharply. 'It is very good of the British Government to take such a deep interest in our affairs and be so lavish with their advice to us that we should behave. I fear I am a little tired of their good intentions and good offices.'[13]

The draft resolution introduced by the British delegate at the Security Council persisted, behind a cloak of seeming impartiality, in ignoring India's version of the case as well as past commitments made by the United Nations commission. India and Pakistan were treated alike and asked to reduce their forces to the minimum, just as the 'Azad Kashmir' authorities were treated on a par with the Kashmir Government; and there was once more talk of a neutral force. This refusal to deal with the issue of aggression and a consideration only of a plebiscite in which India and Pakistan were equal parties exasperated Nehru. 'There can be no right decision based on wrong. That wrong has to be righted first.'[14] The State Department had also been 'made to understand, in the clearest language, that we consider their attitude in this matter completely wrong and unfriendly to India and that this comes more in the way of the development of cordial relations between India and America, that all of us desire, than anything else.'[15] If the Western Powers insisted on passing the resolution, India would take the matter to the General Assembly; but there was no question of accepting the resolution or revising the Kashmir policy.

Despite India's objection, the resolution was passed. Nehru rejected it, and was prepared for a break with Graham if he wished to have talks on the basis of that resolution. But by now the unfriendly attitude of Britain and the United States seemed less important than developments within Kashmir itself. The attitude of Sheikh Abdullah had, over the years,

[11] E.g., Graham suggested simultaneous demilitarization while India was prepared to commence it on her side only after Pakistan had completed it.
[12] See R. G. Casey's diary entries 26 and 27 March 1952, written at Karachi. T. B. Millar (ed.), *Australian Foreign Minister, the Diaries of R. C. Casey 1951-60* (London, 1972), pp. 76-7.
[13] Note, 7 April 1952.
[14] Nehru's telegram to Vijayalakshmi, 10 November 1952.
[15] Nehru to G. L. Mehta, appointed to succeed Vijayalakshmi as Ambassador in Washington, 1 October 1952.

become increasingly a cause of concern to the Government of India. Nehru had, in a sense, built his Kashmir policy round this man. It was the popular support which Abdullah commanded in Kashmir and his commitment to India and secularism which justified prompt military action and saved India's troops from being an army of invasion.

> The only person who can deliver the goods in Kashmir is Abdullah. I have a high opinion of his integrity and his general balance of mind. He may make any number of mistakes in minor matters, but I think he is likely to be right in regard to major decisions. No satisfactory way out can be found in Kashmir except through him.[16]

Such dependence on an individual caused at first no worry. Abdullah's attachment to India and her Prime Minister seemed unshakable and Nehru had to warn him to avoid references to Pakistan in his speeches, for these were always so critical that they were cited in the Security Council to prove that the Abdullah Government was incapable of impartiality at the time of a plebiscite.[17] Nehru was not aware that at the same time Abdullah, who perhaps from the start had nurtured ideas of independence,[18] had spoken to senior officials in the United States of the advantages of independence and hinted at American and British aid for development.[19]

In September 1948 Abdullah's statement that certain people in India believed in surrendering Kashmir to Pakistan drew a protest from Patel, and Nehru had to explain it away.

> Sheikh Abdullah is, I am convinced, a very straight and frank man. He is not a very clear thinker and he goes astray in his speech as many of our politicians do. He is of course obsessed with the idea of meeting the challenge of Pakistan and keeping his own people from being influenced by Pakistan's propaganda. I made it clear to him that while I entirely agree with this, the approach should be different.[20]

But Abdullah himself was unapologetic, and soon the divergence of approach between him and Nehru himself became so marked that in January 1949 the Prime Minister had to appeal to Abdullah not to confuse issues by airing his views in the press.[21] Kashmir, he observed to Krishna Menon a month later,[22] continued to be a headache; there was little

---

[16] Nehru to the Maharaja of Kashmir, 13 November 1947.
[17] Nehru to Abdullah, 3 April 1948.
[18] See Mahajan, *Looking Back* (Bombay, 1963), p. 162.
[19] See Warren Austin to State Dept. on interview with Abdullah, 28 January 1948. *Foreign Relations of the United States 1948*, Vol. 5, Part I, p. 292.
[20] Nehru to Patel, 4 October 1948, *Sardar Patel's Correspondence*, Vol. 1 (Ahmedabad, 1971), pp. 232-3.
[21] Nehru to Sheikh Abdullah, 11 and 12 January 1949.
[22] 19 February 1949.

coordination between the Government of India and Abdullah's Government and this was injuring India's cause. After meeting the United States Ambassador in Srinagar in the spring of 1949, Sheikh Abdullah seems to have got the impression — as against what he had been told in New York in 1948 — that the United States and Britain would favour an independent Kashmir and would provide it with international guarantees.[23] Certainly from 1949 his mind worked clearly on these lines and in numerous speeches and statements he hinted at the advantages of such a development.[24] He was even reported to have suggested this to Sir Owen Dixon in the summer of 1950 as one of the possible solutions of the Kashmir issue and to be contemplating bilateral negotiations with the leaders of 'Azad Kashmir'. All this, of course, embarrassed the Government of India, and Nehru in particular. 'The most difficult thing in life', commented Nehru sadly, having Sheikh Abdullah and Krishna Menon chiefly in mind, 'is what to do with one's friends.'[25]

When Abdullah expressed his resentment at receiving advice from the Government of India on matters lying outside defence, external affairs and communications, the three subjects on which Kashmir had acceded, Nehru wrote directly to Abdullah revealing his distress. Relations with the Kashmir Government were being conducted by India not on a formal footing but on the basis of common objectives and friendship. He had never taken any action with regard to Kashmir without consulting Abdullah fully; but if Abdullah wished only to function on the official level, then Nehru would have to think anew and his interest in Kashmir would be greatly reduced.

> I think I told you once before that if there was any vital difference of opinion between you and me, then I would prefer to drop out . . . I greatly regret that you should have taken up a position which indicates that you do not attach any value to any friendly advice that we might give and, indeed, consider it as improper interference, of which you take a very grave view. If that is so, personally I have nothing further to say. I have not thought of Kashmir or of you in that way and so I am rather at a loss how to act when the very foundation of my thought and action has been shaken up.[26]

Abdullah's defence was that the States Ministry ordered the Kashmir

[23] It has recently been suggested that some Indian leaders believed that it was Mrs Loy Henderson, the wife of the United States Ambassador, and some C.I.A. agents who encouraged Abdullah to think in these terms. See W. Johnson (ed.), *The Papers of Adlai Stevenson* Vol. 5 (Boston, 1974), p. 204 fn.

[24] See, for example, his interview published in the *Scotsman*, 14 April 1949.

[25] To Vijayalakshmi, 10 May 1950. Abdullah's conduct had naturally been seized upon by Nehru's critics. 'I fear Vallabhbhai thinks you have the sole responsibility in respect of Sheikh Abdullah!' Rajagopalachari to Nehru, 23 March 1949.

[26] Nehru to Sheikh Abdullah, 4 July 1950.

Government about too much, that they had done nothing new and that it was embarrassing for him to appeal repeatedly to Nehru.

> I cannot help feeling loss of confidence in myself in this respect. It is clear that there are powerful influences at work in India who do not see eye to eye with you regarding your ideal of making the Union a truly secular state and your Kashmir policy. Their constant endeavour is to weaken you and in order to achieve this purpose they think it necessary to bring down all those who are loyal and attached to you . . . While I feel I can willingly go down and sacrifice myself for you, I am afraid as custodian of the destinies of 40 lacs of Kashmiris, I cannot barter away their cherished rights and privileges. I have several times stated that we acceded to India because we saw there two bright stars of hope and aspiration, namely, Gandhiji and yourself, and despite our having so many affinities with Pakistan we did not join it, because we thought our programme will not fit with their policy. If, however, we are driven to the conclusion that we cannot build our state on our own lines, suited to our genius, what answer can I give to my people and how am I to face them?[27]

This made clear that Abdullah was not merely thinking of independence on its own merits but beginning to contrast India and Pakistan with detriment to the former. He issued a proclamation in defiance of the Government of India which suggested that he was bent on seeking a conflict. Gopalaswami Ayyangar recommended that the central government retort by announcing that the proclamation was not law.[28] But Nehru tided over the problem, and was hopeful that the constituent assembly which Abdullah was establishing for Kashmir would formulate a constitution consonant with the sovereignty of India. Abdullah's first speech to that assembly, stressing the part which Kashmir could play in strengthening secular forces in India, was a hopeful sign.[29] But his speech at Ranbirsinghpura on 11 April 1952 revealed the extent of the gulf which had developed between him and his colleagues at Delhi. He made no distinction between India and Pakistan and criticized the Indian press as a whole. Nehru did not wish to take him up on this, but Abdullah, sensing Nehru's acute concern, complained that his remarks had been distorted by the correspondent of the Press Trust of India because the Kashmir Government had declined to give financial assistance to the Trust for opening an office in the State. He added his grievance that no one in India

[27] Sheikh Abdullah to Nehru, 10 July 1950.
[28] To Nehru, 14 July 1950.
[29] 'From my experience of the last four years, it is my considered judgment that the presence of Kashmir in the Union of India has been the major factor in stabilizing relations between the Hindus and Muslims of India. Gandhiji was not wrong when he uttered words before his death which paraphrase, "I lift up mine eyes unto the hills, from whence cometh my help."'

had defended his proposals of land reform without compensation and even Nehru, instead of first ascertaining his views, had criticized him publicly on the basis of press reports.[30] But even the authorized version of Abdullah's speech was not happy, and his later speeches were in the same strain. Nehru did his best to explain them away to the public in the rest of India by pointing out that, however unfortunately worded, there was nothing in them of substance with which one need disagree. But he himself could not help being disheartened by Abdullah's dispersion of the widespread popular support for him and his policies in India by exaggerating the strength of the communal forces in India. This in itself provided sustenance to these elements and encouraged criticism of India abroad at a time when the Security Council was considering the Kashmir problem.

> I have not the wish or the heart to argue about this or any other matter with you. I have felt deeply about Kashmir, because it represented to me many things and many principles. It always has been an axiom with me, quite apart from constitutional position and the like, that the people of Kashmir must decide their own fate. For me the people of Kashmir were basically represented by you. If you feel as you do, then the link that has bound us together necessarily weakens and I have little heart left to discuss these matters. You will do of course as you think right and I shall certainly not come in the way. My only difficulty is that I happen to hold a responsible position in India and therefore have some voice in fashioning our policy. For the moment, it is not clear to me what I should do.[31]

Abdullah's replies were friendly at the personal level, but unrepentant on the specific issue. He believed that he had been gravely wronged by certain influential sections in India and that this was endangering the communal harmony and goodwill in Kashmir. While claiming that his attachment to Nehru, to their common ideals and to India was unshaken, he insisted that it was necessary to clear up the considerable confusion that seemed to exist regarding the constitutional relationship of Kashmir with India.[32] Nehru could not agree with this, but he decided not to continue a public controversy.[33] 'Some people thought', he assured the Chief Ministers but, in fact, seeking to assure himself,

> that the leaders of Kashmir were not playing quite fair with India and might even think of a breakaway from India. Naturally this thought was rather painful. As a matter of fact, if one thing is certain it is this:

[30] Sheikh Abdullah to Nehru, 23 April 1952.
[31] Nehru's two letters to Sheikh Abdullah, 25 April 1952.
[32] Sheikh Abdullah to Nehru, 1 and 2 May 1952.
[33] Nehru to Sheikh Abdullah, 2 and 7 May 1952.

that not only the leaders but the great mass of the people in Kashmir want to be associated with India and want the accession of Kashmir to India to continue . . . I have no doubt in my mind that the leaders of the people of Kashmir are anxious to continue this accession to India and if there is a plebiscite on this point it will be in India's favour.[34]

Meantime, a step towards cooperation seemed to have been taken when Nehru and Abdullah reached agreement on some general principles which would govern relations between Kashmir and India. The central government's authority would extend to the three subjects covered by the instrument of accession, and residuary powers would be vested, unlike the case of all other States in the Union, in the Kashmir Government. The residents of the State would be citizens of India, but the State legislature would have the power to define and regulate the rights and privileges of permanent residents. It was also for future decision whether a chapter on fundamental rights should be included in the Kashmir constitution; and the Supreme Court would have jurisdiction only in regard to such fundamental rights as were agreed to by the State. The State flag would continue along with the national flag, and the head of the Kashmir State would be chosen by the President on the recommendation of the State legislature. The central government could also intervene in the State only on the request or with the concurrence of the State Government.

Obviously, being an international issue, Kashmir required a special status; but the Delhi agreement was too vague to endure as it stood. To avoid head-on collisions with either Sheikh Abdullah, who toyed with ideas of independence, or those elements in India which demanded closer integration, Nehru suggested a more precise definition of Kashmir's links with India. Abdullah claimed to approve of this, but weakened belief by declining on specious grounds to come to Delhi. He then took steps to provide for the deposition and possible impeachment of the Maharaja and the election of the head of state. While the decision to have an elected head in Kashmir was fully accepted by the Indian Government, deposition and impeachment infringed the President's prerogatives and were bound to rouse discussion and criticism in India. So Nehru advised Abdullah to proceed slowly. 'We are a nation of lawyers and every step is examined with a hawk's eye by the legal fraternity.' The recent debates in Parliament on Kashmir had created a friendly atmosphere which should not be disturbed by fresh issues and doubts. If Abdullah changed the language of the agreement which Nehru had justified in Parliament, Nehru's whole argument would fall to the ground.[35] He also, writing in the general context of the talks with Graham at Geneva, drew attention to the impracticability of an independent Kashmir. The State was so important

[34] Nehru to Chief Ministers, 16 June 1952.
[35] Nehru to Abdullah, 6 August (two letters), and 7 August 1952 (two letters).

strategically that India and Pakistan, as well as other powers, would continue to be interested, and the struggle for influence would ensure that Kashmir was neither independent nor peaceful nor normal. Even the suggestion that Kashmir should be partitioned, with Jammu going to India, the north and north-western areas to Pakistan and the Valley becoming independent under a guarantee of India, Pakistan and the United Nations, was unworkable.

> Most important of all, we should have no doubts in our minds about these matters. Doubts in the minds of leaders percolate to their followers and the people generally. The weakness of the situation in Kashmir is the constant discussions which go on between people holding different views. What is required is a clear and firm outlook and no debate about basic issues. If we have that, it just does not matter what the United Nations thinks or Pakistan does. Personally I have that clear outlook and have had it for these four years and it has surprised me that there should be so much discussion about obvious matters . . . the only possible course for Kashmir is for the state to be closely associated with India, that association not interfering with its autonomy in most respects. If that is so, then it is not wise to say or do things which imperil that association. Our general outlook should be such as to make people think that the association of Kashmir state with India is an accomplished and final fact and nothing is going to undo it . . . I have held these views concisely and precisely for the last four years and nothing has happened during this period which has made me change them in the slightest. So meetings with United Nations officials or developments in Pakistan do not worry me in the least. What has sometimes worried me is what happens in Kashmir, because I have found doubt and hesitation there, and not clarity of vision or firmness of outlook.[36]

Abdullah's ambivalence, however, continued and resulted, as was to be expected, in fanning Hindu communal resentment. By the end of 1952 it was known that the Jan Sangh, a party newly formed by S. P. Mookerjee, the Akali Dal, the Hindu Mahasabha and the R.S.S. had joined hands with the Jammu Praja Parishad (the local Hindu communal party in Kashmir) to spread an agitation from Jammu into the Punjab and up to Delhi and beyond, on the three issues of Kashmir, refugees from East Bengal and the banning of cow-slaughter. The wide appeal of the issues was reinforced by a virulent personal attack on the Prime Minister, and the Sikh leader, Tara Singh, virtually called for the assassination of Nehru. It was likely that the agitation, even if it did not lead to war with Pakistan, might result in

---

[36] Nehru's note for Sheikh Abdullah, 25 August 1952.

killing on much the same scale as in 1947 and the destruction of whatever sense of security had been built in the Muslim mind in India.

Such potential danger called for quick and firm action at many levels; but nowhere was Nehru fully successful, and in consequence the crisis mounted beyond control. His orders that every attempt at disturbance within India should be suppressed were carried out only half-heartedly. The Home Ministry was at this time in the hands of Kailas Nath Katju, a loyal follower of Nehru but long past his prime; and his doddering ineptitude was accentuated by the tardiness of many officials whose communal sympathies were barely concealed. Nor did the effort of Nehru to isolate the agitation, so as to reveal its personal and communal tones, make much headway. He appealed to Kripalani and Jayaprakash Narayan not to support this agitation merely because of their desire to oppose. The possible result was something above parties and politics and might well affect the whole future of India; and for socialists to associate themselves with this agitation was to submerge their hope of progress in communal passion.[37] But Jayaprakash's dusty answer was that anti-communalism did not necessarily mean an acceptance of Nehru's method of handling this problem.[38]

Above all, Nehru failed in his major thrust of seeking to isolate the communal nucleus of the agitation by establishing that Sheikh Abdullah's administration was secular, broad-minded and national. Syama Prasad Mookerjee and his supporters were utilizing the discontent in Jammu to question the authority of Parliament in granting a special status to Kashmir, and to weaken the foreign policy of Nehru's Government; and, by trying to dissociate Jammu from the rest of the State, they were loosening India's hold on the Valley which, of course, was the real prize in the contest with Pakistan. Indeed, Mookerjee made it clear that to him the Jammu agitation was part of his continuous feud with the Prime Minister, whose leadership was to Mookerjee a national liability.[39] So the real attack was not on Abdullah but on Nehru and all the public values for which he stood. 'It is through your mistaken policy and your failure to understand the viewpoints of those who differ from you, that the country is being brought to the brink of disaster.'[40] On this there could obviously be no compromise. But the situation would become easier for Nehru to handle if in Jammu itself the hard core of opposition could be denuded of the support of the large number who were normally non-political but had joined the agitation because of the plausibility of its demands.

As it was, the initiative lay with the agitators and the Kashmir Government was on the defensive. Nehru himself was keen on touring

[37] Nehru to Kripalani, 19 November, and to Jayaprakash Narayan, 19 November 1952.
[38] Jayaprakash Narayan to Nehru, 11 January 1953.
[39] Balraj Madhok, *Syama Prasad Mookerjee* (Delhi, 1955?), pp. 80-84.
[40] S. P. Mookerjee to Nehru, 3 February 1953.

Jammu, but the Kashmir Government showed no great enthusiasm. So all he could do was to appeal to Abdullah to combine a firm attitude, so far as law and order were concerned, with a friendly approach to the large mass of the people in Jammu. Nehru thought this could best be done by implementing all the terms of the Delhi agreement, setting up promptly the commission which Abdullah had offered to inquire into the grievances of Jammu, flying the Indian flag alongside that of the State in two or three prominent places, postponing confiscation of the Maharaja's orchards and bearing in mind, while implementing land reforms, that the lands in Jammu were relatively poorer than those in other parts of the State. A positive, human approach and not mere logic or governmental action would provide a permanent solution by winning over people's minds and not just suppressing their views.[41]

Abdullah, however, was unwilling to oblige. The growing Hindu communal opposition to him seemed to justify all his fears. He did nothing to follow up his tentative suggestion of a commission for Jammu and, instead of taking immediate action on the Delhi agreement, referred its clauses to various sub-committees of the Kashmir assembly, thus ensuring long delays. On the other hand, he expressed concern at the reaction of the Muslims in Kashmir to the communal agitation in other parts of India.[42] This attitude in turn helped to whip up the flagging energies of the agitators in Jammu and elsewhere, and plans were made for concerted demonstrations throughout northern India. There was little that Nehru could do on his own to break this spiral, apart from pointing out to Syama Prasad Mookerjee the international repercussions of his demands and the advantage that Pakistan was taking of them, and urging Sheikh Abdullah to reclaim the initiative. But neither Mookerjee nor Abdullah was in a mood to listen, the one seemingly concerned merely to embarrass Nehru and the other obsessed with Hindu communalism and the fantasy of independence.

> I fear that Sheikh Sahib's mind is so utterly confused that he does not know what to do. All kinds of pressures are being brought to bear upon him and he is getting more and more into a tangle. There is nobody with him who can really help him much, because he does not trust anyone fully, and yet everyone influences him . . . My fear is that Sheikh Sahib, in his present state of mind, is likely to do something or take some step, which might make things worse . . . The fact is that he has so many pulls in different directions, that he just cannot make up his mind.[43]

---

[41] To Abdullah, 1 January, 5 January and 30 January 1953; to Bakshi Ghulam Mahomed, Deputy Prime Minister of Kashmir, 9 February 1953.
[42] Sheikh Abdullah to Nehru, 27 February 1953.
[43] Nehru to Azad, 1 March 1953.

There is a tone of near-despair in Nehru's letter to Abdullah pressing him to act and not merely wait on events.

We all agree that the uncertainty about the state should end as soon as possible. But you say in your letter that you do not know how this is going to happen. It is not enough for us to feel that something should be done. We all want the Korean war to stop. Perhaps everyone wants that. And yet it continues. We want the very serious problems in Europe and Africa to be solved, lest they lead to world war. But thus far no progress has been made and in fact things are a little worse than they were.

It is thus not merely enough to desire that something should happen, but to know how to get that done. The result is never entirely in any one individual's or group's or country's hands, but one works for certain ends and looks at the whole problem with some vision and perspective, not allowing any immediate difficulty to obscure that vision.[44]

But Abdullah did not respond, and even declined Nehru's invitation to come to Delhi to discuss matters. 'He does not quite know what to do and is, at the same time, not prepared to accept our advice. So he is in a complete jam and is very disheartened about everything.'[45] The parallel to this immobility in Kashmir was an intensification of the agitation outside the State. Tara Singh had to be arrested, and thereafter Mookerjee courted imprisonment. 'What is really painful is the extraordinary folly of all this.'[46] Trapped between Abdullah and Mookerjee, for the first time since 1947 Nehru began to feel despondent about the future of Kashmir. He could face Pakistan and the United Nations and even the prospect of war; but with Abdullah and Mookerjee working in tacit concert to divide the State on Hindu-Muslim lines, the problem became almost insuperably complex. The best approach in these circumstances seemed to be to suppress firmly the activities of the Hindu communalists which were little short of treason, thereby giving Abdullah time to recover his nerve. Nehru therefore ordered the prompt arrest of all those who participated in the agitation in Delhi and the Punjab, directed Pant to prevent the movement of volunteers from the U.P. into these areas, and asked Katju to consider the banning of the Jan Sangh.[47]

Nehru's hand, however, was weakened by the persistent inefficiency of the Home Ministry. Katju was unwilling to act on his Prime Minister's

[44] Nehru to Abdullah, 1 March 1953.
[45] Nehru to Vijayalakshmi, 3 March 1953.
[46] Nehru to Vijayalakshmi, 9 March 1953.
[47] Nehru to Pant, 15 March, to B. Sachar, Chief Minister of the Punjab, 20 March, and to Katju, 26 March 1953.

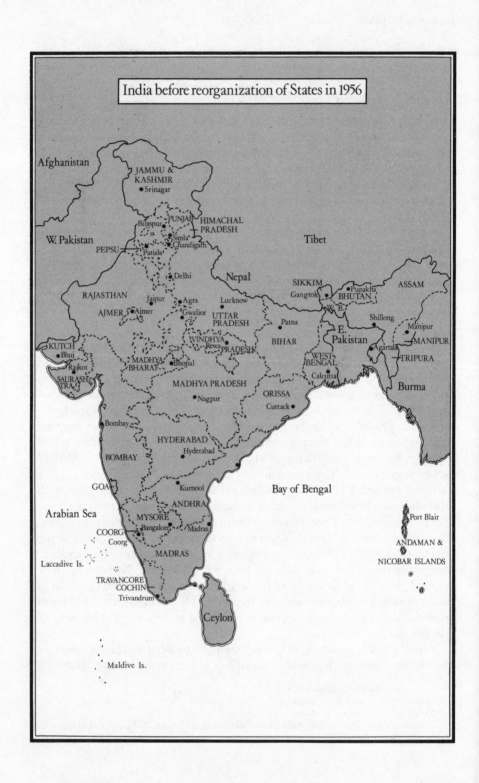

India before reorganization of States in 1956

suggestion,[48] and Mookerjee, whose release was ordered by the Supreme Court on technical grounds, was able again to intensify the agitation and muster support throughout northern India. He then decided to cross over into Jammu without a permit. The obvious step for the Government of India to take was to prevent such action under their own authority rather than place the onus on Abdullah's Government. Incredibly, the local officials in the Punjab travelled with Mookerjee and facilitated his crossing of the State frontier. Incompetence and evasion of responsibility and not, as Mookerjee's supporters suspected, a desire to push their leader into an area where the Supreme Court's writ did not as yet run,[49] seem to have been the reasons for such unpardonable folly. All that Nehru could do, as long as he left the Home Ministry in such shaky hands, was to protest vehemently.[50] Why he did not take immediate action to replace Katju with someone more vigorous is a failure that can be explained only by Nehru's reluctance, even in extreme situations, to hurt an old friend. 'You have surrounded yourself with all sorts of men whom others have rejected.'[51] The security of the state itself took second place in Nehru's scheme of values to personal loyalty. It is a tribute to the man, but not to the Prime Minister.

Abdullah's Government were at least prompt in arresting Mookerjee and placing him under detention; but Nehru could secure little cooperation from them in the positive matter of taking speedy action to defuse the agitation in Jammu.

> I need not tell you how very much concerned I am about this great delay. I cannot understand it. The biggest international matters are decided this way or that way. I do not mind dealing with any matter, but I feel quite helpless about this Kashmir issue because I do not know where I stand.[52]

Abdullah did not seek to explain the delay but invited Nehru and Katju to Srinagar. Overcoming his initial reluctance, Nehru went to Kashmir. Abdullah argued that there was no middle course between full integration and 'full autonomy' (which was his euphemism for independence), and, as the majority in Kashmir would not accept the first alternative, there was no choice but to accept the second, which now seemed to Abdullah, in contrast to his attitude even two months before,[53] to be practicable. He was not convinced by Nehru's reply that there were many intermediate

[48] Katju to Nehru, 16 April 1953.
[49] Madhok, op. cit., p. 261.
[50] To Katju, 8 and 16 May, and to Sachar, 26 May 1953.
[51] Rafi Kidwai to Nehru, 13 March 1953.
[52] To Bakshi Ghulam Mahomed, 27 April 1953.
[53] 'To say that those in whose hands lie the destinies of Kashmir state think in terms of independence is nothing but trash. It is not in the interests of the people of Kashmir to be left alone unprotected.' Speech at Madras, 21 January 1953.

possibilities. But it was also obvious that Abdullah no longer commanded maximum support in the National Conference, and at a meeting of its Working Committee his proposal to negotiate a new status with India was opposed by a majority of the members. Nehru urged all of them not to take any step which might make the situation even more difficult and to stay their hand at least until he returned from the Commonwealth Prime Ministers' Conference.

The tragedy was that the internal situation in Kashmir had deteriorated just when, for the first time since 1947, there was a real chance of a settlement with Pakistan. There the Governor-General, Ghulam Mahomed, had dismissed the Prime Minister, Nazimuddin, and appointed in his place Mahomed Ali—'all', as Nehru summed it up, 'palace politics and palace intrigues — without a palace.'[54] The *coup* was generally believed to have been promoted by the United States; and the Eisenhower administration was willing to consider a bilateral settlement on Kashmir between India and Pakistan. Dulles, on a visit to Delhi in May, added that talk of a plebiscite had little point; such plebiscites had failed elsewhere and only created bad blood, and it would be much better to settle the problem on the basis of partition or some other ad hoc arrangement.[55] Apart from the influence of the United States, there was also for the first time a widespread feeling in Pakistan that mere hostility could not serve for ever as a policy. Conditions in Pakistan, both political and economic, had deteriorated greatly and India could not be blamed for it all. Nehru's assessment was that a

vague regret [had] spread among many people at the fact of partition and its consequences. This must not be taken to mean that anyone really thought of reversing the partition. History cannot be reversed in this way. But all this did mean a reversal of the old habit of mind of blaming India for everything and a toning down of the ill-feeling against India. Probably, at no time during the last five or six years, has the public of Pakistan been more friendly, or to put it better in a negative way, less unfriendly to India than now. There is a genuine desire both in the public and among the leadership for some way to be found to settle the issues between India and Pakistan, which have created so much trouble and ill-will.[56]

Nehru was eager to respond to this new feeling of friendliness in Pakistan. He had already, even before the change of government, ordered his officials to adopt a less rigid attitude on the release of the Indus waters

[54] To Mountbatten, 19 April 1953.
[55] Nehru's note on interviews with Dulles, 22 May 1953.
[56] Nehru's note on relations with Pakistan, 26 April 1953.

12   Nehru and Truman, Washington, October 1949

13   With daughter and grandson Rajiv, October 1950, in the grounds of Nehru's home

14   Nehru, Rajagopalachari and Patel, 1950

and threatened to punish those who avoided execution of his orders and even concealed information from him. This was far too serious and important a matter for the Government of India to behave 'like a petty attorney' and act in a narrow legalistic way.[57] But the main problem was Kashmir. In London Mahomed Ali, while expressing his anxiety for a settlement on Kashmir and other issues, left it to Nehru to make precise suggestions on the ground that his position in his own country was still weak. A determined effort might well have ended in a formal partition of Kashmir; public opinion in Pakistan, the Pakistan Government and the United States would all probably have accepted it. But sadly, in what was perhaps the only hiatus in his long period of ascendancy, Nehru was not in a position to achieve this. The agitation in Jammu, with the support it could claim in the rest of the country, had tarnished India's secular image; nor could the Prime Minister commit the divided Kashmir Government in any way. 'I have not', as he bitterly told Abdullah before leaving for London, 'the ghost of a notion of what I am going to say to him about this because, apart from larger issues, I do not even know for certain what the present position is vis-à-vis India.'[58] So Nehru could do no more than utter platitudes and stress the need for care and caution and goodwill. There should be no external interference; the Government and people of Kashmir would have to be consulted at every step; existing conditions should be upset as little as possible; and rather than follow the detailed lines proposed by United Nations mediators and representatives, the Governments of India and Pakistan should explore fresh avenues. All these admirable sentiments added up to little progress.

At this stage, fate took a hand and gave the crisis a further twist. At Cairo, on his way back to India, Nehru heard that Mookerjee had died in detention on 23 June. The authorities in Kashmir do not seem to have realized that Mookerjee was not a fit man and was uncomfortable in high altitudes; even when he fell ill the doctors did not realize how sick he was, and the end came suddenly. Such was the incompetence of the local administration that Sheikh Abdullah was not informed of Mookerjee's death until the next morning and Karan Singh, the Yuvaraj (crown prince) who was the elected head of state, was told only after the body had been dispatched from Srinagar.[59]

Mookerjee's sudden death led to charges of negligence and even murder, and demands for an impartial inquiry. An emotional storm, particularly in Bengal, drove many who were not political supporters of Mookerjee into a mood sharply critical of Nehru and Abdullah. Nehru kept his balance; but in Kashmir the rift, which had already disrupted the government, became wider. Mookerjee himself, for all his fierce speeches, had no strong

[57] Nehru's two notes, 4 March 1953, and note, 10 April 1953.
[58] Nehru to Abdullah, 27 April 1953.
[59] Nehru to B. C. Roy, 30 June 1953.

commitment to extra-constitutional action,[60] and it was believed that he had, during his last days, been contemplating ways of terminating the agitation. But his death ruled out the thought of any compromise among Mookerjee's supporters just as the reactions to his death in some other parts of India strengthened the support for Abdullah in the Kashmir Valley.

> For the first time public cries are raised in Kashmir that the Indian Army should get out. If I feel strongly on this subject, you will understand me. Nothing more harmful to our cause in the State could have been done even by our enemies. It is for me almost a personal tragedy.[61]

To determine and, if necessary, even to revise policy in the new context Nehru invited Abdullah and some of his colleagues to Delhi.

> Nothing is more depressing than confused thinking in any vital matter. One can face any problem, however difficult, but there is no hope when there is confusion in one's mind. I have, thus far, kept my mind fairly clear on the Kashmir issue in spite of its difficulties. That did not mean that I had an easy solution up my sleeve, but that did mean that I was clear about the line of activity we should pursue. But lately I have not at all been clear as to what you have been thinking, and naturally that has a powerful effect on my own thinking . . . I know that during the past three or four years doubts have risen in your mind and we have discussed them. We did not agree about some things and, on one or two occasions, I even told you that I did not wish to come in your way if you differed from me in any vital matter . . . We have argued enough and must accept each other's present conclusions and then discuss the future on that basis. If that future unhappily leads to divergence with all its consequences we fashion our respective courses accordingly . . . Thus far, I have proceeded on a basis of friendship and confidence in you and have been vain enough to expect the same approach from you. Whether that is justified now or not, it is for you to say. Individual relations should not count in national affairs and yet they do count and make a difference.
>
> To me it has been a major surprise that a settlement arrived at between us should be by-passed or repudiated, regardless of the merits. That strikes at the root of all confidence, personal or international . . . My honour is bound up with my word . . . It is always painful to part company after long years of comradeship, but if

[60] See B. D. Graham, 'Syama Prasad Mookerjee and the Communalist Alternative' in D. A. Low, *Soundings in Modern South Asian History* (London, 1968), pp. 330-66.
[61] Nehru to B. C. Roy, 29 June 1953.

our conscience so tells us, or in our view, an overriding national interest so requires then there is no help for it. Even so we must do it with full understanding and full explanation to each other and not casually.[62]

Yet once again Abdullah declined to come to Delhi. Protesting that he was fully prepared to abide by the Delhi agreement, he blamed not only the agitators and the Indian press of communal vilification, but even the Government of India of failing to state clearly that the status of Kashmir would not be further altered.[63] Nehru merely replied that the criticism was unfair and pressed Abdullah to discuss present issues and not merely repeat past complaints; but Azad offered an explicit assurance that the recognition of Kashmir's special position was not of a temporary nature and India would adhere to this permanently without any reservations.

What I am telling you now is as a personal friend. There is only one way of safeguarding the future well-being of the people of Kashmir and that is the way which we laid down in 1949 and which you had then accepted. Hold steadfastly to this way and be assured that you will never have to regret it.[64]

It was, however, too late by now to shift Abdullah from his course of working for full independence for Kashmir. Believing perhaps that he had in this the support of the United States,[65] and convinced that even Nehru could not subdue communal forces in India, he publicly proclaimed that Kashmir should become independent. Justice had not been done by India to the Muslim majority in Kashmir and he himself was not trusted. 'A time will, therefore, come when I will bid them good-bye.'[66] There was clearly nothing more to be gained by striving for discussions with Abdullah. The Government of India would have either to accept that he spoke for Kashmir and pull out of the State — it was believed that his next specific demand would be for the withdrawal of Indian troops — or to ascertain whether he represented only a minority opinion.

[62] Nehru to Abdullah, 28 June 1953.
[63] Abdullah to Nehru, 4 July 1953.
[64] Nehru to Abdullah, 8 July, and Azad to Abdullah, 9 July 1953.
[65] Nehru thought that Dulles and Adlai Stevenson might have privately put forward the idea of an independent Kashmir; see Foreign Secretary's telegram (dictated by Nehru) to Indian mission at United Nations, 10 July 1953. Stevenson later denied this: 'My talks with Abdullah were the first I had in India regarding Kashmir, and I neither had nor expressed any views ... his casual suggestion that independent status might be an alternative solution ... I could not have given Abdullah even unconscious encouragement regarding independence, which did not seem to me realistic; it made little impression on me. I was listening, not talking, and at that time was most interested in why the United Nations plebiscite idea did not proceed'. Stevenson's cable to United States Ambassador, passed on to the Ministry of External Affairs, 13 August 1953. Abdullah may, of course, have taken silence to denote approval; but Nehru accepted Stevenson's explanation. 'As for Adlai Stevenson, I do not think that he is to blame in any way.' Nehru to Vijayalakshmi, 3 October 1953.
[66] Speech at Mujahid Manzil, 10 July 1953.

This was obviously a matter which would have to be sorted out in Kashmir, and all the documents so far available indicate that Nehru did not interfere or even hint at his own preferences. He did not write to Abdullah and, when Karan Singh came to Delhi, had a long talk with him but gave no advice. Maulana Azad was also told not to suggest to Karan Singh or to anyone else any precise line of action.[67] A visit to Karachi, arranged in London, could not be postponed and Nehru received a popular welcome as warm as that in any city in India. 'I can truly say that I felt among friends and completely at home. The tragedy of the past few years seemed to fade away.'[68] The Pakistan authorities, declaring that to them Kashmir was the only really difficult problem, made 'quite plaintive and almost pathetic' appeals for a settlement; but because of the internal situation Nehru was in no position to offer terms. He could only assert that the status quo should be accepted with minor modifications. Mahomed Ali ruled out independence and seemed to favour a regional or zonal plebiscite on the basis of Graham's proposals. But Nehru did not regard this as easy. India's basic position was not so much concerned with the number of troops as with the fact that all civil and military authority of Pakistan should leave Kashmir.[69]

Meantime the crisis in Kashmir was coming to a head. In the Cabinet itself Abdullah and his supporters were now in a minority, and this was thought to reflect the position in the National Conference. Abdullah, though the head of the Government, was functioning in effect as leader of the opposition. Indeed, he was reported as having said that he would set fire to the State. 'I really cannot explain his new attitude except on the uncharitable assumption that he has lost grip of his mind.'[70] This statement of pique covers a total failure of communication between Nehru and Abdullah. The question now was to determine the measure of support which Abdullah still commanded. The democratic procedure obviously would be for those opposed to Abdullah to resign from the ministry and, if they represented majority opinion, to be asked to form a new government. Nehru knew that such steps were being considered in Kashmir and that, if Abdullah refused to resign, he would be dismissed.[71] His only intervention was, on hearing that the majority group in the Cabinet had requested the local military commander for movement of troops, to order that the Indian army should not be involved.[72]

So Nehru was prepared for the dismissal of Abdullah on 9 August. 'For the last three months, I have seen this coming, creeping up as some kind of inevitable disaster. I did not, of course, know the exact shape it would take.

[67] Nehru to Azad, 19 July 1953.
[68] To Ghulam Mahomed, Governor-General of Pakistan, 29 July 1953.
[69] Note on first meeting with Mahomed Ali, 25 July 1953, to B. C. Roy, 29 July 1953, to Bakshi Ghulam Mahomed, 30 July 1953.
[70] Nehru to G. S. Bajpai, 30 July 1953.
[71] Statement prepared by Nehru, 31 July 1953; secret messages from Srinagar, 1 August 1953.
[72] Nehru to Chief Ministers, 22 August 1953.

To the last moment, I was not clear what exactly would happen.'[73] He certainly does not seem to have anticipated the way in which Abdullah was dismissed, by stealth of night in his absence, and his prompt arrest thereafter. The arrest appears to have been made on the directive of the new Prime Minister, Bakshi Ghulam Mahomed, who felt he could not maintain the administration of the State as long as Abdullah was at large.[74] 'We learnt of these events', Nehru reported later, 'after they had taken place.'[75] He confessed that it left a bad taste in his mouth, but, asserting that the men on the spot knew best, as head of the Central Government he accepted ultimate responsibility for what had happened, although part of it at least had been done without his knowledge.[76]

The whole crisis in Kashmir bore to him the full dimensions of a tragedy. That a close friend and comrade, who had for twenty years played a notable part in the struggle for freedom, should now doubt the bona fides of Nehru and the Government which he headed, and have had to be dismissed and placed in detention was both a personal blow and a setback to national and international policy. 'But we have to face life as it is and carry on to the best of our ability . . . Do not be disheartened by untoward events. We have undertaken big jobs and we must see them through.'[77]

[73] To G. S. Bajpai, 24 August 1953.

[74] Karan Singh to the author, 9 April 1975.

[75] Nehru to Chief Ministers, 22 August 1953. There have been conflicting accounts by those claiming to be participants as to Nehru's role in this crisis; but all are agreed that his consent had been neither sought nor given for the arrest of Abdullah. See B. M. Kaul, *The Untold Story* (Delhi, 1967), p. 144, B. N. Mullik, *My Years with Nehru: Kashmir* (Delhi, 1971), p. 45, A. P. Jain, 'Kashmir', *Imprint*, June 1972, pp. 69-71.

[76] Nehru to Bakshi Ghulam Mahomed, 15 August 1953, and to U. N. Dhebar, 24 January 1955.

[77] To Nabakrushna Chaudhuri, 15 August 1953.

7

The Korean Settlement

ONE

In January 1951 the Commonwealth Prime Ministers met in London. Krishna Menon thought that such a conference at this stage would prove merely a step nearer war-talk than peace-talk. The attitude of the Commonwealth had not really changed despite India's membership; it was still a 'new-old imperialism', with the only difference that India would not now be declared a belligerent without being consulted.[1] Such an analysis from one who had throughout worked for the maintenance of the Commonwealth link was startling enough; but Nehru discerned the underlying cussedness and disregarded the advice that he should not attend the conference. If, as Krishna Menon argued, the assumption of the Western Powers was that communism was a danger to peace and should be resisted everywhere, Nehru speedily rebutted it. At the first session he stressed the importance of befriending China and the danger of becoming involved in war by following the United States in its unrealistic policy. He still believed that China and Russia wished to avoid war, and therefore thought it important to avoid action which increased tension. Bevin argued against him. China might not be a satellite of Russia but the two nations were acting together and their joint strategy seemed clear enough: Chinese manpower would tie down large armies of the Western Powers while the Soviet Union would neutralize Germany and frustrate plans for the defence of Europe. It was not, said Bevin, for him to speak for India, but he feared that in ten or twenty years India might find herself between the pincers of this world strategy.

However, the most powerful support for Nehru's position came from the British Chiefs of Staff, who had already informed their counterparts in the United States that in their view,

open war against China, even without open intervention by Russia,

[1] Krishna Menon's note to Nehru, 3 January 1951.

would almost inevitably involve a major defeat of the Western Powers with consequences that might well be fatal, not only to the unity of the Commonwealth and the United States, but to the whole position of the present free world.

So there was private agreement with Nehru's suggestion that, instead of supporting the United States unquestioningly, an attempt should be made to convince her that, rather than condemn China, the latter's claims to Formosa and membership of the United Nations should be accepted. But the Prime Ministers were not prepared to go along with Nehru to the extent of informing the United States that if necessary they would in the last resort oppose her in the United Nations. All that Nehru could secure was a decision to press at that assembly for a conference of the United States, China, Britain and the Soviet Union to consider all problems of the Far East 'in conformity with existing international obligations' — a phrase introduced by India to cover the Cairo and Potsdam declarations on Formosa.

Nehru also urged China not to reject this formula; the phrase, though worded in general terms, safeguarded her rights, and an invitation to a four-Power conference was even more prestigious than admission to the United Nations, which must inevitably follow. China's response, though it sounded characteristically niggling,[2] was in fact favourable, and Nehru followed it up by seeking to exert pressure on the United States not to precipitate matters[3] and suggesting that the Chinese Government announce their firm desire for peace and for immediate negotiations.

The occasion demands the highest statesmanship which, by its vision and generosity, will upset the forces making for war and give to Asia not only peace and strength but also a moral leadership. The new China is in a position today to give such a far-seeing and generous lead for peace, which can result in an immediate removal of tension and fear from the world. Her position is in fact fully recognized by most countries. Her main objectives have been either openly or tacitly admitted. In these circumstances, arguments about forms of words have little significance when the reality has been gained. Nor is it wise to try to humiliate other countries. We in India and China have suffered enough humiliation in the past and have resented it and fought against it. We should follow a different course and try to secure a stable peace through a peaceful and cooperative approach. This would be no sign of weakness but of strength and confidence in ourselves.[4]

[2] Chou En-lai's telegram to acting Secretary-General, United Nations, 17 January 1951.
[3] Nehru to Attlee, Menzies and St Laurent, 18 January 1951.
[4] Nehru to Chou En-lai, 23 January 1951.

St Laurent, the Prime Minister of Canada, saw in Nehru's message to
Chou 'a classical and momentous document to ensure peace and a mighty
effort of our Prime Minister to save China from the clutches of Russia'.[5]
Certainly the first reactions suggested this. Chou En-lai proposed not a
four-Power but a seven-Power conference including France, Egypt and
India as well, offered clarifications of his proposal which were found
adequate by St Laurent and blamed the action of the United States in
pushing through a resolution branding China as an aggressor for the failure
to start negotiations. Nehru was of the same opinion. He had almost
bridged the gap when the whole attempt collapsed. 'All our efforts failed in
the end before the big stick of the United States. Well, we have the
satisfaction of having done our job. The future will have to look after
itself.'[6]

The efforts of Nehru were not widely appreciated in the West. Even *The
Economist* felt that his peace efforts had misfired.

[He] may be as much an appeaser as Chamberlain; but he is more
dangerous. Chamberlain's assessment of Hitler was straight error. In
Nehru's analysis there is a great deal of truth which the West, in its
annoyance at his conclusions, can disregard only at its peril. Nehru is
strong neither on facts nor on law; but for the expression of Asian
emotions he is unique . . . Nehru brings to the surface, as no one else
in Asia can, the suspicions of his continent . . .[7]

The *Evening Standard*, inspired by its proprietor, Lord Beaverbrook, to a
personal vendetta against Nehru, blamed him primarily for the anti-
Western movement in Asia, of which the oil dispute in Iran was a part.[8] But
it was in the United States that criticism once again mounted to a 'hymn of
hate',[9] and there was canvassing to secure the rejection of India's request
for two million tons of foodgrains on concessional terms. It was then
suggested that one million tons be offered, with the United States
supervising the distribution. Nehru did not like this, but, as the need was
great, he waited to examine the details, and refused to get involved in any
bitter controversy with the United States on food or Korea. But all this was
humiliating, and the Cabinet decided to plan on the basis that foodgrains
from the United States would not be available.

I wish we were in a position to stand on our own feet, even though
that meant a measure of privation. Indeed if we can stand on our feet,
we can get better terms from other countries. I have no doubt,

[5] Indian High Commissioner's report of conversation with St Laurent, 23 January 1951.
[6] To Krishna Menon, 31 January 1951.
[7] 'Nehru — Idealist or Appeaser?' *The Economist*, 28 April 1951.
[8] 21 June 1951.
[9] Vijayalakshmi to Nehru, 5 February 1951.

therefore, that the only possible programme in food we can aim at is one of self-sufficiency. There is no other way out and there is absolutely no reason, except our own ineptness, why we should not attain this objective.[10]

Catching by chance a glimpse of the legislation proposed to be enacted by the United States, Nehru had the American Ambassador informed that, rather than receive a gift which involved a foreign agency controlling India's distribution system and development plans, he would prefer terms of deferred payment.[11] The draft bill amounted 'practically to converting India into some kind of a semi-colonial country or at least a satellite in the economic sense . . . I realize completely the consequence of our refusal of this gift. Nevertheless I cannot bring myself to agree to this final humiliation.'[12] India, he declared publicly, was not 'so down and out as to accept any condition dictated by any foreign country in the matter of importing food that sullies our honour.'[13]

The legislation providing aid, as finally enacted, was unobjectionable, and Nehru acknowledged his gratitude.[14] He also went to the galling extent of authorizing a denial that India was shipping strategic materials to China.[15] This issue of foodgrains faded as the shadow of famine lifted: but then came the problem of the Japanese peace treaty. To sign it as it stood seemed to Nehru tantamount to a somersault in India's policy. The continued presence of American troops, the American trusteeship over the Ryukyu and Bonin islands, and the failure to transfer Formosa to China and the Kurile islands and South Sakhalin to the Soviet Union were the major objections. Again, Nehru was severely criticized.

> Jawaharlal Nehru is fast becoming one of the great disappointments of the post-war era . . . It was an abnegation of greatness — and history is not likely to forgive it. This is the more true because Nehru's attention was primarily turned on a local, national and intensely personal question — Kashmir . . . His statesmanship is not inspiring people and nations to do things but only to leave them undone. How the mighty have fallen![16]

The refusal of India to sign was interpreted in the State Department as not merely a censure of United States policy but part of a general scheme to

[10] Nehru to Chief Ministers, 21 March 1951.
[11] Nehru's instructions to Bajpai, 11 April 1951.
[12] Nehru to Vijayalakshmi, 11 April 1951.
[13] Speech at Srinagar, 29 April, *National Herald*, 30 April 1951.
[14] Statement 12 June, *National Herald*, 13 June 1951.
[15] Nehru's telegram to B. N. Rau, 24 July 1951.
[16] 'The Lost Leader', *New York Times*, 28 August 1951.

bring India, China and Japan into one orbit.[17] Nehru sent for the American Ambassador to explain that it had never occurred to him to try to separate Japan from the United States. There was no ill-will in India towards the United States and differences of opinion on various issues could not blur the basic community of views between the two countries.[18] But the United States Government were not so easily appeased, and, more important, the Indian Government came into conflict — an ominous portent — with Dulles, who was dealing with the Japanese peace treaty and complained to Vijayalakshmi that India seemed to subscribe to the Chinese slogan of Asia for the Asians and to desire to end American influence in Asia.[19] For once Nehru and Rajagopalachari were agreed that the Americans were a psychological case, as summed up by de Tocqueville:

> The Americans, in their intercourse with strangers, appear impatient of the smallest censure and insatiable of praise. The most slender eulogy is acceptable to them, the most exalted seldom contents them; they unceasingly harass you to extort praise, and if you resist their entreaties, they fall to praising themselves. It would seem as if, doubting their own merit, they wished to have it constantly exhibited before their eyes.[20]

Such poor relations with the United States, the result mostly of Nehru's advocacy of China's claims, did not have a counter-reward in warm relations with China. Panikkar continued to be as wishfully optimistic as ever. He reported that the Chinese had not allowed the Tibetan issue to cloud cordiality, there was never any unfriendly comment on India in the Chinese press, and it was India which had blown up the matter out of all proportion to the realities of the situation. There was to him no doubt of the Chinese desire to build up firm friendship with India and not allow small details to come in the way.[21] A Chinese offer of foodgrains lent strength to his contention and Nehru was keen to accept; but lack of shipping virtually rendered the gesture nugatory. Then a Chinese gift of Rs 4 lakhs to the Indian Red Cross was withdrawn when the Indian Government declined to pass on the money to a communist organization. After Truman's dismissal of MacArthur, Nehru, at Krishna Menon's prompting, urged the Chinese to respond positively;[22] as he saw it, however, it was Russia and not India whom China chose to put forward her

---

[17] See Bajpai's report of conversation with Loy Henderson, the American Ambassador, 12 September 1951.

[18] Nehru's note on conversation with Henderson, 15 September 1951.

[19] Vijayalakshmi's report of interview with Dulles, 4 October 1951.

[20] *Democracy in America* (Vintage edition, New York, 1954), Vol. 2, p. 236.

[21] Panikkar to Nehru, 6 January 1951 and to K. P. S Menon, Foreign Secretary, 20 February 1951. See also his *In Two Chinas* (London, 1955), p. 113.

[22] Nehru's telegram to Panikkar, 12 April 1951. But Panikkar himself was not enthusiastic. *In Two Chinas*, p. 134.

proposal for negotiation of a Korean cease-fire and armistice on the battlefield.[23] This led India to withdraw to the background and not seek to force the confidence of the Chinese Government. In Nehru's support of China there was obviously a strong element of enlightened self-interest; it was important for India to be friendly with her powerful neighbour on the basis that China respected the frontiers of India. But there was also much idealism in his China policy. He hoped fondly that friendship with the new China would not only maintain peace in Asia but start a new phase in world affairs, with Asia giving the lead in a more humane as well as a more sophisticated diplomacy. The Chinese took advantage of this and exploited India's goodwill while placing little trust in her. The basic challenge between India and China, as China never seemed to forget and Nehru could not finally help recognizing, ran along the spine of Asia.[24]

For almost a year, therefore, India took no direct interest in the Korean problem. The negotiations at Panmunjom dragged on, and were complicated by Chinese charges against the Americans of bacteriological warfare. Still Nehru kept aloof until the American Ambassador, Chester Bowles, and Mrs Roosevelt, who had come on a visit to India, pushed him into intervention. He asked Panikkar to inform the Chinese leaders of his own conviction that the British and American Governments were anxious for a settlement in the Far East and to suggest an independent investigation into their allegations of bacteriological warfare.[25] Chou En-lai was polite but evasive; and the charges gradually faded out. But, as the United States was insisting on voluntary repatriation of prisoners, the Chinese Government were anxious that India should exercise pressure in their favour on Britain to reach an agreement.[26] Though at Panmunjom China continued to demand the repatriation of all prisoners, Chou proposed to India that as the Americans held, according to Chinese estimates, about 170,000 prisoners, a compromise figure of about 100,000 should be accepted as the number to be repatriated. Nehru was willing to help, but saw no logic in fixing an arbitrary number; and Krishna Menon worked out with Eden a formula for interviews by an independent body of all prisoners who did not wish voluntarily to return. This was acceptable, with minor variations, to China, and a scheme was formulated on these lines. Nehru knew that he was being used by China, but he was willing to be used in the cause of peace, and even considered a visit to Peking.[27]

[23] This was Nehru's understanding at the time of the Soviet proposal of 23 June 1951. But it has now been suggested that the proposal may have come as a surprise even to the Chinese. See J. Gittings, *The World and China, 1922-1972* (London, 1974), p. 185. It was not, however, a surprise to the United States. See D. Acheson, *Present at the Creation* (London, 1969), pp. 532-3.

[24] See Nehru's briefing of the Indian cultural delegation to China in the summer of 1952 as reported in F. Moraes, *Witness to an Era* (Delhi, 1973), pp. 200-201.

[25] 17 March 1952.

[26] Record of interviews of Vijayalakshmi (then visiting China) with Chou En-lai, 6 May and with Mao Tse-tung, 9 May 1952.

[27] Nehru to Bajpai, 8 June 1952.

Then, suddenly, in July 1952 — goaded perhaps by the bombing of power plants in North Korea by the United States — the Chinese retracted, denounced voluntary repatriation, and insisted that all prisoners should be returned. To Nehru this was significant and disturbing, not so much with reference to Korea but as a fresh indication of Chinese unreliability; and as there seemed to be little to choose between China and the United States, he was not inclined to take any further interest. But Chou En-lai indicated a desire for India's support and the United States made signs of wishing to reach a settlement. Nehru therefore decided to send Krishna Menon as a delegate to the United Nations to deal in particular with the Korean issue. This was not just a riposte to Krishna Menon's criticism that India's relations with the Communist Powers had cooled off and Nehru was moving closer to the United States.[28] It was a decision taken as much to solve the problem of Krishna Menon as that of Korea.

TWO

As High Commissioner Krishna Menon had had the advantage of the background of long, even if difficult, years in London, and close association with many leaders of the Labour Party now in office. He was, too, on specially cordial terms with his Prime Minister. Nehru had attached special importance to the efforts of Menon's India League in London before 1947; Menon had served as Nehru's literary agent; and Nehru relished his tart cleverness, the barbed wit, the astringent conversation. 'I have hardly come across a keener intelligence and brain.'[29] Surrounded in Delhi mostly by small men with shallow minds, Nehru admired the quality in Menon's intellectual performance and recognized the mutual sympathy in their viewpoint on most matters. An unexpressed dialogue, in Auden's phrase, underlay even their most casual conversation.

The early years as High Commissioner further strengthened Menon's hold on Nehru's regard and affection. A life of ostentatious simplicity had been combined with diplomatic flair; he had played a prominent role in the Commonwealth negotiations, and Nehru's high opinion of him was backed by Cripps and the Mountbattens. But the powerful drawbacks in Menon's personality and methods of working gradually forced themselves on the Prime Minister's attention; and even he could not fail to see that Menon was becoming increasingly a liability. He distrusted most officials, had no financial judgment and was incapable of delegating authority at any level. Even clerks going on short leave had to secure his permission, and he spent hours every day scrutinizing the use of official cars. An immediate telegram from Nehru to Azad, when the latter was on a visit to London,

[28] Krishna Menon to Nehru, 7 August 1952.
[29] Nehru to C. D. Deshmukh, 26 January 1952.

was not delivered for about a week because Menon insisted on clearing all telegrams and he was then unwell. Even his remarkable political perception tended to be shadowed by such worry about detail; and then it came to light that he had lent his name to dubious transactions involving losses of crores of rupees to the Government of India. The best-known of these was the case of the purchase of a large number of sub-standard jeeps, and it was generally believed that friends of Menon had personally benefited by this contract. The auditor-general and the finance minister favoured pro-secution of those responsible. Nehru stoutly contended that there had been no impropriety, wrongdoing or loss to the state, but even he conceded inadequate inspection and errors of judgment.[30] Obviously, therefore, the case could not be closed.

> As a result of all this, it seems to me that we were the victims of certain rather unusual circumstances. Nevertheless this whole business makes one feel uncomfortable and it is no easy matter to explain it to enquirers. What troubles one is the way some things were done which landed us in this difficulty. Of course our need was great and we had to go through abnormal channels. Nevertheless we were rather badly caught and it is not easy to justify all this to the public, if occasion arises for that.[31]

This, of course, Krishna Menon interpreted as the poisoning by officials of Nehru's mind against him; and as the months passed his physical and psychological condition deteriorated further. Living for years on the drug Luminal, frequently fainting, or speaking incoherently in public, obsessed with an infatuation and closely shut in by an imaginary circle of his enemies, his behaviour had become increasingly unpredictable. Even in 1950 he had denounced Patel to the director of the intelligence bureau when the latter was on a visit to London; and now he sent Nehru a telegram on the Japanese peace treaty which was so clearly dictated while under the influence of drugs that Nehru had to order him to withdraw it.[32] So Nehru advised Menon to give priority to his health. To give strength to his assurance that it was no lack of faith or confidence that prompted his suggestion that Menon should go on leave for two or three months, Nehru reported that he himself was getting nervy and planned to leave off all work for some time.[33]

Menon was not so easily persuaded, but events would not allow Nehru

[30] To Chief Ministers, 10 April 1951.
[31] Nehru to Krishna Menon, 27 February 1951.
[32] 'I beg of you respectfully to give this matter your personal consideration and NOT to be led by the advice of your civil servants. They think like the English . . . Please do NOT put your foot into this. There is no one there except yourself who understands foreign affairs.' Menon's telegram to Nehru, 22 July 1951.
[33] Nehru's telegrams to Krishna Menon, 21 and 22 May, and letter, 5 June 1951.

to let the matter lie. Attlee sent him a message that as some British communists were employed in India House, the British Government would deal in top secret matters only through their High Commissioner in Delhi.[34] Menon objected vehemently to what he regarded as an unjustified slur, made because India would not conform to British policy; either Attlee's suggestion should be rejected or reciprocal action should be taken.[35] But Nehru realized that India could hardly insist on information being channelled through India House; and this embarrassment made it all the more expedient to ease Menon out of this office.

To all this, Menon's main response was to claim a lien on Nehru's affection and to write with yearning tenseness long letters to M. O. Mathai, Nehru's special assistant — letters which he knew Nehru would see — complaining of lack of total support and hinting at suicide.

> I do not think that even you know my mental and emotional relation to Panditji which is now getting on to twenty years although most of it is a one-way traffic as it would be when one party is such a great figure . . . Those who will destroy what is being built up and reduce our independence to a tragedy are in places of power and confidence. He has also made it clear that he resents my submitting advice . . . The fundamental thing is that things have come to an end . . . He is the greatest man in Asia today, may be in the world. My devotion to him will last as long as I live. That devotion now calls for my disappearance . . . He thinks that people like me who think the same way as he does are an embarrassment. That is part of the situation.[36]

To this blend of fawning hysteria and plaintive self-pity Nehru reacted in an unforced but kind-hearted manner.

> You know my attachment to you and you ought to know how I value your judgment. But surely you do not expect me not to exercise my judgment occasionally even though it might not fall in line with yours. I would not expect you to do anything of the kind to me . . . You have a feeling perhaps, and you have hinted at it, that I do not trust your judgment sufficiently. May I say that you show sometimes a great lack of trust in my judgment. I have to deal with the situation here and have to function according to my lights . . . You will not expect me to ignore my own experience or opinion completely.

> We are living through difficult times and I never know what the next few weeks or months might bring. I do not know today whether

[34] Bajpai's report of conversation with British High Commissioner, 14 June 1951.
[35] Menon to Nehru, 19 June 1951.
[36] Krishna Menon to M. O. Mathai, 7 August 1951.

I shall be Prime Minister a month hence or not. All kinds of things are happening which distress me. I try to take them in my usual stride and do not allow myself to get excited over them. I am not responsible for the world or even for India. If I can manage to behave with some decency and in the belief that I am acting rightly, that is about as much as I can do. For me to live on a high plane of excitement would neither help me nor others. For me to get angry with everyone who does not agree with me would also not be helpful at all.[37]

Menon still protested that he was not sick and that his loyalty, though ill-used, would bear the strain of what he felt to be Nehru's cruel letters.[38] But as the evidence mounted, with even Menon's doctor and Mountbatten advising his removal,[39] Nehru sent Mathai to London to report back to him as well as make Menon see sense. His letter to Mathai on receiving confirmation of Menon's desperate condition is a high tribute to his humaneness.

I decided some months ago that Krishna must leave the High Commissionership. But I was not in a hurry and I wanted him to suggest it. I came to this decision partly because of his growing unsuitability for the work in view of his ill-health, but chiefly because this was in his own interest. I saw a progressive deterioration till a time might come when he would disgrace himself not only before others but before himself. That is the only real tragedy in life and the tragedy is all the greater when it comes to a man of Krishna's brilliance and integrity and self-sacrifice. Death or suicide are bad and painful but they do not wipe out the past. They just put a full stop to it. But inner degradation and disintegration are far worse and the memory of old days is largely covered up by recent unhappy memories.[40]

To Menon himself Nehru wrote with warmth but firmness, insisting that he should take leave for six months and then appear before a medical board.[41] Menon would not agree. But he made an effort to pull himself together, and both the doctors and the Mountbattens reported progress. Moreover, with a change of government in Britain and the Conservatives back in office, an immediate removal might be thought of political significance. So Nehru ceased to press Menon to go on immediate leave, but initiated the process of a slow handover. The resistance from Menon continued. He sent long, unintelligible notes, held up the reorganization of India House and objected to any inquiries into any of his actions. He was

[37] Nehru to Krishna Menon, 25 August 1951.
[38] Menon to Nehru, 24 September 1951.
[39] Dr H. K. Handoo to Nehru, 19 September, and Mountbatten to Nehru, 21 September 1951.
[40] Nehru to M. O. Mathai in London, 29 September 1951.
[41] 14 October 1951.

deaf to Nehru's argument that his obstinacy was being used to damage the
Prime Minister's image and that Nehru could not, in the cause of particular
individuals, set aside the general principle he had laid down that necessary
information would be provided in the case of all allegations.[42]

> You are a very sensitive person and I am always a little afraid of saying
> or doing anything which would hurt you or upset you. And yet not to
> say it or do it itself leads to subsequent hurt and, what is worse,
> misunderstanding. Life is difficult enough. It does little good for us to
> make it more difficult. I hope, therefore, that you will consider what I
> have written calmly and think of the wider context in which I have had
> to function and how we can make the best use of our opportunities,
> such as they are.[43]

Nehru first considered the inclusion of Menon in the Cabinet but as
Menon threatened to kill himself rather than return to his own country,[44]
Nehru offered him the Moscow embassy.[45] This too Menon refused. 'All I
now seek is to leave and fade out quietly and with dignity . . . I am sorry
you have come to rate my sense of values as that of a careerist!'[46] Then
Nehru suggested that Menon join the Indian delegation to the United
Nations General Assembly. It would give him some work to do and get
him out of London, where his presence was an embarrassment to his
successor, B. G. Kher. Menon was willing to consider going to New York
only if he were made leader and not sent as deputy to Vijayalakshmi. The
compromise thought up by Nehru was to offer him the Korean question as
a special assignment.

THREE

The General Assembly had before it two resolutions, a Polish one
demanding the return of all prisoners 'in accordance with international
practice', and the other, submitted by the United States, providing for
voluntary repatriation. To meet both viewpoints, Krishna Menon brought
forward in November 1952 a resolution proposing a repatriation commission of four neutral powers, with reference to an umpire or the General
Assembly if no decision could be reached. The weakness of the resolution
lay in the suggestion that any prisoners left over at the end should be
transferred to the United Nations, although that body was regarded by
both China and the Soviet Union not as an impartial international

[42] Nehru to Krishna Menon, 3 and 4 January 1952.
[43] Nehru to Menon, 27 January 1952.
[44] Menon to Nehru, 20 January and to M. O. Mathai, 21 January 1952.
[45] Nehru to Krishna Menon, 25 March 1952.
[46] Menon to Nehru, 29 March 1952.

organization but as a warring party to the dispute. Yet the first reactions of these two countries were not unfavourable and Nehru was hopeful of an advance towards a truce.[47] He sent a message to Chou stressing the importance of a clear attitude in favour of an armistice, especially as, with Eisenhower's election as President, bellicose elements were reported to be gaining influence in Washington. Menon's resolution was based on a full understanding of the essentials of the Chinese position and therefore merited Chou's general approval. That might make it very difficult for the United States to reject the resolution and strengthen the probability of its acceptance by the General Assembly.[48]

It seemed to Nehru that there had not been a better chance for the United Nations to justify itself and help to recover the atmosphere of peace.

> A moment comes in the life of a nation, and sometimes of the world, when the future hangs on a decision that might be taken. That moment is here . . . I speak these words not only with anxious hope but with a prayer in my heart that we of this generation might prove worthy of our inheritance, of the passionate hopes and aspirations of innumerable people who hunger for peace and the future that we claim to build.[49]

But the Indian effort was finally rejected by both China and the Soviet Union. Vyshinsky condemned it in bitter terms while Peking Radio spoke sarcastically of India posing as the voice of Asia. The Communist Powers appeared to be convinced that the resolution was the product of a subtle American move, through Britain, to use India against China; and this feeling was promoted by the fact that Krishna Menon paid more attention at this time to Britain and other countries of the West than to the Soviet Union. The Chinese might have been willing to consider the resolution, but were apparently governed by the Soviet view and what was considered to be a favourable military position in Korea.

One major drawback of Indian diplomacy at this stage was the weakness of its representation. Mehta at Washington was an untried hand and Raghavan at Peking, though less wayward than Panikkar, was also new. At Moscow Radhakrishnan, with his easy personal access to the Kremlin, had been replaced by an official, K. P. S. Menon, who courted the Russians but was not significant politically. This inferior quality of India's ambassadors combined with Krishna Menon's conspiratorial methods of functioning to ensure that the resolution was considered little on its merits by the

---

[47] Nehru to Bajpai, 2 November 1952.

[48] Nehru's telegrams to N. Raghavan (Panikkar's successor as Ambassador), 16, 18 and 20 November 1952.

[49] 21 November 1952. Lok Sabha Debates 1952, Vol. II, Part II, pp. 991-3.

Communist Powers. For the first time, as Nehru regretted,[50] India was driven into supporting one power bloc against the other.

'The world', commented Nehru, 'is determined to commit suicide.'[51] There seemed to be really no common ground between the American and Chinese positions; but he did not allow his disappointment to push him into sulky withdrawal. He directed Krishna Menon not to abandon the resolution, and instructed his Ambassador in Peking to remain cool.

> I want to make it clear that, while we intend maintaining our friendly approach, there should be *no* element of apology on our part as to what we have done. Our attitude towards the Chinese Government should always be a combination of friendliness and firmness. If we show weakness, advantage will be taken of this immediately.[52]

The Chinese Ambassador in New Delhi was informed of India's regret and surprise at the continuous insinuations that the Indian resolution was mischievous and supported the activities of the United States in east Asia. India had persisted with her resolution because the only alternative was an aggressive United States resolution; the Polish resolution demanding forcible repatriation had no chance whatever.

Yet, with the Chinese holding aloof and the United States under Eisenhower not seemingly keen on a settlement, Nehru could do little but wait and watch. This, apart from its unsatisfactory implications in world affairs, had its personal aspect as well; for it left Krishna Menon idle, and he began once more to complain of Nehru's neglect. A mild reference by Nehru to Canadian comment that Krishna Menon had kept away from his own delegation and had spent most of his time with the Canadians[53] evoked the usual tearful reply:

> . . . it is a fact that often times and far oftener than I like I feel almost at the end of my emotional and mental tether in regard to what I feel has, and in fact appears to have, come between us . . . Ours was not a relationship which is very usual and was sustained by ourselves alone . . . I have written to you because I know great realities subsist.[54]

On receiving this letter, Nehru immediately cabled to Menon not to worry,[55] and also wrote a warm letter of assurance deserving full quotation as indicative of the personal side of the Prime Minister.

[50] To Vijayalakshmi and Krishna Menon, 26 November 1952.
[51] Nehru to Vijayalakshmi, 25 November 1952.
[52] Nehru's telegram to Raghavan, 10 December 1952.
[53] Nehru to Krishna Menon, 1 February 1953.
[54] Krishna Menon to Nehru, 12(?) February 1953.
[55] 18 February 1953.

My dear Krishna,

Your letter of the 12th February reached me last evening. I have read it more than once, trying to understand what ails you. I realize of course that you wrote in some distress of mind and that you feel unhappy. You ask me what has come between us. I am not aware of anything having come between us in any real sense. I have the same affection and regard for you as I have ever had. Sometimes I do not understand or like what you might say or do. That happens with everyone. With our most intimate friends we have moments of distance or lack of understanding. That moment passes and the basic feeling remains. Does anyone know or understand another fully? It does not matter very much if one dislikes or distrusts. The real thing is a basic affection and respect and a belief in the integrity of each other. Nothing has happened to shake that so far as I am concerned.

I was happy to have you here and loved the talks we had. I was glad to know that there was a possibility of your coming to India for good, for I wanted you not to be far from me.

So, please do not imagine something that is not there and do not distress yourself about it.

Love

Yours affectionately,

Jawaharlal[56]

Menon's ambition was now expanding; in contrast to his earlier attitude, he was willing to return to India and asked Nehru to appoint him minister without portfolio.[57] Nehru had by this time realized how little Menon was known in India, and was not prepared for this. Instead he offered him, on the suggestion of Radhakrishnan, the vice-chancellorship of Delhi University; this Menon turned down huffily.

However, the question of Menon's future was shelved, for the time being, by developments on the Korean issue. Protests to both China and the Soviet Union that India's good intent and commitment to non-alignment remained unaltered had evoked no response. But in March 1953, after the death of Stalin, the Chinese again changed tack, and proposed that all prisoners who did not wish to be repatriated should be handed over to a neutral state.[58] This was very close to the Indian resolution, and a note of complacency crept into Nehru's reaction.

[56] To Menon, 17 February 1953.
[57] Menon to Nehru, 18 February 1953.
[58] Statement of Chou En-lai, 30 March 1953. This may not have been, of course, solely because China was less dominated by the Soviet Union; the new Soviet leaders may have been keener than Stalin on a Korean settlement and influenced China and North Korea in this direction. See C. E. Bohlen, *Witness to History* (London, 1973), pp. 349-51.

That is all to the good and we need not go about saying that we told you so. In this rapidly developing situation, we have to be wide awake all the time, to maintain friendly relations with the Chinese Government and, at the same time, to keep our dignity. Perhaps, the events of the past few months have, on the whole, yielded good results. The Chinese Government must appreciate that, while we continue to be friendly, we hold to our opinions also and cannot be made to change them by pressure tactics. Anyhow, we must always remember our long-range policy, which is of developing friendship with China, subject always to not giving in on any matter that we consider important or vital to our interest.[59]

The Chinese drew even closer to the Indian position in May when, on the United States objecting to repatriation to a neutral country, they proposed a repatriation commission of five neutral nations. Whatever China's reasons for this step, it was certainly not because of any warning of Dulles, conveyed to China by Nehru after his talks with Dulles in May 1953, that if the truce negotiations failed, the United States would enlarge the war.[60] But India lobbied widely for the general acceptance of the Chinese proposal for a repatriation commission, and on 8 June 1953 the United States and China signed the prisoners of war agreement. The world was faced, in Nehru's phrase, with 'the outbreak of peace'.[61]

[59] Nehru to N. Raghavan, 19 April 1953.
[60] A story to this effect was circulated at the time in the American press, and has since gained wide acceptance. But Nehru, in a note recorded on 16 September 1953, denied this, and there is nothing in the Dulles papers at Princeton University Library to suggest that such a warning was conveyed to Nehru.
[61] To Chief Ministers, 19 April 1953.

8

The Road to Elections

The bickerings between Nehru and Patel on minor issues continued until the end and, sadly, some of the last exchanges of letters between these two giants of the nationalist struggle displayed extreme irritation on trivial matters of administration.[1] This lack of confidence was well known to their followers in the Party; and the intrigues in the Congress did not cease with Patel's death. The AICC in January 1951 passed a resolution on unity brought forward by Nehru, but the atmosphere was not pleasant. Yet Nehru called upon Tandon to act upon it, hinting that if there were any reservation or delay in doing so he would force the issue.

> I believe I have a certain utility in the Congress organization, but I feel that progressively I cannot make myself useful. I seem to be cut off from the working of that organization. I have not had this particular experience previously, and so, with all my desire to be helpful, I find myself a little helpless and I sometimes wonder if it is worthwhile my continuing in this fashion.[2]

In other words, he would resign from the Working Committee; but, at the same time, he was not prepared to leave the Congress. Whatever evils might have crept into the Congress, these evils were to be found outside it too, in perhaps larger measure. The Congress was in a sense indispensable. It still was 'the major fact in India', and if it faded away or ceased to exist, the alternative was a large number of mutually warring groups and political chaos at a time when stability and some form of joint action was most needed in the country. So the Congress had to be improved, and Nehru was

[1] See Nehru to Patel, 21 November, and Patel's reply, 1 December 1950, on the appointment of the Chief Justice of Rajasthan, *Sardar Patel's Correspondence*, Vol. 9 (Ahmedabad, 1974), pp. 502-8; Patel to Nehru, 30 November and Nehru's reply, 1 December 1950, on the grant of a visa to a foreign national, *Sardar Patel's Correspondence*, Vol. 10 (Ahmedabad, 1974), pp. 461-3; and Patel's letter, 11 December, and Nehru's reply, 13 December, on interference in Home Ministry's affairs, Ibid., pp. 468-71. Patel died on 15 December 1950.
[2] To Tandon, 11 February 1951.

still hopeful of 'a slight turn' which might set events in the right direction.[3] It was not just a matter of getting rid of Tandon, but of creating the proper atmosphere in the Congress and the country. As he put it rather clumsily in an interview with Norman Cousins,

> We are — well, in search of our soul. That sounds rather metaphysical, but I am not, of course, discussing metaphysical matters. We are groping and trying for some kind of adjustment — integration, if you like — of our national life, our international as well as individual lives.[4]

Figures somewhat similar to warlords had sprouted in the ideological sphere, deluding the people and injuring the nation with false slogans; and they had to be firmly put down.

> I wonder if I convey to you in any measure any sense of urgency or any idea of the explosive nature of the world we live in. In India too the situation is explosive and I am distressed at the general lack of realization of this. I believe I have faith in India's future, but I cannot ignore the numerous disruptive and fissiparous tendencies I see around me, the strange lack of awareness of people and their occupation in trivial matters, forgetting the things that count. Our democracy is a tender plant which has to be nourished.[5]

As a first step, Nehru wanted the Working Committee to be reconstituted so as to include various viewpoints in the Congress, and a small conference convened thereafter.[6] But Tandon declined to act on this, and advised Nehru to set his own house in order first. If the Congress was unpopular, it was not for any act or attitude of the organization but because of such policies of the Government as controls on food and other articles, rehabilitation and the Hindu Code Bill.[7] The instances given by Tandon were in themselves sufficient to make Nehru bristle, and he now, without Tandon's knowledge, called a few chosen friends among senior Congressmen for an informal discussion.

> I feel, if I may say so, somewhat haunted by the present situation. The burden and responsibility on me, as on you, is great and we have to think outside our narrow grooves of thought and action and face this

---

[3] To J. B. Kripalani, 2 and 5 March 1951; to Chief Ministers, 2 May 1951.
[4] Interview with Norman Cousins, March 1951, printed in *Saturday Review of Literature* (New York), 14 April 1951. The interviews were later published in book form: *Talks with Nehru* (London, 1951).
[5] Nehru to Chief Ministers, 21 March 1951.
[6] To Tandon, 30 March 1951.
[7] Tandon to Nehru, 6 April 1951.

situation squarely . . . History has cast a role upon us and we cannot escape from it.[8]

Meantime the Congress Democratic Front, a small group formed within the Party in opposition to Tandon in September 1950, met in May 1951 to consider secession from the Congress. Already the dissidents in Bengal and Andhra had resigned, and the question now was whether Kripalani and others would follow suit and join the Socialist Party or at least cooperate with it in the elections. Nehru and Azad pleaded with them not to withdraw but to work from within the Congress. Much, of course, depended on Kidwai, who was close to Nehru and had participated in Nehru's discussions and was yet one of the leaders of the Democratic Front. So to him Nehru made a personal appeal.

I am just sending you a few lines written late at night. As you know, I have been greatly distressed in common with you and others at the turn many events have taken. I am quite convinced that it will be a bad day for India if we cannot stop this disruption and rot setting in. We have to act in a big way, each one of us, and not be tied down by prejudices, however justified these might appear to be. We have arrived at a critical stage and what we decide in the course of the next two or three days may mean a great deal for the country. I hope therefore that all of us will decide rightly.

It is impossible in this complicated and rather crooked world to get everything straightened out easily or quickly. One has to take one step at a time. A right step taken leads necessarily to right results. That is my firm opinion. That step must be taken with good heart and with a feeling of confidence and not hesitatingly and with expectation of failure. It should be taken generously and with goodwill. That brings forth goodwill from others.

It rests on you a good deal as to what future developments might be, not only in your individual capacity but as one who can influence others. You can effect the fortunes of the country to some extent at this critical stage. I hope therefore that you will act rightly and with faith.[9]

Kidwai did not let Nehru down. The Democratic Front dissolved itself. However, the issue was not closed, the members deciding to meet again a few weeks later to review the situation; and this disappointed Nehru.

I cannot claim, and have not claimed, that anyone, however close he

[8] 13 April 1951. The invitees were B. C. Roy, G. B. Pant, B. G. Kher, Morarji Desai, Nabakrushna Chaudhuri, A. N. Sinha, S. K. Sinha, D. P. Misra, H. K. Mahtab, G. L. Nanda and Rafi Kidwai. Significantly, Rajagopalachari was not among the number.
[9] Nehru to Kidwai, 3 May 1951.

might be to me, should stand by me or agree with me under any circumstances. But I do claim that I have a right to be consulted. Unfortunately this does not often take place. You consult frequently enough many of your other colleagues and are no doubt influenced by what they say. It is quite possible that I might have gathered some experience in a fairly lengthy career and that this might be useful.[10]

Instead of 'backstair parlour' politics, and cabals meeting in private and taking major decisions, the proper step for senior Congressmen was to state their viewpoints at the AICC or the Congress sessions. Failure to do this could only lead to progressive confusion in the public mind, strengthening of the spirit of disintegration and benefit to the cause they were fighting.

Wrestling with this problem and trying to find assurance about the steps to be taken, Nehru was more depressed than was usual with him. 'I am by nature not constituted so as to function in any narrow party groove; nor have I the makings of a dictator. I feel rather fed up with the low standards, intellectual and moral, that I see around me. I do not know what I shall ultimately do.'[11] On 17 May Kripalani announced his resignation from the Congress; and Nehru appealed to him to reconsider.

Normally speaking, and if it was a question of principle, I think there is much to be said even for a break and the formation of separate groups or parties. But, in existing circumstances, I feel convinced that we shall not be able to serve the country or the cause we have at heart in this way . . . We live in strange and dangerous times both from the point of view of the world and of India. We dare not take grave risks. All of us, whoever we might be, have naturally to think of the bigger issues. You have no doubt given thought to them. I feel therefore that it would be unfortunate in the extreme for this break to continue and to widen. Inevitably, as high principles are not involved, the break must be largely on personal grounds, and that is bad and can only lead to a continuation of personal controversy which does not help even in public education. I see in the paper that you intend forming a separate party. I would beg of you not to hurry and not to take a step which it is difficult to reverse. All of us should be wise enough to find some way out.[12]

While trying to hold the Party together and advising Tandon not to accept resignations,[13] Nehru continued to move along the other track of weakening the influence of reaction in the higher circles of the Party. 'I am a

[10] Nehru to Kidwai, 6 May 1951.
[11] Nehru to B. C. Roy, 13 May 1951.
[12] Nehru to Kripalani, 28 May 1951.
[13] To Tandon, 12 June 1951.

good fighter, provided I have something worthwhile to fight for. It is only when there is doubt about the immediate objective that one's capacity to function effectively becomes a little less.'[14] He resigned from the Congress parliamentary board. The immediate cause was the board's helplessness in face of the defiance of the Chief Minister of the Punjab, who reshuffled his cabinet contrary to the board's directive; but it was also the first move in recasting the approach of the Congress. Nehru's next step was a demand that Tandon reconstitute the Working Committee and the Central Election Committee. Tandon declined to renounce what he regarded as his prerogative and offered to give up the presidentship instead. But as the ground was thus being cleared for the final takeover, Nehru's position was damaged by the activities of Kidwai and his followers. The convention of dissident Congressmen, meeting at Patna in June, had formed a separate Kisan Mazdoor Praja Party. Nehru's reaction was scathing: 'An organization without an ideology should not be called a political party ordinarily, it should be more aptly called a drinking den.'[15] Kidwai's position was characteristically ambivalent. He attended the convention but did not speak; he was still a member of the Congress and of the Cabinet, but was nominated to the central council of the new party. Kripalani stated that Kidwai delayed action to give the Prime Minister time to find a replacement; but Kidwai's intentions were never so uncomplicated. He was really utilizing the new party to strengthen Nehru's hand against Tandon within the Congress. But he acted on his own and delighted in conspiracy. His personal and political loyalty to Nehru was unshakable. As he summed it up, 'The last thirty years' association has so developed me that all you say assumes the form of my ideology.'[16] But his manner of functioning often embarrassed Nehru and made him 'a very unsafe friend . . . Repeatedly my plans have been upset by what he has said or done. He has a great affection for me, but he just cannot restrain himself and thus he plays into the hands of his opponents.'[17] For at this stage, when Pakistan was threatening war, the Socialist Party had decided to organize a railway strike, and Congressmen were in a mood to close ranks, Kidwai, acting under pressure from his supporters, offered his resignation from the Cabinet. Nehru was disinclined to accept it and drew privately a somewhat casuistic distinction between membership of the Party and of the Government;[18] and while blaming Kidwai and his follower Ajit Prasad Jain for offering to resign without consulting him, authorized, with minor changes, their statement to the press.[19] In this statement Kidwai and Jain asserted their liberty to keep free of the Congress, and Nehru had not only

[14] To Mountbatten, 24 June 1951.
[15] Speech at Patna, 19 June, *Hindustan Standard*, 20 June 1951.
[16] Kidwai to Nehru, 7 May 1951.
[17] Nehru to Vijayalakshmi, 24 July 1951.
[18] See Kidwai to Nehru, 17 July 1951.
[19] Nehru to Kidwai, 21 July 1951.

to concede to Tandon that it was improper for any member of the Cabinet to belong to an opposition party, but apologize for encouraging such an attitude.[20]

So Kidwai's resignation was accepted, and Tandon had won this round. Nehru had now to replan his strategy.

> I am troubled and cannot see my way clearly. I doubt if I shall continue in the Working Committee. If I go out of it, that will create another major crisis, for whatever my failings, I still hold the crowd.
>
> We function when we have clear objectives — something to function for. If that goes, then functioning itself becomes rather meaningless. But do not imagine that I have arrived at that stage. I am still in adequate bodily and mental health. Only something seems lacking. I do not quite know what.[21]

Soon his mind cleared, and he saw it as his continuing duty to rid the Congress of the viewpoint which Tandon symbolized. With inner discord and outer weakness, the Party could not fulfil its primary function as a unifying factor in the country, and he himself would be ineffective if he continued to function with a sense of failure. 'The moment you think you are functionless, then you are a dead person, carrying on some dead routine. Now I began to get that sensation about myself.'[22] So he took up the fight again by resigning from the Working Committee and the Central Election Committee. 'I doubt if I have thought about anything more than about this matter. I came to the conclusion that I must wrestle with myself. The responsibility was mine and the decision must be mine.'[23] With the failure of his attempts at unity, the wrong kind of people with the wrong kind of ideas were gaining influence in the Party; and he could not merely stand by. 'The public appeal of the Congress is getting less and less. It may, and probably will, win elections. But, in the process, it may also lose its soul.'[24]

Once more Tandon offered to step down, and the members of the Working Committee, meeting without Nehru, all agreed to resign and request Nehru to reconstitute the Committee, with Tandon remaining the president if Nehru so desired.[25] This was an unworkable half-measure which Nehru was not prepared to accept. No compromise was possible, for the issue was not one of personality or temperament but of basic policy. 'Which viewpoint and outlook are to prevail in the Congress — Tandon's

[20] Nehru to Tandon, 22 and 23 July 1951.
[21] Nehru to Vijayalakshmi, 3/4 August 1951.
[22] Speech explaining his resignation at Congress Parliamentary Party meeting, 21 August, *Hindustan Times*, 22 August 1951.
[23] To Rajagopalachari, 6 August 1951.
[24] Nehru to Tandon, 9 August 1951.
[25] Azad to Nehru, 12 August 1951.

or mine? It is on this issue that a clear decision should be arrived at and any attempt to shirk it will simply mean that the issue will arise every month in an acuter form.' Whether he could help the Congress adequately from outside the Working Committee might be open to question, but it was to Nehru beyond doubt that he would be ineffective within the Committee under Tandon's presidentship.[26] So the AICC, meeting on 8 and 9 September, took the logical and full step of accepting Tandon's resignation and electing Nehru in his place.

Nehru could now wage full war against all communal elements in the country.

> If any person raises his hand to strike down another on the ground of religion, I shall fight him till the last breath of my life, both as the head of the government and from outside.[27]

But even the Congress, of which he was now the head, was not free of this taint; and he had first to cleanse the Party before leading it into battle. Many Congressmen functioned as if they were members of the Hindu Mahasabha, and Muslims who had throughout their lives opposed the League were now being hounded out by men who had not done a day's service in the cause of India or of freedom. The average Muslim was frustrated and there was again a daily exodus of hundreds across the border of Rajasthan to Pakistan.[28] Even the President, Rajendra Prasad, was still prominent in the ranks of medievalism. He insisted, against the advice of his Prime Minister, on inaugurating the rebuilt Somnath temple. Nehru regarded this as totally contrary to the concept of secularism and, while unwilling to veto Prasad's acceptance, sought to make it clear that his government had no part in this decision. But even this sounded hollow as the chief organizer of the function, K. M. Munshi, was a member of the Cabinet. 'I can assure you that the "collective sub-conscious" of India today is happier with the scheme of reconstruction of Somnath sponsored by the Government of India than with many other things that we have done and are doing.'[29] Then, in September 1951, Prasad wished to act unconstitutionally and send a message to Parliament stating his fundamental objections to the Hindu Code Bill; and Nehru, after consulting the Attorney-General, had to make clear that he would resign if the President insisted.[30] 'I regret to say that the President attaches more importance to his astrologers than to the advice of his Cabinet on some matters. I have no intention of submitting to the astrologers.'[31]

[26] Nehru to B. C. Roy, 17 August 1951.
[27] Speech at Delhi, 2 October, *National Herald*, 4 October 1951.
[28] See Nehru to A. P. Jain, 22 September, and to G. B. Pant, 26 September 1951.
[29] Munshi to Nehru, 24 April 1951.
[30] Rajendra Prasad to Nehru, 15 September, Nehru's reply of the same date, Nehru to M. C. Setalvad, Attorney-General, 17 September and to Prasad, 21 September 1951.
[31] Nehru to N. G. Ayyangar, 22 September 1951.

In his efforts to combat communalism, Nehru also came up against Rajagopalachari, Home Minister after Patel's death. There was a minor personal element in this; for it had been suggested by the *Hindustan Times*, a paper known to express Rajagopalachari's view, that there should be two deputy leaders of the Party, and when Azad objected, Nehru denied that he contemplated any such step.[32] Thereafter a tone of acerbity, in contrast to the earlier flattery, crept into Rajagopalachari's attitude to Nehru.[33] But a major difference of policy also emerged. Nehru thought that the main danger now to India's integrity was not the Communists, who were slowly coming to terms with defeat, but renewed agitation by the Hindu Mahasabha, which was believed to be planning riots, particularly in Bengal, Bihar, the United Provinces, Rajasthan and Hyderabad, so as to frighten away Muslims and turn Hindus against the government when action was taken against the rioters.[34] So concerned was Nehru by this that he even secured an amendment of the Constitution to enable 'reasonable restrictions' on the right to free speech and expression in order to curb communal writings. This, of course, aroused criticism which Nehru was, curiously and characteristically, happy about. 'Such public debates waken up people and force them to think, even though the direction of the thought might not always be the right one. Nothing is worse in a democracy than complacency on the part of a government or of the people.' What worried the press was unjustified action by the State governments and assemblies rather than by the Government of India or Parliament from which, so long as Nehru was around, they had little to fear. Sensing this, Nehru ordered that pre-censorship should not be imposed under any circumstances and no action should be taken by the State authorities without reference to the central government.[35]

These amendments were approved by Rajagopalachari, even though he did not agree that communalism was the chief enemy. He was still unwilling to adopt a lenient attitude towards the Communists. He opposed Nehru's desire to commute the death sentences awarded to Communists in Telengana.[36] The Soviet offer of wheat, with Russian ships transporting it to India, in return for raw jute and cotton, was a friendly gesture which Nehru was willing to pursue in detail; but ministers and officials in India were not enthusiastic and only accepted a fifth of the 500,000 tons offered by the Soviet Union. Rajagopalachari too created difficulties by proposing to expatriate some Russians who had been in touch with Indian Communists. 'I am a little tired of this case', wrote Nehru, to which Rajagopalachari retorted, 'I do not like this matter to be disposed of on the

[32] Azad to Nehru, 10 February 1951, and Nehru's reply of the same date.
[33] E.g., when Nehru declined to agree to the deportation of an Englishman: 'It is your desire that should prevail since you press it in spite of my opinion.' Rajagopalachari to Nehru, 11 February 1951.
[34] Nehru to Chief Ministers, 7 and 19 February 1951.
[35] Nehru to Chief Ministers, 2 June 1951.
[36] Nehru to Rajagopalachari, 18 March, and Rajagopalachari's reply, 19 March 1951.

basis of wearisomeness or disgust.' Nehru had also to rebuke Rajagopalachari for a decision of the Economic Committee of the Cabinet showing excessive consideration to a private shipbuilding firm. 'I have a strong feeling that we have got caught up in the toils of out of date policies which imprison us and do not allow even our minds to function in freedom.'[37] Then the Home Ministry shocked Nehru by directing the police to keep a careful watch over schools and colleges, arranging for lectures against communism, and asking guardians to give undertakings that their children would not take part in politics.[38] So when, towards the end of 1951, Rajagopalachari pleaded ill-health and wished to return to Madras, Nehru did not press him too hard to change his mind.

As Congress president, Nehru invited all those who had left the Congress to return.

> I am trying to build up something big and I want every kind of person to help it. I want to immobilize a good deal of opposition and then to go ahead on the lines that the Congress has laid down. I want as far as possible to break through the parties and groups that have arisen in the Congress. I may fail of course, or I may only succeed partially. But it is worthwhile doing so.[39]

Kidwai helped in this by working for the dissolution of the Kisan Mazdoor Praja Party. Nehru also wrote personally to Kripalani, proposing, even if the latter did not rescind his decision to remain away from the Congress, cooperation in what was at this time the chief task of opposing reaction and communalism.[40] Kripalani refused to respond, but Kidwai returned to the Congress.

Having toned up the Party, Nehru turned his attention to the increasing lassitude and lack of coordination in the administration both at the centre and in the States. In the spring of 1951, with foodgrains not available from abroad, it had seemed that vast parts of the country would be overwhelmed by famine. Many States with surplus stocks had been unwilling to dispatch them to deficit areas.

> The time has now come when we face the possibilities of tragedy on a vast scale and we have to think afresh and tackle this problem with all our might to avert this tragedy which, apart from the human sorrow and misery, can only bring shame and humiliation on us and at the same time perhaps shake the whole structure of the state.

It would be a failure of both the political and the economic systems of

---

[37] Nehru to Rajagopalachari, 10 August 1951.
[38] See Nehru's protest to Rajagopalachari, 1 September 1951.
[39] Nehru to S. K. Sinha, 27 September 1951.
[40] Nehru to Kripalani, 23 September 1951.

India.[41] Touring the ravaged districts of Bihar, Nehru is reported to have shed tears at the sight of emaciated children: 'Why do you shout slogans in my praise when I cannot feed you to keep you strong?'[42] But India was able to pull away from the brink of famine and Nehru had hoped that this success might in itself help to produce confidence in the people and to get rid of passivity and submission to fate. But the overall picture was depressing. Politicians, busy with their quarrels, left matters to officials, who sought to carry on as usual.

It was the need for clear objectives which would awaken positive reactions of the right kind among the masses which led Nehru to force the issue with Tandon, as well as to seek to provide an economic programme which would plan to involve a larger number of people. A firm commitment should be made to social justice, which required gradual socialization and redistributive taxation; and if this were to be achieved in a democratic system, it could only be with a new popular drive. This in turn required diffusion of power, an encouragement to the people to throw up their own local leaders. 'It will not be possible to look and walk both ways, as we try to do most of the time with unfortunate results.'[43]

At first Nehru contemplated his favourite remedy of walking out of the Government and jolting the whole system into action.

I have an increasing feeling that such utility as I have had is lessening and I work more as an automaton in a routine way rather than as an active and living person. Throughout my public life, I have drawn my strength chiefly from my contacts with the people. These contacts grow less and less and I find no recompense for them in my new environment. So I grow rootless and feel unhappy. The trend of events and what we ourselves do seems to take me away more and more from many things that I have valued in life and from such ideals as I have nourished. Functioning in such a way ceases to have much meaning.

Many of our policies, economic and other, leave a sense of grave uneasiness in me. I do not interfere partly because I am not wholly seized with the subject and partly because of myself being entangled in a web out of which it is difficult to emerge. We function more and more as the old British Government did, only with less efficiency. The only justification for less efficiency is a popular drive with popular enthusiasm. We have neither that enthusiasm of the people nor the efficiency. We rely more and more on official agencies which are generally fairly good, but which are completely different in outlook

[41] Telegram to Chief Ministers of U.P., Punjab, Madhya Pradesh, Orissa, Madhya Bharat and PEPSU, 23 April 1951.
[42] Message of the Associated Press of America, 20 June 1951.
[43] To Rajagopalachari, 18 May 1951.

and execution from anything that draws popular enthusiasm to it. Complaints grow all round us and we shift about in our policies frequently. In trying to put an end to one difficulty we produce several others. Our economic approach is both conservative and unstable.

I feel that if I have to be of any real use in the future, I must find my roots again. I do not think I can do so by continuing for much longer in my present routine of life. I am prepared to continue for a while, but not too long. I do not think that my days of useful work have ended, but I feel sure that my utility will grow less and less in existing circumstances.[44]

Realizing soon enough that he could not run away, or provide some magic touch such as many seemed to expect of him, Nehru pinned his faith on moving forward on all fronts, social and economic as well as political. Ambedkar resigned because of what he believed to be Nehru's half-heartedness in going ahead with the Hindu Code Bill; but the failure to enact the measure was due to no lack of will on the Prime Minister's part. Even Gopalaswami, on whose advice Nehru depended heavily at this time, had been in favour of postponement until after the elections.[45] On the economic front, Nehru urged the planning commission to finalize a five-year plan with emphasis on self-sufficiency in food and the rapid reduction of unemployment. The Plan outline, as published in July 1951, was, as Nehru stated later, not a plan in any real sense of the term. It merely brought together various projects already started and constituted 'the essential minimum of measures necessary to get some movement into a badly stagnant economy.'[46] It even lacked an ideology. But it at least marked a step in the right direction.

The Congress had been braced up and better equipped by these various measures to offer itself, with some justification, to the people at the coming elections as the party that could lead India forward. But Nehru also sought to improve relations with the Socialists. In the summer of 1951, Jayaprakash Narayan had been sullen. He had been convinced that Nehru had been upholding, no doubt unwillingly and possibly unwittingly, conservatism if not reaction. He publicly denounced 'Nehru's naked, open fascism' and charged his Government with following faithfully in Hitler's footsteps in their dealings with labour.[47] 'Since Patel's death I have, one by one, lost my illusions and it has become a political duty to criticize, even to attack you.'[48] Later, he expressed his approval of Nehru's policies on communalism and towards Pakistan and in consequence postponed the

---

[44] To Rajagopalachari, 9 June 1951.
[45] N. Gopalaswami Ayyangar to Nehru, 21 September 1951.
[46] A. H. Hanson, *The Process of Planning* (Oxford, 1966), p. 98.
[47] 14 July 1951. A. and W. Scarfe, *J. P. His Biography* (Delhi, 1975), pp. 245 and 246.
[48] Jayaprakash Narayan to Nehru, 17 and 25 July 1951.

Hasten Slowly

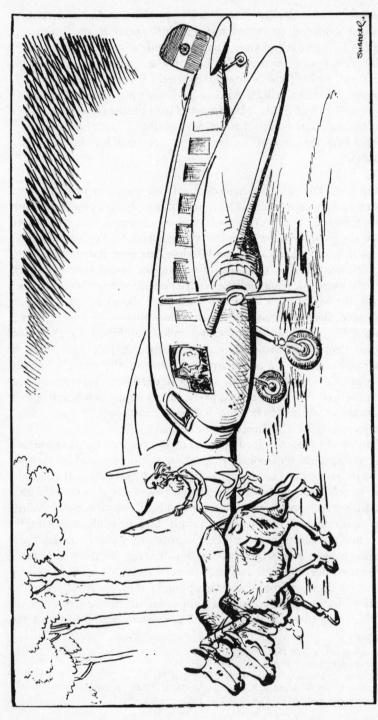

'"To move slowly is dangerous . . . to move fast might lead to conflicts," said Pandit Nehru in his report to the AICC.' Shankar on the Nehru-Tandon differences, *Shankar's Weekly*, 13 June 1951

railway strike.[49] As a response, Nehru arranged that in the elections — the choosing of candidates for which 'is more of a burden and a heart-break than almost anything that I have done'[50] — two Socialist leaders, Narendra Deva and Kamala Devi, should not be opposed by the Congress.[51] When Morarji Desai objected that elections should be fought on principles and not round personalities, Nehru sharply pulled him down to earth. The Congress could hardly talk of high principles when so many of its members were snarling for selection and third-rate individuals were being chosen on grounds of caste and sub-caste. 'I have felt recently as if I was in a den of wild animals.'[52]

The squabbles about selection of candidates filled Nehru with such dismay that he even failed to look forward to campaigning — an event which usually he had found most rewarding. 'One dominant wish overshadows, for the moment, almost everything else in my mind, and of course that wish will be realized. This is for the next hundred days or so to pass and the elections to be a thing of the past.'[53] But once he set out, covering over 25,000 miles and addressing in all about 35 millions or a tenth of India's population, putting in more work in a day than it was meant for and converting weeks into fortnights, the old excitement returned.

Wherever I have been, vast multitudes gather at my meetings and I love to compare them, their faces, their dresses, their reactions to me and what I say. Scenes from past history of that very part of India rise up before me and my mind becomes a picture gallery of past events. But, more than the past, the present fills my mind and I try to probe into the minds and hearts of these multitudes. Having long been imprisoned in the Secretariat of Delhi, I rather enjoy these fresh contacts with the Indian people. It all becomes an exciting adventure . . . I speak to these people and I try to tell them in some detail of how I feel and what I want them to do. I refer to the elections only casually because, I tell them, I have bigger things in my mind. The effort to explain in simple language our problems and our difficulties, and to reach the minds of these simple folk is both exhausting and exhilarating.

As I wander about, the past and the present merge into one another and this merger leads me to think of the future. Time becomes like a flowing river in continuous motion with events connected with one another.[54]

[49] *Bombay Chronicle*, 11 August 1951.
[50] To K. M. Munshi, 14 October 1951.
[51] To Morarji Desai, 22 October 1951.
[52] To Morarji Desai, 27 October 1951.
[53] To Chief Ministers, 1 November 1951.
[54] To Lady Mountbatten, 3 December 1951.

The decision to hold elections on the basis of adult suffrage in a vast country with a large and mostly illiterate population had been a pure act of faith on Nehru's part; and he was vindicated by the result. Nearly a million officials were involved. There was a house-to-house survey to register over 173 million voters. Difficulties of language and physical communication had to be surmounted. Machinery had to be improvised to deal with the inability to read and write of nearly three-quarters of the number entitled to vote. Candidates were given symbols which voters were required to deface and marks, indelible for at least three days, were placed on the fingers of the voters after they had cast the ballot to ensure against double voting. In the elections, spread out on this occasion over six months, from October 1951 to March 1952, candidates of seventy-seven political parties, apart from a number of independents, contested in 3,772 constituencies. Campaigning was vigorous and enthusiastic. Nehru even considered the permitting of election broadcasts but finally decided against it, as there were far too many parties and it was difficult to draw the line.[55] The polling was well organized and all observers, Indian and foreign, were convinced that it was fair.

> The Working Committee of the Indian National Congress can draw pleasure from the extraordinary demonstration which India has given. If ever a country took a leap in the dark towards democracy it was India. Contemplating these facts, the Congress Working Committee may purr with satisfaction.[56]

The exercise of the franchise had been a prized privilege, and at many booths there had been a carnival atmosphere with women coming out in their jewels and finery. Nowhere had there been, in Nehru's phrase, 'sheep voting';[57] with the heightening of political consciousness, local and general issues had been carefully considered and the quality of candidates assessed. As before 1947, all the speeches of Nehru were part of a process of adult education, of teaching the masses that they had minds which they should use. Of course, local influences, factions and organizational pulls played a part in these elections. But recognizing that the Prime Minister, with his glamorous record and his immediate presence, was the trump card of the Congress, all the opposition parties had joined in attacking him from every possible viewpoint. So, in a sense, the overall victory of the Congress was a personal referendum in Nehru's favour, overriding all other issues. The crowds took to him with, not the hypnotized reverence they had reserved for Gandhi, but the easy idolization earned by the leader who held out the hope of a worthwhile future.

[55] To R. R. Diwakar, Minister for Information and Broadcasting, 4 August 1951. Prime Minister's Secretariat, File 16(55)/51-PMS, Serial 17A.

[56] *Manchester Guardian*, 2 February 1952.

[57] To C. D. Deshmukh, 26 January 1952.

Though the Congress had secured a majority of seats in the House of the People, it had not had it all its own way everywhere. It fell back in Rajasthan because feudal allegiance overshadowed Nehru's popularity and in the south because even his reputation could not smother particular grievances. To Rajagopalachari, whose intellectual idiosyncrasy had been sharpened by smarting under loss of central office, the lesson of these elections was the need to replace the Congress. 'After these elections are over and we scrape through, we must scrap the Congress organization and rebuild a proper political party. I hope the gods will help you to do it.'[58] That a politician of such mental alertness should be blinded to the national acceptance of the Congress under Nehru by personal chagrin and the reverses in his own part of India was surprising enough; but even more startling was the naivety of Mountbatten. He counselled Nehru, after his

[58] Rajagopalachari to Nehru, 8 January 1952.

PERSONALITY AND THE PRESIDENT

R. K. Laxman's cartoon in *The Times of India*, 28 November 1951

triumph, to depute Rajagopalachari to scour the country to find a successor to Nehru whom Nehru could train by taking him round, introducing him to crowds and getting him to attend Cabinets.

> Please forgive my going on worrying you about this, but I am so concerned about the future of India, and so horrified at the mere thought that you might slip on a banana-peel one day before you had a successor ready, that I feel that nothing is more important than to get you to do something about it.[59]

The suggestion of Rajagopalachari Nehru brushed aside; and to Mountbatten he replied to some extent tongue in cheek.

> You never fail to astonish me with your practical and methodical approach to life's problems. Your writing to me about my ultimate successor was a special example of this foresight. What you say is, logically speaking, absolutely correct. But logic does not go too far in this complicated world of ours; and when the democratic method flourishes, it fails even more often. Nevertheless, there is much in what you say. I am not thinking of it so much from the point of view of an individual who might succeed me, but rather of a group who might be in a position to take charge. In a sense I am always on the look-out for such persons. The demand for right persons to take charge of responsible positions in India is great and growing and it is exceedingly difficult to find the right person often enough.[60]

Sorting out his own multitude of impressions and ideas, Nehru felt that the electioneering had restored to the forefront the shared feeling of kinship between the Congress leadership and the masses, and this mutual awareness and appreciation could be far more important than logical arguments. The renewal for vast numbers of the Indian people of direct contact with Nehru was also, as Nehru could not fail to see, healthy and refreshing. He, more than most Congress leaders, realized how close disruptive elements were to the Indian surface; and, in these early years of the Republic, even the armed services were an unknown quantity. 'Few people think of the Army, Navy and Air Force. They take them for granted. Our Defence Services are good and loyal. But if any sudden changes took place in India, nobody can say what the Defence Services might do.'[61] But the elections and the national vote of personal confidence in Nehru strengthened stability. 'It is true that without me in the Congress,

[59] Mountbatten to Nehru, 18 February 1952.
[60] Nehru to Mountbatten, 16 March 1952. This attitude of Nehru to the question of his successor never wavered.
[61] To Krishna Menon, 27 January 1952.

there would have been no stable government in any State or in the Centre, and a process of disruption would have set in.'[62] So this in itself was ground for active optimism. The elections had given the Congress a fresh mandate to ensure unity and secularism — and this was important enough; for no other party or group in India seemed to Nehru to evince both the intent and the ability to fulfil this role. But in addition the Congress would have to provide for continuous cooperation with the people by quickening the pace of economic advance, raising the tone of public life and developing local leadership in the small towns and villages. Apart from local problems, the measure of unpopularity from which the Congress suffered was due to the belief that it was conservative and did not represent the growing desire in the country for economic progress. The Socialists had not been able to take advantage of this and had proved 'completely ineffectual'. The Communists had been slightly more successful and could be said to have established themselves. Nehru, without making any specific promises, had created a feeling that something would be done. This would now have to be followed up, and if the Congress took up the Five Year Plan and pushed through land reforms, it could recover lost ground.[63] But it was not sufficient to draw up plans in remote offices; the minds and hearts of the people had to be touched by speedily involving them in worthwhile projects and offering quick results. As he had written years earlier to Bidhan Roy, probably the most conservative of the Congress Chief Ministers, 'it is not good enough to work *for* the people, the only way is to work *with* the people and go ahead, and to give them a sense of working for themselves.'[64] The Congress Party workers would have to serve as the links between the government and the people, and for this the Party would have to shed cliques and 'bossism' and find room for young men and women who had not money but enthusiasm for work. 'We progressively become elderly men with elderly ways, interested in small committees and reluctant to go to the people.'[65]

[62] Ibid.
[63] Nehru's note for Working Committee on elections, 31 January 1952. AICC Papers, File No. G-43/1952.
[64] 25 December 1949
[65] Nehru to presidents of Pradesh Congress Committees, 8 February 1952.

9

The Zenith of World Influence 1953-1954

ONE

The Commonwealth Prime Ministers met in London at the time of the Coronation in a euphoric atmosphere; and the key position was held by India's Prime Minister.[1] Following a distinctive policy of his own, Nehru had yet chosen to remain within the Commonwealth, thereby both assuring the positive continuance of that association in a changed context and enabling Britain to claim an influential role, if in a new guise, in world affairs. So Nehru's general analysis of the world situation was heard with respect. He stressed the need for a clearer understanding of the possibly explosive situation in parts of Asia and Africa. He expressed his conviction that the death of Stalin had led to a change of emphasis in Soviet policy, and reminded the other Prime Ministers that their distrust of the Soviet Union and China was matched by the distrust in those two countries of the United States. It was the mutual suspicion and fear which had to be gradually got over. These assessments seemed to make a considerable impression. Such recognition of India's role and significance gave Nehru, of course, much satisfaction.

> I have been watching, with restrained pride and pleasure as well as an evergrowing sense of responsibility and humility, the growth of India's prestige in the world. It is not for us to talk about this and I have deliberately not attempted to praise India or to say much about any success that she may have achieved in her policy. That praise will remain locked up in my mind and heart and will give me strength for greater effort in the cause of the country we hold dear. Why should we talk of this to others? It is for others to do so, if they so choose. Facts are more important than praise or blame, and facts are compelling the world to give a new status and position to India in the larger scheme of

[1] J. D. B. Miller, *Survey of Commonwealth Affairs: Problems of Expansion and Attrition 1953-1969* (Oxford, 1974), p. 1 ff.

things. But this, though pleasing, is also a little terrifying, for it brings tremendous responsibilities in its train.[2]

Despite his irritation with Britain's attitude on Kashmir, Nehru's general attitude to that country was cordial.

It is rather odd that on the whole our relations with the United Kingdom are in some ways more friendly than those of almost any other country. They have behaved decently towards us during these past five years and I think they appreciate that we have behaved decently towards them and not tried to take advantage of their difficulties, which are very great. Indeed I have great sympathy for England in her present plight.[3]

He assured Krishna Menon that he would not allow the recruitment of Gurkhas for the British army to develop into a major issue.[4] But relations were not without stress. The chief issue was British policy in East Africa. To Nehru, apart from his general interest in the battle against colonialism, Africa was a neighbour across the sea and of direct concern to India. Churchill, resentful of the Labour Government's withdrawal from Abadan, wished to adopt a firm attitude elsewhere, and Oliver Lyttelton, the Colonial Secretary, appeared to Nehru to be 'exceedingly narrow-minded and vengeful' and unsuited for dealing with Africans.[5] Therefore, while he regretted the Mau Mau movement and the recourse to violence and discouraged the convening of an all-African conference in Delhi,[6] he came round to the view that, in face of British provocation, the Africans had really no alternative to resistance. 'How any decent person who is an African can be a "loyalist" passes my comprehension.'[7] Talk of a multi-racial society, condemnation of terrorism and emphasis on the need to safeguard the interests of the Indian communities in Africa was all meaningless in face of the heavy offensive that the British were mounting against the African people. In this respect Nehru was ahead even of Apa Pant, the Indian representative in East Africa, whom the British disliked as too committed and outspoken. 'We are all for the multi-racial society, but I am getting a little tired of the repetition of this phrase when the African is being kicked, hounded and shot down and the average Indian prays for safety first.'[8] The conviction of Kenyatta was a purely political act which the Africans could not be expected to accept. Nothing that the Africans had

[2] Nehru to Chief Ministers, 2 July 1953.
[3] Nehru to B. G. Kher, new High Commissioner of India in London, 9 August 1952.
[4] Krishna Menon's telegram 28 August, and Nehru's reply, 2 September 1952.
[5] Nehru to Apa Pant, 6 August 1953.
[6] To Chaman Lall, 1 January 1953.
[7] Nehru's note, 25 March 1953.
[8] Ibid.

done was as bad as the naked and brutal racial domination of the white
settlers. 'At present, there is no question of our teaching the Africans
anything. You do not teach anyone when his house is on fire.'[9] Repetition
of axioms divorced from reality would have little effect on a people in
agony and torture of spirit.

> I am not interested at present in petty reforms for the Africans; that is a
> matter for them to decide. I am interested in standing by people who
> are in great trouble and who have to face tremendous oppression by a
> powerful Government. I should condemn of course every species of
> violence and give no quarter to it. But I shall stand by the Africans
> nevertheless. That is the only way I can serve them and bring them
> round to what I consider the right path.[10]

A public speech on these lines criticizing the British Government and
assuring the people of Kenya of India's sympathy[11] evoked the wrath of
Lord Swinton, the British Commonwealth Secretary, who deemed it to be
interference with British domestic interests: 'how would it strike you if we
criticized your policy in regard to say the separation of Andhra state or
untouchability?'[12] Nehru replied that racialism in Africa was a world
problem on which Indians held strong opinions, and if he had not stated his
views moderately and without ill-will, others would have said much more.
He had repeatedly supported India's membership of the Commonwealth
and praised British policy on many matters; but his arguments would have
been weakened if he had remained silent on this issue. However, Swinton
persisted and said that he had nothing to retract; so Nehru sent a sharply
worded protest.

> Our Government is not used to being addressed in this way by any
> Government and I can only conclude that he has for the moment
> forgotten that he is addressing the independent Republic of India. We
> have endeavoured on all occasions to observe the proprieties of
> diplomatic intercourse and have often suppressed our strongly felt
> feelings. It has been our constant endeavour not to embarrass the
> British Government and we have tried to cooperate with them to the
> largest possible extent subject to adhering to our own principles and
> policies. We shall continue to do so, but we are not prepared to change
> these principles and policies because of any pressure exercised on us
> by an outside authority.[13]

[9] Nehru to Apa Pant, 8 April 1953.
[10] To Apa Pant, 20 April 1953.
[11] Speech at Delhi, 13 April, *National Herald*, 14 April 1953.
[12] Telegram from B. G. Kher, Indian High Commissioner, reporting Swinton's protest, 17 April
1953.
[13] Nehru's telegrams to Kher, 18 and 21 April, Kher's reply, 21 April and Nehru's telegram, 25 April
1953.

The same views were expressed by Nehru in London to Churchill, at the Prime Ministers' Conference, to the press and in a television interview. But there was no angry reaction such as that of Swinton. Churchill, in particular, was appreciative of Nehru's standing and significance. Whatever his attitude to Indian nationalism before 1947, he was willing thereafter to develop a personal relationship with Nehru over which the shadow of the past did not fall. In 1949, he had welcomed India's continuance in the Commonwealth. When Smuts, then out of office, cabled to him deploring this decision, Churchill replied, 'When I asked myself the question "Would I rather have them in, even on these terms, or let them go altogether," my heart gave the answer, "I want them in." Nehru has certainly shown magnanimity.'[14] He was still occasionally capable of denouncing India's leaders, but on returning to office as Prime Minister, he put such irresponsibility behind him. He paid attention to Nehru's views on Africa, agreed with him on the anomaly of Portuguese imperial policy and sought his assistance in recasting Britain's relations with Egypt.

Before 1947, Nehru had not disguised his sympathy for the Arab cause, which he had regarded as part of the general struggle against imperialism. As Prime Minister, he sought to take a neutral attitude on the Arab-Israel question, but a neutrality slanted towards the Arabs — as he himself described it, favourable to the Arabs but not hostile to the Jews. The weight carried by Muslim opinion in India and the need to prevent this issue from intensifying bad relations with Pakistan or poisoning relations with Indonesia strengthened his inclination to support the Arabs; but he carefully refrained from criticizing the Jews. What he would have liked was a federation in Palestine with fully autonomous Jewish and Arab units and a special status for Jerusalem, and a review, if necessary, of the whole problem after ten years.[15] When Israel was established, he realized that it had come to stay; and the vote cast by Farouk's Egypt against India on the Hyderabad issue in the United Nations disposed him towards accepting the fact of Israel and recognizing her. Visiting Cairo in November 1948, he was disgusted by what he saw. 'I found Farouk to be one of the most repellent individuals I had met. All that I could do was not to be rude to him.'[16] So, on the question of Israel's admission to the United Nations, his first reaction was to abstain. Later, as part of the policy of cooperation with the Islamic states, he ordered the Indian delegation to vote against; but he recognized that the general policy of supporting the Arabs required reconsideration. 'It is about time that we made some of these Arab countries feel that we are not going to follow them in everything in spite of what they do.'[17] A few months later, he recognized Israel. He did not

[14] Quoted in H. Tinker, *Separate and Unequal* (London, 1976), p. 388.
[15] Nehru's note on Palestine, 4 April 1948.
[16] To Vijayalakshmi, 17 November 1948.
[17] Note, 12 May 1949.

immediately follow this up with the establishment of a legation in Tel-Aviv, perhaps mainly because of Muslim sentiment within India; and the Israeli insistence on reciprocity created a deadlock.[18] In March 1952 Nehru informed the Israeli Government that there was no major objection to the exchange of diplomatic representatives, but it might be better to wait for the formation of a new government after the elections.[19] Even then nothing was done. This inaction has been attributed to the influence of Azad.[20] Nehru probably attached no importance or urgency to the matter. There was certainly no closeness to the Neguib regime which, though clearly a great improvement on Farouk's Government, was thought to be a creation of the United States.[21] But it was believed that the new rulers of Egypt would listen to Nehru. At Cairo, on his way back from London, Nehru advised Nasser and Salah Salem not to use harsh language against Britain even while standing firm on the issue of sovereignty. The tone of their speeches became milder thereafter, making discussion with Britain easier; and Churchill acknowledged Nehru's assistance. 'Thank you so much for your message and for the help you gave us over Egypt and Israel — Winston.'[22]

There was, however, no change in British colonial policy. 'It is clear that whether in Kenya or Egypt or British Guiana or Central Africa, this policy is of aggressive colonialism. We cannot even passively acquiesce in it, though no doubt we have to take certain accomplished facts for granted.'[23] The leaders of nationalism in British Guiana were disappointed on finding that the Government of India could go no further than an expression of general sympathy.[24] But it was with Africa that Nehru was most concerned, and here he resisted, in all ways possible to him, the attempt not merely to hold on to empire, as was the case of other European powers, but to promote domination by settlers under the guise of self-government, on the model of South Africa. He repeatedly drew attention to the way in which Africans were being treated 'almost as wild animals'[25] and promised that India would do everything in her power, short of war, to oppose racial discrimination.[26]

> While we cannot do anything directly, India's position is such in the world today that even expressions of opinion from us carry some weight. Therefore we should be clear in enunciation of our policy and

[18] M. Brecher, *The Foreign Policy System of Israel* (Oxford, 1972), pp. 386-7.
[19] Nehru's note on conversations with Eytan, 4 March 1952.
[20] M. Brecher, *The New States of Asia* (London, 1963), pp. 129-30.
[21] Report of K. M. Panikkar, then Ambassador in Egypt, 27 January 1953.
[22] Telegram forwarded by British High Commissioner in Delhi, 1 July 1953.
[23] Nehru's note, 14 October 1953.
[24] C. Jagan, *The West on Trial* (Berlin, 1972), p. 151.
[25] Speech at Agra, 6 July, *National Herald*, 7 July 1953.
[26] Press conference at Delhi, 30 July, *National Herald*, 31 July 1953.

following it up in so far as we can without needlessly getting ourselves entangled in any conflict.[27]

This might not result in much; but it was keeping faith with the African people which was important.

TWO

Such influence of India was not confined to the Commonwealth. By the Korean settlement, India was made the chairman of the commission which would provide explanations to the prisoners of both sides and arrange for repatriation if so desired. That this was going to be no mere routine operation became clear at the very start when President Rhee of South Korea suddenly released a large number of North Korean prisoners, thereby increasing the difficulty of concluding any armistice or long-term settlement.

> The issue is a straight one. Who commands in South Korea? Are there two different commands — the United Nations and Syngman Rhee? Either the United Nations Command has full control over Syngman Rhee and South Koreans or it has not. If the former, then they should do something about it and, as you suggest, should smack him down. If they do not wish to do so, then they are equally incapable of signing the armistice with effect. The Chinese can hardly be expected to sign an armistice for two-fifths of the front and carry on a war on three-fifths. It is a bad look-out and the credit of the United Nations has been badly damaged. Indeed, one might say that the future of the United Nations is at stake, apart from the major question of war and peace in the Far East.[28]

Nehru requested that the General Assembly be convened early to consider this failure on the part of the United Nations Command to carry out its obligations.[29] Unless the United States controlled Rhee, disaster seemed inevitable; and when Rhee violently abused India, the State Department was informed that India could not function without satisfactory assurances. The Government of India 'cannot be expected to accept a position which is not in keeping with their self-respect or in which they are called upon to function in a furtive manner where the movements of their own representatives are limited and confined.'[30]

[27] Note on Africa, 16 October 1953.
[28] Nehru to Mountbatten, 24 June 1953.
[29] Nehru to Pearson, President, United Nations General Assembly, 24 June 1953.
[30] India's *aide-memoire* to the United States, 15 July 1953.

AT THE U N — INDIAN NON-DISAPPEARANCE ACT

Low's cartoon on the Korean political conference in the *Manchester Guardian*,
18 September 1953

The United States did bring Rhee under control, but probably by a
promise that India would be excluded from the political conference that
was to follow the armistice. So, after the armistice was signed on 27 July
1953, the United States took the line that only nations directly involved in
the Korean war should participate in the conference. When the matter came
up at the United Nations, the United States saw to it that a majority voted
against the inclusion of India.

> Some countries who had openly stated that they would vote for us had
> to back out. Not only that, but American Ambassadors brought this
> pressure on countries in their respective capitals. It really has been an
> extraordinary experience to see how a great Power behaves.[31]

In fact, 'the Americans were at their most bloody-minded vis-à-vis the
Indians in this period.'[32] China wanted India to make an issue of this
exclusion, but Nehru felt such undignified behaviour was perhaps exactly

[31] Nehru to M. S. Mehta, 28 August 1953.
[32] Later comment of Mr Escott Reid, Canadian High Commissioner in Delhi during these years.
D. Stair, *The Diplomacy of Constraint* (Toronto, 1974), p. 282.

what Rhee wanted, as it would lead to a breakdown of negotiations. So Nehru made clear that he did not wish a vote on India's inclusion to be taken at the plenary session; and Churchill sent a private message of approval.

> I thought you were very wise to help the United States out of their difficulty with Syngman Rhee. I cannot forget how he cheated about the prisoners and the fact that the negotiations went forward notwithstanding encourages the hope which I cherish that better days are in store. You must be gratified by the general recognition of the wisdom and dignity of India's withdrawal.[33]

That, in fact, India was in a thankless position became manifest from developments in Korea on repatriation, culminating in both sides accusing India of partisanship. First, some prisoners in the United Nations camps assaulted the guards and attempted mass break-outs, and Nehru had to make personal appeals to Winston Churchill and St Laurent.

> You will appreciate that the situation is a very grave one and the Repatriation Commission and the Custodian Force are entitled to full support from the nations at whose instance they went there. The honour of India is concerned in this matter, but I would specially lay stress on the consequences to world peace in which you are so greatly interested.[34]

The United States agreed that India had every right to expect proper protection and peaceful conditions, although it was felt that the explaining procedures were slanted in favour of China and North Korea and worked on the premise of repatriation rather than free choice.[35] The Repatriation Commission itself was split on the question as to whether force should be used to compel prisoners to appear before explainers. Poland and Czechoslovakia were in favour of force, while Sweden and Switzerland opposed it. India was for the use of force; but the crucial question was the degree of force. It seemed to India, though it was difficult to prove, that terror and intimidation prevailed in the camps on both sides.

The crisis was reached on 16 October 1953. A thousand North Korean prisoners refused to appear before explainers and, when troops encircled the compound to force them to appear, threatened a break-out. As this might well have meant mass slaughter, the matter was referred to the Commission. Poland and Czechoslovakia said this was a matter for India as the Custodian Force and not for the Commission, while Sweden and

[33] Churchill to Nehru, 31 August 1953.
[34] 6 October 1953.
[35] G. L. Mehta's report of interview with Walter Robertson, Assistant Secretary of State, 7 October 1953.

Switzerland sought instructions from their governments. The Government of India authorized General Thimayya to use measures of compulsion short of producing a major conflict which would lead to mass killing, and sought the assistance of the Secretary-General, Britain and the United States.

The situation took a bizarre turn when *People's China* criticized India for failure to take effective action,[36] and Chou En-lai charged the Indian Custodian Force with 'weakness and connivance'.[37] Even India's refusal to become a subordinate partner of the United States was interpreted as a result of British machinations.[38] Nehru firmly rejected all such criticism from China. India had withstood the general attitude of the United Nations Command and had left no doubt that she was prepared to take all necessary steps, including pressure and compulsion. But large-scale killing would lead to a break-up of the Commission and a breakdown of the armistice, which was in no one's interest. 'It is easy to point out the grave difficulties of the situation, but much more difficult to suggest a way out which will not completely break up the work of the Commission and endanger the armistice.'[39]

The result was a deadlock, with no Koreans coming forward for explanations. Nehru blamed both sides but did not take the easy way of giving up the effort.

It was not possible for us to refuse this responsibility which meant so much to the world. If we had not accepted it, because of fear, we would have sunk in our own estimation as well as that of others, and we would have helped in aggravating the perilous situation in the world. There was no other country that could do it or that would have been acceptable to both the parties. In any event, to talk of calling back our troops now is to say something that is rank nonsense and the height of irresponsibility.[40]

36 22 October 1953.
37 Message to Indian Ambassador, 22 October 1953.
38 'India advocates a peaceful settlement of the Korean question. Why does she dare do so? It is because England is at her back. England has still large capital investments in India. Out of the total industrial and commercial enterprises capital in India of Rs 320 crores, England controls Rs 220 crores while America controls only 20 crores. Ninety per cent of India's external trade is in the hands of England. In recent years England has made some recovery of her economic conditions and therefore she has become slightly stiff. At the Roosevelt-Churchill talks in 1945, Churchill said that so long as he lived he cannot see England being sold to America. The British bourgeoisie wants to stage a comeback to her former position and does not want to be deemed a small nation. Churchill wants England to return to her pre-war international status. For over a hundred years England has shown great cunning in diplomacy and, while openly showing great frankness towards America, actually she is making trouble for her behind her back. Such is the background of the Indian attitude.' Report on the international situation by Wu Ling-si, head of the New China News Agency, to the National Committee of the Chinese People's Political Consultative Council, 25 October 1953, published in *Min Ko Huei Kan,* February 1954.
39 Nehru's oral communication to Chou En-lai, 23 October 1953.
40 To Chief Ministers, 6 November 1953.

The stalemate in Korea could obviously only be resolved by the United Nations. But Lester Pearson, as President of the General Assembly, was not keen on summoning that body, and was still hoping for diplomatic pressures on the Americans and the Chinese.[41] The Americans had decided to release all prisoners to civilian status after 120 days, regardless of whether the political conference met or not. When Nehru pointed out at a press conference that India could not approve of this and would prefer that the question be referred back to the two commands or to the General Assembly,[42] he was strongly criticized in the United States. On his part, Nehru rejected the suggestion of the United States that India should attend any political conference as an observer.

Chou, on his side, objected to the Indian Ambassador that Thimayya was being weak about recalcitrant prisoners.[43] But Nehru clearly instructed Thimayya that when the 120 days lapsed on 22 January 1954, prisoners were not to be released but restored to detaining sides. If the Commission did not agree, the Chairman should decide this on his own.[44] Any other step might result in anarchic conditions and violence, endangering even Indian soldiers. Those prisoners who did not wish to be handed over could remain with the Custodian Force for the time being. He also asked Vijayalakshmi, who had succeeded Pearson as president, to take steps to convene the General Assembly — a suggestion not to Hammarskjöld's liking.

Chou was now even more upset and, while supporting the convening of the General Assembly, wanted the Commission to extend the explanation period. He even preferred a mass break-out to the handing back of the prisoners.[45] But Nehru was not prepared to change his mind. He knew that the United Nations Command would most probably hand over their prisoners to the South Korean and Taiwan authorities; but India was powerless to prevent this. All he could do to meet Chou's viewpoint was to direct the Commission to declare that the receiving sides should not alter the status of the prisoners,[46] and to refuse to hand over prisoners accused of murder and other crimes.

However, the majority of the members of the United Nations did not favour the convening of the General Assembly. Even Britain opposed, and Churchill sent a personal telegram explaining that while great issues, including a Five Power Conference, were being discussed in Berlin it would be premature and might well be harmful to have simultaneously a wide discussion on Korea in New York.[47]

[41] Pearson to Escott Reid, 26 October 1953. This message was passed on by the Canadian High Commission to the Ministry of External Affairs.
[42] 15 November 1953.
[43] Raghavan's telegram, 22 December reporting interview with Chou, 21 December 1953.
[44] Nehru's telegram to Thimayya, 8 January 1954.
[45] Raghavan's telegram to Nehru, 10 January 1954.
[46] Commission's resolution, 21 January 1954.
[47] 28 January 1954.

THREE

China's shifting attitude towards India on the Korean question underlined the importance of formulating a policy regarding India's direct relations with China. Obviously a prime element in this was the question of India's northern frontier, which, with the movement of China into Tibet, became a long common frontier from Ladakh in the north-west to the tri-junction with Burma in the east. In the middle sector lay Nepal, Sikkim and Bhutan, of varied status, but for the frontiers and integrity of all of which India had assumed responsibility. Nehru did not expect armed attack on India by China from Tibet, but he did not rule out infiltration by groups or even occupation of disputed areas.[48] To forestall this, it was necessary to be clear as to where the boundary lay and to strengthen both administration and communication. Nehru's attitude from the outset was that the frontier was firm, well-known and beyond dispute. 'About Tibet, our position is first of all that our frontiers with Tibet, that is the McMahon Line, must stand as they are. There is no room for controversy over that issue.'[49] There is a looseness about such statements, because India's frontier with Tibet was more than the McMahon Line, which was only the north-eastern frontier from Bhutan to Burma, settled at the Simla Conference of 1914, attended by Britain, China and Tibet. It did not cover the western and the middle sectors, from the north-western tip of Kashmir to the western end of Nepal. But, speaking in Parliament the next month, Nehru was more precise.

> Tibet is contiguous to India from the region of Ladakh to the boundary of Nepal and from Bhutan to the Irrawaddy/Salween divide in Assam. The frontier from Bhutan eastwards has been clearly defined by the McMahon Line which was fixed by the Simla Convention of 1914. The frontier from Ladakh to Nepal is defined chiefly by long usage and custom . . . Our maps show that the McMahon Line is our boundary and that is our boundary — map or no map. That fact remains and we stand by that boundary, and we will not allow anybody to come across that boundary.[50]

Even here, however, there is a difference of emphasis and Nehru's assertion of India's rights is more definite as regards the eastern sector. But there was yet another problem. The border had, except as regards Sikkim, not been demarcated on the ground; the boundary in the western and middle sectors had been defined, as Nehru said, by custom, usage and tradition, but not by treaty; and even as regards the McMahon Line, while

[48] Nehru's note, 18 November 1950.
[49] Nehru to Panikkar, 25 October 1950.
[50] 20 November 1950. Parliamentary Debates, 1950, Vol. V, Part I, pp. 155-6.

the Chinese delegation at Simla had initialled the map on which it was shown, the Chinese Government had not ratified it. So, although the People's Government were left in no doubt as to India's position on the frontier, there would be much advantage, even though they knew where it lay, in securing a fresh acceptance of every stretch of the delineation.

Panikkar thought there would be no difficulty about this[51] and that relations between the two countries were again as good as they had been before the exchange of sharp notes on Tibet.[52] On the Korean question there appeared to be no great appreciation in China of India's efforts, but her refusal to sign the Japanese peace treaty evoked a warmer response and Chou's analysis, as reported by Panikkar, was encouraging.

Events in Asia are moving fast. The Japanese treaty is one example. Much depends on India and much is expected of her by the peoples of Asia. She has won a great position of leadership by her courageous policy of independence. I hope she will maintain that leadership.[53]

A few weeks later, referring directly to Tibet, Chou stated that there was no difference of viewpoint between India and China and he was particularly anxious to safeguard in every way Indian interests in Tibet. There was no territorial dispute or any controversy in this matter between India and China; and the question of 'stabilization of the Tibetan frontier', which was a matter of common interest to India, Nepal and China, could best be done by discussions between the three countries.[54]

The Government of India took this to mean that the Government of China accepted the boundary, and particularly the McMahon Line sector, as depicted by India. To say that there was no territorial dispute and the frontier required to be stabilized certainly suggested this. Chou could not have been thinking, at best, only of the eastern sector, for Nehru in his statement in Parliament the previous year had spoken specifically of the entire length. Even so, this shrouded sentence was not an explicit recognition of the frontier, and the senior officials at Delhi favoured making such a recognition part of a general settlement. India should not withdraw her garrisons from Gyantse and Yatung without securing this.[55] In the instructions drawn up for Panikkar and approved by the Prime Minister and Panikkar himself, it was stated that one of India's interests in the negotiations with China on Tibet was the affirmation of the McMahon

[51] Telegram to Foreign Secretary, 29 December 1950.

[52] Panikkar to Nehru, 6 January 1951.

[53] Record of Panikkar's conversation with Chou En-lai, 5 August 1951.

[54] Panikkar's telegram to Nehru, 28 September 1951, reporting conversation with Chou En-lai the previous evening.

[55] Notes of G. S. Bajpai, Secretary General, 21 November, and K. P. S. Menon, Foreign Secretary, 22 November 1951.

Line and the rest of the frontier with Tibet.[56] But when, on return to Peking, Panikkar met Chou, the latter confined the discussions to trade and cultural interests and appeared to the Ambassador anxious not to open up wider issues; and Panikkar, ignoring his instructions, fell into line and did not refer to the frontier.[57] Neither did he mention the subject in the note on India's interests in Tibet which he formally presented to the Chinese Foreign Office. In the same vein Panikkar, at his next interview with Chou, stated that the main item for consideration was the establishment of some kind of relationship for economic, commercial and other purposes.[58] Again nothing was said about the frontier and Nehru sent a telegram pointing out in passing that Chou himself had, earlier in September, agreed to discuss this among other issues.[59] Then, as at further meetings Chou continued to remain silent about the boundary and made no reference to any political problems, Nehru's surprise turned to ill-ease. Friendship with China was of more concern to India than with almost any other country, and to ensure its continuance India had taken care to avoid futile gestures in support of Tibetan autonomy. But she could not abandon any of her vital positions.

> We think it is rather odd that, in discussing Tibet with you, Chou En-lai did not refer at all to our frontier. For our part, we attach more importance to this than to other matters. We are interested, as you know, not only in our direct frontier but also in the frontiers of Nepal, Bhutan and Sikkim, and we have made it perfectly clear in Parliament that these frontiers must remain. There is perhaps some advantage in our not ourselves raising this issue. On the other hand, I do not quite like Chou En-lai's silence about it when discussing even minor matters.[60]

The obvious step for India to take, in face of this studied silence of China, was to raise the matter herself, but Panikkar argued that India's position being well-known, Chou's silence should be presumed to be acquiescence, if not acceptance, and it was wisest to ignore the subject.[61] Though Nehru, against his better judgment, first allowed himself to be convinced,[62] he soon after had second thoughts, prompted by China's volte-face on the Korean issue, his awareness of Panikkar's 'habit of seeing further than perhaps facts warrant',[63] and the protests of Bajpai, even

[56] Instructions drawn up by K. P. S. Menon, 26 January 1952, shown to Panikkar and approved by Nehru, 27 January 1952.
[57] Panikkar's telegram to Nehru, 13 February 1952.
[58] Record of Panikkar's interview with Chou, 5 April 1952.
[59] Nehru's telegram to Panikkar, 12 April 1952.
[60] Nehru's telegram to Panikkar, 16 June 1952.
[61] Panikkar's telegram to Prime Minister, 17 June 1952.
[62] Nehru's telegram to Panikkar, 18 June 1952.
[63] Nehru's note, 9 April 1952.

though now out of the Ministry of External Affairs.[64] 'But I am beginning
to feel that our attempt at being clever might overreach itself. I think it is
better to be absolutely straight and frank.'[65] Panikkar, however, on his
transfer from Peking, was at this moment at Nehru's elbow and again the
Prime Minister was persuaded to treat the border as a preclosed issue.[66]
But, perhaps as a concession to Bajpai, he instructed the Embassy at Peking
not to pass unchallenged vague statements, which could be interpreted in
many ways, about unequal treaties and past British aggression in Tibet.[67]

Mao's remark to Panikkar's successor that India had nothing to fear
from China and China had no fears on her south-west frontier[68] confirmed
Nehru's conviction that India need expect no aggression from China and
the border was not an immediate issue. China should be in no doubt that
any modification of or intrusion across the frontiers would be unacceptable to India and India should be strong enough to prevent this; but such
strength lay not in the prompt location of frontier outposts but in a long-
term effort of building up the country politically and economically over a
period of five to ten years. 'No major challenge to these frontiers is likely in
the near future. If we are alert, no challenge will take place within a
reasonable time and possibly even later.'[69]

This was a sound formulation of India's objectives; but it gave room for
bureaucratic delays in pushing the administration in all its aspects into the
frontier region. Of even greater consequence was its reflection in India's
attitude on the proposed treaty with China on Tibet. As suited the Chinese,
the negotiations were carried on piecemeal on specific issues which were
'ripe for settlement' — an ominous masked phrase — and India weakly
made no attempt to secure an overall settlement. By asserting that not only
questions ripe for settlement but 'all outstanding questions' were being
settled, the Indian side sought to score a debating point of no value.
Semantics cannot guarantee an international frontier. The official involved
in the discussions did once more suggest that the Indian side might include
in its general statement a definite declaration about the boundary; but
Nehru ruled that the matter need not be raised 'for the present'.[70] There
seemed to him no reason to depart from the well-declared stand that the
alignment was a settled one except for a few minor tracts. India's policy
towards China should be one of friendliness and coexistence, allied with
firmness in regard to any interference with India's basic rights. 'Ultimately
the basic right is the preservation of the frontier.' But the best way to

[64] Bajpai, Governor of Bombay, to N. R. Pillai, Secretary-General, 14 July, and to Panikkar,
7 August 1952.
[65] Note, 23 July 1952.
[66] Note, 29 July 1952.
[67] Telegram from Ministry of External Affairs to Embassy at Peking, 31 July 1952.
[68] Raghavan's telegram, 26 September 1952, reporting Mao's speech at presentation of credentials.
[69] Nehru's note, 5 March 1953.
[70] Note of T. N. Kaul, 27 August, and Nehru's directive, 30 August 1953.

prevent this frontier from becoming a dangerous one was to have friendly relations with China, develop the border regions and win over the local inhabitants to the conception of India.[71] Panikkar, advising from his new post at Cairo, went even further and thought that the Indian side should break off negotiations if the Chinese themselves raised the question of the frontier; for to agree to discuss would mean that there was something to discuss.[72] Nehru agreed that the Indian side should refuse, and express surprise at the Chinese reopening a settled issue; but any walk-out should require specific reference to Delhi.[73] A map in *People's China*, on too small a scale to permit precision, yet showed the boundary with India as a settled one, and roughly followed the alignment as depicted on Indian maps from Kashmir to Bhutan. Even in the eastern sector, while the delineation was unclear, no large territorial claims were made.[74] Nehru saw in this map further justification for not raising the border issue with China. He seems by now to have got over his earlier uncertainties on this question and to have come round fully to Panikkar's point of view — a shift of attitude which was to have disastrous consequences in the long run.

The treaty, signed in April 1954, provided for the withdrawal of all Indian influence from Tibet. Nehru had no regret about this, for it embarrassed him to lay claim to the succession of an imperial power which had pushed its way into Tibet. Anxious to make the agreement purely non-political, the Chinese at first resisted mention of the Five Principles which they themselves had elaborated, but ultimately agreed to it as a concession.[75] India was keen on the inclusion of these principles as explicit reference to mutual respect for each other's territorial integrity and sovereignty, and mutual non-aggression suggested, at least by implication, that China had no frontier claims; but this was clutching at straws after the main opportunity had been deliberately discarded. The only real gain India could show was a listing of six border passes in the middle sector, thereby defining, even if indirectly, this stretch of the boundary. On the other hand the Chinese had secured all they wanted and given away little; and that they regarded even this sanction of some Indian trade agencies and markets in Tibet as an interim concession was made clear by their objection to automatic renewal of the treaty after its first term of eight years.

The recognition of Chinese sovereignty over Tibet was no new step, and to this extent the 1954 treaty marked only a formalization of the developments of 1950. The withdrawal of military escorts and the abandonment of extra-territorial privileges inherited from the British were

[71] Note, 25 October 1953.

[72] Panikkar to Foreign Secretary, 31 October 1953.

[73] Nehru's note, 3 December 1953.

[74] Nehru's note, 9 April 1954.

[75] The Five Principles, known as *Panchsheel*, were mutual respect for each other's territorial integrity and sovereignty, mutual non-aggression, mutual non-interference in each other's internal affairs, equality and mutual benefit, and peaceful coexistence.

also logical consequences of the assertion of Chinese authority in this region.

> We have only given up what in fact we could not hold and what in fact had in reality gone. We have given up certain rights that we exercised internally in Tibet. Obviously, we cannot do that. We have gained instead something that is very important, i.e., a friendly frontier and an implicit acceptance of that frontier.[76]

But the chance of securing a clear and explicit recognition of India's frontier at a time when India had something to offer in return had been lost. This was not because of Nehru's unrealistic assessment of China's intent and strength or of his failure to attach importance to this issue but because he allowed his own views, and those of his senior advisers, to be set aside by an ambassador who rationalized a shirking of unpleasantness. The argument that the best defence of the frontier was a friendly neighbour was sound, provided the frontier was a settled one. This was India's case. But that case could have been immeasurably strengthened by directly making it a part of the negotiations leading to the 1954 treaty. In the face of that omission, the best Nehru could do was to insist that now at least the central ministries and the provincial governments should act on the directives he had been issuing since 1947. Administration should be pushed right up to the border and check posts strung out along its entire length, priority should be given to the building of communications, the intelligence system should be strengthened, and the border areas developed economically and their inhabitants integrated in the national life of India. The impact of government would have to make up for remiss diplomacy.

FOUR

Growing influence in the world and concern about the borders of India could not diminish the preoccupation with Kashmir. The removal of Abdullah, though constitutionally a matter of domestic politics, had an obvious bearing on India's moral case. Abdullah might have lost command of the majority in the party, but he still had a large following, and his dismissal and detention were bound to weaken the support India enjoyed in the State. Far from underrating this psychological setback, Nehru had for weeks been adjusting himself mentally to what could well result in the loss of the Valley. He had no intention of retaining Kashmir at the point of the bayonet.

> Obviously I cannot ignore the wishes of the people of Kashmir. If our

[76] Nehru to G. L. Mehta, 29 June 1954.

efforts thus far have been, as it now appears, in vain and the only result that we can expect is some sort of a tragedy, even so we have to behave decently and honourably, adhering to what we have stood for.[77]

Now, therefore, disregarding the threats and invective which filled the air in Pakistan,[78] he agreed to receive Mahomed Ali, and Delhi gave the Prime Minister of Pakistan a welcome such as no one, except Gandhi, had until then received. 'I have seldom felt so proud of my people as I did when I saw the men and women of Delhi behaving in this big way, in spite of the wild outbursts in Pakistan.'[79]

Reversing his position that any settlement in Kashmir could only be broadly on the lines of accepting the status quo, Nehru now offered Mahomed Ali a plebiscite for the entire State; and for this purpose, after the two Prime Ministers had decided on preliminary issues, a plebiscite administrator should be appointed by the end of April 1954.[80] These were, as later correspondence shows,[81] terms offered by Nehru rather than imposed on him. What he had in mind, and indicated to Mahomed Ali, was voting in the whole State rather than in regions predetermined on the basis of Hindu and Muslim majorities, and partition of the State on the basis of the results of the plebiscite. If this meant the loss of the Valley, Nehru was prepared for it.

> The situation in Kashmir and as between India and Pakistan has become a very dynamic and indeed an explosive one. It cannot be treated in a static way. We have to consider the various forces at work and, understanding them, try to fashion our policy so as to get the best advantage out of it. In particular, we have to look a little ahead and think of the future . . . We have to choose the lesser evil and we have to choose a path which not only promises the greatest advantage but is dignified and in keeping with our general policy.[82]

The new government in Kashmir resented Nehru's offer to Pakistan, and the Chief Minister, Bakshi Ghulam Mahomed, threatened to resign;[83] but, after the first shock, the Prime Minister's view was accepted.

Abdullah's conduct, therefore, coupled with the recognition that Ghulam Mahomed and Mahomed Ali were representative of a new, basic goodwill in Pakistan towards India, now brought Pakistan within reach of

[77] To Bakshi Ghulam Mahomed, 30 July 1953.

[78] For example, Khaliquzzaman, the Governor of East Bengal, asked Muslims to be ready with their swords and horses as enjoined in the Koran.

[79] To Chief Ministers, 22 August 1953.

[80] Joint communiqué of the two Prime Ministers, 21 August 1953.

[81] Letter to Mahomed Ali, 3 September 1953.

[82] To Bakshi Ghulam Mahomed, 18 August 1953.

[83] Karan Singh to Nehru, 19 and 25 August 1953.

a settlement in Kashmir on her terms. An overall plebiscite in Kashmir was at this time a real possibility. But the chance was thrown away by what Nehru described as 'mere cleverness or trying to overreach each other.'[84] Nehru wished to have as plebiscite administrator someone from the smaller states in place of Admiral Nimitz, selected earlier by the United Nations. Apart from his desire to insulate Kashmir from the rivalry of the great powers, Nehru was sore with the attitude of the United States, which had been canvassing for the exclusion of India from the political conference on Korea, and was believed to have encouraged Abdullah and to be instigating a revolt in Nepal.

> I have no doubt that American agents have been the cause of some mischief both in Kashmir and Nepal. I have little doubt that it is American help that has brought about the last change in Iran. With all this background, I am not prepared for an instant to accept an American nominee whoever he might be.[85]

While in Delhi Mahomed Ali had not objected to the replacement of Nimitz, but on return to Karachi he pressed that no change be made. He also raised petty, imaginary issues as to the way in which regions should be organized for the plebiscite (although Nehru had ruled this out) and the interim administration of the State — a matter which had been settled earlier by the United Nations.[86]

During the time wasted by such unnecessary niggling, other developments compelled Nehru to revise his position. Towards the end of 1952, there had been talk of Pakistan joining a Middle East Defence Organization (MEDO), sponsored by the United States. From the viewpoint of the Western Powers themselves, such an organization in West Asia seemed to Nehru ill-advised.

> As far as I can see, the position of the United States and the United Kingdom has tremendously deteriorated there from the political point of view. The result is that they rely more and more on the military aspect. That is a bad foundation to build upon in distant countries.

But India was particularly concerned with the possible inclusion of Pakistan and Nehru recognized that, though the Western Powers would not take such a step casually, it could not be ruled out. 'India counts for them and they will not easily adopt such a policy. But if military opinion is dominant, they might very well override political considerations.'[87]

---

[84] To Mahomed Ali, 3 September 1953.
[85] Nehru to M. S. Mehta, 28 August 1953.
[86] Letters of Mahomed Ali to Nehru, 27 August, 5 September and 31 October 1953.
[87] Nehru's note, 25 November 1952.

Acheson assured India that though some thought had been given to the extent to which Pakistan could participate, no approach had been made to her.[88] Nehru was convinced, despite this assurance, that Pakistan had discussed with the United States her participation in any such military association;[89] but he decided not to show great concern.[90] When Dulles came to Delhi in May 1953, he told Nehru that MEDO, a conception of the British, had little current relevance. While the United States would like some form of defence organization in this area, she would prefer the initiative to come from the Arab countries rather than impose a defence system on them.[91] Nehru made no comment. But his indifference to American policy in this respect could not obviously continue if it involved Kashmir and dragged parts of that State into American military preparations. Considering his objection to an American even as a plebiscite administrator, it could be expected that he would react sharply to a military alliance between the United States and Pakistan. He hinted almost from the start that Mahomed Ali's Government would have to make the choice between a fair chance of acquiring the Kashmir Valley after an impartial plebiscite and closer military partnership with the United States. 'While the interests of the people of Kashmir are paramount, there are also certain national interests of India and Pakistan which come into conflict over this Kashmir affair.'[92] Then, on 10 November, he wrote a personal letter to Mahomed Ali — 'I would have hesitated to write it to anyone else but you' — stating frankly his fears about Pakistan's policies. The decision of the Pakistan Constituent Assembly to convert their state into an Islamic republic was a contradiction of the Prime Ministers' Agreement of 1950 and the assurances then given by Liaqat Ali Khan. Apart from weakening the minorities in Pakistan by converting them virtually into second-class citizens, this would come seriously in the way of restoring normality and friendliness between the two countries. The other matter 'of the gravest importance' was the seemingly imminent military alliance with the United States.

> Again, it is not for us in India to come in the way of Pakistan's foreign or internal policy. But, when we are affected by it powerfully, we cannot ignore it . . . If such an alliance takes place, Pakistan enters definitely into the region of cold war. That means to us that the cold war has come to the very frontiers of India. It means also that, if real war comes, this also reaches the frontiers of India. This is a matter of serious consequence to us, who have been trying to build up an area of peace where there would be no war whatever happens elsewhere. It

[88] G. L. Mehta to Foreign Secretary, 15 January 1953.
[89] Letter to Krishna Menon, 14 February 1953.
[90] Note, 13 March 1953; letter to G. L. Mehta, 14 March 1953.
[91] Nehru's note on interview with Dulles, 22 May 1953.
[92] To Mahomed Ali, 3 September 1953.

must also be a matter of grave consequence to us, you will appreciate, if vast armies are built up in Pakistan with the aid of American money . . . All our problems will have to be seen in a new light.[93]

It can, of course, be argued that this was an excuse trumped up by Nehru to ensure an escape from his commitment to a plebiscite in Kashmir. But the evidence suggests that his offer to Mahomed Ali had been genuine and would have held if the prospect of a military alliance between Pakistan and the United States had not impinged on it. Nehru disliked such an alliance not so much because it would increase the armed strength of Pakistan as because the United States appeared to regard it as a means of extending the cold war and weakening the policy and security of India. One reason for the alliance with Pakistan was the pressure it would bring to bear on India and perhaps compel a revision of policy. The United States throughout made it clear that if India sought military assistance of the same kind it would be promptly provided. The makers of policy at Washington must, of course, have known that any such reversal of Nehru's attitude was highly unlikely and, therefore, probably relied more on the counter-effects of their decision to arm Pakistan. It looked as if the United States, resenting India's refusal to be a subordinate partner and her plans to develop into an independent centre of power, was seeking to contain India by building up Pakistan.[94]

In effect Pakistan becomes practically a colony of the United States . . . The United States imagine that by this policy they have completely outflanked India's so-called neutralism and will thus bring India to her knees. Whatever the future may hold, this is not going to happen. The first result of all this will be an extreme dislike of the United States in India. As it is, our relations are cool.[95]

The American Ambassador was, on Nehru's instructions, sent for and warned of the repercussions of any such alliance on India's relations with both Pakistan and the United States. Nehru told U Nu of Burma that, with this general attack on the concert of non-aligned countries, it had become all the more incumbent on these countries to hold together. 'This is not only practical politics but is the only way to save our real freedom and, if I may say so, our soul.'[96] Asian countries, lacking power and prestige, would be even more subservient than the countries of Europe to any dominant power providing military assistance, with the consequence of not only entanglement in case of war but the loss of freedom in peace. India's envoys in other countries were ordered to bring to the notice of governments at

[93] To Mahomed Ali, 10 November 1953.
[94] For an elaboration of this argument, particularly for an even later period, see B. R. Nayar, *American Geopolitics and India* (Delhi, 1976).
[95] To K. M. Panikkar, 12 November 1953.
[96] 11 November 1953.

the highest level what seemed to Nehru a reversal of the process of the liberation of Asia, and to create, if not a world opinion on this subject, at any rate an Asian opinion which might influence, if not Pakistan, at least the United States.[97] In the hope that this might yet lead to a revision of the decision, Nehru directed the Kashmir Government to continue to work on the assumption that a plebiscite administrator would be selected.[98]

The American Ambassador denied all knowledge of a military alliance with Pakistan and added that the advantages would be so greatly outweighed by the hostility it would create in India and Afghanistan that the United States would hardly be likely to contemplate such a step.[99] But the State Department acknowledged that military thinking was now focused on Pakistan,[100] and Dulles was so obsessed with anti-communism that he was in no mood to listen to India. He informed Nehru that the disparity in population and area between India and Pakistan ruled out any reasonable possibility of Pakistan exploiting American assistance to menace India, and the United States could not indefinitely postpone the military strengthening of a vital area because India and Pakistan were not on friendly terms.[101] The Pakistan Government were less honest and both publicly and in private denied that any such pact was being negotiated. There had been some exploratory discussions, but the matter was still being deliberated and was nowhere near conclusion.[102] Pakistan did not share India's views about communist infiltration and regarded India's China policy as a dangerous one; but nothing would be settled with the United States without Nehru's knowledge. Ghulam Mahomed offered to visit Delhi for this purpose. He added that if a military alliance were concluded, Pakistan would be willing to sign an agreement that equipment received would not be used against India, to issue a no-war declaration and to consider joint defence arrangements.[103]

These assurances could hardly have satisfied Nehru, who saw in the alliance both an immediate and a long-term threat. Free military aid to Pakistan could not but affect that country's relations with India. 'I agree with you that we are in danger of losing all the ground we have so far gained. But I would like you to consider who is to blame for this.' It seemed unimportant that the United States intended to sign no formal alliance or acquire any bases in Pakistan. Free military aid was as good as a military alliance, and bases could be set up within a day or so when the need arose.

[97] See Nehru's notes to N. R. Pillai, Secretary-General, 14 and 27 November 1953.

[98] To Bakshi Ghulam Mahomed, 12 November 1953.

[99] Report of N. R. Pillai, Secretary-General, on conversation with American Ambassador, 16 November 1953.

[100] Report of minister, Embassy of India, Washington, on conversation with Byroade, Assistant Secretary, State Department, 5 November 1953.

[101] G. L. Mehta's telegram, 16 November 1953.

[102] Statements of Mahomed Ali and Ghulam Mahomed; Mahomed Ali to Nehru, 9 and 17 December 1953.

[103] M. S. Mehta's telegram reporting conversation with Ghulam Mahomed, 11 December 1953.

Nor was the quantity of such aid of much relevance, for what concerned him was the qualitative change which he thought would occur. Pakistan was lining up with one of the parties in the cold war, and thus changing the whole context of her relations with India. 'Behind Pakistan would stand a great and powerful country, the U.S.A. In fact the giving of military aid to Pakistan was an unfriendly act to India.' But there were also broader issues.

> We, in India, have endeavoured to follow a foreign policy which we feel is not only in the interests of world peace but is particularly indicated for the countries of Asia. That policy is an independent one and of non-alignment with any power bloc. It is clear that the policy which Pakistan intends to pursue is different. It is one of alignment with one group of nations and, in particular, of close military association with one great nation . . . If our approaches are so different, the ends we strive for or that are likely to take shape, are bound to be different. It is not enough to talk of peace; one has to shape one's policy to that end. Otherwise we go straight to the atomic bomb and all its progeny.

So he urged Mahomed Ali to consider these matters from the wider point of view, not only of relations between the two countries but of the future of Asia and of the world.[104]

It was, however, by now too late to prevent the conclusion of this military alliance. Mahomed Ali persisted in his assertion that this had nothing to do with friendly relations between India and Pakistan,[105] although he announced publicly that with equality of military strength there would be a greater chance of a settlement on Kashmir.[106] The State Department took the line that India's public denunciation of any such agreement had made it impossible for the United States to reconsider the position. Congress would regard it as a complete surrender to India, Mahomed Ali's government would be overthrown, and no country in West and South Asia would ever come forward again with an offer of friendship with the United States.[107] 'General indication', Nehru cabled to Krishna Menon, 'appears to be to give every help to Pakistan and to take tough line with Delhi. Fact of India getting stronger in South Asia not favoured as coming in way of American policy.'[108] But efforts were made, both by Eisenhower in a personal communication and by St Laurent, the Prime Minister of Canada, on a visit to Delhi,[109] to render the alliance with Pakistan more acceptable to Nehru.

[104] Nehru to Mahomed Ali, 12 and 21 December 1953.
[105] Mahomed Ali to Nehru, 14 January 1954.
[106] Interview in *U.S. News and World Report*, 15 January 1954.
[107] G. L. Mehta's telegram from Washington reporting a conversation with Byroade, Assistant Secretary, State Department, 28 January 1954.
[108] 11 December 1953.
[109] D. C. Thomson, *Louis St Laurent: Canadian* (Toronto, 1967), pp. 360-1.

These efforts failed. Nehru had now no doubt that the United States was following an imperialist policy, not in the normal sense of conquering a weaker country, but in that she was seeking to force the countries of Asia to conform to her own attitudes. In resisting this, India would have not only to reject offers of military aid and denounce its granting to other nations, but also consider the refusal of economic assistance. Without going out of his way to announce that India would not accept such assistance, Nehru ordered budgeting on the basis that it might not be available.[110] The occasion could also be utilized to press forward with developmental programmes and harness the public emotion which had been aroused for constructive work rather than spend it in demonstrations of feeling against Pakistan and the United States. Attempts to expand the defence services and buy equipment elsewhere, in competition with the United States, would be futile and serve only to weaken the nation. He rejected Krishna Menon's suggestion of a radar screen along the whole border with West Pakistan as being beyond India's financial and technological capacity.[111] Even the decision to demobilize 10,000 men each year for the next five years was, after consideration, not reversed.[112] But what could be done was to improve and tighten the existing defence forces and establishments and expedite the completion of sanctioned projects. 'A country's defence potential is, if I may put it in some kind of equation, defence apparatus plus industrial growth plus economy of the country plus morale.'[113] The long-term policy should be to promote basic industrial strength and go ahead with indigenous tank and aircraft production even if not of the latest models; but to counter the immediate danger of sophisticated weapons in Pakistan's control, purchase of foreign aircraft could not be avoided. Nehru directed his officials to begin their inquiries in Britain and Europe, in line with the existing defence system and training in India; the United States should be avoided for the time being. 'As for the U.S.S.R., we should proceed very cautiously and let it be known privately that we are prepared to consider suitable offers provided they fit in with our requirements.'[114] There had been the previous year the first formal indication of a change in the Soviet attitude towards India when India's role in the Korean negotiations had been acknowledged;[115] and a trade agreement had been signed in December 1953, at a time when Vice-President Nixon was on a visit to Delhi. Nehru thought this could be followed up by suggestions of possible purchase of military equipment.

The announcement of the military alliance further stiffened India's

[110] To T. T. Krishnamachari, Commerce Minister, 25 January 1954.
[111] Krishna Menon's note, 27 February and Nehru's reply, 12 March 1954.
[112] Nehru's note, 14 March 1954.
[113] Nehru's address to Congress members of the Mysore Assembly, 4 January 1954.
[114] Note, 21 February 1954.
[115] Malenkov's speech in August 1953. H. Kapur, *The Soviet Union and the Emerging Nations* (London, 1972), p. 43.

attitude towards both Pakistan and the United States. Though earlier Nehru had rebuked the Kashmir Government for certain decisions in the Kashmir constituent assembly which ignored India's international commitments,[116] he now informed Mahomed Ali that the whole context of the Kashmir issue had been changed and India had perforce to resist what was clearly an attempt to settle the matter by force of superior American arms. All earlier agreements had become irrelevant and India could now take no risks with the quantum of forces in the State. The decisions of the Kashmir constituent assembly had nothing to do with this and were fully valid in their setting.[117] Hammarskjöld was informally requested to remove American members of the United Nations observer team in Kashmir.[118] When the Secretary-General protested that once a person had been selected for United Nations work his nationality was of no concern, Nehru retorted that all facilities would be denied to Americans in United Nations service in Kashmir.

> To give military aid to one party to a conflict and when armies stand on either side of the cease-fire line is obviously a breach of neutrality. No person coming from that country can be considered as disinterested or impartial by us. The argument that United States officers are functioning not as United States nationals but on behalf of the United Nations is flimsy in the extreme. In any event, these persons are persona non grata and even as such they have to be removed.[119]

Ultimately Hammarskjöld agreed to replace them when their terms lapsed at the end of the year.

It was not, however, only the alliance with Pakistan that sullied India's relations with the United States. The approach to world affairs of that country under the guidance of Dulles was squarely in confrontation with that of Nehru. Men like Chiang and Rhee, who to Nehru symbolized the most decadent aspects of Asia, were regarded by Dulles as modern-day equivalents of the founders of the Church.[120] While recognizing that the United States was not a committed foe of India, Nehru allowed his antipathy to its activities abroad to colour his general attitude towards the United States. 'I dislike more and more this business of exchange of persons between America and India. The fewer persons that go from India to America or that come from the United States to India, the better.'[121] Americans in India produced an impression of having partly taken charge of many activities which were normally the responsibility of the govern-

[116] To Bakshi Ghulam Mahomed, 14 February 1954.
[117] To Mahomed Ali, 5 March 1954.
[118] Nehru's telegram to Krishna Menon, 4 March 1954.
[119] Nehru's telegram to Indian Mission at the United Nations, 6 March 1954.
[120] T. Hoopes, *The Devil and John Foster Dulles* (London, 1974), p. 78.
[121] Nehru's note, 6 May 1953.

ment.[122] 'We have had quite enough of American superiority.' Americans carried their politics and their peculiar outlook on the world wherever they went, and these were becoming more and more irritating.[123] But there was no blind, romanticist idealism about his assessment of the Soviet Union and China. He did not assume that these two countries were peace-loving friends of India. He knew that the attitude of China, in particular, lacked warmth and cordiality, that India's support for China was being played down and her friendship was being exploited without any commitment. Even on Kashmir China, unlike the Soviet Union, took no position, and Pakistan's alliance with the United States led to no change in this neutrality. 'In the final analysis', Nehru wrote in a letter which was manifestly intended for the Burmese Prime Minister, U Nu, 'no country has any deep faith in the policies of another country, more especially in regard to a country which tends to expand. Obviously we cannot be dead sure of what China may do in the future.'[124] No country, he reminded his own officials, 'can ultimately rely upon the permanent goodwill or bonafides of another country, even though they might be in close friendship with each other.' Both the Soviet Union and China pursued long-term expansive policies, and communism was only a tool for the purpose. Chinese expansionism had been evident during various periods for about a thousand years, and a new period of such expansionism was perhaps imminent. 'Let us consider that and fashion our policy to prevent it coming in the way of our interests or other interests that we consider important.'[125] But at this particular time, for reasons of their own, the two Communist Powers seemed eager for peace while the United States appeared to be willing to wage war and, particularly in Asia, was busy concerting a holy alliance to protect feudal reaction. After she had carried out a nuclear test in the Pacific, Winston Churchill wrote to Nehru about his intense concern.

> I am sure that you will share my feelings of anxiety on the momentous issue involved. We are indeed at a turning-point in the world's history and very grave responsibility rests on those of us in authority. I wish that at this moment it had been possible for us all to take counsel together — as we did at the time of the Coronation. I am devoting my mind as to how best any words of mine can help, conscious as I am of all that is involved for the future of mankind.

Nehru replied promptly, suggesting an immediate standstill agreement on nuclear explosions and welcoming a conference of Prime Ministers.[126] But

[122] Nehru to Deshmukh, 7 May 1953.
[123] Nehru to Amrit Kaur, 30 August 1953.
[124] Letter to Indian Ambassador in Rangoon, 9 May 1954.
[125] Note, 18 June 1954.
[126] Churchill to Nehru, 4 April 1954, and Nehru's reply of same date.

Churchill's speech in Parliament the next day did not accord with his moving message. He now contended that the American test had increased the chances of world peace;[127] and a week later he wrote to Nehru that there was no need for a meeting of the Commonwealth Prime Ministers.[128]

Nehru attributed Churchill's change of attitude to the pressure of the United States, and it therefore appeared all the more important to him that India should continue to oppose publicly the policy of the United States and muster as much support for this as possible. However averse the Soviet Union and China might be to war at this stage, they could not totally surrender; and Dulles appeared willing to consider the alternative of a major conflict. Indeed, the United States was forcing the issue politically and militarily in Indo-China.

> Asia has been and will continue to be the scene of hydrogen bomb experiments and of war in which Asians are made to fight Asians. It may be that it will be Asians again who will have the unfortunate privilege of experiencing the effects of atomic bombing.[129]

But to most other people mutual adjustment between the two blocs appeared indispensable; and this could only come from the initiative of a third power. 'Between these rival giants and their loud trumpeting, there is the small and perhaps feeble voice of India.'[130] So, even though he had earlier not favoured the proposal for a conference of a few Asian Prime Ministers, he went to Colombo for such a meeting in April. Mahomed Ali of Pakistan took a strident line in support of the United States and spoke, as Nehru was reported to have said, as the 'voice of America'.[131] Even U Nu, irritated by Chinese support for Burmese communist parties and regional separatist movements, was inclined to lean towards the United States. But Nehru was determined to secure a unanimous resolution on Indo-China which could be considered to represent an Asian, as against an American, European or communist viewpoint. He won over U Nu by requesting China to give satisfactory assurances to Burma[132] and, by drafting the resolution in such a way as not to imply criticism of Pakistan's new association with the United States, obtained unanimous backing for a resolution urging that Indo-China be allowed to settle its own future without intervention by the Great Powers.

Armed with this resolution, Krishna Menon set off for Geneva. In the course of about three weeks he had about 200 interviews, each lasting nearly two hours, with the various heads of delegations. He had no specific

[127] Hansard 1953-54, Vol. 526, p. 44.
[128] Churchill to Nehru, 10 April 1954.
[129] To Chief Ministers, 14 April 1954.
[130] To Chief Ministers, 26 April 1954.
[131] M. O. Mathai's report of Krishna Menon's account of the Colombo conference, 3 May 1954.
[132] Nehru's telegram to N. Raghavan, Ambassador in Peking, 8 May 1954.

proposals to present but informed the principal parties of the views and interests of India and the other members of the Colombo conference in this matter; and the fact that, apart from China and the Indo-China states, no Asian country was represented at Geneva, enhanced the importance of Menon's presence. He was, from all accounts, also able, by talking to the various leaders informally and ignoring the rigidities of conference procedure, to help in smoothing over minor issues of difference. Britain and the Soviet Union were keen on a settlement while the United States stood angrily aloof and China appeared edgy. Menon, representing a country with no formal standing at the conference, suggested possible ways of meeting such objections as were raised. 'Opinion at Geneva has converged on India.'[133] After long and separate discussions with Eden, Chou and Molotov, he contrived agreement on Laos and Cambodia. The decision to withdraw all foreign troops from these two states marked the successful conclusion of the first phase of the Geneva conference.

Never had India's — and Nehru's — reputation stood higher in the world. Menon's assiduous efforts could succeed only because of the unchallenged integrity and commitment of his Prime Minister and government. Nehru's sustained endeavour in the face of discouragement to control the development of nuclear weapons, his courageous and out-spoken resistance to United States policy and his achievement in holding together the South Asian governments in support of his views on Indo-China ensured for him a commanding stature in world politics. In India, Nehru's dedication to democratic principle and method was beyond doubt. The unquestioned leader of the Indian people, he was keenly conscious of the urgency of progress, yet willing to slow down the pace rather than ride rough-shod over resistance and incomprehension. The mere fact of continuous progress on a stable basis would be a triumph for democratic functioning on such a vast scale. There was danger in moving slowly; but it was equally dangerous to try and move faster than circumstances and resources permitted. To Krishna Menon this appeared basically unsound and likely to lead to subservience to foreign powers; but Nehru was not shaken. 'The advice you have often given me is not precise and you seem to indicate that the only worthwhile thing to do is to reverse engines completely. It is not even clear to me how this is to be done.' The human factor was important in India and, in guiding events in one direction, he had to carry people with him.[134] 'I have been convinced', he wrote to his party henchmen

> of the high importance of the Congress functioning today, carrying on its work of unifying and integrating India, laying stress on peaceful and cooperative methods, and carrying our people along the line of

[133] Krishna Menon's telegram to Nehru from Geneva, 23 May 1954.
[134] Krishna Menon to Nehru, 12 April, and Nehru's reply, 24 April 1953.

15   A morning ride, 1953

16   Driving a tractor, 1951

17   With Nasser in Cairo, June 1953

18   With U Nu and a Naga chief, March 1953

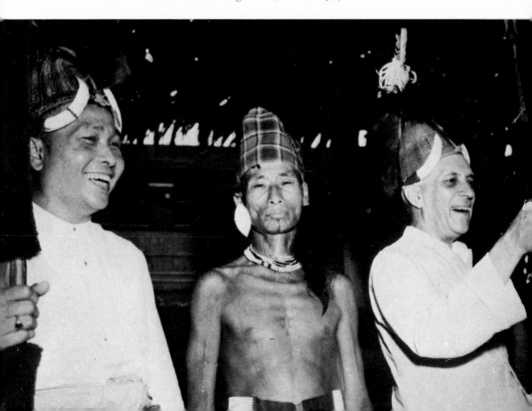

progress. We are not a sectarian body consisting of the elect. We are fellow-travellers with the people of India.[135]

He had laid, in a vast and diffuse country, the foundations of representative government and, at a time when the United States was bolstering petty dictators all over the Asian continent, shown that a poor, battered, ill-educated people could operate a sophisticated process of democratic rule. Nehru himself stood forth, in all his majesty, in Parliament and lent the power of his name to building up the prestige of that institution.

All that is happening in Asia throws a spotlight on the Indian Federal Parliament at Delhi as the one institution of the kind which is working in an exemplary way. Pericles said that Athens was the school of Hellas; Mr Nehru, without boasting, may say that Delhi is the school of Asia.[136]

This participation of the Indian people in politics provided a stimulus to effort in other fields. There was a growing sense of confidence in the air, and pride at India's expanding role in the world was matched by a feeling of domestic achievement. The total production of cereals in 1953-4 was three million tons higher than the target that had been fixed for 1955-6. This had enabled the government to abolish all controls on foodgrains. The massive Bhakra-Nangal Dam had been completed and other such multi-purpose projects, the temples, in Nehru's phrase, of the new India, were making progress. There was clearly still much to be done. As Nehru put it in human terms,

I travel about a great deal in India and see vast crowds of people. They are friendly crowds and they give me a feeling of basic strength. And yet the sight of a child or a boy or a girl without adequate food or clothing or house to live in always produces a sense of shock in me as well as a sense of shame. I compare my own comfort and well-being with the lot of that child of India who is our responsibility.[137]

The first results of planning were only just beginning to come in, land reforms had far to go and unemployment was widespread. The basic problem of poverty had been hardly touched and the growing population was beginning to cause concern. The change in the social climate, so necessary if India was to rise to her full stature, was not as yet marked. Yet to most Indians progress, however slow, did not seem to be blocked; and of this itself exhilaration was born. It was the vision that Nehru gave his

---

[135] Nehru to Presidents of Pradesh Congress Committees, 30 May 1954.
[136] *Manchester Guardian*, 26 May 1954.
[137] To Chief Ministers, 6 November 1953.

people, the prospect that seemed not too remote of *les lendemains qui chantent*, that was perhaps his greatest achievement in these years.

Strong on his home ground, Nehru could adopt firm attitudes abroad. His policy was backed by a moral strength which was independent of economic primacy and which even criticisms of his Kashmir policy could not seriously tarnish. Many, of course, disliked his growing influence.

> There is a great deal of resentment and even jealousy at the part India, almost against her will, is playing in world affairs. There are plenty of intrigues going on to create trouble for us just to show us that we are not so big as we imagine.[138]

Yet to demand that no step be taken towards war, that Asia be left to mind its own affairs and that Africa be rid of racism — and to suggest all these in practical, constructive terms — was to enlist widespread support outside India. His aid was sought by Sir Anthony Eden at Geneva and his policies were taken over by the Opposition in Britain. 'At the moment Labour's attitude to the Indian Prime Minister falls little short of canonization. Most Labour questions to Sir Winston implied that he should not move a step in Asia without Mr Nehru's approval.'[139] Even in the United States, outside the government, Nehru had an audience that could not be ignored.

Not surprisingly, therefore, in the summer of 1954 Chou En-lai planned a visit to Delhi on his way from Geneva to Peking. The support of India was at this time obviously worth cultivating. Krishna Menon was already on his side. Chou, reported Menon to Nehru after their meetings at Geneva,

> is a fine and I believe a great and able man. I do not believe that the Chinese have expansionist ideas . . . I found little difficulty in getting near him. He was never evasive with me even on difficult matters after the second day. He is extremely shrewd and observant, very Chinese but modern.[140]

But it was Nehru that mattered, and Chou well knew that Nehru's stronger sense of realism about China's policy had not faded. The agreement on Tibet had not given Nehru a sense of complete satisfaction; and the frequent double-tracking by China on the Korean question was of recent memory. So Chou set out to talk directly to Nehru and win him over. He referred repeatedly to India being industrially and economically ahead of China and asserted that he was anxious for peaceful conditions and for the countries of Asia to advance. He agreed with Nehru that South East Asia

[138] To B. G. Kher, 5 November 1953.
[139] *The Economist*, 1 May 1954.
[140] Menon's telegram from New York, 21 June 1954.

should be developed into 'an area of peace', asked him to arrange a meeting with U Nu and sought Nehru's assistance in improving China's relations with Indonesia. He hardly mentioned communism or the Soviet Union or European politics, and requested that India should remain in the Commonwealth because it was good for India and the world. 'That remark of his', commented Nehru later, 'shows his realistic appreciation of the situation which many of our own people have not fully grasped yet, because they live in a world of out-of-date slogans and have little understanding of today.'[141] Above all, a clever flatterer, Chou concealed his personality and sought Nehru's advice on all matters.

> Your Excellency has more knowledge about the world and Asia than I have. I am not being modest. Your Excellency has participated much more in international affairs than I have. We have been shut up in our own country dealing with our own human problems.

Nehru was not immune to such deference. He was aware that this could be smart tactics, but did not think it was. 'He strikes one as a frank and forthright person, which is rather unusual in the average Communist leader. He speaks with some authority and is receptive to ideas.'[142] The result was that the element of uneasiness in Nehru's attitude to China was much weakened. Even Chou's reference to the border, that although it was long and not fully demarcated the two peoples alongside it had been living in complete amity, did not revive his earlier concern. He realized that this would give rise to misunderstanding and secured Chou's consent to omitting any such sentence from the joint communiqué. But he was lulled into ignoring the dangerous possibilities in the long term of such an attitude on the part of China.

To Nehru the question of cooperation or conflict between India and China, on which depended the future of Asia, did not now need to be answered fully one way or the other. For a third alternative had emerged, of containment of China through friendship. It was not just a matter of believing that China would abide by the Five Principles which she had accepted. An environment should be created in which China would find it difficult to break her word. Such an effort would be possible only if China came at least half-way, and this China now seemed to Nehru to have done.

[141] Nehru to Chief Ministers, 1 July 1954.
[142] Nehru to U Nu, 27 June 1954.

10

The Fine Art of Government

ONE

Nehru was human enough to enjoy the prestige which he commanded abroad. Many of his fellow-countrymen with sufficient awareness to appreciate the trends of international events also basked in India's dazzling, even unnatural, ascendancy in world affairs. But it was within the country that the real problems lay, and these were more intractable and less responsive to reason and argument than the issues in foreign affairs. Not that the great powers were willing to be talked into a more peaceful state; but as India was as yet not directly involved in these major rivalries, what to some seemed mere attitudinizing on Nehru's part in itself took shape as a policy and influenced opinion in many parts of the world. But in India mere influence and commitment to a respected line were no longer enough. Such success as there had been in creating an atmosphere for progress meant that it was now time for hard decision-making at all levels. Objectives had to be formulated more precisely, the area of popular participation had to be carefully extended, national fusion had to be ensured, and government by consensus sensitively tended. Nehru realized that these were matters of the first priority. By the mid-fifties, he would have happily given these problems all his attention and allowed the world to look after itself without his assiduous nursing. It is one of the myths of recent history that Nehru, and the Indians who shared his thinking, concentrated on foreign affairs to the detriment of their country's domestic demands. But certainly the achievements on this plane were less spectacular. In some cases, while policies were clear, their implementation was erratic; in a few others, the proper solutions evaded his grasp. Neither was his own handling of men at other levels than control of the crowds wholly to his satisfaction. To Nehru democratic government was a fine art, the achievement of a cooperation within a series of widening circles which gave a sense of participation to everyone involved. He exploited his personal dominance to secure, as he hoped, its own destruction. It was a magnificent effort which did not quite come off.

TWO

The reorientation of Nehru's thinking on economic and social matters, brought about by the election campaign and results of 1952, was clearly reflected in his directive to the planning commission, written within a week of his forming a new ministry. The first Five Year Plan had been an exciting venture, if only because of its pioneering quality; but it was mainly a preparatory effort, a collection of projects giving a general indication of priorities. It could be taken no further for lack of information. Even the drawing up of this Plan was indispensable work, the best work, in Nehru's opinion, done by the central government during the four years of its free existence.[1] At the meeting of the planning commission to discuss the various drafts, there had been 'electricity in the air'.[2] But within two years of its formulation, the purpose of the first Plan had been served, and more positive, determined action was now required. Even after five years of freedom, India appeared more or less static. The central and state authorities were on the defensive and seeking to do no more than avoid the blows of untoward happenings. 'We cannot go ahead because of circumstances and circumstances will not change until we go ahead.' Dependence on foreign assistance, apart from its political disadvantages, encouraged this lack of self-reliance and confident effort. Production was to Nehru no longer all that mattered; consumption and purchasing power also demanded attention. Indeed, if they declined, production would slow down as well. The main aim should be the increase of both production and purchasing power — and this should be the purchasing power of not merely a handful of the rich but of large numbers of the relatively poor. Widespread development in production, providing employment for many, was the chief requirement; and budgetary and financial restrictions which stood in the way should be surmounted by an unorthodox, New Deal approach.

> In war one takes great risks, because one must and there is no other way. One lives on the next generation. In any productive drive on a large scale in peace-time, however, we are building up wealth and not destroying it as in war. Therefore, we are not really living on the future. Such a risk is far less than the risks involved in war-time and far more profitable. The situation we have to face is, in a sense, as serious as any war situation and we should look upon it, therefore, from a special point of view and not allow ourselves to remain in very orthodox, set grooves of thought.

Large-scale productive works spread out all over the country would, above

---

[1] Speech at Ahmedabad, 24 December, *National Herald*, 25 December 1951.
[2] Nehru's address at meeting of planning commission, 27 May 1955.

all else, create a new atmosphere of aggressive and forward action in place of timid defence. No doubt there was some risk in this policy, but probably the greatest risk was an over-cautious approach to these major problems. A certain boldness in outlook had become essential.[3] The government should plan for bringing about, in an orderly and democratic manner, large changes which would result in greater production and equality of opportunity. They should go all out to prepare the people for these changes and then proceed as fast as the people could be carried along.[4]

To the planning commission, immersed in the immediate problems of existing commitments and paucity of resources, such a wide-ranging survey of future policy seemed wholly unreal. The burden of day-to-day management of even the first Five Year Plan had brought the commission to 'a stage of something approaching mental disintegration. How to provide for a number of more excellent and important schemes with the resources at their disposal? Arithmetic does not help and magic is not available.'[5] In fact, the effort, which Nehru had seen as the basis of the first Plan, to bring the whole picture of India's future — agricultural, industrial, social and economic — into a single framework of thought and action,[6] went awry. Kidwai at the centre and Rajagopalachari in Madras acted on their own and spoke publicly in favour of progressive removal of controls on the prices and movement of foodgrains. Krishnamachari, the Commerce Minister, by threatening resignation, overcame Nehru's disapproval of his encouragement of foreign firms and stifled any revival of the old *swadeshi* urge.[7] During the five years of the first Plan, there was, despite Nehru, progressive liberalization of foreign imports. Irritated by the political hindrances to the technical implementation of the Plan, Deshmukh, the Finance Minister, offered repeatedly to relinquish office. Nehru dissuaded him but did not discipline the central and state governments. Moreover, though chairman of the planning commission, he knew little of what it was doing.

> I am almost completely out of touch. Occasionally some paper may come to me. But the real job of planning is to think and discuss vital matters. Either this is done without my knowledge or this is not done at all, because I have no information about it.[8]

The fault was not the planning commission's; the fact was that Nehru's interest now lay mostly elsewhere. At this time he was looking not to the

[3] Nehru's note to planning commission, 16 May 1952.
[4] Nehru to Chief Ministers, 20 June 1952.
[5] Nehru to Morarji Desai, 3 August 1952.
[6] 15 December 1952, Lok Sabha Debates 1952, Vol. VI, Part II, pp. 2367-81.
[7] Nehru to T. T. Krishnamachari, 29 September and 3 October 1952, and 5 March and 26 August 1953.
[8] To V. T. Krishnamachari, deputy chairman, planning commission, 2 August 1953.

large projects, which were the heart of the Plan, but to small schemes, cottage industries and community development, for the increase of production and purchasing power which seemed to him so important. He was no longer fascinated by huge multi-purpose dams, for social welfare had become to him of as high a priority as economic progress. A sight of the hovels in which the workers of Kanpur lived caused him such intensive shame that he developed a sort of fever. 'I have no need for any industrialization which degrades a human being and sullies his honour.'[9] Besides urban housing, there were the problems in the rural areas of not just habitation, but sanitation, water supply and lighting. 'We might not be able to change the face of India quickly but we should proceed about it with some speed.'[10]

All specific schemes for improving living conditions in the countryside and providing the ordinary peasant with an interest in the future were soon included in Nehru's mind in the need for integrated development of the village communities, with the active assistance of the local inhabitants. This would encourage growth from the bottom and enable the ordinary villager to a certain extent to govern his own destiny. The initiative had to be given to the people and they had to be vested with a sense of partnership and purpose. Backwardness was not an attribute of a few sections of Indian society; basically ninety-six per cent of the Indian people were backward, but they had all to be involved in the building of a new India, and a measure of equality in opportunity and fulfilment progressively produced.[11] Nilokheri, a township in the Punjab created by cooperative effort for the settlement of refugees, which Nehru thought was 'the brightest example of rehabilitation that I have seen anywhere',[12] served as the model for community centres to be set up all over the country. The object was to encourage the villagers to participate and even take the lead in all aspects of rural development. The inauguration on 2 October 1952 of fifty-five community projects, covering about 17,000 villages, offered to him the promise of the small beginning of something big. 'That idea is to change the whole face of rural India and to raise the level of the vast majority of our population.'[13] In the same vein he suggested, only half in banter, that it would be a good thing if the planning commission or part of it lived in village surroundings.[14]

In 1953, as a development of the community projects programme, the

[9] Speech to the Federation of Indian Chambers of Commerce and Industry, 29 March, *National Herald*, 30 March 1952.

[10] Nehru to Chief Ministers, 16 March 1952.

[11] Nehru's speech at conference of development commissioners, May 1952, and talk to the first set of community project officers, August 1952. *Jawaharlal Nehru on Community Development, Panchayati Raj and Co-operation* (Delhi, 1965), pp. 2-3 and 12.

[12] 2 March 1950, Parliamentary Debates, Vol. 1, Part I, 1950, pp. 586-8.

[13] Nehru to Chief Ministers, 2 October 1952.

[14] To V. T. Krishnamachari, 2 August 1953.

national extension service, whose purpose was to provide trained workers, was formulated. This service was intended to lay the broad foundation over the whole country for the community projects. Nehru saw in these twin programmes the possibility of a great revolutionary change carried out peacefully and without conflict.[15] As the two schemes proliferated, almost every part of India came within their reach, and by 1955 there was no gap of more than fifty miles between any two areas touched by either one or other of them. This rapid progress was even, in a way, a cause for alarm, lest the government should fail to keep pace with it, mainly for lack of trained personnel.[16]

THREE

Community projects and the national extension service were expected to form the base for the national edifice of 'a socialistic pattern of society' — the odd, half-hearted phrase adopted by the Congress at its session in January 1955. Nehru himself preferred straightforwardly to use the word 'socialist', and 'socialistic' soon dropped out of use. But the word had its advantage at the start, even if it was not coined by Nehru, in suggesting what he had in mind, that the country was accepting not a rigid or doctrinaire framework of ideology but certain methods of economic and social change. Rationality in long-term planning was to be taken seriously. The socialism to which Nehru committed India was, to adapt the definition of a modern philosopher, not so much a certain desirable set of social relations as a way of solving social problems.[17] The goals were clear enough to Nehru soon after the elections and within two years of initiating the first Plan.

> I will not rest content unless every man, woman and child in this country has a fair deal and attains a minimum standard of living . . . Five or six years is too short a time for judging a nation. Wait for another ten years and you will see that our plans will change the picture of the country so completely that the world will be amazed.[18]

To move towards this, the second Plan would have to be qualitatively different from the first. That had been a relatively easy ride, beginning at a slow pace, gradually gathering speed and finishing at a good canter. Its very success had brough the country not only to a promising stage of growth but also to a much more difficult one. So the second Plan would have to

---

[15] Nehru to Chief Ministers, 27 September 1953.
[16] Nehru to Chief Ministers, 15 April 1955.
[17] S. Hampshire in L. Kolakowski and S. Hampshire (ed.), *The Socialist Idea* (London, 1974), p. 43.
[18] Speech at Sholapur, 30 April, *National Herald*, 1 May 1953.

look far ahead and concern itself with structural changes in the country's economy and society. It should provide for rapid industrial development which would result by ten years in full employment and a society which gave priority to equality. Emphasis would be placed on the building of heavy industry for the production of capital goods as a base for a modern and strong country, and on the wide expansion of village industries for producing consumer goods as well as employment. If enough were produced to meet the growing needs of the community, deficit financing would not necessarily result in inflation.

The ways in which this socialism was to be made possible were very similar to those which Anthony Crosland formulated for Britain a year later.[19] India was striving to move ahead from a low stage of economic backwardness whereas Britain was an advanced capitalist society, and the programme was necessarily very different. But the approach which Nehru favoured was on the lines of British left-wing thinking. The ownership of industry was in itself unimportant, and nothing was gained by nationalizing existing industries solely in order to gain control. But it was important for the state to control the strategic points of production. The discussion on the relative merits of the public and private sectors — an issue on which T. T. Krishnamachari once again offered to resign — was unrealistic. There was no doubt that the public sector would grow and gradually dominate the scene. 'The argument that private enterprise is sacrosanct does not hold good in India today.'[20] But both sectors had their roles in increasing production within the broad limits of general control by the state, and could even help, by healthy rivalry, in keeping each other up to the mark. Indeed, the kind of socialism which Nehru had in mind would be more easily achieved in a mixed than in a wholly state-owned economy.

The second Plan involved vast investments and a considerable measure of foreign assistance; but it also required the training of a large personnel and a careful balance at various levels, and this demanded 'physical' planning rather than merely regard for financial considerations. It was 'this mighty problem', rather than foreign affairs and the 'unavoidable nuisance' of domestic politics, which now began to claim more and more of Nehru's attention. There was no comparable example elsewhere in the world to the task which India had set herself and the way in which she was proposing to deal with it. Indian planning had suddenly caught the imagination of the world. 'It is for us now to make good the anticipations that we have aroused and the promises we are making. It is an exciting prospect and an adventure worthy of this great country.'[21] It was much more than a matter of dry figures and statistics; it was a 'living, moving process, affecting hundreds of millions', which could succeed only by the combined and

[19] C. A. R. Crosland, *The Future of Socialism* (London, 1956).
[20] To S. S. Bhatnagar, 8 April 1952.
[21] Nehru to Chief Ministers, 13 January 1955.

cooperative efforts of all the Indian people.[22] The government and the planning commission should provide the lead — clear and single-minded, 'as it were, an arrow going straight from the bow'[23]; but the achievement could only be that of the ordinary man and woman.

As the first step towards this goal of a socialist pattern, Nehru formulated a new resolution on industrial policy, replacing that issued eight years earlier. The public sector would necessarily be dominant, with a complementary private sector organized on cooperative lines. For achieving rapid economic growth, industrialization, particularly the development of heavy and machine-making industries, would have to be speeded up. These industries, and the material on which they were dependent, would necessarily have to be in the public sector. So too would transport, public utilities, drugs and industries of strategic importance or requiring large investments. Even in areas which normally would be left to the private sector, it would be open to the state to develop any industry. There would also be a growing sphere of state trading. But such stress on the role of the state was, in a paradoxical sense, intended to assure private enterprise of the government's goodwill and promise it relatively free play in secondary fields which were not of vital national interest. As technology and monopoly had not in India reached the stage which endangered society as a whole, the steps necessary in Western countries to control monopoly capitalism were not as yet required in India. There was enough time for the public sector to grow both absolutely and relatively, and gradually secure control of the whole economy. Thus the economic foundations of a socialist society would be gradually laid and, without a major and immediate assault being mounted on private enterprise, steps would be initiated to reduce disparities in income and wealth, weaken private monopolies and disperse the concentration of economic power in the hands of a few individuals.[24] This appealed to Nehru as a realistic and yet a dynamic and even revolutionary programme. 'Our way has been to bring about changes as rapidly as possible and at the same time to keep up the continuity of national life and tradition.'[25]

The second Five Year Plan, seeking to give form and shape to the new resolution on industrial policy 'in as large a measure as our strength and resources and our will to success permit',[26] was published soon after. In agriculture, from both the economic and the social viewpoints, preference was given to cooperative farming as a replacement of the *zamindari* system and not to the only other alternative of state ownership. Indeed, with smallholdings, cooperative farming seemed inevitable. The Indian farmer,

[22] Nehru to Chief Ministers, 15 April 1955.
[23] Nehru's address at meeting of planning commission, 27 May 1955.
[24] Nehru to V. T. Krishnamachari, 1 April 1956; Government of India resolution on industrial policy, 30 April 1956.
[25] Nehru to Chief Ministers, 10 May 1956.
[26] Ibid.

though not well educated, seemed intelligent enough to be able to understand this arrangement if it were explained to him.

> I have not heard of the argument that we should not increase our railway system or even scrap the railways that we have, because the Indian farmer is used to the bullock-cart. We live in a different age and, indeed, even the age we live in is, perhaps, ending before long, to give place to yet another age, the atomic age. If we are not wide awake to these obvious facts, then we fail as a nation and as individuals.[27]

The life of the village should revolve round the multi-purpose cooperative, the *panchayat* and the school and foster local democracy and self-reliant growth. Cooperation was more than an economic technique; it was a means by which social change could be effected. Nehru recovered his old faith in cooperation and talked once again of the ultimate objective of a cooperative commonwealth.[28]

FOUR

The formal decision in 1955 to erect a socialist pattern of society had been preceded by a long-drawn-out effort by Nehru to reach an understanding with the Socialist Party; but the result was that relations became much worse than before. After the elections, Jayaprakash Narayan had accused Nehru of weakening the Socialist Party by claiming agreement with its leaders even while he emasculated the concept of socialism. Jayaprakash was worried, not so much by sneering references by Congressmen to the Socialists as Nehru's second eleven, as by what seemed to him Nehru's proneness to run down all forms of socialist thought and practice without elucidating his own ideas as to their true content.[29] Nehru replied that he had never said a word against socialism and had criticized the Socialist Party only with regard to its electoral alliances and its views on foreign policy. 'I do not pretend to be a socialist in any formal sense of the word but surely socialism is not the monopoly of any particular group.'[30] Moreover, while he realized the importance of a coherent and healthy opposition, it appeared to him unnecessary to have two parties indulging in semantic quarrels while sharing broadly common objectives. So, early in 1953, he initiated talks with the Socialist leaders to explore the chances of working together. But a general agreement on the principles and aims of national reconstruction did not seem enough to the Socialists, especially as Nehru's personal cordiality was not shared by many other members of his party, and

[27] Nehru to Chief Ministers, 12 August 1956.
[28] Nehru to Chief Ministers, 16 April 1952.
[29] Jayaprakash Narayan to Nehru, 25 May 1952.
[30] Nehru to Jayaprakash Narayan, 27 May 1952.

particularly by the State governments. So Jayaprakash drafted a programme specifying constitutional amendments, administrative and land
reforms and nationalization of banks, insurance and mines.[31] Nehru,
however, preferred to move cautiously and pragmatically; rather than the
formalization of a joint programme he hoped for general cooperation
between the Congress and the Socialist Parties.

> Reading your letter, I realized not only how much we had in common
> in regard to our basic outlook, but also the differences in our
> approach. It may be that those differences are partly at least due to our
> viewing our problems from different angles. It is fairly easy to make a
> list of what we would like to have. It is more difficult to get that done
> in the proper order of priority. To attempt to do many things at the
> same time sometimes results in nothing being done.

No intelligent person could quarrel about the goals of socialism, but the
many uncertain factors, including the human material in India, meant that
one could only grope forward step by step. So he was seeking assistance
from the Socialists, not in drawing up a precise programme but in
promoting a sense of urgency in the country and accelerating the rate of
progress. 'I feel after your letter and our talk that perhaps any kind of a
formal step at the present moment would not be helpful. We have to grow
into things, not bring them about artificially.'[32] His public statement the
next day made clear that he had no longer any thought of cooperative
activity, let alone a merger of the two parties.[33]

Thereafter, even personal understanding between Nehru and the
Socialist leaders weakened. They believed that Nehru had given up his
plan for a political partnership not for the reasons he had stated but after a
talk with his Chief Ministers, who had no wish to share power. This
particular suspicion that narrow party interests had prevailed seems to
have been unfounded, though the Socialists may have been near the truth in
believing that Nehru's general attitude suggested an unwillingness to
cooperate with them at the price of splitting his own party. But the
bitterness increased. Far from appreciating the help given by Nehru in
securing Kripalani's unopposed return to the Lok Sabha, the Socialists
resented the Congress taking credit publicly for its generosity.[34]
Jayaprakash condemned the Kashmir Government for the death of
Mookerjee, and told Nehru that his explanation was unconvincing.[35] 'It
seems to be my misfortune', replied Nehru, 'that I get out of step with you

[31] Jayaprakash Narayan to Nehru, 6 February and 4 March 1953.
[32] Nehru to Jayaprakash Narayan, 17 March 1953.
[33] 18 March 1953.
[34] Nehru to Chief Minister, Bihar, 5 May, Kripalani to Nehru, 6 May, and Nehru to Kripalani, 6 May 1953.
[35] Jayaprakash Narayan to Nehru, 25 July 1953.

however much I may try to do otherwise.' His effort to draw closer to the Socialists had ended in controversy and imputation of motive, and both personal and party relations had become much worse than they had been at the start. 'Evidently some evil fate is pursuing us and I have begun to think that the safest policy might well be not to tempt that fate and to remain quiet.' He had made a mistake by writing to Jayaprakash about Mookerjee's death, and had had his punishment. 'If you feel that I am behaving in this matter or any other matter like some High Authority which considers itself infallible, then, of course, there is nothing more to be said by me. If I have fallen from grace, nothing can justify what I do.'[36]

After the formation of Andhra province, Prakasam, who had joined the Socialist Party mainly because of dislike of Rajagopalachari, returned to head the first Congress ministry in the province. Jayaprakash saw in this personal manoeuvring by Prakasam an attempt by Nehru to weaken the Socialists.[37] The relationship between the parties had clearly got beyond rational argument. At the Avadi session of the Congress in January 1955, Nehru was contemptuous of the Socialist Party as one which appeared to have lost its moorings and was tending to disintegrate.[38] That process was accelerated by the explicit commitment of the Congress to socialism; but the commitment did not improve Nehru's relations with Jayaprakash. The two friends continued to carp publicly at each other. When Jayaprakash termed Nehru's criticism of student agitation in Bihar as a 'command performance', Nehru protested that facts should be investigated fully before such 'unbalanced' statements were made. 'You refer to Congressmen's behaviour having fallen. Perhaps you are right. But I think the remark would apply to others' behaviour at least as much if not more. I may be wrong, but is it not possible that you may also be wrong?'[39] Obviously, for the time being at least, in his efforts to build socialism as he saw it, Nehru would have to go it alone, without the support of the Socialist Party. Even the broad cooperation he had hoped for, not compromising the individuality of either party, proved unattainable. 'Privately, of course, we meet many of them often. But what is one to do when Jayaprakash Narayan talks the most unmitigated nonsense and hates the Congress so much as to prefer the devil to it?'[40]

FIVE

Much as Nehru desired to concentrate on economic issues and ignore all else, some domestic problems continued to force themselves on his

[36] Nehru to Jayaprakash Narayan, 29 July 1953.
[37] Jayaprakash Narayan to Nehru, 10 October 1953.
[38] Report to the AICC, *National Herald*, 17 January 1955.
[39] Nehru to Jayaprakash Narayan, 1 September 1955.
[40] Nehru to V. N. Sharma, 7 October 1956.

attention. Although secularism had gained strength, it could still not be taken for granted. The fall of Abdullah in Kashmir had inevitably promoted communal feelings. Muslim communalism might have been sharpened, but it was the reaction on the same lines of some elements in the majority community which caused Nehru concern, for it was this which ultimately mattered.

What real Hinduism may be is a matter for each individual Hindu to decide. We can only take it as it is practised. In practice, the Hindu is certainly not tolerant and is more narrow-minded than almost any person in any other country except the Jew. It does not help much to talk of Hindu philosophy, which is magnificent. The fate of India is largely tied up with the Hindu outlook. If the present Hindu outlook does not change radically, I am quite sure that India is doomed. The Muslim outlook may be and, I think, is often worse. But it does not make very much difference to the future of India.[41]

As one means of countering this growing communal attitude, Nehru pressed his colleagues at the centre and in the States to provide adequate representation for the minorities, especially the Muslims, in the armed and civil services. As it was, these minorities felt that they were being considered aliens in India. 'All our ideals will go to pieces if we don't pull ourselves up.'[42] In a vast and mixed country like India it was vital to produce in every citizen a sense of partnership.[43] He urged incessantly the importance of generous treatment of the minorities so that they would feel that they were Indians, and be completely at home.

I do not wish to exaggerate this matter and I do not think it has gone deep yet. But the mere presence of these tendencies is dangerous. What troubles me most is the way most of us do not attach much importance to this.[44]

But his words were scarcely heeded by those to whom they were addressed. Far from trying to remove this feeling of frustration by steps which might well, if taken on a large scale, reduce the economic and social dominance of the majority community, fresh issues which fanned the fears of the Muslims were being opened up. In the two provinces of Uttar Pradesh and Madhya Pradesh, low priority was being given to the teaching of Urdu in schools and Hindi and Sanskrit were sought to be imposed on both Hindus and Muslims.[45] The working of the Evacuee Property Act was regarded by

[41] To K. N. Katju, 17 November 1953.
[42] To A. P. Jain, 3 August 1953.
[43] To Chief Ministers, 20 September 1953.
[44] Nehru to Chief Ministers, 26 April 1954.
[45] Paul R. Brass, *Language, Religion and Politics in North India* (Cambridge, 1974), p. 211; Nehru to R. S. Shukla, 20 March 1954.

many Muslims as a threat to their security. It was repealed in 1956, but the pending exceptions ran into many thousands and the custodians continued to exercise their inquisitorial powers in a manner which looked to Nehru as a vendetta against a large section of Indian citizens.[46]

Another group in India which raised problems causing Nehru considerable vexation was not, like the Muslims, a religious minority; but it had a certain individuality. The Nagas, in the farthest north-eastern corner of the country, had received special treatment from the British. Indeed, when the time came for them to withdraw from India, the British considered seriously the possibility of joining the Naga hills with the upper part of Burma and retaining the area as a Crown Colony. Administration in the Naga hills had always been carried out with a light hand; there had been little integration of the Nagas with the rest of the Indian community; and the influence of foreign missionaries was particularly strong. So it was not surprising that within a few years of India becoming independent a demand arose among the Nagas for breaking away from India and becoming independent themselves. While not prepared even to consider the grant of such independence, Nehru was willing to sanction a much greater measure of autonomy than was enjoyed by other States in the Indian union. He had promised this even in 1946, and he was prepared to respect his assurance.[47] The Nagas were a tough people who could give much trouble and Nehru saw the danger of any hurried attempt to absorb their areas into standard administration. Between this and the isolation of British days there was a middle way, a friendly rather than a coercive attitude, an acceptance of their social structure, protection from encroachments and advance in such fields as education. They should neither be treated as anthropological specimens nor drowned in the sea of Indian humanity. They could not be isolated from the new political and economic forces sweeping across India; but it was equally undesirable to allow these forces to function freely and upset the traditional life and culture of the Nagas. It was presumptuous to approach them with an air of superiority and try to make of them second-rate copies of people in other parts of India.

Therefore, while authorizing the Government of Assam to reject the demand for independence and to make clear that incitement to violence would not be tolerated, Nehru emphasized the importance of dealing with this problem as a psychological rather than a political one, and instructed that punitive measures should as far as possible be avoided.[48] As part of the same approach, he planned to visit the Naga hills and talk directly to the people.[49] He was even willing to receive Phizo and other members of the Naga National Council, the group campaigning for independence, if they

[46] Nehru to G. B. Pant and to M. C. Khanna, 11 June 1956.
[47] See his letter to Naga leaders reported in *National Herald*, 6 August 1946.
[48] To J. Daulatram, Governor, and to B. R. Medhi, Chief Minister, Assam, 2 February 1951.
[49] To J. Daulatram, 9 May 1951.

came to Delhi.[50] The Government of India were big enough to be generous and to declare their willingness to consider any proposals short of independence. Further, three million rupees were granted as compensation to the Nagas for damage suffered during the war. 'It is likely that if government keeps its head cool and restrains its hand, the whole movement may gradually fizzle out, because it leads to nothing.'[51] Phizo's influence appeared to be waning, and the government let it be known that they did not attach much importance to him and his followers. Phizo himself was informed that the Government of India could in no event recognize any attempt by any section of the people of India to claim an independent state.[52]

In March 1952, Nehru met Phizo and told him bluntly that he would not listen to any talk of independence; but he was prepared to help the Nagas to maintain their autonomy in cultural and other matters and he would see to it that there was no interference.[53] As this did not satisfy Phizo, the authorities, instead of waiting for the independence campaign to fade away, had to take steps which would weaken the support for Phizo among the Nagas. Nehru had no doubt that it was right in itself as well as politically expedient to create among the tribes a feeling of kinship with the rest of the country. 'The movement for independence among the Nagas is entirely based on the assumption that Indians are foreigners ruling over the tribes. Our policy must be aimed at removing this impression.'[54] They should feel part of India and sharers in its destiny, but free to live their own lives, with opportunities of advancement along their own lines.

To give a lead to this policy, in April 1953 Nehru, accompanied by U Nu of Burma, toured the Naga areas. A group of Nagas ostentatiously walked out of a public meeting, which was being addressed by the two Prime Ministers, in protest against an official order prohibiting the presentation of petitions. This deliberate discourtesy, not so much to him as to U Nu, stiffened Nehru's attitude. The Naga leaders were sent for and informed that by such behaviour the Naga National Council had put itself outside the pale and the government would not hereafter recognize or deal with it. Immediate counter-measures would also be taken in case of any unlawful action.[55]

This incident also brought to the fore the whole question of foreign missionaries in India. Nehru had not wished to lay down any general rules about them, but to leave each case to be considered on its merits by the central and state governments. Christians in India should not develop a sense of persecution. So, although foreign missionaries should not

[50] To J. N. Hazarika, 13 May 1951.
[51] To B. R. Medhi, 25 May 1951.
[52] Nehru's principal private secretary to Phizo, 7 August 1951.
[53] Nehru to B. R. Medhi, 13 March 1952.
[54] Nehru to J. Daulatram, 4 April 1952.
[55] Nehru to J. Daulatram, 3 April 1953.

normally be encouraged, and the Church in India should learn to stand on its own feet, there should be no bar on any person of whatever nationality who was clearly and solely engaged in evangelical work.[56] The President, the Home Minister, Katju, and the Chief Minister of Madhya Pradesh, R. S. Shukla, were all rebuked by the Prime Minister for giving credence, even remotely, to the charge that the authorities in India were anti-Christian or interested in any way in conversions.[57] The government were concerned only with foreign missionaries because they were foreign and not because they were missionaries; and even in their case the government were concerned only with any political activity in which they might indulge. If they hindered their evangelical work with spiritual or racial arrogance, this was their affair.[58] But it did seem that in the Naga areas foreign missionaries, enjoying considerable influence with the inhabitants, were involved in fostering anti-national sentiments. A letter had been circulated to pastors requesting them to celebrate 5 April as Naga Independence Day in their churches and chapels. So Nehru ordered that foreign missionaries in this area be informed that they would have to leave India if their complicity in such activity were established. It was also decided that no new missions should be opened and no more foreign missionaries should be allowed into the Naga area, and the antecedents of the foreign missionaries already functioning there should be checked.[59] That this decision was independent of any prejudice is demonstrated by the freedom with which a British missionary, Verrier Elwin, roamed these tribal areas. Indeed, Elwin, rather than any Indian, was Nehru's trusted adviser on all tribal problems.

Elwin, however, was an exceptional character whose dedication to Christianity was not irreconcilable with a deep respect for India's national sovereignty. Some of the other British missionaries in the Naga hills were former officials who had not yet come to terms with the political changes in India. There had also been, since 1947, a heavy influx into India of missionaries from the United States. Nehru suspected that, even if they did not interest themselves in politics, their very presence might have a political impact. 'Americanism is not only a particular way of life but a particular way of thinking in politics. In the present context of the world this becomes politics directly.'[60] But to avoid injustice to any individual and enable free entry without political embarrassment to the Government of India, he conveyed informally the message to foreign governments that the Government of India would deal with the principal missionary organi-

[56] Nehru's note, 23 February 1953.
[57] Nehru to Rajendra Prasad, 10 August 1953; to K. N. Katju, 10 July, 29 July and 13 October 1953; to R. S. Shukla, 27 May 1955.
[58] See Nehru to the Archbishop of Sweden, 22 August 1953.
[59] Nehru to J. Daulatram, 3 April 1953.
[60] Nehru to Amrit Kaur, 30 October 1953.

zations abroad rather than consider the case of every applicant separately.[61]

As regards general policy towards the Nagas, the incident of the walk-out made little difference. Nehru still insisted on a gradual spread of administration and its adaptation to local conditions. The situation was fluid and could with care be made to take the right shape; but it was equally easy for it to take the wrong shape. Possibly Nehru would have slowed down the pace of administrative permeation even more but for the necessity created by these tribal areas also being border areas. However, he laid emphasis on the presence of government being imposed more in the form of roads, dispensaries, and schools than in the enforcement of law and order. He directed also that a cadre of senior officials, specially selected and trained for these areas, be built up, and that their subordinates be drawn from the local tribes. A feeling should be created among the Nagas that responsibility would be cast increasingly on them and that the authorities regarded them as partners in development.[62] In fact, there was no alternative, for total suppression was out of the question and partial suppression would have served only as an irritant. The Nagas 'are a tough and fine lot of people and we may carry on for a generation without solving the problem.'[63]

At a political level, the kind of solution Nehru had in mind at this time was not a Naga province within the Indian union but a district with considerable autonomy so as to give 'a sensation of self-government' and check the widely resented growth of Assamese influence and control of the local economy.[64] But neither prong of Nehru's policy made any marked impression, chiefly because of the inertia of the Assam Government, and he had to concede some months later that the effort to win over the people of these areas had largely failed. The 'law and order' approach had become the norm, and this could not be the basis of any policy. The adverse and not surprising result of this was a non-cooperative attitude on the part of the Nagas. There was now a growing demand not so much for independence as for separation from Assam; but if this were not controlled or diluted, it might well add to the feeling against India itself.[65] One way of initiating a friendly and constructive approach would be to extend the community project scheme to these tribal areas, but it would have to be followed up by more positive action. 'We are in a deadlock and we should explore ways of getting out of it.'[66]

As for the rebel Nagas, Nehru refused to meet Phizo unless he gave up the demand for independence and publicly condemned violent activities.[67]

[61] Nehru's note, 24 January 1955.
[62] Nehru's note on the north-east frontier area, 24 April 1953.
[63] Nehru's note, 9 December 1953.
[64] To S. Fazl Ali, Daulatram's successor as Governor, 10 August 1954.
[65] To B. R. Medhi, 9 March 1955.
[66] To B. R. Medhi from Bandung, 21 April 1955.
[67] To J. Daulatram, 27 July 1955.

'We have to steer the middle course between a complacent approach to the problem and an over-dramatized approach. We must proceed calmly, without excitement, without shouting and yet with strength.'[68] But this was rendered impractical by the renewal of violent activities by Phizo's followers, and Nehru ordered the arrest of Phizo and his henchmen and the suppression of their activity.[69] Slow action gave them opportunities; the government should, therefore, hit hard and swiftly. It should become clear to the Nagas that the government would not deal with Phizo or weaken as a result of violence; nor would political or other changes be considered till complete calm had been restored.[70] When three Nagas came to Delhi, claiming to be acting in an independent capacity, but obviously in contact with Phizo and probably sent by him, it was made clear to them that the first task was to restore law and order, and anyone not cooperating would be punished severely. There was also no question of any talks or negotiations.[71] Confronted with an open, armed rebellion by the Nagas in which a number of Indian officers and troops had been killed in regular battles, the Government of India concluded that they had no option but to deal with it as a purely military situation. But Nehru vetoed suggestions for machine-gunning from the air.[72]

Suppression of violent revolt, even if it were the first step to be taken, obviously could not be the only one. Once the back of resistance had been broken, a political approach would have to be renewed. The time for this had clearly not yet come, but as a prelude Nehru explained to the army and the civil authorities that nothing should be done which widened the gulf between the government and the mass of the Naga people.

We must not judge them as we would others who are undoubtedly part of India. The Nagas have no such background or sensations and we have to create that sensation among them by our goodwill and treatment. We shall have to think how we can produce this impression and what political steps may be necessary.

This was important both for internal stability and to counter the use being made of trouble in the Naga area for international propaganda against India.[73] One administrative measure Nehru had in mind was to remove the Naga hills from the control of the Assam Government and attach the area to the frontier division so as to bring it directly under central control. But any such step required careful consideration. There was a growing

[68] To B. R. Medhi, 8 September 1955.
[69] Nehru's telegram to Governor and Chief Minister of Assam, 25 January 1956.
[70] Nehru's telegram to Chief Minister, 28 February 1956.
[71] Nehru to J. Daulatram, 8 and 9 March 1956.
[72] Note to Defence Secretary, 19 June 1956.
[73] Nehru to B. R. Medhi, 13 May 1956.

inclination to be hustled into some kind of political action. 'It does not help in dealing with tough people to have weak nerves.'[74]

The army, however, failed to deal decisively with the rebellion. Its efforts, reminiscent of what T. E. Lawrence once described as eating soup with a knife, served only to alienate even many loyal Nagas and to provoke criticism of India abroad. So Nehru urged the army to act swiftly but not brutally, and pressed ahead with many minor political changes while working out the major political decision on the future administration of the area.

> It must always be remembered that if the Nagas are made to feel that they have no other alternative but to fight and die, they will prefer doing so. We must give them a better alternative and seek their cooperation or at least [that] of those who are prepared to cooperate. This has not been done so far either by the Assam Government or by our military.[75]

Thimayya, the most distinguished of the senior army commanders, was ordered to take charge immediately.

The Naga problem was, therefore, nowhere near solution. There was to Nehru no question of political or any other form of surrender to a small group in active revolt. 'It is fantastic to imagine that the Government of India is going to be terrorized into some action by Phizo and company.'[76] Weakness in dealing with such people appeared to him to be almost a sin. But the military approach, while necessary, was not adequate; and Nehru insisted that soldiers and officials should always remember that the Nagas were fellow-countrymen who were not merely to be suppressed but, at some stage, had to be won over. They should be permitted the fullest freedom subject to the two overriding demands of national unity and national security. How this was to be worked out remained a problem for the future. Indeed, this postponement was a deliberate decision of policy. Nehru had no intention of making any precise commitments as long as the revolt was not called off. But the Naga problem remained a messy situation which his government had not, in these years, succeeded in tidying up. A correctly formed policy had not been effectively executed.

SIX

The Naga problem was created by some Indian citizens who were wishing to secede from the republic; the problem of the French and Portuguese settlements was the reverse: many — if not all — of their inhabitants were

[74] Nehru's note, 21 May 1956.
[75] To K. N. Katju, Defence Minister, 28 July 1956.
[76] Nehru to Fazl Ali, 9 September 1956.

eager to merge their territories with the mother-country. This problem straddled the domestic and foreign policies of India. The Indian people regarded these demands for integration as part of their national movement. The Congress had always encouraged this view and Nehru, more than any other leader before 1947, had involved Pondicherry and Goa in the effort to defeat imperialism. 'Wherever human liberty and human suffering are involved, the problem is not a little one. Wherever people struggle for freedom and against repression they enact a drama which is always full of vital interest to lovers of liberty all over the world.'[77] Colonial domination, for however long, could not result in the assimilation of the occupied territory by the imperial power. Pondicherry and Goa were geographically and culturally parts of India and had to be so politically as well. It was only a matter of time and circumstance as to when this happened.

To assume, however, that the withdrawal of the British would be followed rapidly and inevitably by the liberation of other foreign possessions in India was to sink into facile optimism. The negotiations with the French dragged on till 1954, when M. Mendès-France found an honourable way of handing over Pondicherry and the other bits of French territory. But the Portuguese had no intention of leaving Goa at any time and, recognizing that the Government of India could not compromise on this issue, adopted an attitude of aggressive hostility. For example, they offered assistance to the Nizam in his attempt to keep Hyderabad aloof from the Indian union. Nehru realized that the Portuguese were beyond persuasion and would only yield under pressure, either from other powers or from the people of Goa. 'Sometime or other these people are going to have a rude awakening to the twentieth century.'[78] But building up international support was a gradual and heartbreaking process, while there was considerable support for the Portuguese among the vested interests in Goa that had grown in strength over the centuries. It was not certain that, if a plebiscite were held immediately, India would win. So Nehru discouraged the States peoples movement and the Bombay Government from promoting a popular campaign on the borders of Goa, preferring to start negotiations with the Portuguese Government, 'exceedingly stupid and sticky' as they might be.[79]

As expected, no progress resulted. Neither were the efforts to keep the situation from freezing any more effective. To work out a sanction to buttress the written note offering to commence consultations on the transfer of Portuguese territories, and the public declarations that Goa would have to become part of India,[80] an examination of Goa's economic

[77] Nehru's statement on Goa, 22 July 1946.
[78] Nehru to Chandralekha Mehta, 11 July 1949.
[79] To B. P. Sitaramayya and to B. G. Kher, 24 May 1949; also see Nehru to Patel, 5 June 1949, *Sardar Patel's Correspondence 1945-50*, Vol. 8 (Ahmedabad, 1973), pp. 136-7.
[80] Statements in Parliament, 4 and 9 February 1950. Parliamentary Debates, Vol. I, Part 1, 1950, pp. 81 and 164-5, respectively.

relations with the rest of India was undertaken. But nothing emerged from this. In 1952 Nehru again considered economic action. 'The attitude of our Government, though perhaps justifiable, is exceedingly demoralizing.'[81] But, chiefly because of the fear that economic sanctions might hurt the people of Goa more than the Portuguese authorities, Nehru was reluctant to order positive steps.

In this dilemma, it became increasingly clear that only military pressure would tell; but Nehru was even more determined to avoid taking this easy step than using economic sanctions. So, apart from closing the legation at Lisbon, he did nothing in the hope that time was an ally and the force of world opinion might eventually secure Goa for India. The Government and people of India, being mature and not 'children at play', would quietly wait.[82] 'Generally it is recognized that both the Portuguese and the French possessions must come to India. Sir Winston Churchill said so to me and remarked on the extreme backwardness of Portuguese thought.'[83]

Nehru's decision to set an example to the world of postponing the attainment of a legitimate objective because the quickest means was questionable did not, however, shame the foreign powers into exerting diplomatic pressure on Portugal. Indeed, in the summer of 1954, when the Government of India made clear that they would not permit Goa to be used by any foreign power for military purposes, the British Government — whatever Churchill might think of Portugal — gave an oral reply that old treaties made it obligatory for them to defend any Portuguese colonies if the need arose.[84] This woke Nehru up to the disregard of moral principle in international relations. 'If it is logic for Britain, having given up her empire, to protect other people's empires by force of arms, I am unable to comprehend it.' India would continue to seek a solution of this problem by peaceful methods but there could be no commitment to future policy; that would depend entirely on circumstances. A situation might well arise when a continuation of Portuguese domination over Goa would become a direct threat to India's security and welfare, and then India would be obliged to consider what steps should be taken.[85]

These were brave words, but Nehru, because of his ethical commitments, was still unwilling to act upon his threats. He had the previous year decided that the Bombay Government and the district officials on the borders of Portuguese territory should give no direct or indirect assistance to the Portuguese authorities even if such abstention hurt the people of Goa; and he authorized the Congress Party in India to assist any effort in

[81] Nehru's note on Goa, 8 July 1952.
[82] Nehru's statement at press conference at Delhi, 2 November, *National Herald*, 3 November 1952.
[83] Nehru to Chief Ministers, 2 July 1953.
[84] Secretary-General's note on interview with acting British High Commissioner, 11 June 1954.
[85] Nehru's note, 11 June 1954.

Goa for integration with India.[86] Goans settled in India were not stopped from entering Portuguese territory,[87] but all other Indians were discouraged from supporting what should essentially be regarded as a freedom movement within Goa. Nehru was not prepared to go further than this and restrained the eagerness in India for more positive action lest the Portuguese retaliate with the use of firearms, thereby forcing his hand.

> The Portuguese are bent on violence and are inciting us to commit violence. They have prepared themselves well for this kind of thing. On no account must we fall into that trap and our people should realize that . . . Thus we shall put the Portuguese into a false position and they will make themselves rather ridiculous. The Portuguese live in a medieval climate of mind and are rather melodramatic. If their melodrama is made to appear completely ridiculous, their case suffers greatly . . . Circumstances have made Goa a first-class issue and the Portuguese have been driven to take all kinds of steps. I have no doubt that Goa will come to us, but we must adhere to non-violence.[88]

This would seem to be the naivety of the over-sophisticated. But the policy bore, at the beginning, a few results. Diplomatic relations with Portugal were not severed, but when the Salazar government spoke in terms of defending Christianity, and Roman Catholicism in particular, in India, Nehru made sure of the sympathy of the Vatican and left it to Indian priests to answer the propaganda.[89] Aid to resistance within Goa took the form only of economic measures. Suspecting more, the Portuguese proposed international observers. Nehru agreed promptly and the Portuguese, fearing that their proposal might lead unavoidably to negotiations, retracted. They were happier expressing their objections by shooting down some Indian volunteers who sought to cross into Goa. The Government of India protested formally but were still reluctant to react to this brutality with force.

> We have to take not only the right steps but also in the right way. We have also to keep in view our general world policy because we cannot isolate one action from another. I have no doubt that we shall win in Goa. But I am anxious to do so without giving up in the slightest the basic policy that we claim to pursue.[90]

[86] To Morarji Desai, Chief Minister of Bombay, to Secretary-General, Ministry of External Affairs and to General Secretary, AICC, 29 October 1953.

[87] Speech at New Delhi, 13 August, *National Herald*, 14 August 1954.

[88] Nehru to Morarji Desai, 12 August 1954.

[89] Nehru to Morarji Desai, 11 August, and to Cardinal Gracias, 23 August 1954.

[90] Nehru to Chief Ministers, 3 September 1954.

Confidence in the ultimate outcome enabled Nehru to be still very much the narcissist saint in world affairs. Krishna Menon, it may be added, approved wholly of this policy of restraint.[91]

To give the Portuguese no scope for complaint, Nehru vetoed the establishment in India of a provisional government of Goa. Organizations working for the merging of Goa with India were viewed with a little more tolerance than before; but this did not involve any alteration of policy, which was still one of inaction and patience, waiting for the popular movement in Goa to gain strength, for the colonial economy to weaken, for the transfer of Pondicherry to have an influence in Lisbon and for sympathy in world opinion to prevail. 'To expect sudden changes and always to think in terms of bringing about a big crisis is wrong both from the general political point of view and that of *satyagraha*.'[92]

Impeccable in theory, this policy assumed a high degree of understanding in India as well as sensitive reaction on the part of the Portuguese. The political parties in opposition to the Congress saw in Goa a chance to criticize Nehru. They organized a campaign for Indian volunteers to cross into Goa and compelled him to warn them that he would take whatever action became necessary to prevent this.[93] As for the Portuguese, Nehru accepted the advice of Morarji Desai, the Chief Minister of Bombay, that if the Portuguese gave provocation, such as deporting Indian persons, all diplomatic relations should be severed;[94] but every step would have to be carefully considered.

> Goa continues to be a headache. It is natural for people to demand strong action but we must always remember that we should not, in the excitement of the moment or because of anger and resentment, undertake any action without thinking out all the possible consequences. I need not tell you that we are giving continuous and earnest thought to this Goa situation. We do not propose to allow ourselves to be hustled into wrong action.[95]

It was, in a sense, more to embarrass Nehru than to secure any concessions from the Portuguese that the Jan Sangh and the Socialist and the Communist Parties organized a mass *satyagraha* campaign; and the Portuguese opened fire on unarmed volunteers when they tried to cross the border. Passions rose sharply in India and Nehru was severely criticized for not retaliating and ordering Indian troops to advance into Goa. But Nehru stood firm and argued in detail the case for patience. India was afraid of

[91] Krishna Menon's telegram to Nehru from New York, 30 September 1954.
[92] Nehru's note on Goa, 2 December 1954.
[93] To Peter Alvares, 28 March 1955.
[94] Nehru's note on Goa, 6 May 1955.
[95] Nehru to Chief Ministers, 20 May 1955.

nothing except of doing anything which did not fit in with her larger policy. She would not be stampeded into forgetting or bypassing those principles of her foreign policy which had grown since 1947.[96] 'I say there is nothing more scandalous on God's earth today than the Portuguese occupation of Goa, historically, factually, religously if you like or from any point of view.'[97] The Pope, when Nehru met him, had agreed that Goa was not a religious issue.[98] The world, and particularly the Atlantic Powers, should take note that India would tolerate no nonsense about Goa. But the peaceful approach was the right one not only from the point of view of Goa and India but also because of major issues in the world. The Government of India were not pacifist but they would only go to war in case of an armed attack.

> If you are under the impression that the Government will take police action or use force to liberate Goa from Portuguese domination, you are entirely mistaken. I am not going to do any such thing . . . Wars and armed actions have never solved any problem anywhere in the world.[99]

It was easy enough to occupy Goa, but that would be unfair to the people of Goa, form a betrayal of India's policies and result in many undesirable consequences.

> We have set our face against the solution of problems by warlike methods, and we intend to adhere to that decision. Once the necessity of war on some occasions was accepted, who was to define the occasion? Every country would decide for itself, and the floodgates would be opened. Let no man think that a little war is justifiable though a big war will not be so. If once the principle is given up, then we are anchorless and cannot work for peace in the world, which is so essential for the future of humanity.[100]

If the Government of India sought to solve the problem of Goa by other than peaceful methods, they would be regarded as 'deceitful hypocrites' and opportunists with no principles and the whole edifice of their foreign policy would come down.[101]

Abroad, and especially in the neighbouring countries, this policy was regarded as weakness. The Pakistan Government spoke in terms of support to Portugal and, striking a pose emulating the Indian example,

[96] Statement at press conference, 31 May, reported in *Hindustan Times*, 1 June 1955.
[97] Press conference, 19 July, *National Herald*, 20 July 1955.
[98] Nehru's statement in Rome, 8 July, *National Herald*, 9 July 1955.
[99] Speech at Poona, 4 June, *Times of India*, 5 June 1955.
[100] Address to U.P.P.C.C. at Sitapur, *National Herald*, 21 August 1955.
[101] Speech (in Hindi) in Lok Sabha, 17 September 1955.

organized a crossing of the cease-fire line in Kashmir by a large crowd of armed civilians. Kotelawala of Ceylon offered to mediate between India and Portugal and, when reminded that he was committed by the Bandung resolution, if nothing else, to an anti-colonialist position, allowed his prejudice against India to express itself in sympathy for Portugal.[102] It was not generally appreciated that Nehru had in fact shown a gritty resolution in adopting his policy of restraint. 'It has been no easy matter for us to stop *satyagraha* and I doubt if any other government anywhere in the world could have had the courage and strength to take such an unpopular step.'[103] The only action he took to counter this misunderstanding of his policy was to send an official note to all the Bandung countries reminding them that India was entitled to their support on this issue. Adherence to peaceful methods despite flagrant provocation could not blur the fact that Goa was a symbol of intransigent and oppressive colonialism, completely out of keeping with the spirit of Asia and Africa and indeed of all freedom-loving people all over the world.[104] Refusal to react to Portugal's use of force and the decision to stop the *satyagraha* should not be interpreted as acceptance of the 'monstrous anomaly'[105] of Portuguese rule in Goa. The only settlement which India would accept was, as in the case of Pondicherry, an early withdrawal of the foreign power followed by a formal transfer of authority. 'A flash of anger shot through his eyes as he said, "There are some questions over which it is permissible to have two points of view, but over this one, that is the Goa issue, it seems to me that only one view is possible." '[106] But the very belief in Nehru's dedication to peaceful methods weakened the pressure that foreign governments were willing to exert on Portugal and confirmed them in the even-handed attitude that was all in favour of the status quo. Those who had faith in Nehru could not take seriously his assertion that India would not accept indefinitely the continuance of Portuguese rule in Goa. The adamant Portuguese attitude and the failure of other powers to interfere meant that the dilemma could not be solved by Nehru's methods. It would have to be broken, at the cost of Nehru's principles, or the Portuguese left undisturbed, in defiance of Nehru's commitments. Nehru was as yet not prepared to take what he considered adventurist action. 'We have to act with some responsibility and some wisdom in this matter, even though we may be very angry. We have got entangled in an international knot and we cannot untie it by pulling in the wrong direction. Untie it we will.'[107] How this was going to be done was not clear. For the time being the situation was at a standstill, and Nehru was worried but helpless.

[102] Indian High Commissioner in Colombo to Foreign Secretary, 19 August 1955.
[103] Nehru's telegram to Vijayalakshmi, 14 September 1955.
[104] Nehru's note to Ministry of External Affairs, 8 September 1955.
[105] Nehru's message to mass rally of Goans, 25 September 1955.
[106] Taya Zinkin's dispatch in *Manchester Guardian*, 29 February 1956.
[107] Nehru to Peter Alvares, 27 August 1956.

SEVEN

Nehru's various public activities were held together by a general theory of government. Ruling India was to him not just a matter of dealing with files or issuing executive orders. These were important duties, but only a small part of the whole. Democratic government 'is not something which we can deal with merely because we have some general knowledge or ability.' Regard had to be paid to the deeper issues beneath the day-to-day concerns.

> The fact is that often we are struggling with major problems without the larger experience which gives assurance to the mind. We have to be firm and we have to be flexible. We must not be undecided and unable to make up our minds. But we can only be firm if our minds are clear about major problems, and they seldom are . . . There should always be the human touch, but behind the human touch one should give the feeling of firm decisions. That is, while one should be flexible, one should not be weak in handling an issue and our approach to the party and to the public should always be friendly.[108]

Neither firmness by itself nor a flabby friendliness was enough. Nehru wished his followers, like himself, to have clear, long-term objectives, such as socialism and community development, and to work for them persuasively and not solely on the basis of dry logic.

> A leader must always have a sense of the public. He cannot do some things, because he senses they would create difficulties . . . We have to deal with human beings as individuals and in the mass, and we must know the art of getting into their minds and hearts and not merely imagine that any logical argument must prevail.[109]

This art of human management had in these years to be exercised by Nehru at every level, both in the larger, impersonal context of binding the masses to the government and in the more delicate task of holding his colleagues together. 'This country requires such a tremendous deal of managing in a variety of ways, that sometimes I wonder how it holds together. And yet, I suppose there are stronger forces than individuals which hold us together.'[110] This, of course, was true of India in general; but in dealing with narrower, personal problems Nehru was indispensable. He alone, in the higher ranks of the Congress, because of his undisputed command over the Party and the people, could keep individuals and groups from dissension. 'It seems to me that the most difficult job in the world is to

[108] Nehru to H. Upadhyaya, 29 October 1953.
[109] To B. K. Kaula, 29 October 1953.
[110] Nehru to Mountbatten, 16 November 1953.

deal with human beings, especially those one has to work with. It is relatively easy to deal with opponents . . . I really do not know who else could succeed even in this measure.'[111] In the central Cabinet Deshmukh, T. T. Krishnamachari and Kidwai pulled in different directions, bitterly denouncing each other and repeatedly offering to resign. Kidwai continued to snipe against Pant in Uttar Pradesh and Deshmukh fell foul of Rajagopalachari in Madras. In New York, Vijayalakshmi resented Krishna Menon's secretive handling of the Korean question. Nehru devoted considerable time to patching up these quarrels — advising, mollifying, sometimes even shouting a little.

> It seems to me, whether in Delhi or elsewhere, that far the best part of my time is taken up in reconciling people or in soothing them when they get ruffled with each other. It is extraordinary how little our capacity is for friendly cooperation . . . I do not know if in other countries people are continually faced with these difficulties of individuals behaving too individualistically. In the Soviet, I suppose, when this happens somebody is liquidated.[112]

Nehru was generally successful in guiding his team, with its clashing temperaments and holders of conflicting opinions; yet on some major problems of human management he had to accept defeat. He could not subdue Abdullah's political tantrums. He could not harness to the public service the mutual affection between himself and Jayaprakash Narayan. Neither could he, after Rajagopalachari's departure from the Home Ministry, vest his relations with Rajagopalachari with any measure of cordiality and understanding. From 1952 their personal friendship plunged in a steep downward curve. Absence from Delhi did not, to a man like Rajagopalachari, mean retirement from politics. In the elections in Madras province the Congress had fared badly. Its local leaders had lost touch with the people, in the Andhra districts there was much soreness at the failure to secure a separate province, the belief was widely prevalent that the central government cared little for the interests of southern India, and the food shortage, particularly the lack of rice, was keenly felt. As the Congress Party was now in a minority in the Madras Assembly, Nehru recommended the democratic procedure of allowing the other parties, if they could muster a majority, to form a ministry. 'The one thing we must avoid is giving the impression that we stick to office and that we want to keep out others at all costs.'[113] But Sri Prakasa, the Governor, Rajagopalachari, whom he consulted, and most Congressmen in Madras favoured executive government. They were agreed that the Communists

[111] Nehru to Krishna Menon, 13 November 1953.
[112] To Vijayalakshmi, 4 November 1953.
[113] Nehru to Rajagopalachari, 29 January 1952.

should be kept out of office and it should be asserted as an axiom of Indian politics that the Congress ruled India, whatever the electoral setbacks in certain parts of the country. 'I do not think it would be justifiable from any point of view, even of ideological democracy, to leave patches of rebel areas and go into disorder. We cannot work out democracy in fractions of India.'[114] Nehru vetoed this suggestion of permanent Congress hegemony, particularly in a State where the local Congress leadership had shown itself to be so incompetent. The electoral defeat of the Congress did not amount to a failure of the Constitution.[115] This annoyed Rajagopalachari:

> I can see how you and friends there have given the best consideration to the situation here and have on grounds of expediency, logic and democratic principles come to conclusions wholly contrary to my view. Let us agree to differ and let it rest there. Please do not therefore seek to explain to me. I can see the Euclidean steps that lead to the conclusions you have arrived at, and who can question Euclid?[116]

Nehru, however, had no intention of giving way. It was evident that the Congress had failed in the primary business of winning the people to its side, and till it recovered its vitality by building up a new set of leaders, Nehru was convinced that others outside the Congress would have to be given a chance to function.[117] To get round such obstinate commitment to democratic principle, Sri Prakasa and Rajagopalachari resorted to deviousness. Without informing Nehru, the Governor nominated Rajagopalachari to the upper house; thereupon Rajagopalachari was elected leader of the Congress Party and the Governor, ignoring Nehru's specific reminder that a chief minister should be a member of the lower house,[118] invited Rajagopalachari to form a government. For once the President and the Prime Minister were united in disapproval of both the decision to recall Rajagopalachari to the leadership of the Congress in Madras and the manner in which this was done.[119] But as there was no way of reversing the situation, Nehru decided not to object officially and to give Rajagopalachari such help as he could to stabilize his position.

From every wider point of view, the second term of Rajagopalachari as Chief Minister of Madras was a disappointment. He felt, as did Bidhan Roy, that Nehru's decision to release détenus and his attempts to deal with communism by methods within the democratic tradition were in effect assisting the Communist Party. Nehru was second to none in his

---

[114] Rajagopalachari to Nehru, 10 February 1952.

[115] To K. Kamaraj, 11 February, to T. T. Krishnamachari, 13 February, to P. Subbarayan, 13 February, to P. S. K. Raja, 14 February, to V. V. Giri, 17 February, and to Rajagopalachari, 17 February 1952.

[116] Rajagopalachari to Nehru, 1 March 1952.

[117] Nehru to Rajagopalachari, 4 March 1952.

[118] Nehru to Sri Prakasa, 5 March 1952.

[119] Nehru to Rajagopalachari, 7 April, and to the President and to Sri Prakasa, 8 April 1952.

denunciation of the methods followed by the Communists in India. He informed them sharply that their movement was not democratic and that there was considerable evidence to confirm the general belief that their policy was directed from outside; and he did not hesitate to tell them what he thought of their propaganda. 'I have seldom come across a greater bunch of falsehoods and distortions of truth.'[120] But he was willing to accept and to act on their assurance that their party had now turned from violence and subversion to parliamentary activity. Rajagopalachari and Roy were unconvinced; and they regarded as weakness Nehru's contention that communism was a faith which force alone could not combat as some of its tenets were admired and believed in by most intelligent and sensitive persons. Rajagopalachari laid stress on routine administration rather than on economic planning and land reforms, which were so important to Nehru; and the strengthening of the Congress as a conservative party became to him the purpose of office. 'As Prime Minister, I am not concerned with parties but am only concerned with good and progressive government in the interests of the people.'[121] Such sentiment was at this time unacceptable to Rajagopalachari. As a private citizen before becoming Chief Minister, he had recommended, on hearing of the electoral reverses of the Congress in southern India, that the Party be dissolved; but inconsistency was to Rajagopalachari always a cause of satisfaction. Deliberate perversity was a major facet of his intellectual arrogance. He now, for example, to the annoyance of Azad, excluded Muslims from his ministry on the ground that it would displease the remnants of the Muslim League in Madras.[122]

Differences also arose on administrative matters between Rajagopalachari and the central government, and Nehru had repeatedly to smooth matters over. Rajagopalachari's proposal to reduce the salaries of members of the Indian Civil Service, while acceptable to Nehru on principle, was turned down by the Cabinet because of the constitutional aspects of the question. Then Rajagopalachari threatened to resign because a large subvention sought by the Madras Government had been refused.

You know very well that your advice is more important for me than from anyone else. India is some kind of a jigsaw puzzle with a tendency for separate parts to jump out. It is no easy matter to keep them together. Indeed, I am sometimes a little surprised that they do hold together . . . I am sorry I cannot think of releasing you, as you say. What am I to do when all our wise men go one after the other leaving me with some capacity but little wisdom to shoulder the burden of the country?[123]

[120] Nehru to A. K. Gopalan, 2 July 1952.
[121] Nehru to Gyan Singh Rarewala, 24 April 1952.
[122] Azad to Rajagopalachari, 19 April, and Rajagopalachari to Nehru, 22 April 1952.
[123] Nehru to Rajagopalachari, 12 February 1953.

But finally Nehru's patience broke. Within the Congress Party in Madras, especially after the separation of the Andhra areas, discontent against Rajagopalachari's high-handedness had become widespread. Nehru strove loyally to smother this feeling[124] but Rajagopalachari was not satisfied. He gave no help in smoothing over the situation, sneered at Kamaraj and his hopes of 'running chief ministership with the help of literate stooges',[125] and was offended by Nehru's suggestion that he keep in touch with and humour local Congressmen.[126] A prompt apology by Nehru for daring to offer advice did not help.[127] Even after this, Nehru sharply rebuked forty members of the Congress Party in the Madras Assembly who had demanded that Rajagopalachari be replaced.[128] But Rajagopalachari, far from appreciating such support, even objected to Nehru having acknowledged this letter and forwarded it to him. Nehru would not accept that he had erred in this matter.

It is perfectly true that I make myself accessible to every disgruntled element in India. That is my consistent practice. In fact, I go out of my way. That does not mean that I encourage them; but it does mean that I am accessible to everyone, time permitting. I propose to continue this because that is the way I control these people and, if I may say so, to some extent, India. If Rajaji does not want me to send these letters to him, I shall not do so, but that will be a wrong policy both for me and him. It is difficult enough to hold this country together. If I followed Rajaji's policy, I would fall out with most people. It may be a logical policy, but it will result in failure.[129]

However, he decided to keep away from Madras politics and say or do nothing in any matter concerning Rajagopalachari. But it seemed as if even this were not possible. In accordance with Rajagopalachari's advice, he instructed Kamaraj to choose between the chief ministership and the presidentship of the Party in Madras. Informing Rajagopalachari of this, he added,

The situation is obviously not a happy one, but there it is, and we have to face it. We cannot permit the Madras government or the organization to go to pieces. We shall, therefore, give him [Kamaraj] such help as we can and I have no doubt that you will also help him to the extent possible in the circumstances.[130]

[124] Letters to P. S. K. Raja and to K. Kamaraj and two letters to C. Rajagopalachari, 6 September 1953.
[125] Rajagopalachari to Nehru, 5 September 1953. Kamaraj had had no regular education.
[126] Nehru to Rajagopalachari, 6, 7 and 8 October 1953.
[127] Rajagopalachari's telegram to Nehru, 8 October 1953.
[128] Nehru to P. V. Naidu, 29 October 1953.
[129] Nehru to Sri Prakasa, 18 November 1953.
[130] Nehru to Rajagopalachari, 6 April 1954.

Even these seemingly platitudinous remarks caused Rajagopalachari grave offence. An unrelenting hostility to Kamaraj was extended to include Nehru when it was realized that opposition to Kamaraj would not succeed unless Nehru was weakened.[131]

Yet, what Nehru himself would have rated as his greatest failure in these years in political relationships was over his inability to secure immediately what he wanted for Krishna Menon. Deeply impressed by Menon's efforts at Geneva and under the usual pressure from him, Nehru planned to appoint him a cabinet minister. Azad, who felt strongly about the charges of financial irregularity against Menon, immediately offered to resign in protest.[132] Nehru tried hard to persuade Azad to withdraw his objection and finally made a personal appeal:

> My dear Maulana,
>
> I shall be grateful if you will let me have your decision about the matter we have discussed so often recently regarding Krishna Menon. I have been working under great strain for some months. To this has been added mental anguish during the past two weeks. The issues before me are far-reaching and involve my future life. It is becoming difficult for me to concentrate on my work till I know clearly what I shall have to do.
> Should you so wish it I can come over to see you again.
>
> Yours affectionately,
>
> Jawaharlal.[133]

Azad, however, would not give way and Nehru had to shelve the proposal for the time being. The disappointment influenced his announcement a few weeks later that he would like to retire from office, at least temporarily. He himself claimed that it was merely to shake off a feeling of physical and mental staleness and regain freshness and creativeness by going round the country mobilizing opinion and whipping up public enthusiasm in favour of official plans for development. Unlike previous occasions when he had offered to step down, his ideas and policies at this time did not run counter to those of the Party; he felt basically fit and was determined to remain so; he had a sense of confidence and fulfilment and believed he had still work to do; and relinquishing office would not mean retirement from public life. The country had reached a stage-post in its progress and could carry on for at least a short while without him. He wanted leisure to read and think and

[131] M. Desai, *The Story of My Life* (Delhi, 1974), Vol. 2, p. 31.
[132] Azad to Nehru, 1 August 1954.
[133] Handwritten letter, 12 August 1954.

19   Nehru in 1954   20   At a charity cricket match, 1953

21   Presiding over a speech by Jayaprakash Narayan

22   Nehru, 1954

to establish the irrelevance of the irritating question, 'After Nehru, who?'[134] All these were arguments planned to convince. But no doubt the failure to obtain Azad's assent to Menon's return to Delhi, the inability to add to his team the man with the closest intellectual affinity without losing the colleague nearest to him in politics, helped to create a feeling of tiredness and disillusion in the midst of all-round success.

[134] Nehru's speech to Congress Parliamentary Party, 30 September 1954; Nehru to Chief Ministers, 1 October 1954; Nehru to presidents, Pradesh Congress committees, 11 October 1954; Nehru to Sir Charles Trevelyan, 21 November 1954.

11

'The Light of Asia'

ONE

From the summer of 1954, the drift away from the United States and towards the Communist Powers continued steadily. Nehru became increasingly alienated by the strident bellicosity of the State Department. 'And yet, no one knows what it [American policy] is, except strong language and powerful emotions . . .'[1] Americans, he commented later, 'seem to imagine that every problem can be solved if there is enough talking and shouting about it. My own view is that a little silence might help.'[2] It was almost as if he could not approve of any facet of the United States. On a project for Indian scholars visiting the United States, he wrote

> I am all for broadening the outlook of the person. But mere breadth is not enough; there must be some depth also. As far as I can see, there is neither breadth nor depth about the average American. There is technical knowledge in a special field which is certainly important. The United States is hardly a place where one could go at present in search of the higher culture.[3]

The dislike of United States policy, while it helped to expose a prejudice against the United States, did not immediately result in India drawing closer to the Soviet Union. When the Soviet Ambassador suggested, and even produced a draft of a non-aggression treaty embodying the Five Principles delineated in the Tibet agreement, Nehru shied away from signing and used the chairmanship of the Indo-China commissions as the excuse.[4] All he was prepared to do was to accept more technical and

[1] To K. N. Katju, 3 July 1954.
[2] Note, 24 July 1954.
[3] Note, 18 July 1954.
[4] Nehru to K. P. S. Menon, Indian Ambassador in Moscow, 8 August 1954; note, 17 August 1954.

scientific assistance; and the fact that this would entail the presence of a large number of Soviet citizens in India caused him no worry.

> In these international matters, there is always an element of risk in whatever one might do. The friends of today might be the enemies of tomorrow. Our main objective is to build up India and we should take advantage of any proposal to that end, unless it is clearly undesirable. At the present moment, I would almost say that, owing to various circumstances, we have rather undermined the Communist position in India.[5]

There was less hesitation in Nehru's response to China, and his visit to that country in October was to him part of his continuing discovery of Asia. En route he spent a few days in the states of Indo-China, where the only event of significance was a meeting with Ho Chi Minh.

> He came forward — almost leapt forward — and embraced and kissed me. Obvious that this was not a showpiece. He felt it and meant it. Fine, frank face, gentle and benign — not at all one's idea of a leader of a rebellion.[6]

On arrival in Peking, he found that about a million people had turned out and crowded the twelve-mile route from the airport to give him what Desmond Donelly, a witness to the scene, described as 'a Roman triumph'.[7] For the only time on Nehru's visit, the hosts dispensed with the bullet-proof car with window glass nearly four inches thick, and Nehru and Chou rode in an open car. This was the first occasion that Chou, or anyone else in high office in the People's Republic of China, had so appeared in public, and it was clearly done to prove to Nehru that the leaders of the new China could, if they chose, behave as Nehru did in India. There were few men in police uniform to be seen on this drive but, as Nehru commented later, 'no doubt there must have been plenty of other people to maintain this order.'[8]

It was not, therefore, the number of people gathered to welcome him, but their enthusiasm which impressed Nehru, for it seemed to him to possess an element of spontaneity. 'I make myself deliberately receptive when I go to any place, critically receptive if you like, but receptive. And I sensed such a tremendous emotional response from the Chinese people that I was amazed.' It was almost an upheaval of sentiment, representing the basic urges of the people for friendship with India.[9] That India, not a member of the Communist fold but a fellow-Asian state, should be friendly

---

[5] To K. N. Katju, 28 August 1954.

[6] Diary entry, 17 October 1954. During his seventeen years as Prime Minister, Nehru kept a diary for only five days, from 15 to 19 October 1954.

[7] *Daily Mail* (London), 8 July 1955.

[8] Nehru to Lady Mountbatten, 2 November 1954.

[9] Nehru's talk to the Congress Parliamentary Party, 17 November 1954, Tape 1, N.M.M.L.

to China perhaps served to increase the self-assurance of the Chinese people and strengthen a traditional outlook. For both the government and people of China still seemed to him, in spite of a new ideology, strongly Chinese; and a deep nationalist sentiment went along with an attachment to old-world virtues of courtesy, artistic sense and hospitality, and a sympathy for much of classical literature and culture.

Nehru still found Chou 'very India-conscious' and as eager as at Delhi to be as friendly as possible. It was Nehru who did not go out of his way to extend the area of assent. He pointed out the fear of China (and also perhaps of India) that prevailed in the minds of the smaller nations of Asia, drew attention to the problem of overseas Chinese and referred to the possibility of interference in the internal affairs of other countries through the medium of local communist parties. When Chou spoke of the expansionist policy of the United States and their effort to bully weaker nations and rule the world, Nehru replied that he did not think that the American people wanted war; but they were undoubtedly afraid of communist aggression and wanted to take action to protect their interests. Nehru also refused to discuss the future of Taiwan and the other islands under Taiwanese rule; but this did not seem to be resented although the Chinese attached much importance to this question, especially as they knew that the United States was negotiating a mutual defence treaty with Taiwan. Chou, however, hinted that he would welcome Nehru's assistance in securing an invitation to any Asian-African conference, and also requested Nehru to sponsor a proposal for a conference on the Korean question. Chou added, as obvious testimony of goodwill, that he had repeatedly advised the Pakistan Government to draw away from the United States and improve relations with India. Nehru raised the question of India's frontiers and their erroneous delineation on Chinese maps. Chou replied that this was a historical question and they had been mostly reprinting old maps as they had had no time to revise them. While the Kuomintang could be charged with intentional tampering with the delineation of boundaries, the People's Government had no such motive. But one would always find some differences between maps because none of the boundaries of China, including those with the Soviet Union and Mongolia, had been precisely demarcated. This was a satisfactory answer as far as it went, and Nehru replied that the error in printing the boundary with India did not worry him much because India's boundaries were quite clear and were not a matter for argument. He could understand that the revision of Chinese maps had not yet taken place, and expressed the hope that the depiction of the boundary with India would be corrected before long. 'But I wondered how China would feel if a part of Tibet had been shown as part of India in our maps.'[10] Chou was later reported to have said that he had intended to

10 Nehru's note on his visit to China, 11 November 1954; Nehru to Chou En-lai, 14 December 1958.

discuss the frontier question, but in view of Nehru's 'strong attitude' had not pursued the matter.[11] It was a pity that Nehru rejected Chou's suggestion of a final joint communiqué. Much later trouble on this question of maps could have perhaps been avoided if Nehru had not had to depend solely on his own record of the talks.

With Mao also Nehru had long talks, described by James Cameron as 'clearly a punctuation mark in the history of Asia,'[12] Mao, talking, as Nehru later recorded,[13] like an elderly uncle giving good advice, referred to the ancient ties as well as the new friendship between India and China, their common experiences and their need for peace to reconstruct their backward economies. There were no quarrels between them, and cooperation between two countries of different ideologies was fully possible. China needed at least twenty years of peace — time for four five-year plans — for economic development, and was willing to cooperate with any country, even the United States, in pursuit of this objective. But the United States would not permit China to live in peace; 'we cannot have even good sleep, you know.' The United States was occupying or helping in the occupation of Taiwan and many other islands near the mainland, and from these bases air-raids and bombardment were carried out frequently. American imperialism had made profits in two wars, but a third war might not be to her advantage, for then revolution would spread. Atomic weapons had made no basic change in warfare except that more people would be killed. Nehru ventured to disagree. Mao's arguments led to the conclusion that war, though bad and to be avoided, should be welcomed if it came, and this Nehru could not accept. Atomic warfare was not a matter of a greater quantity of deaths, but of qualitative change in killing, and a third world war would be quite different from earlier wars.[14] But Nehru agreed with Mao that no country would benefit from such a war, and this

[11] Chou to U Nu, December 1954, as reported by Burmese Ambassador. See Raghavan's telegram to Nehru, 28 October 1956.

[12] James Cameron in a dispatch from Peking, *News Chronicle*, 20 October 1954.

[13] Nehru's note to his principal private secretary, 25 November 1959.

[14] Mao's version of this part of the discussion, as said to have been given at Moscow on 18 November 1957, was: 'I had an argument about this with Nehru. In this respect he is more pessimistic than I am. I told him that if half of humanity is destroyed the other half will still remain but imperialism will be destroyed entirely and there will be only socialism in all the world, and within half a century, or a whole century, the population will again increase by even more than half . . .' See J. Gittings, *Survey of the Sino-Soviet Dispute* (Oxford, 1968), p. 83.

Mao gave another account seven years later, on 9 January 1965. 'As he remembered it he had said China did not want a war. They didn't have atom bombs, but if other countries wanted to fight there would be a catastrophe in the whole world, meaning that many people would die. As for how many, nobody could know. He was not speaking only of China. He did not believe one atom bomb would destroy all mankind, so that you would not be able to find a government to negotiate peace. He had mentioned this to Nehru during their conversation. Nehru said that he was chairman of the Atomic Energy Commission of India and he knew about the destructiveness of atomic power. He was sure that no one could survive. Mao replied that it would probably not be as Nehru said. Existing governments might disappear but others would arise to replace them.' Edgar Snow, *The Long Revolution* (New York, 1971), p. 208.

led Mao to suggest that Nehru use his influence with the United States to point this out.

> If we act as chief of staff to Eisenhower, we would advise him not to go to war. This work, however, can be more easily done by the Prime Minister rather than us. If we do it, he will think we are intimidating him with revolution and he will say 'I am not afraid of revolution.'

Mao also proposed the convening of a world peace congress, in which over a hundred nations could participate and sign some form of treaty for peace and non-aggression. Nehru did not respond with much enthusiasm; with every passing year the possibility of war diminished, and if fifteen years went by without a war and there was an increasing fear of using weapons of such total destruction the time might then come for a world agreement. 'Of course', replied Mao, 'it is difficult to sink entire China into the sea and so India too, no matter how many people are killed.'[15]

The major impression left on Nehru by this visit to China was of a country smoothly running, with enormous potential power which was being translated gradually into actual strength. China was large not only in size but in spirit and character, and the Chinese people, unified, organized, disciplined and hardworking, exuded a tremendous sense of vitality. Arguments about recognition of the People's Republic of China or its admission to the United Nations seemed absurdly irrelevant when considered from China, for this enormous population lived in a world in itself. The question of accepting the new China was of crucial importance to the rest of the world, but China herself had passed the barrier when it could be made to suffer much from non-recognition.[16]

Nehru was appreciative of what he saw, but by no means overwhelmed or cowed. 'I am impressed by China. Having said that, I may also tell you that, having been to China, I am very much impressed by my own country.'[17] There had been nothing in China to give him a sense of inferiority about India. He was neither thunderstruck by admiration nor paralysed by fear. He was conscious of how important India and Indian support were to China's leaders at this time and how keen and careful they were to retain his sympathy; and he did not feel that India was likely to be outstripped by China economically. The initial start that India had was still secure. But the pace the Chinese had set for themselves was swifter than that of India; 'we have to be very, very wide awake.' Though there was no unfriendly rivalry, and it seemed to him without doubt that the two countries could live together peacefully, 'there is something all the time there which we will

[15] Record of Nehru's talks with Mao, 19 and 23 October 1954. Nehru minuted on the file that this record was not always accurate.

[16] To Lady Mountbatten, 2 November, note, 13 November, and to Chief Ministers, 15 November 1954.

[17] Address to Congress Parliamentary Party, 2 December 1954, Tape 1, N.M.M.L.

have to watch to see that we do not fall back, something to keep us up to the mark all the time . . .'[18] But he saw no reason for India to change her ways of functioning. Before his visit he had been committed to democratic socialism.

> I take it that our objective is to have ultimately a socialist economy. I am not using the word in any doctrinaire sense, but in its broad meaning. That economy as well as any planning requires an organized approach based on adequate data with definite targets. It requires various kinds of controls at least at strategic points. It is clear that we cannot proceed along authoritarian lines, such as in the Soviet Union or even as in China. The problem for us, therefore, is how far we can achieve our objective through democratic planning without too much compulsion. It may be that this kind of planning does not yield those spectacular results which might be obtained by an authoritarian approach to this question and a great deal of compulsion. Even so, we prefer the democratic approach because of certain values and standards we cherish.[19]

First-hand knowlege of China provided him with no reason to change his general view. Each country had to develop according to its own genius and the fact that he did not criticize or condemn what took place in the Soviet Union or China did not mean that he wanted to act in similar vein in India. 'But I have the strongest objection to India being made a rootless pale shadow of some other country.'[20] Indeed, to some it seemed that he felt more strongly about this now than ever before.[21] But there was, after his visit to China, an added degree of urgency to his thinking on democratic socialism.

> For my part, I believe in parliamentary democracy and in individual freedom. But I also believe that it is essential to have rapid economic progress. We have to combine the two. That is a great test for us and it will require all our wisdom and all our strength and unity of purpose.[22]

[18] Address to Congress Parliamentary Party, 17 November 1954, Tape 1, N.M.M.L.

[19] To Chief Ministers, 15 September 1954. This incidentally disposes of the contention of some critics of Nehru that he had been frightened by evidence of China's rapid progress, and it was only on his return from China that he began, for the first time since 1947, to speak of the necessity of socialism in India. See A. & B. Rao, *Six Thousand Days*, (New Delhi, 1974), pp. 9-10.

[20] To Chief Ministers, 9 December 1954.

[21] 'I thought, too, that on his return from Communist China he felt consciously satisfied — more than before — that his way of running a country was better than Mao Tse-tung's. This feeling, whether correct or not, was so strong that I have come to the conclusion that Nehru's visit to Red China was a good thing for all the friends of democracy in India and the world, for his observation of Chinese communism strengthened his conviction that democracy is better.' Robert Trumbull, 'Portrait of a Symbol named Nehru', *New York Times Magazine*, 12 December 1954.

[22] To Chief Ministers, 15 November 1954.

232   JAWAHARLAL NEHRU

India still led, and was on the path which to Nehru was the only correct
one; but the lead could not be taken for granted and the direction taken had
to be justified by results.

TWO

At the Colombo conference, Indonesia had suggested the holding of a
wider conference of Asian and African states. Nehru had not been in favour
of providing what he thought would be a forum for heated discussion on
local and regional matters, particularly Israel and Palestine.[23]

> Egyptian or indeed Arab politics appear to me to be extraordinarily
> immature and wrapped up in their petty problems with little
> understanding of what is going on in the world. When I met Nasser, I
> was attracted to him; he is a likeable person. When I read a little book
> of his, I felt disappointed, that is, in regard to his intellectual calibre.[24]

He had indefinitely postponed an exchange of embassies with Israel
because he believed that it would hamper India's chances at an appropriate
moment in mediating in the West Asian problem;[25] and a general
discussion of the whole matter at this stage and in the setting of an Asian-
African conference could only prove an embarrassment. But gradually
Nehru came round to accepting the utility of such a conference, and saw in
it perhaps a possible platform for refuting the United States policy of
imposing military alliances on Asia and Africa. That India, Burma and
Indonesia held together augured well; together they formed an area of
peace which could be extended and buttressed.

Nehru, therefore, now gave serious thought to the details of such a
conference. As the main purpose was to create an atmosphere of
cooperation and improve the projection of Asia and Africa in the world
picture, there should be no formal agenda and specific controversies should
be avoided. Krishna Menon was for an invitation to Israel with an
explanation to the Arab states that the presence of Israel committed them to
nothing; Nehru, wishing to avoid dissension even on the question of the
composition of the conference, agreed with reluctance that an invitation to
Israel should be extended only if the Arab countries agreed to it.[26] But he
was firm that China, who was eager to be present, should be invited. A hint
by Eden that this would create a bad impression in Britain and the United
States was sharply rejected. India had no desire to irritate opinion in these

[23] Note, 8 August 1954.
[24] To Ali Yavar Jung, Indian Ambassador to Egypt, 8 September 1954. The book was Nasser's *The Philosophy of Revolution*.
[25] Nehru's note, 3 June 1954, and letter to M. Sharett, 5 June 1954.
[26] Krishna Menon's note, 18 December, and Nehru's note, 19 December 1954.

two countries but the world was larger than them and account had to be taken of views and reactions in the rest of the world.

> For us to be told, therefore, that the United States and the United Kingdom will not like the inclusion of China in the Afro-Asian conference is not very helpful. In fact, it is somewhat irritating. There are many things that the United States and the United Kingdom have done which we do not like at all.[27]

So the five Colombo powers, meeting at Bogor, decided to invite all the independent countries of Asia and Africa barring South Africa and Israel. The first was an obvious omission, but Nehru conceded that the second was an illogical surrender to Arab susceptibility.[28] The People's Republic of China, recognized by all the inviting powers, was asked to participate, despite Pakistan's initial opposition; and this ruled out Taiwan, for it enjoyed no separate statehood. All four states of Indo-China were included as they presented an urgent problem of peace and the Colombo powers had special responsibilities with regard to the Geneva agreements. There was no basic objection to inviting the two Koreas but on balance it was decided not to do so. The borderline cases of states on the verge of independence were considered each on its merits and invitations were sent to the Gold Coast, the Sudan and the Central African Federation — the last in order to establish the principle that the conference would not be merely a gathering of coloured races.

Though the mere fact of such a wide membership would give the conference high and unique importance of a general nature, the development of the crisis in East Asia added a topical relevance. The United States argued that the continued detention of American prisoners in China was a breach of the Korean armistice agreement, while China took the line that these were spies who had been parachuted directly into China. Nehru passed on a message that there was such strong feeling in the United States over this that the Canadian Government feared serious consequences;[29] but Chou assumed an attitude of indifference. Though China wanted peace, she would not beg for peace.'[30] The United Nations Secretary-General, Hammarskjöld, then offered to visit China to mediate on this issue and Nehru advised Chou to receive him. To refuse to do so would give some handle to China's enemies, while his visit might well help in stating China's case fully before the world.[31] This was all the more important as the United Nations had one-sidedly condemned China. Hammarskjöld claimed that as

[27] Memorandum of British Foreign Office on Eden's conversation with Krishna Menon, 10 December 1954, and Nehru's note, 18 December 1954.

[28] Nehru's telegram to all Indian missions, 4 January 1955.

[29] Nehru's telegram to Raghavan, 6 December 1954.

[30] Raghavan's telegram to Nehru after interview with Chou, 9 December 1954.

[31] Nehru's telegram to Chou, 13 December 1954.

he did not approve of the resolution he had not forwarded it; but he hoped
that some good might result from his direct approach to China and open
out fresh avenues.[32]

The Chinese Government agreed to receive Hammarskjöld, and this in
itself strengthened their diplomatic position by bringing them, despite
non-recognition by the United Nations, more fully into the international
system. But any quick settlement of this question was thwarted by the
deeper involvement of the United States with Chiang Kai-shek.[33] At the
Commonwealth Prime Ministers' Conference, Churchill, in 'a kind of
second childhood',[34] fully supported the United States; but Eden,
R. A. Butler and Pearson were keen to exercise a restraining influence, and
Eden requested Nehru to persuade China to refrain from interfering with
the evacuation of the coastal islands and to send a representative to Lake
Success.[35] If Chou's words were any indication, India still had some
influence.

> As I have said before, the Chinese people are very glad to have such a
> friendly neighbour as India in the common cause of defending peace. I
> have the firm conviction that the deep friendship between our two
> peoples and their common desire to work for peace have provided the
> prospect of broad development for the friendly cooperation between
> China and India.[36]

So Nehru sent messages from London to Chou to isolate the Taiwan issue
and give it low priority; agree to negotiations on other issues; not to insist
on total withdrawal by the United States; to accept even an informal
conference unconnected with the United Nations such as the Geneva
conference on Indo-China; and to foster Sino-British relations by not
raising the question of Hong Kong. A merely negative attitude, however
strong one's case, was neither adequate nor proper when the alternative was
a major war; so one should proceed step by step, and start with diplomatic
soundings and informal undertakings in order to lower tension. There was,
for example, no reason why, if the United States desisted from action and
restrained Chiang, China should not acquiesce in the evacuation of the
coastal islands.[37] Chou's response was not very helpful. He complained of
active provocation, observed that friendship with Britain would be as easy
to secure as 'fish on tree-tops' and said nothing about any Chinese moves to

[32] Nehru's telegram to Raghavan, 3 January 1955.

[33] On 1 December 1954 the United States had concluded a military security alliance with Taiwan, and
on 24 January 1955 Eisenhower followed this up by speaking of military action to counter any effort
from the mainland.

[34] Nehru to Indira Gandhi, 1 February 1955.

[35] Eden to Nehru, 2 February 1955.

[36] Chou to Nehru, 28 December 1954.

[37] Nehru's telegrams to Raghavan, 4, 5, 9 and 10 February 1955; Krishna Menon's telegram to
Raghavan, 6 February 1955.

reduce tension. The only positive reaction was support of the Soviet proposal for a great power conference on the lines of Geneva.[38] But this in itself was insufficient to thaw the attitude of the United States, and the prospect of a general war remained as menacing as before.

So the Asian-African conference could be of more than general significance, and Nehru was determined that it should succeed. No detail of organization was too trivial for him.

Above all, one fact should be remembered and this is usually forgotten in Indonesia. This fact is an adequate provision of bathrooms and lavatories, etc. People can do without drawing rooms, but they cannot do without bathrooms and lavatories.

It was such deficiencies which upset people, and frayed tempers were no good when considering important problems.[39] It was generally recognized that he himself would be the most important figure at Bandung. Though People's China was mustering strength and prestige, India was still the political pivot of Asia, and in India Nehru was more than ever the pre-eminent figure. He spoke for almost every shade of opinion. The resolution of the Congress in January 1955 to build a 'socialistic pattern' of society blurred differences between the Congress and left-wing parties. To Rajagopalachari this was 'the crazy piloting of the nation'[40] but to the country as a whole it was a major step forward. Most Socialists felt there was now no basic reason why they should not return to the Congress fold, but Nehru dissuaded them. He claimed to have done so because of his belief that the Socialists still had a role to play as a responsible opposition party;[41] but he was probably also influenced by the desire not to hurt Jayaprakash. In the elections in Andhra province the Communist Party, which had earlier exercised considerable influence, was now routed. Eden, then on a visit to Delhi, remarked to Nehru that this was an event of greater world importance than anything else that had happened recently.[42] This triumph was the result not so much of a positive failure on the part of the Communists as of the new mood of hope and expectation created by an improved food situation, a successful foreign policy and the commitment of the Congress to socialism. For much of this Nehru could, and did, take personal credit. 'No, I don't believe it [communism] is at all a threat to my country. I can't speak of every other country, only that I feel reasons — well, frankly, because I think I'm quite good enough to prevent that.'[43]

[38] Raghavan's telegrams to Nehru, 6, 8 and 11 February 1955.
[39] Nehru to B. F. H. B. Tyabji, Indian Ambassador in Indonesia, 20 February 1955.
[40] B. Chatterjee, *Thousand Days with Rajaji* (New Delhi, 1973), p. 136.
[41] Nehru to U.N. Dhebar, reporting conversation with Sucheta Kripalani, 1 April 1955.
[42] Nehru to Vijayalakshmi, 5 March 1955.
[43] Interview with Margaret Chase Smith on television, 15 March 1955.

The Communists themselves were dejected, having little to criticize in Nehru's policy at home or abroad. A. K. Gopalan, a generally respected Communist leader, called on Nehru, evidently on instructions from his party, to apologize for some objectionable remarks made during the election campaign. He assured Nehru that it was now the policy of his party not to create trouble in any way.

> He reminded me that he was an old Congressman and even though he had become a Communist he could not forget what he had learned as a Congressman. There was a difference between those Communists who had been Congressmen and had worked hard for the Congress and newcomers who did not have that past experience or discipline.[44]

In fact, Nehru now needed to worry only about lone assassins, either those encouraged by the Salazar government or unbalanced individuals. He was told that the Portuguese had offered a considerable amount as payment for his murder;[45] and at Nagpur a man jumped on the foot-board of his car with a large, razor-sharp knife. But Nehru vetoed any tightening of security.

Abroad, his status was equally unchallenged. No single individual had done more, in the years since the Second World War, to project Asia on to the world stage. Consistently, as at the Commonwealth Prime Ministers' Conference earlier in the year, he had given expression to the general Asian viewpoint and drawn attention to the ferment taking place on the Asian continent. This basic upheaval of ideas had to be understood and come to terms with if it was not to become explosive. Even Churchill, though his mind and memory were clouded, grasped the pre-eminence of India's Prime Minister and cast him in a crucial role.

> I hope you will think of the phrase 'The Light of Asia'. It seems to me that you might be able to do what no other human being could in giving India the lead, at least in the realm of thought, throughout Asia, with the freedom and dignity of the individual as the ideal rather than the Communist Party drill book.[46]

The Commonwealth members as a whole relied heavily on Nehru to give value to their association. Others turned to him with particular problems. Ollenhauer, leader of the opposition in West Germany, travelled to London to explain to Nehru the viewpoint of his party on rearmament and reunification; Adenauer, the Chancellor, then expressed a desire for a meeting to argue the counter-case of the West German Government, but

[44] Nehru's note on interview with Gopalan, 1 April 1955.

[45] Nehru's note to his secretary, 11 March 1955.

[46] Churchill to Nehru, 21 February 1955. Churchill referred again to this phrase in his letter of 30 June 1955.

WESTERHAM 3344

CHARTWELL.
WESTERHAM.
KENT.

PRIVATE. ‚ó June 1955.

My dear Nehru,

I hope you will forgive the lapse of time in
replying to your letter of April 8. Events following
upon my resignation, and the General Election here, have
delayed my correspondence greatly.

I was much touched by what you said. One of
the most agreeable memories of my last years in office is
our association. At our conferences your contribution was
a leading and constructive one, and I always admired your
ardent wish for peace and the absence of bitterness in your
consideration of the antagonisms that had in the past
divided us. Yours is indeed a heavy burden and
responsibility, shaping the destiny of your many millions
of countrymen, and playing your outstanding part in world
affairs. I wish you well in your task. Remember

"The Light of Asia!"

With warm personal regards,

I remain,

Yours sincerely,

Winston Churchill

Winston Churchill's letter to Nehru, 30 June 1955

an interview could not be fitted into Nehru's schedule. Mendès-France came to the airport at Paris for a *tour d' horizon*. Casey of Australia requested Nehru to restrain Indonesia on the question of West New Guinea. 'It is clear that you will personally be the leading figure at the Bandung Conference — although I expect that Chou En-lai will endeavour to make the most of the opportunities that the conference will provide.'[47] Eden and Hammarskjöld sought his personal intervention with Chou to persuade China to respond to the permission granted to seventy-six Chinese students to leave the United States by releasing the American airmen.[48] The Dutch Government desired him to speak to Sukarno and secure a fair and quick trial for thirty-five Dutch prisoners in Indonesia.[49] Non-official opinion also had faith in him, and Einstein, shortly before his death, passed on to Nehru Leo Szilard's suggestion that China agree not to occupy the offshore islands for some time after their evacuation.[50]

The sabotage in Hong Kong which led to the crash in the Indian Ocean of the *Kashmir Princess*, the Air India Constellation carrying the advance party of the Chinese delegation, set a sombre note for the Bandung Conference. The chronic crisis in East Asia had escalated to the verge of war,[51] the formation of SEATO had muddied the waters in South East Asia and, with both Britain and Pakistan linked with the Baghdad Pact, tension had increased in West Asia. Given the imperative of the 'soul' of Dulles,[52] to throw a military harness not only round China but around communism everywhere, one could expect a crisis to develop at any place. In this context, the very fact of a meeting of the representatives of the peoples of Asia and Africa was of enormous importance; and it was, therefore, vital to Nehru that the conference should not end in failure. Agreement on specific issues was not possible; nor was it necessary. The broad purpose of the Bandung Conference, in line with the Asian Relations Conference at New Delhi in 1947, should be to reassert the importance of Asia and Africa in the world. For too long they had been treated as outer fringes of Europe; but now they had their own views on world affairs and these could not be ignored. They had no wish to intervene in other people's problems but to the extent that these problems impinged on Asia and Africa, their views

[47] Casey to Nehru, 6 April 1955.

[48] Personal message from Eden transmitted by British High Commission in Delhi to Secretary-General, 10 April 1955; telegram from Indian Permanent Mission at United Nations to Foreign Secretary, 14 April 1955.

[49] Secretary-General's record of conversation with Dutch Ambassador, 12 April 1955.

[50] Einstein to Nehru, 6 April 1955.

[51] Dulles publicly warned China on 8 March not to underrate United States determination to meet what it regarded as aggression, and Eisenhower later revealed that the United States had even selected targets on the Chinese mainland that might have to be hit. A number of senior officials in Washington expected in late March that war would break out within a month. J. H. Kalicki, *The Pattern of Sino-American Crises* (Cambridge, 1975), pp. 149-52.

[52] The phrase was Chou's years later, in an interview with an Australian delegation, 5 July 1971. See R. Terrill, *800,000,000 The Real China* (Penguin, 1975), p. 148.

would have to be heard. Whatever the differences among the nations of these continents, they had inherited common social and economic problems, and on these perhaps there could be some unity of opinion. Certainly they would not accept any decisions imposed on them by others, however powerful, and particularly on issues created by the interference of other states in Asia and Africa.

All these aspirations could easily be lost in a mass of verbiage about the spirit of Asia and Africa; and aware of this, Nehru set out to keep the Bandung Conference firmly rooted to the fundamental issues. He spoke, like almost everyone else, of the new surge of feelings in these two continents, and of marching in step with history; but the course he sought to steer was one of 'practical idealism'. The first task was to hold together these variegated nations, covering all attitudes from military alliance with the United States to communism as the official creed. As the impact which the conference made on the outside world was as important as the relations which member countries developed among themselves, it was essential to conceal differences beneath wide generalizations and assert, wherever possible, common viewpoints. If the Bandung Conference were to be a success, it could only be as a *tour de force*. Without sleight of hand or trickery, an assembly which included so many allies of one side or the other would have to find ways of presenting themselves convincingly to the world as possessing, beneath their varied policies, a genuine sense of shared interest.   To avoid each nation stating at the very outset its own attitude on various problems, thereby reducing elasticity of discussion, Nehru proposed that the conference dispense with opening speeches. Mahomed Ali opposed this and Nehru had to give way, but himself refrained from speaking at the inaugural sessions. Nehru was by now rousing considerable hostility among the other delegations by what was suspected to be a calculated effort at personal leadership.[53] It was decided, after much discussion, to reach a consensus on general issues while reserving controversies for informal discussions. When a resolution condemning colonialism was being considered, Sir John Kotelawala of Ceylon raised the issue — which, apart from everything else, was far removed from Asia and Africa — of Soviet dominance in eastern Europe.[54] Nehru's sharp reaction revealed his annoyance. This was a conference of governments and should function within that limitation. The countries of eastern Europe were sovereign states and members of the United Nations, and for the conference to treat them as colonial territories would be 'a most extraordinary position to take up'. If, however, the delegates wished to review the pressures and coercion to which independent countries were subject, 'you enter into a region of doubt, uncertainty, difficulty and

[53] I. A. G. Gdo Agung, *Twenty Years Indonesian Foreign Policy 1945-65* (The Hague, 1973), pp. 223-5.
[54] Sir J. Kotelawala, *An Asian Prime Minister's Story* (London, 1956), p. 187. Personal relations between Nehru and Kotelawala had never been happy.

international confusion about which you can argue day in and day out. Whatever the result you may arrive at, it will be a confusing one.' He was not an admirer of the Soviet Union. 'I dislike many things they have done as I dislike many things the Western Powers have done and at the proper moment, if members consider it necessary, we will give expression to it in our own language.' But this question of conditions in eastern Europe could not be raised as a formal matter and the policies of any country criticized. It would be enough if members emphasized, in general terms, that no country should interfere in the internal affairs of another.[55]   This hurdle was got over by condemning 'colonialism in all its manifestations' as an evil which should be speedily ended, but without making any specific reference to independent countries, or, as suggested by Turkey, to 'international doctrines resorting to the methods of force, infiltration and subversion'. But even more fraught with difficulties was the question of military alliances, which was of direct concern to many participants. Nehru elaborated with some impatience on the meaning and virtues of non-alignment for the countries of Asia and Africa. NATO might have advantages for Western Europe, but to the rest of the world it assumed the face of colonialism, while SEATO was no more than an angry reaction to the Geneva agreements. Every nation had the right to defend itself but such a right would not be strengthened by joining either the Western or the Soviet bloc or even by forming a separate bloc. For the newly free and under-developed countries, potential strength lay not in piling up arms, but in industrial progress and the fostering of a spirit of self-reliance. Peace might well come through strength, but not, for the Bandung countries, through military strength or alliances. 'We do not agree with the Com-munist teachings, we do not agree with the anti-Communist teach-ings, because they are both based on wrong principles.' India certainly would not belong to either bloc whatever happened, and would cherish her identity. Non-alignment, however, was not just a matter of ideology. If the whole world were divided up between two big blocs the inevitable result would be war. But India could utilize her present position to promote the forces working against war and for friendly coexistence. A military alliance increased the insecurity of its members while commitment to the Five Principles lessened tension and harmed nobody.[56]

This was not an issue on which Nehru could hope to persuade the representatives of governments which were already signatories of military pacts. Indeed, by conceding that they could organize for self-defence, he virtually recognized that he had no hope of securing the acceptance of his views. The clause in the final communiqué of the Bandung Conference, that every nation had the right to defend itself singly or collectively in conformity with the United Nations Charter, while stating nothing new,

[55] Nehru's speech at a closed session of the conference, 22 April 1955.
[56] Nehru's speeches at the closed sessions of the Bandung Conference, 22 and 23 April 1955.

seemed to Nehru not to cover the Manila treaty, because the Charter only provided for self-defence in case of armed attack.[57] But no direct condemnation of that treaty was feasible at Bandung. The most that the non-aligned countries could secure was an indirect censure of SEATO by stipulating that such collective defence arrangements should not serve the particular interests of any of the big powers.

So the Bandung Conference was in no solid sense a victory for Nehru, if by that be meant the imposition of his outlook on a large number of the participating countries. In fact, he sacrificed his views in order to secure the maximum harmony and only asserted himself when the proceedings threatened to get out of hand. Yet he was satisfied, not so much with the trend of the formal discussions and the final communiqué drafted in such a way as to enable all to sign, as by the very fact that the conference had met and the leaders of the two continents had got to know each other. Nasser, who had never before left Egypt except for the pilgrimage to Mecca, was 'excited like a little boy'.[58] Nehru himself, who was attending for the first time since 1947 a full-scale international conference, had to revise his opinions of many foreign statesmen, and was particularly impressed by Prince Wan Waithayakon of Thailand.[59] But the conference was really a stage set by Nehru, with not naivety but conscious deliberation, for the Chinese Prime Minister. He saw himself as a producer-manager rather than as a hero; and had he not willingly abdicated, Chou would not have been the central figure. If Chou appeared to many to be the star of Bandung, frequently timing his diplomatic operations so as to overshadow the Indian Prime Minister,[60] Nehru regarded Chou's success as his own personal triumph.

Chou, expectedly, made the fullest use of the occasion presented to him and projected an image of smiling friendliness.

He conducted himself with ability and moderation in the Conference and its committees. Whenever he spoke, he did so with authority. He took particular pains to meet delegates and went to many parties given by heads of delegations. He had private talks also with them. He did not put forward any important proposal but objected to something if it seemed to him to be opposed to any principle for which he stood. He was obviously anxious that the Conference should succeed and, therefore, tried to be as accommodating as possible. He was patient even when he had to put up with rather offensive behaviour, which sometimes happened. Only once did he lose his temper for a short while in a committee and said that China would not be bullied.[61]

[57] Address to Congress Parliamentary Party, 3 May 1955. Tape 2, N.M.M.L.
[58] Nehru to Lady Mountbatten, 30 April 1955.
[59] Note, 28 April 1955.
[60] Gdo Agung, op. cit., p. 257.
[61] Nehru's note on the Bandung Conference, 25 April 1955.

He told Nehru that the People's Government had practically decided to release the American airmen when the *Kashmir Princess* was blown up; but he promised to review the matter and invited Krishna Menon to Peking for this purpose.[62] At a meeting with the four sponsoring Prime Ministers, Prince Wan and Romulo of the Philippines, he laughed out the idea of introducing communism into Tibet, and invited them all to visit that region.[63] He expressed publicly his willingness to hold direct talks with the United States on Taiwan and added in private that, while he could make no further commitment till the American reaction was known, he was anxious to seek a peaceful settlement. Though China could not accept a cease-fire as this implied acknowledgment of Chiang's possession of Taiwan and the presence of United States forces on the island, his government had no desire to punish Chiang's officers and men and would gladly absorb them in the Chinese army. He approved of the idea of recognizing the neutrality of Laos and Cambodia, and supported Nehru's rejection of U Nu's suggestion (made with the consent of Dulles) that India should channel economic and military aid to these two countries. Chou's own proposal, which was that India, Burma and China should jointly address Britain and the United States, seeking clarification of their suggestion, was turned down by Nehru.[64]

On relations with other countries, Chou stated that China, though under a communist government, desired no expansion or internal subversion; so he had come to Bandung to reach a common understanding on the basis of the Five Principles. Each country should respect whatever way of life and economic system had been chosen by another, and he was prepared to give every assurance to remove apprehensions. He specifically mentioned that China respected the ways of life of the American and Japanese peoples, but claimed the same right, to be respected, for herself. China wanted no special privileges or status but only equality of treatment. Chou followed up this statement by personal discussions with the various participants. Talks were begun with Indonesia on the question of overseas Chinese, and even with the Thai delegates on possible improvement of relations. Indeed, Chou, a hard-headed communist beneath an exterior of 'reasonableness, restraint and good breeding',[65] was not influenced by such infantile notions as friendship or a sense of obligation. Convinced that each country was utterly alone in the world, with nothing but its own self-reliance and resources to protect it, he had no qualms about acting to weaken India's position. When he found that Nehru had thrown his weight against a condemnatory resolution on Palestine, Chou carefully cultivated the Arab representatives and contended that the creation and support of Israel was an even more

[62] Nehru's notes on talks with Chou, 23 and 26 April 1955.
[63] Nehru's notes on talks with Chou, 23 and 28 April 1955.
[64] Nehru's notes, 25 and 26 April 1955.
[65] Nehru to C. Rajagopalachari, 28 April 1955.

flagrant case of interference by the Western Powers in Asia than Taiwan.[66] He also quietly established relations on a cordial footing with Pakistan. Mahomed Ali informed him that Pakistan was not hostile to China, did not fear Chinese aggression and would not be dragged into any war between the United States and China. It is said 'on unimpeachable authority' that in return Chou assured Pakistan that there was no conceivable clash of interest which could imperil the friendly relations between the two countries, but that this was not true of relations between India and China and a definite conflict of interests between them could be expected soon.[67] If this report be accurate and even if Nehru had known of it, he would probably not have minded or even have been surprised. He had no wish to see the leaders of Bandung become yes-men of each other any more than of the Western or Communist Powers, and he was aware of the priorities of national interests. Even so, Chou saw fit to keep these overtures hidden. He was clearly not Nehru's equal at this time in international trust and goodwill.

THREE

After Bandung, Nehru continued to maintain contacts with the two blocs. He had been severely critical of many aspects of American policy, while his opposition to the creation of a circle of alliances and to the extension of spheres of influence in Asia brought him in line with the current policy of the U.S.S.R. Large-scale economic assistance had also been inaugurated in a spectacular manner in February 1955 with Soviet agreement to build a steel mill with an annual capacity of one million tons. Yet Nehru regarded as unfair any suggestion that he was non-aligned more in favour of one side than the other. 'I belong', he had asserted at Bandung, 'to neither [bloc] and I propose to belong to neither whatever happens in the world. If we have to stand alone, we will stand by ourselves, whatever happens . . . and we propose to face all consequences.'[68] On his return from Indonesia, he sent for the American Ambassador to assure him that there was no truth in the suggestion that his government was hostile to the United States. They wanted to be friends, although they certainly felt that American policies had been wrong and encouraged the very tendencies which they sought to end. Too much talk of communism or anti-communism confused the issue,

---

[66] Report by S. Dutt, Foreign Secretary, of conversation with Foreign Minister of Jordan, 19 April 1955.

[67] L. F. Rushbrook Williams, *The State of Pakistan* (London, 1962), pp. 120-21. The establishment of good relations between China and Pakistan may explain the omission in the Soviet press of any mention of Pakistan's anti-Soviet attitude at the conference. See G. Mc. Kahin, *The Asian-African Conference* (New York, 1956), p. 20 fn.

[68] Speech at the closed session, 22 April 1955.

and the world crisis was better interpreted as one of large, dynamic countries inevitably trying to expand in various ways.[69] It was as part of this attempt to facilitate a *modus vivendi* between the clashing powers that Krishna Menon shuttled between Peking, London and Washington; for it was in this manner, outside the realm of formal diplomacy, that Nehru believed the principal non-aligned power could play its most effective role.

> There are no affirmatives and negatives about it. There are fine shades of opinion, hints thrown out, general impressions created without commitments, reactions awaited and so on. If a reaction is favourable, one takes another step forward. Otherwise one shuts up . . . What do we try to do? To soften and soothe each side and make it slightly more receptive to the other. This is not a matter of formal messages at all . . .[70]

Few today would question the wisdom of Nehru's analysis and of his hopes of moving gradually towards a peace based on firmer foundations. Even then in the United States there were some far-seeing enough to discern that it was not the pursuit of a mirage.[71] The *New York Times* agreed that there was enough development to allow hope that the cold war was growing lukewarm.[72] But to those sections of opinion in the United States that were guided by Dulles and the 'nationalism-anti-communism-warfare coalition',[73] Nehru's reasoning seemed an over-subtle apologia for partisanship. He was regarded as a declared protagonist, and his failure to steer the Bandung Conference clear of ideological dispute was received as a triumph for the allies of the United States.[74] Propaganda was set afoot claiming that India was inclined to communism and was encouraging its spread, that she and, in particular, her Prime Minister, were arrogant, sought the leadership of Asia and were striving to develop into a strong and dominating power, and that India was opposed to Arab interests.[75] Official American agencies were suspected of giving wide circulation to a

[69] Nehru's note on talk with John Sherman Cooper, 5 May 1955.

[70] Nehru to G. L. Mehta, Indian Ambassador in Washington, 1 June 1955.

[71] Cf. Professor George Kennan: 'In certain relatively powerless sectors of the American government establishment people continued to explore, patiently and with insight, the possible channels of approach to a less dangerous and more hopeful state of affairs. But in other and more powerful echelons other people continued to carry on with the concepts born of the Korean War, as though Stalin had never died, as though no changes had occurred, as though the problem were still, and solely, the achievement of superiority in preparation for a future military encounter accepted as inevitable, rather than the avoidance of a disastrous encounter for which there was no logical reason at all and which no one could expect to win . . . And who does not remember the result?' 'The United States and the Soviet Union 1917-1976', *Foreign Affairs*, July 1976, p. 685.

[72] 1 June 1955.

[73] The phrase is Professor J. K. Galbraith's, 'America's Undercover Coalition', *New Statesman*, 13 August 1976.

[74] See dispatch from Washington in *The Hindu*, 27 April 1955.

[75] Nehru's notes on interview with Prince (later King) Faisal, 5 and 7 May 1955.

vicious article by Nehru's younger sister denigrating the Nehru family;[76] and American money was being spent within India not merely to gain support for American policy but even to weaken Nehru's hold over his own followers.[77] All this might have embittered a smaller man and led to an open breach with the United States — a step which would have been received with considerable acclaim in India. Even Rajagopalachari, bothered by the growing American programme of nuclear armament, pressed Nehru to reject financial assistance from the United States. 'Sometime or other you will have to take the great step of not taking American aid. I hope I am not becoming a visionary, but it seems it is inevitable we take this step to complete the moral structure of our freedom.'[78] But it was precisely because the United States Government were so angry and promoting a widespread campaign against India and her leader that Nehru declined to take any step, however justified, that might further worsen relations between the two countries. Rajagopalachari was mixing up moral and political issues. 'Will it help from any moral or other point of view for us to take up a line which makes us appear to be actually hostile to the United States and not to be understood or appreciated by any country? An act must bear some relation to the existing circumstances.'[79]

Nehru, therefore, had no intention of being deflected from his genuine commitment to non-alignment by provocation or blandishment from either side, his general policy thereby being weakened and his personal integrity endangered. As a result, he exercised immeasurable influence in the world at large. It was India and not the United Nations whom China selected to announce the release of four American airmen. It was Nehru whom Hammarskjöld invited to wind up the tenth anniversary celebrations of the United Nations[80] — an invitation which Nehru had to decline because he could not fit in his schedule a journey to San Francisco. Nehru knew the sources of his strength in international affairs and had no intention of throwing them away. Visiting the Soviet Union that summer, he was not surprised to find that his hosts had organized an unprecedented welcome. For many months the Soviet leaders had realized how helpful to their own interests Nehru's general policies had been. Soon after the Geneva Conference Bulganin, referring to one of Nehru's speeches in Parliament, had remarked, 'All I can say of that speech, so full of wisdom

[76] Krishna Hutheesing's article in the *Ladies Home Journal* (January 1955) was distributed freely in India and abroad, allegedly by United States authorities, and efforts were made to secure its republication in some Indian newspapers. Nehru was also told that the *Pratap*, a Hindi journal of Delhi, was paid substantially by the United States Embassy for this purpose. See Nehru's note, 15 May 1955.

[77] 'It might interest you to know that some little time ago I received definite information that the United States were looking for agents in the Congress Party in India.' Nehru to S. N. Agarwal, secretary of the Congress Party, 24 May 1955.

[78] C. Rajagopalachari to Nehru, 4 May 1955.

[79] Nehru to C. Rajagopalachari, 9 May 1955. See also his statement at press conference, 31 May, *Times of India*, 1 June 1955.

[80] Dag Hammarskjöld to Nehru, 3 June 1955.

and vision, is may Nehru live long.' He knew of India's difficulties; he also knew that some people might even call Nehru communist. All that the Soviet people wanted was that Nehru should remain Nehru.[81] Now they had the chance to demonstrate to the world their growing empathy and perhaps even to draw and bind Nehru closer. All the members of the presidium were present at the airport in Moscow, and Bulganin, for the first time in his career, drove with Nehru in an open car through the milling streets of the capital. It was clearly an effort both to outpace the reception in China a year earlier and to demonstrate to Nehru that the regard for him in the Soviet Union was in converse proportion to that in the United States. But even foreign observers in Moscow conceded that there was a spontaneous element in this reception for the man who had become a symbol of the world's hope for peace.[82]

Nehru himself, back in the Soviet Union nearly thirty years after his first tour, which had so impressed him, was in a receptive and inquiring mood. He went 'with an open mind and, I hope, with an open heart'[83] to find out what he could for himself.

I remember reading in the thirties the great work of the Webbs: *Soviet Communism — A New Civilization.* I wondered then and I wonder still what this new civilization is. What are the enduring elements in it, what are superficial and will pass away. Is this a new religion that has appeared in human history with all the vitality and aggressiveness of a new faith, even though it puts on an economic garb? Is it a basic philosophy which gives us some understanding of the complexities of human relations and of the great and often tragic drama of man's adventure since first homo sapiens appeared on the surface of the earth? Does it give us some glimpse of the future?

The Soviet experiment had an economic appeal, but those bred in the Gandhian tradition of peaceful action and high standards of behaviour could not avoid doubt and distaste when techniques of unscrupulous violence were even made into a philosophy. Could the new economic approach, shorn of its violence and coercion and suppression of individual liberty, be helpful in solving India's problems or the world's problems?

There was no easy answer. Only by action and continuous effort and trial and error, could we proceed along the dimly lit path of the present towards an uncertain future. And whatever our decisions might be, events in other parts of the world could come in our way and influence them and even obstruct them.[84]

[81] K. P. S. Menon's telegram to Foreign Secretary, 31 August 1954.
[82] See, for example, dispatch from Moscow in *New York Times*, 12 June 1955.
[83] Interview with Ralph Parker, *Blitz* (Bombay), 4 June 1955.
[84] To Chief Ministers, written on the plane en route to Moscow, 5 June 1955.

To deal with such questions, obviously an official visit as Prime Minister to a closed society would not provide full information. Though Nehru saw much more than he had in 1927, he knew that even now he was not shown all. He was aware, for example, that labour camps existed, although he did not see or hear of them. But what did strike him was that the general look of the people — and he saw millions of them in far-flung parts of the Soviet Union — was happy and cheerful. They looked well-fed and were adequately clothed. Stress was being laid on the needs of children and on the importance of games and athletics. There was no civil liberty as Indians knew it, but this did not seem to be missed because, Nehru thought, it had never been known in Russia. Virtually all persons under fifty, that is, a very large part of the entire active population, had grown up under the Soviet system and been fully conditioned by it. So, 'the general impression I got was one of contentment, as practically everyone is occupied and busy and no one seems to get much time for complaining, or if there are complaints, they are about relatively minor matters.'

It seemed to Nehru that a new type of society was developing in the Soviet Union, a vital society, expanding in numbers, pushing ahead in the construction of new towns and cities and factories, and fully believing in its environment. Its production was increasing, its standards were rising, and its citizens were gaining the reading habit and were becoming attuned to thinking scientifically. Such a society, if it could shake off the war atmosphere which had enveloped it since its inception, was almost certain to settle down to normality. A measure of individual freedom might also follow. 'I do not think this will lead to the type of individual freedom that is known in some of the countries of the West, but a well-read and well-trained society is not likely to submit for long to many restrictions on individual freedom.'

With so much to safeguard and so much yet to be done, the people and rulers of the Soviet Union appeared eager for peace; for they were confident that given time they could do as well economically as the United States. Communists in the Soviet Union formed the government, daily facing national and international problems, and they were in touch with reality and responsibility. This made them very different from communists in non-communist countries, whom they cared little for and only utilized for political purposes when necessary.[85]

In his talks with the Soviet leaders, Nehru was concerned to put forward the case for the United States and to make clear that his independent thinking could not be submerged by cordiality and the current coincidence of his outlook with the Russians. He argued that China's release of four American prisoners had been appreciated in Britain and, to some extent, even in the United States; so the Soviet Government should use their

[85] Nehru's note on visit to the Soviet Union, 1 August 1955.

influence with China to secure the release of those still under detention. He advised against any proposal for a conference of six powers, including India and China, to consider East Asian problems, as this would immediately raise the question of Chiang's attendance. It would, therefore, be far better to encourage bilateral talks between the United States and China. He rejected the Soviet offer to propose India as the sixth permanent member of the Security Council and insisted that priority be given to China's admission to the United Nations. Bulganin and Khrushchev severely criticized the United States for aggressive attitudes. 'I don't see', replied Nehru, 'why a strong man should always go about showing his muscles.' It was a remark seemingly made in agreement but in fact it had a double edge. Nehru then drew attention to the more hopeful elements in United States policy: the eclipse of Knowland and McCarthy, the differences between Dulles and Eisenhower and the more conciliatory attitude of the President, and the general friendliness of the people of the United States. He pressed the Soviet leaders not to be despondent about the Four-Power Conference soon to be held in Geneva, for Britain and France could be expected to side with the influences in United States decision-making that were keen on a settlement.

So clearly Nehru, while responsive to the enthusiastic reception he had received, had not lost his balance. 'A combination Cambridge man, Oriental sage and twentieth-century politician,' reported the correspondent of the *New York Times* at the start of the visit, 'he moved confidently and easily among the heirs of Bolshevism.'[86] But as the days passed and Nehru's reaction to the sustained plaudits seemed to get more emotional, the comment of the *New York Times* turned sour.

> The intentions, certainly on Mr Nehru's part, were good. One cannot doubt his desire to contribute to world peace and to act as a mediator or pacifier, as he sees it, between the two great powers of the United States and the Soviet Union. It is a pity that Mr Nehru's contribution to this ideal should have been a general acceptance of the Soviet policies. If that is the way he feels he cannot be blamed for saying so, but he is surely too intelligent a man not to realize that in espousing the Soviet cause he can only antagonize the American side of the balance. That could hardly have been his desire . . . He said as he took off from Moscow: 'I am leaving part of my heart behind.' We might be forgiven for thinking that he also left a part of his common sense behind.[87]

This assessment was unfair as well as harsh. Whatever the emotional tone of his speeches, the final communiqué, which was wholly the draft of

[86] Dispatch of 7 June, published 8 June 1955.
[87] Editorial in the *New York Times*, 24 June 1955.

the Indian side,[88] was in line with Nehru's arguments in the discussions, and committed the Soviet Government to the Five Principles of coexistence, the Bandung declaration and complete nuclear disarmament.[89] 'The curious thing', commented *The Times*, more discerning than its counterpart across the Atlantic, 'is that his Russian hosts let him put forward views — and they themselves endorsed them — not altogether in line with those which Mr Molotov was putting forward in their name at San Francisco.'[90] The Chinese claim to Taiwan was accepted, but the stress was on peaceful means of acquisition, in contrast to Chinese threats of assault, and no time limit was set. The commitment to non-interference in each other's internal affairs was amplified to cover all aspects, whether economic, political or ideological. This reference was clearly to the Cominform, and the Soviet Union was virtually renouncing it. But Nehru rejected a Soviet suggestion, made somewhat half-heartedly, that both sides condemn the policy of military blocs and agree not to participate in any coalitions or actions directed against each other. Even such a negative alliance, as Nehru described it, was not acceptable to him, and his hosts were obliged to drop the proposal.

While in Moscow, Nehru received an invitation from Eden to visit London on his way home, and the Soviet leaders approved of his acceptance. 'It would be', said Bulganin, 'a good thing for the world if the West would understand you as much as we did.' Nehru now, on leaving the Soviet Union, saw his task as being that of conveying to the Western Powers his understanding that there had been a real change in Moscow. It would be folly to assume that because of a grave shortfall in agricultural production the Soviet Union could be driven to retreat; but it did seem that Soviet policy was now genuinely projected towards coexistence.

> My general impression was that a marked change had come over Soviet policy and that this was not a mere temporary phase. This gave me hope for the future and indicated that more than at any time in the past, there was substantial reason for hoping for peaceful approaches and settlements.[91]

He gave the same appraisal in his talks with Eden and Macmillan and, after the Four-Power Conference at Geneva, Macmillan informed the Commonwealth High Commissioners that

> his Government were under a debt of deep gratitude to the Indian Prime Minister, whose assessment of the Russian situation had been

[88] K. P. S. Menon, *The Flying Troika* (Bombay, 1963), p. 119.
[89] Joint declaration of Bulganin and Nehru, 23 June 1955.
[90] 24 June 1955.
[91] Nehru to Eisenhower, 27 June 1955.

their guide throughout the talks and proved correct every time. He said he had taken notes of the conversation at Chequers and was amazed to find how closely the Russian approach followed the line indicated by the Prime Minister.[92]

The world, then, seemed to Nehru to have reached a turning point, moving away from the attitudes of the cold war and towards real peace; and the Geneva Conference marked the first stage on the new road. 'There has been, I believe, a turn in the tide.'[93] He was hopeful that thereafter, step by step, the specific problems of the world would be brought nearer solution and there would be a gradual approach towards normality, less excitement and tension, and a stronger understanding by the leading military powers of each other's views and fears. To him the greatest iron curtain was the one in people's minds.[94] As we know, these hopes soon faded. Neither can the temporary lifting of the clouds at Geneva be regarded as a triumph for India or the personal achievement of Nehru. Great powers know their own interests and act on them. The most that can be said is that India had helped in bringing about a mutual comprehension; but this in itself was no small effort. With a commitment to international goodwill and morality that was compelling to all sides, Nehru had narrowed the interstices in the relations between the Western Powers and the Soviet Union. 'Ours is not a loud voice. We speak in a soft, gentle voice because that is the tradition of India.'[95] It was this performance behind the scenes, on the lines of what Nehru had indicated as the role of Menon, rather than the speeches and communiqués at Bandung and other conferences, that was the real service of non-aligned policy in these years and justified the comment of Radhakrishnan a few months earlier that if non-alignment did not exist it would have had to be invented.[96]

FOUR

Appreciative of the friendship with the Soviet Union, Nehru was yet concerned that India should not be tied up too closely with any country or give the impression that she was becoming dependent on the help from that country. Neither could India afford to let herself appear cheap.

Our prestige in the world today is largely because we maintain our self-respect and independence, at the same time being friendly. Therefore we must proceed with a certain restraint in all these matters.

[92] 27 July 1955. But Eden makes no mention of Nehru's visit to London in his memoirs.
[93] Note of Nehru, 1 August 1955.
[94] Address to the Parliament of Yugoslavia, 2 July, *National Herald*, 3 July 1955.
[95] Speech at the Kremlin, 10 June, *National Herald*, 11 June 1955.
[96] Cited in M. Brecher, *Nehru* (London, 1959), p. 571.

Restraint does not necessarily mean delay. Indeed, if an eager step is taken, the reactions may well be delay.[97]

He ordered the organization of a cordial welcome to Bulganin and Khrushchev, who were visiting India that winter, but proposed to go no further than discuss Soviet assistance in training Indian technicians in heavy-machine building and drug manufacture.[98] He rejected a suggestion that the draft Second Plan be placed before the Soviet leaders and possibilities of collaboration explored. But circumstances, and the exuberance of the Soviet visitors, combined to vest the occasion with a significance and a spontaneous enthusiasm both far beyond Nehru's intent. The meeting at the same time in Baghdad of the MEDO powers, the formal alignment of Britain with the Baghdad Pact and the close association of the United States with it, came close to being an unfriendly act towards India. An official assurance from the British Government that they were most anxious to avoid doing anything against India's interests gave little satisfaction, for the arming of Pakistan, for whatever reason, this time by another Commonwealth country, in itself created a new and worse situation for India.[99] Taken with the Manila treaty, the Baghdad Pact suggested that Pakistan had succeeded in encircling India with a ring of hostile alliances. The tempo of violent denunciations of India in Pakistan was promptly raised. It must have been clear to Britain that her relations with India would be affected by this alliance; yet no reference had been made to India on this subject.

All this reacts on our public opinion. You know how we have consistently sought to foster and promote understanding and cooperation in all fields with the United Kingdom. We have looked upon the Commonwealth relationship as something of great importance and have supported it in spite of criticism in India. We have referred to the Commonwealth as a pillar of strength in the cause of peace and cooperation. Recent developments will give a handle to many of our critics and it will be difficult for us to explain them.[100]

The United States were not far behind in taking steps which were bound to irritate Indian opinion. Provoked by some forthright speeches in India by Bulganin and Khrushchev which were critical of the Western Powers, Dulles issued a joint statement with the foreign minister of Portugal recognizing Goa as one of the 'Portuguese provinces' in Asia. It

[97] To K. D. Malaviya, 25 October 1955.
[98] To T. T. Krishnamachari, Commerce Minister, 13 November 1955.
[99] Nehru's note on interview with Malcolm MacDonald, British High Commissioner, 26 November 1955.
[100] Nehru to Eden, 2 December 1955.

overshadowed all the friendly assistance given by the United States over the years and brought Indian feeling to a peak of anger. The American Ambassador later explained that the statement had been meant only to call attention to the attacks on the policies of the United States by Bulganin and Khrushchev, and did not commit the United States on the Goa issue or imply that the NATO treaty extended to Goa.[101] If so, it betrayed a naïve failure to anticipate the impact that such a statement, coming soon after Portuguese firing on Indians on the Goa border, would have on Indian opinion. Nothing could have been better calculated to weaken Nehru's effort to impress on his Soviet guests the nature of non-alignment and the inappropriateness of criticizing other governments while on Indian soil. Indeed, even Nehru now saw some advantage in the spiralling of unqualified Soviet support of India's policies on Goa and Kashmir and the consequent intensification of the welcome which the Soviet leaders received. 'People in England and America are very courteous to us and friendly but, in the final analysis, they treat India as a country to be humoured but not as an equal.'[102]

While the British press severely criticized Nehru for seeming to have fallen a victim to Soviet blandishments, the British Government hastened not only to seek to explain away the Baghdad Pact but to prevent Indian purchase of Soviet military aircraft. An under-secretary of the Ministry of Supply flew out to finalize the sale of Gnats and possibly of more Canberras, while Malcolm MacDonald conveyed the 'grave concern' with which Britain would view any purchase by India of military ware from the Soviet Union.[103] Even Nehru's Defence Minister thought it necessary to voice his fears that acquisition of Soviet bombers might affect India's non-alignment.[104] But all this was to underrate Nehru's shrewd sense of business as well as the strength of his independent outlook. He saw no reason why purchase of Soviet aircraft should in itself undermine India's basic policies. 'But we should always be careful not to appear to be too eager to the other party. That is bad tactics. They are clever people and we gain our ends much better by keeping our dignity and restraint.'[105]

The progress of Bulganin and Khrushchev through India gathered popular momentum till finally, at Calcutta on 1 December, a crowd of over two millions gathered to hear them speak and mobbed them in the streets. The visitors were both impressed and taken aback. When, as a measure of security, they were transferred from an open car to a prison van, they looked extremely frightened, and Serov, the K. G. B. official, suggested that troops be called out and, if necessary, ordered to fire.[106] Nehru took

[101] Note of Foreign Secretary, 6 December 1955.
[102] To Vijayalakshmi, 2 December 1955.
[103] Nehru's note of interview with Malcolm MacDonald, 26 November 1955.
[104] K. N. Katju to Nehru, 29 November 1955.
[105] To Mahavir Tyagi, 4 December 1955.
[106] Note of G. K. Handoo, security adviser, 5 December 1955.

advantage of 'this feast of friendliness between the Soviet leaders and the people of India'[107] to secure not immediate material assistance but commitments on political and international issues. There was firstly the question of Soviet relations with the Indian Communist Party. Nehru had no high opinion at this time of Indian Communists.

> My own experience of Communists has been that it is exceedingly difficult to rely on their word or on their basic integrity . . . Their loyalty to their party overrides all other loyalties and, therefore, they are prepared often to function in a way which cannot be reconciled with my standards of personal behaviour . . . Personally I have had no animosity against the Communists at all but I have come to feel increasingly how quite out-of-date Communist parties in non-Communist countries are . . . they are like the Jesuits belonging to the strict Order and not over-scrupulous in their dealings with others, provided they carry out the dictates of that Order to whom they owe their basic loyalty.[108]

These loyal followers of the Party were now puzzled, perplexed and embarrassed by the Soviet cordiality towards Nehru and the fading Soviet interest in international communism and the Cominform. Nehru, on his part, well in control of the domestic scene, did not, at the start, raise this issue with Bulganin and Khrushchev. He merely noted that when some Communist members of Parliament were introduced to them, they did not give their fellow-Marxists much encouragement; however, they pointedly mentioned to Nehru their interest in meeting Indian nationals as such rather than any specific category.[109] But later, as Bulganin and Khrushchev relaxed and became more expansive, Nehru conveyed to them his feeling that, if the past were any guide, the Communist Party would often indulge in violent outbreaks and rely on instructions from Moscow. He also hinted that the party was receiving considerable funds from abroad. Khrushchev replied that the role of the Soviet Communist Party in leading the communist parties of other countries was exaggerated. Communist doctrines and activities would exist and expand whether the Soviet Union supported them or not, and it was unrealistic to ask the Soviet Union to order communist parties all over the world to cease to function. Naturally the Soviet authorities, as communists, had sympathy and understanding for communists elsewhere; but they had no intention of leading these communists. In fact, by abolishing the Cominform, they had dissolved any organization for doing so. Khrushchev then added, on his 'word of honour', that the Soviet Communist Party had no connection with the Communist

[107] Nehru to Lady Mountbatten, 5 December 1955.
[108] Nehru to Zakir Husain, 12 August 1955.
[109] Nehru to U Nu, 1 December 1955.

Party of India, and this was confirmed by the very fact that Soviet policy
had placed the Indian Party in an awkward position. When Nehru
mentioned that the claims of the Indian communists to have contacts with
the Soviet leaders endangered Indo-Soviet relations, Khrushchev said that
he too was depressed by this. 'Our relations should not be disturbed by
misunderstanding.' As for foreign subsidies to the Indian Party,
Khrushchev asserted that he knew nothing about any such payments. Nehru
then expressed the general belief that Indian nationals were employed in
communist embassies on the recommendation of the Indian Communist
Party, and that the peace movement was intended to encourage communism more than peace. Khrushchev replied guardedly that he was not in a
position to say anything about employment in embassies, but the Soviet
Ambassador should be very careful. Generally the Soviet Government
would abide by the Five Principles, and did not wish anyone to weaken the
Indian Government and its Prime Minister.[110] In a way, therefore, the
commitment to keep aloof from India's internal affairs was blurred at the
edges; but to Nehru it was at this stage satisfactory.

On the eve of the departure of Bulganin and Khrushchev, Nehru raised
the question of the Soviet veto on the admission of eighteen countries to
the United Nations. As a parting gift to their host, the Soviet leaders agreed
to the entry of all but Mongolia and Japan. It was a demonstration of both
flexibility and cleverness. In contrast to British clumsiness in promoting,
perhaps without intent, the encirclement of India by the Manila treaty and
the Baghdad Pact, and to the 'astounding stupidity'[111] of Dulles in lining up
thoughtlessly with Portugal, Bulganin and Khrushchev demonstrated their
recognition of India's importance and of Nehru's role in the world. The
spectacular withdrawal of the Soviet veto, as a response to the Indian Prime
Minister's 'grand gesture'[112] in appealing to them on this matter, came as a
climax to Soviet support for India's policies on Kashmir and Goa, the offer
to negotiate economic and military assistance on India's terms and the
promise to deny support to the Communist Party of India. The Soviet
Government had realized that, although the summit conference at Geneva
and even more so the meeting of the foreign ministers had led to no precise
agreements, the cold war had to some extent diminished. There was now a
new phase in world affairs, and in this the countries of Asia and Africa, and
particularly India, would have a major part to play. So it was worth
cultivating India, and this was best done with tact, and without seeking to
push her into commitments. Support and assistance were, therefore,
offered with no obvious expectations of response. As Khrushchev observed
to Nehru on the last day of his visit, 'We want to be friendly with you but

[110] Nehru's note on talks with Bulganin and Khrushchev, 12 December 1955.
[111] Nehru to Vijayalakshmi, 15 December 1955.
[112] Press statement by José Maza, President of United Nations General Assembly, *Hindustan Times*, 22
December 1955.

not to separate you from your other friends. We want to be friendly with your friends.'[113] Britain and the United States were not so percipient. While Eden was seeking to placate Nehru and assuring him that there could be no question whatever of Britain giving military support to one Commonwealth country against another,[114] the Commonwealth Secretary, Lord Home, annoyed Nehru by suggesting to the Indian High Commissioner that India make 'a gesture of goodwill' on the Kashmir question. 'I am afraid Lord Home and most of his colleagues in the United Kingdom Government still live in a past age and imagine that they can treat India as some casual third-rate country.'[115] The United States, particularly with Dulles in charge of their foreign policy, seemed to Nehru no better: 'the great access to financial and military strength since the war has made them look down on almost every country, friend or foe, and they have developed a habit of irritating others by their overbearing attitudes.'[116] Such short-sightedness of Britain and the United States weakened the goodwill they had earned by the large amount of economic assistance they had provided. Khrushchev was blunt and crude, but also wiser.

[113] Mentioned by Nehru to Pineau. See Nehru's record of interview with Pineau, 11 March 1956.
[114] Eden to Nehru, 12 December 1955.
[115] Nehru to Vijayalakshmi, 15 December 1955.
[116] Nehru's note on the visit of Bulganin and Khruschev, 18 December 1955.

12

The Problem of Linguistic Provinces

The frustrations on Goa and the Naga question, the inability to communicate the intensity of his anxiety that various religious groups in India be treated fairly, the inadequacy of his effort to transform his personal authority into democratic administration – all these caused Nehru concern. But to his countrymen they were overshadowed by what appeared as a continuous weakness in taking decisions on the issue of the formation of linguistic provinces. Towards the end of 1955, a problem that had been simmering for a long time came to the boil. For many years before independence, the Congress had been committed to the creation of provinces on a linguistic basis. The formation of composite units, consisting of people speaking different languages, had been one of the ways adopted by the British to dissipate the force of nationalism, and as a counter-measure the Congress had framed its own organization on linguistic lines. It seemed, therefore, a matter of course that a free India would recast the internal map in accordance with these principles. Some members of the Constituent Assembly pressed that steps be taken in this direction even before the introduction of the new Constitution. But Nehru gave the matter low priority. The country was facing a series of extreme crises and there were numerous and urgent demands on the government's attention. 'First things must come first and the first thing is the security and stability of India.' A strong India had to be established before details about its component parts could be considered.[1] The desire of the Andhras for a breakaway province raised relatively few difficulties, but if a start was made in any one area there would be demands from many others; and the whole problem of provincial boundaries bristled with difficulties. As the best way of postponing decisions on this subject and avoiding the government themselves taking any step which would raise a large number of issues and precipitate a minor crisis, Nehru favoured the appointment by the Constituent Assembly of a committee to investigate and report on the

[1] Nehru in Constituent Assembly, 27 November 1947, Constituent Assembly (Legislative) Debates, 1947, Vol. I, pp. 793-5.

23 Receiving Chou En-lai
    in Delhi, June 1954

24 With Mao Tse-tung in
    Peking, October 1954

25   At a Congress session, 1955: throwing a pillow

feasibility of linguistic provinces. If this committee obtained a large measure of agreement, then one or more specific boundary commissions could be appointed.[2] He therefore, at the last stage, abandoned the idea of listing an Andhra province in the first schedule of the Constitution.[3] Even if the creation of new provinces like Andhra and Karnataka had to be taken up later, it should be a very limited operation and the provincial boundaries should not be altered. The Congress was not committed to this and, considering the vast problems facing the country, it would be a disservice to divert interest to what seemed to Nehru to be petty issues.[4]

The committee set up by the Constituent Assembly received evidence, to Nehru's surprise,[5] in public and thereby helped to sustain an atmosphere of argument and passion. Its recommendations against the formation of linguistic provinces and in favour of the later recasting of some existing provinces on administrative considerations[6] did not, therefore, enable the problem to be shelved. Nehru ordered the dissatisfied Andhra leaders to be silent. 'I should like to have a little peace or the semblance of peace for sometime. After that we can go ahead in many directions.'[7] But in February 1949 the legislative assembly of Bombay passed a resolution recommending the creation of a province of Maharashtra including Bombay city. As clearly the issue could not be avoided, Nehru thought the best course would be for himself, Patel and the President of the Congress to form a committee which could report to the Party; the government could then express their general agreement with the report.

Nehru drafted the report, which suggested that, in view of the unsettled conditions in the country, the consideration of linguistic provinces might be postponed for ten years; but some steps could be taken in individual cases if there was agreement between the parties. Accepting the report, the Constituent Assembly merely provided, in Article 3 of the Constitution, for the creation of such provinces sometime in the future. Nehru directed the Working Committee and the Parliamentary Party of the Congress not to press for early action on this.[8]

As it appeared that there was agreement between the Andhras and the Tamils on the details of an Andhra province, the Working Committee, despite Nehru's known reluctance, asked the Government of India in November 1949 to form immediately an Andhra province, consisting of the undisputed Andhra districts but without Madras city; and Nehru

[2] Nehru to Rajendra Prasad, 16 and 17 February 1948.

[3] K. V. Narayana Rao, *The Emergence of Andhra Pradesh* (Bombay, 1973), pp. 202-3.

[4] To N. Dutt Majumdar, 22 May 1948.

[5] Nehru to Rajendra Prasad, 22 September 1948.

[6] Report of the Linguistic Provinces Commission, 10 December 1948, printed in B. Shiva Rao, *The Framing of India's Constitution*, Vol. 4 (Delhi, 1948), p. 439 ff.

[7] Nehru to T. Prakasam, 10 January 1949.

[8] Note on linguistic provinces, 2 October 1949, read out at Working Committee and Parliamentary Party meetings during Nehru's absence in the United States.

decided to act on this resolution.[9] But then it transpired that the two sides could not agree on the temporary location of an Andhra capital; and the financial and other consequences also required careful investigation. With the elections drawing near, Nehru was able thankfully to avoid immediate action.

Even after the elections Nehru argued that, with economic problems assuming importance, the time was not right for forming linguistic provinces.[10] As he repeatedly emphasized, once the government opened the issue, they would be dragged into a turmoil all over India. On the Andhra demand in particular Nehru was inclined to be sympathetic, for he realized that it had its root not so much in a narrow love of language as in a widespread feeling among the Andhras that they were not getting a fair deal in the composite province; but he feared that the creation of psychological satisfaction might well lead to greater financial, economic and other difficulties.[11] Rajagopalachari, now Chief Minister of Madras, too, advised Nehru not to take up the question of linguistic provinces for at least another year, though his recommendation was based not on the priority of other issues but the fear that communist influence would be strong in an Andhra or Kerala province.[12] He had also a marked streak of linguistic bigotry, which led him to adopt an attitude of cussed vindictiveness and, for example, object to the appointment of a senior civil servant, who happened to be an Andhra, as adviser to the planning commission on the ground that this official was touched with 'Andhra shortsightedness.'[13] Nehru pointed out that he was committed to the creation of an Andhra province if there were general agreement and the Government of India could not be passive or on the defensive in this matter.[14] He, too, thought that an Andhra province would be a mistake, but if the Andhras wanted it he would not stop them.

> I am quite sure that it is not a good thing for the Telugu-speaking areas to be formed into a separate state. Their state will be a backward one in many ways and financially hard up. They cannot expect much help from the centre. However, that is their look-out. If they want the state, they can have it on the conditions we have stated.[15]

On 19 December, after three days of rioting in the Andhra districts consequent on the death of an Andhra leader by fasting on this issue, the

[9] Nehru to Patel, 18 November 1949.
[10] Speech in Parliament, 22 May 1952. Lok Sabha Debates, Vol. I, Part II, pp. 374-97.
[11] 21 July 1952. Rajya Sabha Debates, 1952, Vol. I, pp. 1583-93.
[12] Rajagopalachari to Nehru, 27 and 30 May 1952.
[13] Ibid., 1 November 1952.
[14] Nehru to Rajagopalachari, 26 and 28 May 1952.
[15] Ibid., 16 December 1952.

Government of India announced their decision to establish an Andhra province.[16]

Rajagopalachari now sought to block progress on points of detail. He vetoed a common capital, governor or high court for Madras and Andhra or any joint property at all. ' If the Andhras wanted separation, they must get out lock, stock and barrel.'[17] Nehru agreed — despite the recommendation of a senior judge commissioned to examine this matter, that the Andhra capital should be located in Madras for a temporary period of about three years — that the Andhras should have their own capital and should not maintain even a temporary headquarters in Madras city; but he could not persuade Rajagopalachari that the process of transfer was bound to take some time, and there were many minor matters which could not be settled in a hard and fast way. Then the grant of an interview by the President to the Andhra leader, Prakasam, further fanned Rajagopalachari's wrath. 'The slender threads of my faith and courage are weakening rapidly. Forgive me if I make any decision at any time without consulting anyone any more.'[18] He ignored Nehru's suggestion that he make friendly statements offering help to the Andhras in setting up the new administration.[19] When the Union Cabinet decided that 'most' of the offices of the Andhra government might continue to be located in Madras till arrangements were made for their transfer to an Andhra capital, Rajagopalachari insisted on the replacement of the word 'most' by 'some'.[20] It is one of the sadnesses of personal history to observe Rajagopalachari utilizing the enormous weight of his prestige for the petty purpose of spiting the Andhras.

The decision to create an Andhra province encouraged similar demands throughout the country. 'You will observe that we have disturbed the hornet's nest and I believe most of us are likely to be badly stung.'[21] It had become clear that few shared Nehru's view that the Andhra province was an exceptional case which should not form a precedent. Even so, the general aspirations for comprehensive linguistic provinces might have been kept in control had Nehru declared firmly that there was no question of recasting India at this stage. His failure to do so was not solely a consequence of weakness. He felt that it would be undemocratic to smother this sentiment which, on general grounds, he did not find objectionable. Indeed, a

[16] Nehru has been criticized for not making this announcement a few days earlier and saving the life of the leader on fast. Narayana Rao, op. cit., pp. 252-3. It seems really to have been a matter of circumstances overtaking procedural delays. Nehru had, however reluctantly, decided on principle on the creation of an Andhra province; but he had to overcome Rajagopalachari's resistance.

[17] Rajagopalachari to Nehru, 17 December, and Sri Prakasa to Nehru, quoting Rajagopalachari, 20 December 1952.

[18] Rajagopalachari to Nehru, 24 February 1953.

[19] Nehru to Rajagopalachari, 19 and 21 March 1953.

[20] Minutes of Union Cabinet, 18-19 March; Rajagopalachari's telegram, 24 March; Nehru to Rajagopalachari, 25 March 1953.

[21] Nehru to K. N. Katju, 13 February 1953.

linguistic mosaic might well provide a firmer base for national unity. What concerned him were the timing, the agitation and violence with which linguistic provinces were being demanded and the harsh antagonism between various sections of the Indian people which underlay these demands. He therefore sought to delay matters and to wait until the Andhra province had been fully established before taking the next step, which would be the setting up of yet another commission to examine carefully the whole question, not just of linguistic provinces but of the redistribution of provincial areas on the basis of all the factors involved.[22] Then, instead of isolated, random decisions being given, a general policy could be implemented, bearing in mind every aspect of the problem — the maintenance of national cohesion, the cultural and linguistic pulls, the considerations of finance, security and economic progress. 'I have to look at things from the all-India point of view. Otherwise I am not worthy of the place I occupy either in the Government or in the Congress.'[23]

However, despite a clear declaration by Nehru that a commission for this purpose would be appointed by the end of the year, agitation and hunger strikes for the creation of particular provinces continued. There was a growing mood of provincial expansionism and claims were made by linguistic chauvinists for extra territory, forgetful of the fact that internal boundaries should be primarily a matter of administrative convenience. Nehru reacted vigorously. If national policies were to be controlled or influenced in this manner, both progress and unity would be destroyed. If the people regarded this matter to be of such vital importance as to be given precedence over all other questions, then they would have to find another Prime Minister. 'I cannot be responsible for taking a step which, I am convinced, means injury to the cause of India and to something which I have cherished and worked for.'[24] At the inauguration of the Andhra State he stressed most the need for all Indians to grow into the thought of India.[25] But the agitation in various parts of India continued and, even after the commission was appointed, there was no diminution of these pressures. Nehru's appeal to Congressmen to recall the role which the Party had played in the past as a cementing and unifying force[26] was virtually unheeded. Shankarrao Deo, a senior Congressman who had been a prisoner with Nehru at Ahmadnagar fort, accused him of scorning the deeply felt sentiments of the people. Nehru pointed out the importance of acting in this matter at the right time and with the goodwill of all concerned; 'otherwise all attention and resources would have been taken up by this and we would have had to say a long goodbye to planning and economic

[22] Nehru to Morarji Desai, 19 February 1953.
[23] To S. Nijalingappa, 10 May 1953, rejecting the demand for the immediate creation of a Karnataka province.
[24] Nehru to Chief Ministers, 2 July 1953.
[25] Speech at Kurnool, 1 October, National Herald, 2 October 1953.
[26] Nehru to presidents of Pradesh Congress committees, 13 November 1953.

progress.' The whole future of India was involved in this question and it could not be dealt with in a casual or partisan way. He himself had no fixed opinion and wanted more light.[27] But no one listened. Throughout the two years that the commission gathered evidence the problem was clouded by intense public feeling. Some provincial governments were known even to be spending the secret funds at their disposal to further territorial claims on the basis of language.[28]

In this atmosphere, it was clear that, when the commission submitted its report, the agitation would increase, for obviously, whatever the recommendations, they would not be to the liking of everybody. Nehru had been arguing for months that the only statesmanlike approach would be to accept unquestioningly the proposals made, after careful deliberation, by a commission consisting of experienced men with no partisan viewpoints; but he knew that there was little likelihood of this and girded himself for trouble. 'As a matter of fact, life is becoming very complicated here and the report of the states reorganization commission is going to be the last straw.'[29] The report, published in October 1955, revealed, it must be said, no basis of logic or principle. It recommended the establishment as separate provinces of Kerala and Karnataka because of the common language of the people; but Bombay would continue as a bilingual province, including people speaking Marathi and Gujarati. The Marathi-speaking districts of Hyderabad were transferred to Bombay but certain other Marathi-speaking areas were taken away to form the separate State of Vidharba. The Telugu-speaking districts of Hyderabad were also not to be transferred to Andhra till 1961.

The popular reaction to the report, therefore, was intense. 'One might almost think from reading reports of speeches etc. that we were on the verge of civil war in some parts of India.'[30] Nehru yielded ground to the extent of conceding that, if the principal parties concerned reached agreement on any particular issues, the government would accept this, as it had done in the case of the Andhra province; otherwise, the recommendations of the commission should be broadly followed.[31] But in most parts of India the only agreement that could be reached was in rejection of the commission's proposals; and all sides looked to the Government of India for fresh decisions. However, the very nature of the problem ensured that Nehru would not be seen at his best. The redistribution of provincial areas was to him too trivial and tedious a matter to engage his full and sympathetic attention. While he appreciated the importance of language in a community, he was not wholly committed to monolinguistic provinces.

[27] Nehru to Shankarrao Deo, 26 November 1953, AICC Papers, Box 10. File PG-29/1953-55, N.M.M.L.

[28] Nehru's letters of rebuke to Chief Ministers of Bengal, Bihar and Orissa, 6 July 1954.

[29] Nehru to Vijayalakshmi, 13 September 1955.

[30] Nehru to Mountbatten, 12 October 1955.

[31] Nehru to Chief Ministers, 14 October 1955.

The British might have established composite provinces for their own reasons but such provinces had other virtues too. A province like Hyderabad, with people speaking various languages including Urdu, appealed to Nehru as a potential centre of composite culture in south India, while Bombay had built up a rich cosmopolitan tradition which it would be vandalistic to throw away. So he could not comprehend the intense passions which the issue of linguistic States aroused; and, faced with such strong feelings, his idea of a solution was not the search for merits, which did not to him exist in any sharply defined sense, but producing the largest consensus and avoiding, as far as possible, compulsion. In his eagerness to get rid of this problem so that it would not continue to erode the unity of the country, and to concentrate on such matters as planning which were to him of far greater importance, Nehru seized on every proposal, regardless of its intrinsic soundness, which appeared to offer the chance of a settlement. Too sensitive to public feeling to impose decisions and yet anxious to reach them as quickly as possible, he allowed himself to be dragged along, shifting course and revising policy as the agitation demanded, appeasing the most influential sectors and hoping that every compromise arrangement would be the conclusive one. In this matter, of relatively little importance to him and in which right and wrong hardly figured, Nehru relied too much on the correct decision turning up and did not set out to find it.

> This is a terrible job, and I do not see much light yet. Passions have been roused and old friends have fallen out. However, I suppose we shall see this through also with our usual luck. I do think we are rather lucky. Looking back, I am surprised at many of the things we have managed to do and the difficulties we have overcome.[32]

The chief centres of unrest were the Punjab, where the Sikhs wanted a state of their own, and Bombay city and the Marathi-speaking districts, where the people demanded a separate State of Maharashtra instead of being cobbled together with the Gujaratis in a bilingual province. A visit to Amritsar enabled Nehru to reduce the tension and animosity in the air and, without making any concession, to convince Tara Singh and his followers of his good intent.[33] The welcome he was given in that town was, even to him, a new experience.

> On two or three occasions I did something which I take it few prime ministers have done in the past. I climbed up a lamp-post in order partly to see the crowd and partly to exhibit myself to them so as to lessen the pressure. However, everything passed off well and

[32] Nehru to Lady Mountbatten, 5 December 1955.
[33] Nehru to Pratap Singh Kairon, 24 November 1955.

Amritsar, from being a scene of conflict, suddenly became a place of overflowing friendship and goodwill. I do not know how long this will last.[34]

The situation in Bombay city was less easily brought under control. That recognized political parties should organize violence on a mass scale, involving students and factory workers, and that society as a whole should remain strangely silent and not condemn it severely, worried Nehru, not just in itself but because of what it might mean for the general progress of India. It did not immediately strike him that in this case it might well be because many people felt strongly about the issue which sparked off such rioting. He tended to assume that his own list of priorities, in which the fresh demarcation of provincial boundaries hardly figured, was widely accepted. He took it for granted that the effort to decide issues in the streets by bludgeoning passers-by and committing arson could only be the work of a minority seeking to impose its view by almost fascist methods; a majority would not need to do this because it could secure its objectives by democratic processes. He failed to recognize straightaway that even a majority might, in desperation, tolerate such methods if it were driven to the feeling, however erroneous, that the government were wilfully refusing to appreciate its viewpoint.

So Nehru's first reaction was to refuse to consider the demand for Maharashtra so long as it was backed by such violent agitation.

Obviously no Government can be coerced by such methods. Indeed the Government will cease to function if it tolerated such methods and the success of this behaviour would lead to its being followed in many other places. Our country would be reduced not only to chaos but to chaos of the lowest and most vulgar type.[35]

But, realizing that it was the rival claims to Bombay city which mainly stood in the way of dividing the Bombay province into Maharashtra and Gujarat, Nehru began to think by December 1955 in terms of converting Bombay into a separate city-state.[36] At the meeting of the Working Committee in October, when the formula had first been suggested, the representatives of Maharashtra had welcomed it;[37] but when the plan was publicly announced, the Maharashtrians denounced this as a compromise wholly at their expense. So Nehru thought again. 'I have even thought of what Bapu might have advised us if he had been present.' Gandhi would obviously have placed emphasis on the long-term aspect of the question

---

[34] Nehru to Lady Mountbatten, 13 November 1955.
[35] Nehru to Chief Ministers, 26 November 1955.
[36] Nehru to Shankarrao Deo, 20 December 1955.
[37] T. R. Deogirikar, *Twelve Years in Parliament* (Poona, 1964), p. 198.

and would have disliked bargaining. So Nehru switched back to the idea of a large, composite State, consisting of Bombay city, and all the Gujarati and Marathi-speaking areas, including Vidarbha, at least for five years, when the whole question could be reviewed. To make this palatable to the Marathis, he hinted that Morarji Desai, the Gujarati Chief Minister who had become unpopular with the Marathis, should step down. Gandhi would have favoured some gesture which would at least lay the foundation for better relations in the future, and his advice would naturally have been directed more to the Gujaratis than to the Maharashtrians. The initiative for this proposal of a composite State would have to be taken by Desai, but his continuance as Chief Minister should not be made part of the bargain. 'That would not suit your dignity and you could very well make this perfectly clear. Later, when things are calmed down, this question can be considered in a more reasonable atmosphere and decisions can be taken then.'[38]

The proposal for a composite State of Bombay fitted in with the latest trend in Nehru's thinking, that India should have fewer and larger States. He was sufficiently persuasive to get the Chief Ministers of Bengal and Bihar to agree to merge the two provinces, while Madras agreed to join Travancore-Cochin. There was even talk of a larger Dakshina Pradesh, covering all the Tamil-,Kannada- and Malayalam-speaking areas. But these proved short-lived products of utopian imagination, with no influence on opinion in Bombay. Riots continued in the city and the Marathi districts against the continuance of a bilingual province, and even Deshmukh, the Finance Minister at the centre, protested sharply. Nehru had brought Deshmukh, a senior member of the Indian Civil Service, into the Cabinet in 1950 and had respect for his technical proficiency. There was even a little warmth in their relationship in the early years; but this was gradually demolished by the acidity of Deshmukh's correspondence, his temperamental aversion to Krishna Menon and his inability to get on with Chief Ministers or other members of the Cabinet. He was too hard-minded to realize that adequate financial control was but a small part of the task of a finance minister. 'Running the government', Nehru gently reminded him, 'as a competent business concern is not the whole of the picture.'[39] The advice was of little avail, and repeatedly Deshmukh, in letters that verged on personal discourtesy, offered to resign because some central department or State government had ignored financial decorum or demanded more money. Nehru did not let him go because he knew Deshmukh was honest and, in his limited way, able; but by 1956 Deshmukh was in Nehru's tired disfavour.

The break with Deshmukh, however, came not, as in the case of Matthai, on matters of financial policy but on a purely political issue. Though a

[38] Nehru to Morarji Desai, 1 January 1956.
[39] 29 June 1952.

member of the Cabinet, Deshmukh had initially, to Nehru's irritation, been reluctant to join the Congress Party and had only at the last moment agreed to contest the elections in 1952 as a Congress candidate and not as an independent. But, once elected from a constituency which was a part of Bombay city, he took his duties as a member seriously and developed close relations with Congressmen and other members of Parliament from Maharashtra. He had little knowledge of politics; but he seems to have begun to nurture political ambitions, and in 1956 he stepped forward as a spokesman of Maharashtrian interests. He pressed his resignation in protest at what he said was Nehru's failure to consult the Cabinet before making his proposals for a separate city-state of Bombay.[40] Nehru's recollection was that the matter had been generally discussed in the Cabinet. If a composite Bombay province were not feasible, the other alternative was three States of Maharashtra, Bombay city and Gujarat; the only question was whether the city should govern itself or be centrally administered. Deshmukh had thought that the three-State formula was acceptable to Maharashtrians, but the Congressmen of Maharashtra had later said that they would prefer the city to be centrally administered. It would have been better to have taken the whole matter to the Cabinet again; but Nehru himself had been clear about the Cabinet's views on the subject when he publicly made the proposal.[41]

Deshmukh was not mollified. The punctilious custodian of the public revenue was by this time lost in the committed politician. But Nehru let Deshmukh's resignation lie; and the leaders of Maharashtra were also willing to await developments. Nehru was now searching for some solution which would hold at least for a while without irritating anyone by suggesting finality. His task was not made easier by the Bombay Government, which permitted the police to open fire on a number of occasions to subdue the agitation. The demands for inquiries into alleged excesses were rejected by the Chief Minister, Morarji Desai, and Nehru supported him on the ground that such investigations would only keep alive passions and hatred.[42] Deshmukh again protested.[43] Nehru authorized him to bring up the matter at a Cabinet meeting and added that he had called for a full report. But he himself was inclined to believe that, while unnecessary force might have been used on occasions, organized hooliganism had created a situation which had made any kind of orderly government almost impossible.[44] As Nehru announced that no inquiry would be ordered, Deshmukh, under protest, did not pursue the matter.[45]

This did not mean that the problem of Bombay was any nearer solution,

[40] Deshmukh to Nehru, 22 and 26 January 1956.
[41] Nehru to Deshmukh, 28 January 1956.
[42] Nehru to Pant, 15 February 1956.
[43] Deshmukh to Nehru, 19 February 1956.
[44] Nehru to Deshmukh, 20 February 1956.
[45] Deshmukh to Nehru, 24 February 1956.

and Nehru was subdued by a sense of inner failure. He had suggested the three-State formula, and even the formula of two States with Bombay as a centrally administered city, not as a final settlement but as a halfway house which would enable calm thinking and the adoption of long-term solutions at the right time and in the right spirit. His rejection in this particular case of his normal approach of a judicial inquiry into the use of firearms by the police had been motivated not by any desire to protect the Bombay Government from censure but because, whatever other consequences might follow, one certain result was an increase in bitterness and conflict. But it worried him that for once he had failed to maintain a spirit of understanding with a large section of the Indian people. He had lost his usual, intimate touch with the minds and hearts of Maharashtrians; and this lessening of the spirit of community sapped his self-confidence, limited his capacity for action and made him feel a little helpless.[46] Deshmukh continued to be angry and opposed to a centrally administered Bombay city, especially as he thought that this would probably mean its administration 'by those who are primarily responsible for ruining the relations between Maharashtrians and Gujaratis, particularly Shri Morarji Desai, owing to their overbearing and inequitable conduct of the affairs of the present Bombay state during the last five years.'[47] Nehru hotly defended Desai:

> It is not necessary to agree with a person in everything in order to recognize the person's worth. I do not agree with some of the views of Morarji Desai. But in my large acquaintance in India I know very few persons whom I respect so much for their rectitude, ability, efficiency and fairness as Morarji Desai. I have known him and the general course of his life for a long enough time to be able to judge.[48]

As this suggested that Nehru would abide by the formula of establishing Bombay as a centrally administered city, Deshmukh proposed to appeal to Parliament to include Bombay in Maharashtra with safeguards for its special interests, and offered to resign before doing so. Nehru appealed to him not to take a step which would only add to tension and ill-will, but made clear that if he insisted on stating his case in Parliament, he would first have to resign.[49] Deshmukh promptly resigned but Nehru, concerned more about the reaction in Maharashtra than the loss of Deshmukh's services, prevailed on him to wait a little longer.[50]

It was now Morarji Desai's turn to express resentment at Nehru's policy.

[46] To Shankarrao Deo, to V. V. Nene, and to T. R. Deogirikar, 15 March 1956.
[47] Deshmukh to Nehru, 16 April 1956.
[48] Nehru to Deshmukh, 16 April 1956.
[49] Deshmukh to Nehru, 20 April 1956, and Nehru's reply of the same date.
[50] Deshmukh to Nehru, 23 April, Nehru to Deshmukh, 24 April, and Deshmukh to Nehru, 24 April 1956.

He believed that the continuous insistence that the three-State formula need not be a final settlement was helping to keep alive the agitation in Maharashtra. He threatened to retire from active political work if Nehru agreed to further changes and believed that any such action would weaken the influence of the Congress Party in the rest of India.[51] The people of Gujarat also now began to agitate against the decision about Bombay, although it lay outside their area. The problem as it had developed was well beyond Nehru's intellectual horizons and accentuated his bewilderment and depression.

> I have always considered it a great privilege for people of this generation to live during this period of India's long history and to take some little part in the shaping of that story. I have believed that there is nothing more exciting in the wide world today than to work in India. That very thought fills me with vitality and a desire to get the most out of this passing show in our fleeting lives.

But there could be too much excitement or the wrong kind of excitement. They had for nearly seven months been preoccupied with a question which had nothing to do with high political or economic or social policy and which had aroused such passions as to endanger the whole fabric of India. He had tried to convince himself that this was a relic of the narrow regionalism and parochialism which had been India's failing in the past and which were having a final burst before the ghost was laid.

> For the moment the ghost is there and we live a somewhat haunted existence. We may well blame each other, but that brings little solace or solution, for, in the context of India, we are all to blame and we have all to suffer the consequences. I have tried to search my mind and heart to find out where I have erred. What should I have done that I have not done and what should I have avoided doing that I have done? It is easy to be wise after the event. But the basic fact remains that we have yet to develop a unified nation. We distrust each other and sometimes even dislike each other.

Religion, caste, language and provincialism all served as separating factors and kept India in a tribal age. The country had undertaken tremendous tasks demanding all the strength and energy of her people, and yet these were frittered away in dealing with insubstantial problems, using coercive methods.[52]

Nehru had virtually allowed the making of decisions on this matter to fall from his hands and was prepared to accept any solution that might be proposed by the contending groups. Even *The Hindu*, the Madras

[51] Morarji Desai to Nehru, 27 April 1956.
[52] To Chief Ministers, 10 May 1956.

newspaper, the chief characteristics of which have always been timidity and
an inclination to please whoever is in power in Delhi, was driven to criticize
Nehru for his inability to make up his mind.

> The root of the violence we see creeping over our country today does
> not lie truly with the people but the politicians. Those who resort to
> violence at least know their minds. But it is indecision in high places
> on both planes, economic and political, that threatens to loose on our
> country an orgy of highly decisive violence.[53]

However, it now looked as if some agreement was at last in the offing.
Towards the end of May, the leaders of opinion in the Congress in
Maharashtra, including Deshmukh, suggested that Bombay city be
centrally administered for a fixed period, after which the issue should be
reviewed by Parliament. Meantime, the administration of Maharashtra
should be carried on from Bombay city.[54] Acting on this suggestion, Nehru
announced in Bombay on 3 June that the city would be centrally
administered with some representatives of Bombay associated with this
administration; and after a certain period, which might be about five years,
the people of the city should have the opportunity to decide their own
future. How this was to be done could be decided later in consultation with
the people concerned.[55]

This firm decision seemed to have a healthy effect at the start. But soon
violence was again the master. Nehru blamed the Communist and the
communal parties. The Communist Party, bewildered by the changing
attitudes of the Soviet Union, and struggling to formulate a new policy,
publicly denounced the call of the Congress to abandon violence, while the
R.S.S. and the Jan Sangh were active in both Maharashtra and the Punjab.
The approach of the general elections encouraged such behaviour and
Nehru appealed to his own party not to be influenced by this.

> We are apt to take many things too much for granted and to forget
> that unless certain basic assumptions are agreed to generally, the
> superstructure that we try to build will have weak foundations . . .
> Above all, we have to adhere to certain basic principles of group and
> personal behaviour and to maintain certain standards. That is more
> important than some minor advantage or even some victory in an odd
> election.[56]

Despite the violence, the Government of India persisted with the
proposal of a centrally administered Bombay. Deshmukh awaited Nehru's

[53] 'Violence in the Air', editorial in *The Hindu*, 31 May 1956.
[54] H. V. Pataskar, Law Minister in the Government of India, to Nehru, 28 May 1956.
[55] Speech at AICC, 3 June, *National Herald*, 4 June 1956.
[56] Nehru to Chief Ministers, 15 June 1956.

return from Europe and again resigned, sending Nehru a copy of the statement he intended to make in the Lok Sabha. On this occasion Nehru made no attempt to dissuade him and accepted the resignation.[57] Deshmukh's statement was a severe criticism of both the official policy on Bombay and Nehru's functioning as Prime Minister. Nehru, in dealing with the latter charge, gave as good as he got; but feelings in Maharashtra were even more inflamed by Deshmukh's resignation. It was now suggested by Pataskar, a sober Maharashtrian Congressman and a member of Nehru's government, that the province be split and it be agreed that by a certain date Bombay city would automatically revert to Maharashtra. Nehru suggested as an easier compromise that Parliament consider the question at a later date.[58] But, in fact, Nehru was coming round with great reluctance to the natural conclusion, which should have been accepted from the start, that Bombay's place was in Maharashtra. His own predilection for a composite State, the influence of Morarji Desai, the naïve political stances of Deshmukh and the distaste for seeming to yield to violence had all helped to prevent Nehru from comprehending the strength of the case for a Maharashtra inclusive of Bombay. It was as if it required the departure of Deshmukh for Nehru to see reason.

As you well know, I have been greatly distressed about the Bombay and Maharashtra matter and the fact that practically the entire people of Maharashtra feel almost unanimously and strongly on this subject, is rather an overwhelming one. Nobody can deny that there is a good deal of logic in what they say, although there is some logic for the other view too. Anyhow, we have landed ourselves in a position where we are doing something which intimately hurts the whole people of Maharashtra and their representatives. That is a bad position.[59]

At this stage, 180 members of Parliament, belonging to all parties, no doubt influenced by a knowledge of Nehru's private wishes in the matter, revived the scheme for a bilingual State. It embarrassed the government officially, for they were on the eve of enacting the bill creating three States; but Nehru personally was far from unhappy.[60] Consideration of the bill was promptly postponed and, after various consultations, the proposal for a composite State was approved by the Cabinet and accepted by the Congress Parliamentary Party amid scenes of general rejoicing. 'All this has been rather exhausting business, but I feel as if a burden was off me. And this is a common feeling in Parliament and outside here.'[61]

[57] Deshmukh to Nehru, 23 July 1956, and Nehru's reply of the same date.
[58] Nehru to H. V. Pataskar, 29 July 1956.
[59] To G. B. Pant, 29 July 1956.
[60] See his letter to K. M. Munshi, 4 August 1956.
[61] Nehru to Lady Mountbatten, 6 August 1956.

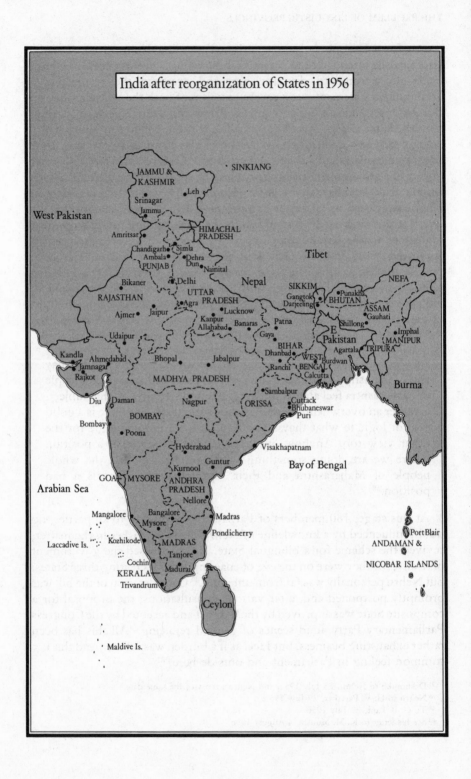

India after reorganization of States in 1956

The relief did not last long. This time it was in Ahmedabad and other parts of Gujarat that violence and arson spread. Preaching amity and peaceful settlements of disputes to the world, India seemed unable to evoke the same spirit of concord in dealing with her own problems. 'We talk of indiscipline, but the gravest of all indisciplines is emotional indiscipline which upsets the balance of the individual. We have seen in India these emotional upheavals and, what is worse, we have seen them take to violence.' At a time when India was playing for high stakes and striving to infuse a new life into the country,

> suddenly all the evil hidden in our hearts came out and took possession of us, blinding us and leading us to wrong action. We stood out before ourselves and the world as narrow and parochial-minded, caste-ridden people who were unworthy of what we had ourselves proclaimed . . . Whether we like it or not, a high destiny has caught us in its grip. We may master it and shape it to our will, or fail and prove ourselves false to the opportunity that came to us.[62]

But, dejected as he was, Nehru was unwilling to consider further changes in the reorganization of western India. A return to the starting point of a multilingual province even larger than before was, after months of violence, accepted with relief as the solution of the crisis.

> The past is done with and it is no good grieving over what has happened. I have no doubt in my mind that the final decision was a good decision and a right one . . . I am sure that on calm consideration even those who reacted strongly against it will realize that it was a right decision. It was right for the constituent parts of this great state, it was even more right for India.[63]

---

[62] Nehru to Chief Ministers, 16 August 1956.
[63] Nehru's message on Bombay State, 8 September 1956.

13

Suez

The problems created by the reorganization of States and the drafting of the second Plan diverted Nehru's attention from foreign affairs; and the lack of any pressing crisis in the world justified this. For nearly a year relations with Pakistan had been at fairly low pressure. Early in 1955 the President had urged military action in retaliation for border raids by the Pakistan police and accused Nehru of 'nothing short of supine cowardice'.[1] Ignoring such bloodthirstiness, Nehru invited the new rulers of Pakistan, Ghulam Mahomed, Iskandar Mirza and Khan Sahib to pay a goodwill visit to India. Such goodwill cannot by itself solve a basic problem of national conflict, though it did help in relaxing tension. The Baghdad Pact reversed this trend and it was feared in Indian army circles that with the continuous and rapid flow of American arms Pakistan would, within a year, be in a superior military position to India. Nehru did not show his concern and continued to suggest a settlement on Kashmir broadly on the lines of the status quo. But the advocacy of an early settlement on Kashmir in the resolution of the SEATO Conference in Karachi in March 1956 was an irritant. The United States, which had the authority to prevent such a reference, had presumably not wished to do so, and three Commonwealth countries had sided with Pakistan against another member of the Commonwealth. The Foreign Ministers of the United States and France, who, unlike Selwyn Lloyd, came to Delhi after the meeting, were left in no doubt about Nehru's views on their having virtually placed a military alliance behind Pakistan on this issue. Of the three ministers, Pineau impressed Nehru the most. Perhaps this was because he apologized for what had been said about Kashmir, showed a willingness to conclude the treaty for arranging the transfer of the French possessions in India, publicly criticized the Baghdad Pact, and gave a sympathetic hearing to Nehru's analysis of the world situation. Nehru referred to the change in Soviet thinking and the growing similarity between the United States and the Soviet Union, and expressed half jokingly his fear at the distant prospect of

[1] Rajendra Prasad to Nehru, 6 January 1955.

these two countries coming to an agreement and sitting on the rest of the world — probably the first reference in high diplomatic circles to the détente that was to crystallize nearly twenty years later. But what, according to Nehru, stood in the way of a continuous lessening of tension were regional pacts and unnecessarily generalized thinking. Rather than condemnation of communism or capitalism, as the case might be, effort should be made to reach solutions on specific problems. With all this Pineau broadly agreed. He was most concerned with Algeria; but on this too Nehru thought Pineau's attitude was reasonable and, as Pineau was going on to Cairo from Delhi, Nehru suggested to Nasser that he talk frankly to Pineau.[2]

Selwyn Lloyd, after the demonstrations against him in Bahrain and the news of Glubb Pasha's dismissal, did not appear to Nehru to be in a condition for a calm discussion. Lloyd pleaded that Britain had practically been driven by the United States into SEATO and they had gone in with the object of toning it down and keeping Chiang Kai-shek out of it. Nehru stressed the concern felt by India at the arming of Pakistan and, when Lloyd suggested that Kashmir be settled on the lines of the Trieste agreement between Italy and Yugoslavia, replied that a partition was exactly what he had proposed to Pakistan.

> Generally speaking, our talk was friendly and frank, and one had the impression (which he confirmed) that in spite of our differences of opinion in regard to some matters, our basic approaches were not far apart and there was much in common. We can at least talk in the frankest manner with each other.[3]

Britain's chief concern at this time was to ensure that India made no purchase of Soviet military aircraft. Nehru, who thought that India was committed in this matter,[4] told Lloyd that the Government of India would like to buy Gnats[5] and Canberras but also a squadron of Ilyushins, which were liked by the Indian Air Force and which would be delivered quickly and at a reasonable price. This was a purely commercial transaction, and care would be taken to see that Soviet technicians did not have access to the secrets of new devices in British aircraft. But, even with these safeguards,

---

[2] Nehru's record of interview with Pineau, 11 March; telegrams to Krishna Menon in New York and Ali Yavar Jung in Cairo, 12 March, and letter to Chief Ministers, 14 March 1956.

[3] Nehru's record of talks with Selwyn Lloyd, 4 March 1956.

[4] See Nehru's letter to Krishna Menon, 8 March 1956.

[5] It is worth observing, in view of the splendid performance of the Gnats in the war with Pakistan in 1965, that in taking the decision to equip the Indian Air Force with Gnats, Nehru had to overrule Krishna Menon, who had a poor opinion of them. 'Those little things would be blown out of the air by the fire-power of the American Sabres. You have said to me something about the psychological effect of these Gnats flying about. There is something in that so far as our own people are concerned, but I doubt whether this is so in regard to the other side, which is armed with Sabres against which we have no fighting and intercepting equivalents.' Krishna Menon to Nehru, 1 July 1956.

the British were not satisfied. Eden wrote to Nehru that delivery of Gnats
and Canberras would be speeded up, at the cost of supplies to the Royal
Air Force; and the price of these aeroplanes, superior to anything the
Soviet Union had to offer and containing highly secret equipment, had
been reduced to the minimum. The British Government would be willing
to consider any other proposal from India, but all this was on the
understanding that no Soviet aircraft would be bought.[6] This letter from
Eden was followed by a visit from Mountbatten, who is said to have
protested that if India purchased Ilyushins his own position would become
impossible and he would be unable to arrange for the supply of Canberras
with secret devices. India should buy arms only from Britain and nothing
from the Soviet Union, whose Ilyushins were no match for the Sabre jets
being provided to Pakistan by the United States.[7] Nehru gave way, not so
much out of conviction as out of friendliness. He agreed not to buy any
Soviet military aircraft for the time being and, although no guarantee could
be given for the future, promised not to take any such step without
informing and consulting the British Government.[8] While many aspects of
British policy exasperated Nehru, in the spring of 1956 his basic goodwill
for Britain and the Eden Government was without reserve.

Of all these visits of foreign ministers, that of Dulles was the most
pointless. He could not have arrived in Delhi at a worse moment. The
references to Goa the previous year and to Kashmir the week before had so
angered the public that special precautions had to be taken by the Government of India to prevent demonstrations against him. The talks themselves, lasting five and a half hours, brought Dulles and Nehru no closer
in ideas or intentions. 'The most that we can expect out of his visit here
is that he has got some idea into his rather closed head as to what we feel
about various things.'[9] Nehru believed that the policy of the United States
had reached a dead end and, if not altered, could only lead to war. To talk of
containing communism was to miss the issue, which was basically a
struggle for mastery between two powers. This, of course, made no sense to
Dulles. When Nehru interpreted the developments at the twentieth Party
Congress in Moscow as forming a further stage in the return of the Soviet
Union to normality, Dulles politely assented, but added that it would
probably take a generation before these changes could have full effect, and
meanwhile the Western Powers should maintain their strength. So on the
primary problem of world affairs the two men were really as far apart as
ever. But Dulles used the occasion to try to clear the air on other topics. He
blamed Britain for the Baghdad Pact and for embarrassing the United
States by dragging them in. He was critical of French policy in Algeria and

[6] Eden to Nehru, 8 March 1956.
[7] K. N. Katju, Defence Minister, to Nehru, 15 March 1956.
[8] Nehru to Eden, 23 March 1956.
[9] Nehru to Padmaja Naidu, 10 March 1956.

Indo-China; and again the burden, said Dulles, had fallen on the United States to help France out. He agreed that Pakistan had no place in SEATO, attributed to others the initiative in making her a member and disowned major responsibility for the reference to Kashmir in the latest communiqué. As for the military alliance of the United States with Pakistan, Dulles repeated the assurances that the United States would never permit an attack by Pakistan on India, and had taken express guarantees from Pakistan on this score. These assurances had never carried conviction with Nehru; and he was confirmed in his lack of confidence by Mikoyan's report a fortnight later in Delhi, that he had been informed in Karachi by the Pakistan Government that the defence pacts were intended solely to strengthen Pakistan's military capacity against India and Afghanistan.[10] In fact, Dulles informed Nehru that the Pakistan army would soon be of the same size as the Indian army and with superior equipment. This, in a way, was to lay bare the hollowness of his own assurances; and Dulles acknowledged that he had not realized till his visit to Delhi that India genuinely feared that Pakistan was growing in military strength and would use such strength against her.

Nehru then mentioned, as Dulles must have expected, the strong reaction in India to the statement on Goa issued by Dulles with the Foreign Minister of Portugal. Dulles replied that his chief anxiety was not to say anything which might hurt India. The Portuguese minister had suggested something very much worse and this had been turned down repeatedly. He had only agreed to the final communiqué after it had been approved by the experts on India in the State Department — which only showed, commented Nehru, how poor was the official advice Dulles received on India. Dulles agreed that the Portuguese could not remain in Goa, asked how he could help in settling this issue and remarked in passing, while discussing other matters, that it would be difficult for India to renounce the use of force completely in the matter of Goa.[11]

All Nehru's impressions regarding the attitudes of the Western Powers were reinforced during his visit to Europe in the summer of 1956. He liked Eden and had appreciated his role at the Geneva Conference; they had got on well when Eden visited Delhi in the spring of 1955; and Nehru sent a handwritten letter of warm congratulations when Eden succeeded Churchill as Prime Minister.

> This is just a brief personal note of welcome to you on your assumption of the high office of prime minister of the United Kingdom. I am happy that in England and in India we have had occasion to know each other a little more intimately. I am sure that this is of importance not only in the personal sense but in the larger

[10] Nehru's record of talks with A. Mikoyan, 26 March 1956.
[11] Nehru's two notes on talks with Dulles, 10 March 1956.

sense also. I hope that, whatever occasional differences of opinion we might have, we shall be able to cooperate in a large measure in the great causes that confront us. In this you have not only my personal goodwill but the goodwill of many in India.[12]

At the Conference of Commonwealth Prime Ministers, even Nehru could not have improved on Eden's analysis of Soviet policy, which was the main item on the agenda. Reporting on the visit to Britain a few weeks earlier of Khrushchev and Bulganin, Eden said there was not so much a fundamental change of heart in the Soviet Union as a change of outlook and of direction. There was no reason to suppose that the Soviet Government had modified their ultimate aim for communism of world domination, but they were moving from the fixed positions implied by the cold war to more flexible policies. They wished to avoid a major war and to establish better and more normal relations with other countries. There was, as a result, a new element of flexibility in Soviet domestic policy also, and this provided new opportunities.

Nehru's already high opinion of Eden's diplomatic maturity and sophistication was enhanced by this analysis and the report from Moscow that both Khrushchev and Bulganin had been deeply impressed by Eden.[13] At the Conference he urged that the improvement in world affairs effected by the new Soviet attitudes be supported by bringing China into the United Nations or, if this were too much to expect of the United States on the eve of a presidential election, at least by loosening the ties of the United States with Taiwan. The other prime ministers agreed but were unwilling to embarrass the United States by recommending China's entry into the United Nations, or even by making a general reference to the need for the United Nations to be more fully representative.[14] Nehru, who had been invited to Washington by Eisenhower, proposed to press the matter at a personal level. He intended, as it were, to talk above the head of Dulles — who had recently criticized non-alignment as immoral and shortsighted — [15] just as he rejected Krishna Menon's offer to join his party.[16] No one else should be present when he talked to Eisenhower. But Eisenhower's illness and the consequent suggestion from Washington that Nehru should seek a postponement led to Nehru putting off his visit.[17] Nehru thought that possibly Dulles had manoeuvred this; certainly

[12] Nehru to Eden, 8 April 1955.
[13] K. P. S. Menon's telegram to Nehru, 10 July 1956.
[14] Record of discussions at the Conference of Commonwealth Prime Ministers, 27 June to 5 July 1956.
[15] New York Times, 10 June 1956.
[16] Nehru's telegram to Krishna Menon, 14 June 1956.
[17] G. L. Mehta's telegram reporting conversations with J. F. Dulles and Sherman Cooper, 20 June, 1956.

Krishna Menon and Rajagopalachari were pleased, both taking the view that the invitation was part of electioneering.[18]

It was not, therefore, to Washington but to Paris that Nehru went from London. It had already been agreed by Nehru, after his talks with Pineau in Delhi — to the disappointment of the British Government and of Krishna Menon, who was negotiating without authority for the purchase of Hunter aircraft — to buy French Mystère planes.[19] Now Nehru met Mollet, and came to believe even more in the moderation and good sense of the French Government. He thought France was willing, once the military position in Algeria improved, to offer a generous settlement, and he sent word to the Algerian nationalists, who were sore that he had not helped their cause in Paris, to take advantage of the French offer.[20]

Such sunshine in Nehru's relations with the British and French Governments helped in shaping his position at the start of the crisis over Suez. Neither at Brioni, where Nasser, Tito and Nehru had met, nor later at Cairo, to which city Nehru and Nasser had travelled together, did Nasser mention to Nehru that he was considering the possibility of nationalizing the Suez Canal — a not surprising omission in the light of Nasser's later statement that he had not thought of nationalization at this time.[21] Indeed, at Brioni, war in West Asia had seemed far away, for an informal message had been received from the Prime Minister of Israel to the effect that Israel had made a mistake in leaning on the Western Powers and the Israelis now realized more than ever that they were of Asia and must look to Asia.[22] But Nasser showed Nehru on the aircraft flying to Cairo a radio version of Dulles's speech announcing withdrawal of assistance for building the Aswan dam, and the speech seemed to Nehru very discourteous and almost contemptuous in tone.[23] Nasser's only reaction at this stage was that he would abandon the Aswan dam project; and Nehru approved. It seemed wiser to distribute Egypt's resources among a large number of small projects yielding quick results rather than concentrate on one major project which would not begin to function for at least another ten years and would vest any country providing major assistance with a commanding control of the Egyptian economy.[24]

Nationalization of the Canal came, therefore, to Nehru as an unpleasant

[18] See G. L. Mehta, Indian Ambassador in Washington, to Nehru, 25 July 1956; Rajagopalachari to Nehru, 26 July 1956.

[19] Nehru's note to Defence Ministry, 13 June; Eden to Nehru, 15 June 1956 and Nehru's reply of the same date.

[20] Nehru's telegram to Krishna Menon, 17 July, and note to Foreign Secretary, 25 July 1956.

[21] See A. Moncrieff (ed.), *Suez Ten Years After* (London, 1967), pp. 43-4.

[22] Nehru's note, 9 September 1958.

[23] Nehru's background note for missions, 31 July 1956. M. H. Heikal reports Nehru as having commented, 'These people, how arrogant they are.' Heikal, *The Cairo Documents* (New York, 1973), pp. 67-8.

[24] Nehru's telegram to Ali Yavar Jung, Ambassador in Cairo, 27 July 1956.

surprise. 'I feel that the Egyptian Government is undertaking more than it can manage and is being pushed by some extremist elements and by angry reaction to American and British refusal to help the Aswan dam project.'[25] There was to Nehru an element of warmongering in Egypt's action. Rajagopalachari, who at this time, in contrast to Nehru, was adopting a pronouncedly anti-Western attitude, favoured prompt and pre-emptive action on the side of Nasser. He suggested an immediate declaration by all the Bandung countries clearly expressing their support for Egypt so as to prevent any intimidation by the Western Powers.[26] But Nehru preferred to hold his hand and instructed that all governments be informed that India would make no commitment of support to either side and would merely watch developments.[27] No one could doubt Egypt's right to nationalize the Canal, but the manner in which it was done and the offensive language employed made it difficult to reach any acceptable agreement providing for what Egypt had already promised, the continuance of the Canal as an open international waterway.[28]

This was obviously an effort by Nehru to play fair by Britain and France who had, in his opinion, been behaving commendably on other matters in previous months, and not to be swept along by the deep tides of nationalism and anti-colonialism. But, thanks to Eden, he could not long maintain this attitude. Unlike Pineau who, after meeting Nasser had been persuaded that he was not a second Hitler, Eden, enclosed in the walls of his past career, regarded Nasser as 'an Asiatic Mussolini',[29] felt that no honourable agreement could be reached with him, and even thought it possible that Nehru might be willing to accept action against Egypt.[30] Any such illusion was shortlived, for the fierce reactions in Britain to the nationalization of the Canal led Nehru to advise the British Government against any attempts at coercion. But hopes of Nehru's support in securing a diplomatic settlement[31] were not baseless. On hearing that Britain intended to convene a conference to consider international control of the Canal, Nehru suggested to Nasser that Egypt herself might take the initiative and call together, on the basis of Egypt's sovereignty, all those interested in the international aspects of the issue.[32] The crisis could be settled by negotiation if rigid attitudes did not result in further unilateral decisions, for the demands of the two sides were not contradictory. 'But

[25] Nehru's telegram to Vijayalakshmi in London, 27 July 1956.
[26] Rajagopalachari to Nehru, 28 July 1956.
[27] Nehru's directive to Foreign Secretary, 29 July 1956.
[28] Nehru's background note for missions, 31 July 1956.
[29] The phrase is, in fact, Macmillan's: diary entry 27 July 1956; *Riding the Storm* (London, 1971), p. 101.
[30] I. McDonald, *A Man of the Times* (London, 1976), p. 144.
[31] Britain rejected Pearson's suggestion that the Suez crisis be discussed by the NATO Council before the meeting of the London conference, because this might antagonize and alienate Nehru who would play a key role in the dispute. Pearson, *Memoirs*, Vol. 2, p. 229.
[32] Nehru's messages to Lord Home and to Nasser, 2 August 1956.

how the question is going to be settled by show of force is more than I can understand.'[33]

While the tone of Nasser's speeches had become more moderate, his reply to Nehru's suggestion was not helpful. He requested Nehru to join him in declining the invitation to the London conference, and his positive counter-proposal was to offer to discuss the problem of all international waterways at the United Nations.[34] He must have known that this was virtually a meaningless offer, for the waterways Nasser had in mind were the Panama Canal, the Dardanelles, Gibraltar and Aden;[35] and the countries concerned with these would obviously not agree to multilateral discussions. So Nehru ignored Nasser's suggestion and declared his willingness to participate in the London conference. 'Our object would not be to weaken your position, but as you yourself have been doing, to work for conciliatory approaches. In this way, it may be possible to prevent the proposed conference from becoming a barrier to settlement.' He added, in what was clearly a rebuke to Nasser: 'We wish to emphasize these aspects and not to support any unilateral action taken by one nation or any group of nations.'[36] But to Eden Nehru pointed out that the list of invitees was too partial and required expansion. He would also be reluctant to send a delegation to the conference if it was committed to consideration only of an international authority to manage the Canal. Attempts to impose a solution on Egypt would lead to armed conflict and powerful reactions all over Asia and large parts of Africa. If the conference were to have positive results, the whole approach would have to be different.[37]

Taking seriously a polite request from Nasser for advice, Nehru rashly sent a draft of the reply which Nasser should send to Britain. He should express surprise at the convening of a conference without reference to the Egyptian Government, but state that Egypt would be willing to attend if there were an agreed list of invitees and no prior conditions and commitments. While Egypt could not accept any challenge to her sovereignty, she would be willing to execute a fresh agreement which would guarantee freedom of navigation. Disillusioned by the United Nations himself, Nehru cautioned Nasser against any reference of the issue to that organization.[38] But Nasser rejected this draft and said his government would not be represented, under any circumstances, at a conference convened by Britain.[39] So a lack of whole-hearted support by

[33] Nehru to Mountbatten, 3 August 1956, the *New York Times* was of the same view: 'This is no time for battleships and planes. It is a time for sober and responsible talk.'
[34] Nasser to Nehru, 4 August 1956.
[35] Egyptian Ambassador's conversation with Indian High Commissioner in Pakistan, 4 August, reported in High Commissioner's telegram of same date to Ministry of External Affairs, New Delhi.
[36] Nehru to Nasser, 5 August 1956.
[37] Nehru to Eden, 4 and 5 August 1956.
[38] Nehru to Nasser, 5 August 1956.
[39] Report to Nehru of Indian Ambassador in Cairo after meeting Nasser, 7 August 1956.

India of Egypt's action had been followed by a disagreement on tactics. With Nasser standing aloof, Nehru announced that India would attend the London conference on the basis of Eden's assurance that participation need not imply acceptance of the British demand for an international authority.[40]

> It seems to me that the London conference cannot possibly come to any settlement as Egypt will not be there. Our main purpose at this conference has, therefore, to be to prevent any wrong and dangerous steps being taken and to leave the door open for a further conference or consultations in which Egypt must necessarily play an important part.[41]

A conference without Egypt's participation could only be a prelude to real discussions; but even this might not be without value. Nehru was continuing his balancing act, assisting Egypt without standing forth as her unhesitating champion. He suggested to the Speaker of the Lok Sabha that he disallow discussion on a private member's motion advocating withdrawal from the Commonwealth.[42] He discouraged the Egyptian Government from adopting the rupee as the medium of exchange for her trade with third countries. He directed Krishna Menon to break his journey at Cairo on his way to the London conference to explain to Nasser that it did not follow from Egypt's refusal to attend that it would be best for her friends also to stay away, for they might be able to prevent foolish decisions being taken. But mediation without unqualified acceptance of his bonafides by either of the parties was not enviable. 'This is far the most difficult and dangerous situation in international affairs we have faced since independence. I do not think we can do very much, but it is just possible that we might stop the rot. Probably we shall end by displeasing our friends on both sides.'[43]

At Cairo Krishna Menon found Nasser more mellowed but, while appearing 'to realize in his mind that perhaps he was precipitate', unyielding on such issues as international control.[44] At the conference in London Menon sought to persuade the Western Powers to negotiate with Egypt on the basis of her sovereignty, and was embarrassed by the Soviet Union taking the same line.[45] His compromise formula provided for minority representation of international user interests, without ownership rights, on the Egyptian corporation for the Canal, a consultative body of user interests, and transmission by Egypt to the United Nations of the

---

[40] Eden to Nehru, 7 August, and Nehru's statement in Parliament, 8 August 1956.

[41] Nehru to S. W. R. D. Bandaranaike, Prime Minister of Ceylon, 8 August 1956. Nehru had rejected suggestions for a preliminary meeting of the Colombo powers (particularly as Burma had not been invited to the London conference) but kept these powers informed of his thinking.

[42] Nehru's note to Speaker, 9 August 1956.

[43] Nehru to Rajagopalachari, 10 August 1956.

[44] Krishna Menon's telegram to Nehru, 15 August 1956.

[45] Krishna Menon's second telegram to Nehru, 15 August 1956.

annual reports of the Canal corporation. The first two parts of the formula appeared inadequate to Britain and France and really an appeasement of Nasser; but the formula as a whole was disliked by Egypt. Neither could Nasser have liked Menon's suggestion that if the Egyptian Government claimed to bar Israeli ships from the Canal as a legitimate act of war, they should abide by any decision of the Hague Court on this subject.[46] So far from the Indian delegation virtually functioning, as Eden and Lord Home have later alleged,[47] as Egypt's spokesman and egging on Nasser, at the time Krishna Menon had to press the Egyptian Government to counter the growing impression that India had no influence in Cairo by giving a measure of support to India's proposals. But Nasser could not be persuaded.[48] Nehru was probably not surprised for, though he urged Nasser to be a little more flexible,[49] he also directed Menon to formulate some 'more constructive proposal',[50] implying that the earlier suggestion leant too much towards the British side. This lack of close accord between India and Egypt made it easier for the majority at the London conference to support the Dulles plan for an international board of control. Krishna Menon's wish to walk out of the conference was overruled by Nehru, who had never attached much significance to it. Such a dramatic step was, in fact, not necessary, as the conference decided merely to forward its proceedings to Nasser without any specific recommendation.[51]

The retrospective bitterness of Eden and Home about India's activity at this time is not justified by contemporary evidence. For, after the conference, both Eden and Selwyn Lloyd sought to utilize India's general standing in Egypt to secure some arrangement which would provide international control of the Canal. But at Cairo, on his way back, Menon made no suggestion, as the Egyptian Government were still somewhat chary of India,[52] wisely leaving any initiative to come from Nasser. On 6 September, when it became clear that the Menzies mission would be fruitless and the threats of the use of force by Britain and France became more open, Nasser requested Nehru to get negotiations started on the basis of the legitimate concerns of user interests, but without acceptance of international control. Nehru agreed to help, but again dissuaded Nasser from approaching the United Nations.[53] So the Egyptian Government

[46] Menon later recorded that he had been surprised that Nasser agreed to this, and thought he had done so 'because he had no anti-Jewish feeling personally, and part of him was a statesman even then, and he wanted a settlement.' M. Brecher, *India and World Politics* (London, 1968), p. 68.

[47] A. Eden, *Full Circle* (London, 1961), p. 444; Lord Home, *The Way the Wind Blows* (London, 1976), p. 140.

[48] Menon's telegram from London to Indian Ambassador in Cairo, 20 August, and telegram to Nehru, 21 August 1956.

[49] Nehru's telegram to Indian Ambassador in Cairo, 21 August 1956.

[50] Nehru's telegram to Krishna Menon, 21 August 1956.

[51] Menon's telegram to Nehru, 22 August and Nehru's reply, 23 August 1956.

[52] Menon's telegram to Nehru from Cairo, 31 August 1956.

[53] Nasser to Nehru, 6 September, Nehru to Nasser, 7 September, and Nasser to Nehru, 8 September 1956.

announced their proposal for the formation of a negotiating body representative of all views among the user nations, and Nehru pressed Eden to react constructively.

> The position of the two sides and the points of difference as between them, though they appear to be wide apart and seemingly difficult to reconcile, do not appear to me to be so in fact. I believe we could discover and establish some common ground from which a settlement on the points of difference can emerge.[54]

He also wrote to Eisenhower, who had by now rejected the possible use of force, seeking American support for a negotiated settlement.[55]

Eden paid no heed. The British Government announced that a Suez Canal association would be set up, virtually taking over the operational control of the Canal. It was added that other steps in assertion of British rights were being contemplated, and this was thought to mean that the British Government would try to adopt successively stronger measures in the hope that somewhere along the line Nasser would crack or Arab support for him would weaken or a plausible excuse for military action would be provided.[56] In view of this, Nehru advised Nasser, as the plan for a users' conference had seemingly become out of date, to consider a reference to the Security Council. This would have the advantage of at least delaying a crisis.[57] He also complained to Eden about his endangering whatever prospects still existed of a peaceful settlement.

> In my mind and in my approach to you I do not contemplate or advocate appeasement to which references are frequently made, but a settlement that is satisfactory and honourable. This should be fully consistent with the interests and the position and prestige of the United Kingdom, which you know are our concern as well.

There should be an emergency meeting of the Commonwealth prime ministers before any steps leading to conflict were taken.[58]

War now seemed possible, and Nehru ordered the various departments in Delhi to plan the measures that would be required in the event of hostilities. The consequences of a stoppage of traffic through the Canal had to be examined and suitable action considered.[59] But he still could not

---

[54] Nehru to Eden, 11 September 1956.
[55] Nehru to Eisenhower, 11 September 1956.
[56] Vijayalakshmi's telegram to Nehru, 13 September 1956. As we now know, on 1 September Israel had been informed of Anglo-French plans to seize the Canal Zone. M. Dayan, *Story of My Life* (London, 1976), p. 151.
[57] Nehru to Nasser, 13 September 1956.
[58] Nehru to Eden, 14 September 1956.
[59] Nehru's minute for the Cabinet, 14 September 1956.

believe that Britain would be so lacking in good sense as to wage war on this issue;[60] so he persevered with his efforts to create some basis for future negotiation by informal soundings on both sides. A broad sympathy for Egypt need not mean support of every action taken by her or deliberate humiliation of Britain and France. Krishna Menon sought to persuade the Egyptian Government to be a little more cooperative even though the plan for a users' association was totally unacceptable.[61] Nehru was due to go to Saudi Arabia a few days after Nasser's visit to that country; but to avoid any suggestion of ganging up, Nehru asked Nasser not to stay on in Riyadh to meet him.[62] He also declined to supply to Egypt bren-guns and spare barrels and fuses for mortar bombs.

> For us to supply arms to the Egyptian Government at this stage would naturally be greatly resented by the United Kingdom and other Western Governments and make them feel that we are supporting Egypt one hundred per cent in peace and war. Our capacity for playing a mediatory role would disappear.[63]

This continuous reluctance to side unquestioningly with Egypt was not supported by a less bellicose approach from the Western Powers. Eden still favoured a users' association and told Nehru that Egypt should be persuaded to agree. An immediate meeting of Commonwealth prime ministers would be difficult. 'In any event we will maintain close touch with Commonwealth Governments by every means.'[64] Dulles too, to whom Nehru had appealed,[65] replied that while the United States would not support any disregard of Egypt's rights, it was not clear what precisely these rights were. Her legal title to the Canal was coupled with an international easement across her territory. The United Nations could deal with any overt violation of this easement, and the users' association would provide a comparable sanction against covert violations.[66] These were not helpful attitudes; but, as the days passed, the threat of war seemed to Nehru to retreat a little, giving way to what would probably be a long period of cold war.[67]

In such a new phase, while the Western Powers had much to lose, Nasser could not be complacent. He had, as Tito said, in his inexperience reacted too quickly and too sharply to the American withdrawal of assistance to the Aswan dam project; if he had been put in a very difficult position by that

[60] See Menon's account in Brecher, op. cit., p. 65.
[61] Krishna Menon's telegram from Cairo to Nehru, 19 September 1956.
[62] Nehru's telegram to Indian Ambassador in Cairo, 21 September 1956.
[63] Nehru's note to Foreign Secretary, 17 September 1956.
[64] Eden to Nehru, 16 September 1956.
[65] Nehru to Dulles, 14 September 1956.
[66] Dulles to Nehru, 16 September 1956.
[67] Nehru to Chief Ministers, 20 September 1956.

withdrawal, now his position was even more difficult.[68] In the Arab world, too, the situation was turning against him and the Egyptians were showing signs of nervousness. The British Ambassador in Cairo reported at the beginning of October that the situation appeared to be moving in favour of Britain, and the near future appeared a favourable moment for any negotiated settlement.[69] Krishna Menon worked out a fresh set of compromise proposals, providing for an Egyptian Canal authority whose annual report would be forwarded to the United Nations, a broad-based users' association with advisory functions and an agreement to settle all disputes in accordance with the United Nations Charter. He thought that he had persuaded Eden and Lloyd to accept these proposals and Nasser should now be pressed to accept.

> For your information only we have got somewhere. If we can get over one or two smaller hurdles in Cairo, which should be possible with the weight of your backing, we would have turned the corner. Subsequent stages are largely methodological problems.[70]

From this predicament of being pushed into a settlement not to his liking, Nasser was repeatedly rescued by Eden. Krishna Menon had been over-optimistic in his assessment of the British Government's reaction. Nehru was informed by Eden that Menon had put some hypothetical questions and the British Government could not commit themselves by answering these questions. They still stood by their earlier insistence on international control of the Canal, and Menon's proposals left Egypt in unfettered grasp of the waterway and provided no means of enforcing whatever arrangements might be reached.[71] Discussions now shifted to New York, where Hammarskjöld kept Menon out of the picture and secured an agreement on principles between Egypt, Britain and France.[72] Egypt, reported Menon,[73] had given in far more than she ever gave India to understand she would, and on points which on the face of them were vital to her sovereignty. Dulles thought that this was the best opportunity that there might ever be for a reasonable and honourable solution peacefully arrived at.[74] Nehru was confident that the problem had definitely reached a negotiating stage and it would be difficult to go back on this.[75]

Even if, on this last lap, Nehru and Menon had played little part, their

[68] Report of Indian Ambassador in Belgrade on conversation with Tito, 15 September 1956.
[69] H. Trevelyan, *The Middle East in Revolution* (London, 1970), pp. 101-2.
[70] Krishna Menon's telegram from London to Nehru, 29 September 1956.
[71] Nehru's note on interview with British High Commissioner, 1 October 1956; Eden to Nehru, 9 October 1956.
[72] B. Urquhart, *Hammarskjöld* (London, 1972), pp. 166-8; Heikal, op. cit., p. 167.
[73] Krishna Menon's telegram from New York to Nehru, 14 October 1956.
[74] Dulles to Nehru, 18 October 1956.
[75] Press conference, *The Hindu*, 26 October 1956.

contribution to the maintenance of peace over the whole period from the time of nationalization of the Canal had been massive.

I want to help in letting you know how large a volume of support you have in this country, and how deeply grateful most people here are for the stand you have made from first to last. Your first outspoken statement in your Parliament was, in my view, of immense value, and I think it did more than anything else to give our hotheads pause. Krishna's work all through the Conference and ever since has been of immense value, and if in the end your solution of the Canal problem is adopted, as I hope and believe it will be, not only Britain but the whole world will owe you very much. In any case, I think the Labour Party, with Liberal and other support, are now strong enough to prevent the Government pursuing the suicidal course which was nearly taken.[76]

Noel-Baker was, of course, wrong in this forecast. Eden, unknown to Nehru and Dulles and even to his ambassadors,[77] was working out other plans. The secret arrangements with Israel necessitated a request for postponement of further explanatory talks with Egypt, scheduled to begin in Geneva on 29 October. The Egyptian Government believed that this meant a lull[78] and were as startled as everyone else by the Israeli attack and the Anglo-French ultimatum. The invasion of Egypt was clearly no matter on which Nehru could refrain from taking sides. 'This is a reversal of history which none of us can tolerate.'[79] Apart from public condemnation of the aggressors, he called on Hammarskjöld to ensure that the procedures of the United Nations were swifter than those of invasion and aggression, and urged the United States to intervene.

I cannot imagine a worse case of aggression. If this aggression continues and succeeds, all faith in international commitments and the United Nations will fade away, and the old spectre of colonialism will haunt us again . . . The whole future of the relations between Europe and Asia hangs in the balance. There can be no peace, howsoever it might be imposed, if it means conquest by force of arms.[80]

[76] Philip Noel-Baker to Nehru, 26 October 1956. In earlier years Nehru had often justifiably been irritated with Noel-Baker.

[77] 'Lately he [Nasser] has been telling me that he was quite prepared to believe that Britain was restraining the Israelis. Trevelyan told me this was so, and that the Israeli Ambassador in London had expressed to the British Foreign Office his country's dissatisfaction at the British attitude. I conveyed this information to Nasser for whatever it was worth.' Report of Indian Ambassador in Cairo to Ministry of External Affairs, 22 October 1956.

[78] Telegram of Indian Ambassador in Cairo after talks with Egyptian Foreign Minister, 26 October 1956.

[79] Nehru to Nasser, 31 October 1956.

[80] Nehru to Dulles, 31 October 1956.

To Eden himself, who sent a formal letter of explanation, Nehru did not
mince his words.

> It seems to us that this is clear aggression and a violation of the United
> Nations Charter. For us in India and, I believe, in many other
> countries of Asia and elsewhere, this is a reversion to a previous
> and unfortunate period of history when decisions were imposed by
> force of arms by Western Powers on Asian countries. We had thought
> that these methods were out-of-date and could not possibly be used in
> the modern age. The whole purpose of the United Nations is
> undermined and the freedom of nations imperilled if armed might is
> to decide issues between nations . . . it is a matter of the deepest regret
> to me that the United Kingdom, with her record of liberal policies,
> should be associated now with aggression and invasion and, in the
> minds of many countries where memories of colonialism still linger,
> should become a symbol of something that they have fought against
> in the past and dislike intensely in the present. Our sympathies must
> necessarily be with Egypt in these circumstances . . . nothing can
> justify aggression and the attack on the freedom of a country. I have
> set down my feelings freely and frankly for I think it is due to a friend
> that I should do so. Unless these wrong courses are halted the future
> appears to me to be dark indeed.[81]

It was now a matter of almost hourly activity to obtain a cease-fire and
prevent the spread of military action, to shelter the honour of Nasser, to
safeguard the sovereignty of Egypt and to save the Commonwealth. Nehru
rejected as impractical the suggestion of the Soviet Union, Egypt and
China for an immediate reassembling of the Bandung countries[82] and
thought it best to seek solutions at the special session of the United Nations
assembly. He supported a proposal, which was acceptable to Egypt, of a
contingent from the United States to re-establish armistice lines between
Israel and Egypt, and an observer team manned by India, Canada and
Czechoslovakia. An international police force would be acceptable on the
old Arab-Israeli armistice line for a temporary period but not in the Suez
Canal area or anywhere else in Egypt.[83] When the United Nations set up an
emergency force, both Pearson and Hammarskjöld requested India to
participate and Krishna Menon was for agreement, 'both to give it moral
support and character and indeed to make it possible . . . It may be the only
way of terminating hostilities and saving the Egyptian Government.' It

[81] Nehru to Eden, 1 November 1956.

[82] Bulganin to Nehru, 2 November and Nehru's reply of same date; Foreign Secretary to Indian
chargé d' affaires in Cairo, 2 November; Chou En-lai's message to Nehru, communicated by Indian
Ambassador, 3 November 1956.

[83] Telegram from Indian delegation in New York to Foreign Secretary, 3 November and Foreign
Secretary's reply, 4 November 1956.

would operate for a temporary period on Egyptian soil with Egypt's consent, not as a successor of the invading forces but to push them back behind the armistice lines. But, whatever the merits of the proposal, Nehru was prepared to agree only if the Egyptian Government expressed an unqualified desire for Indian participation. 'You can assure the Egyptian Government of our complete solidarity with Egypt whatever happens.'[84]

The Soviet proposal for a joint Soviet-American military effort to stop the fighting was obviously unacceptable to Eisenhower.[85] But the threat to use rockets remained. The British Ambassador in Moscow, who did not think the threat an empty one, advised the Foreign Office to mobilize the United States and Nehru to warn the Soviet Union of the danger of such action.[86] But this was a matter in which Nehru needed no prompting. He appealed to Bulganin not to take any steps which might lead to a general war but to agree to act through the United Nations.[87] He also welcomed the Swiss proposal of a meeting of the heads of government of the United States, Britain, France and the Soviet Union, and expressed his own willingness to attend if desired.[88] But there were other problems than the restoration of peace. Egyptian military resistance was disintegrating and Ali Sabry reported that Nasser proposed to lay down his life fighting.[89] Though a cease-fire was accepted by Britain soon after, Nehru sent Nasser a warmly worded note of encouragement.

Recent developments indicate definitely that the tide has turned in favour of Egypt. I am sure that this process will continue and not only bring relief to Egypt but ultimate removal of all aggression wherever it may come from. I should like to congratulate you on this turn of events and to assure you that we shall stand by the independence of Egypt. World opinion has been largely with you and has undoubtedly helped greatly, but it is essentially your leadership and the determination of the Egyptian people to preserve their freedom that has made the difference. I trust that Egypt will long have your leadership and prosper under it.[90]

Nasser replied that no expression of thanks or gratitude was necessary as he and Nehru had reached such a stage of close friendship and understanding; even now he suspected some political trick in the cease-fire and asserted

[84] Telegram from Indian delegation in New York to Foreign Secretary, 4 November; Krishna Menon's telegram from New York to Nehru, 5 November; Nehru's telegram to Indian chargé d'affaires in Cairo, 5 November 1956.
[85] Bulganin to Nehru, 5 November, and Eisenhower to Nehru, 5 November 1956.
[86] Sir William Hayter, *The Kremlin and the Embassy* (London, 1966), pp. 147-8.
[87] Nehru to Bulganin, 6 November 1956.
[88] Nehru to the President of the Swiss Confederation, 6 November 1956.
[89] Telegram from Indian chargé d'affaires, 6 November 1956.
[90] Nehru to Nasser, 7 November 1956.

that he would accept nothing which limited Egypt's sovereignty.[91]

In India itself, Nehru had to subdue the growing storm of hostility to Britain as well as to the Commonwealth as a whole. In both his private communications as well as in his speeches he never criticized Britain or even the British Government, but only Eden; and he always expressed his disapproval more in sorrow than in anger.[92] To Nehru the Suez adventure was the aberration of one man; and the Indian public should remember that Eden did not symbolize the totality of British opinion. He knew that there was opposition even among the Conservatives and in the British Foreign Office to Eden's policy, while Pethick-Lawrence appealed to him to take into account the fact that the Labour Party was severely critical.

> A rumour has reached me that there is a possibility that in view of your profound disapproval of what our United Kingdom Government is doing in the Middle East you may be considering withdrawal from the Commonwealth.
>
> As one who is equally an out-and-out opponent of Sir Anthony Eden's policy, may I say that I should regard any such decision as a disaster. There is as you know a great number of people here in the United Kingdom whose views are similar to yours, and we hope you will not desert us in our struggle to rescue the Commonwealth from the disgrace which our Prime Minister has put upon it.[93]

The demand for withdrawal from the Commonwealth came not only from left-wing parties and within the Congress but from even the conservative leader Rajagopalachari. But Nehru withstood the pressure. The Commonwealth connection had not inhibited India from expressing her opinions in the strongest possible manner, and any severance of this relationship should be not the result of an angry reaction to a particular crisis but a cool decision taken after consideration of every aspect of the issue. Britain had no monopoly of the Commonwealth, and India had been able to make her efforts more effective by acting in close collaboration with other members such as Canada.[94] So, when the storm passed, the Commonwealth, despite the British Government's neglect of their obligations and the heavy volume of criticism in India, remained intact. Nehru was not only among the creators of the new Commonwealth; he was also, in its first major crisis, it saviour.

After the cease-fire, Britain requested India to 'come in heavily and assist

---

[91] Report of Indian chargé d'affaires to Foreign Secretary of interview with Nasser, 8 November 1956.

[92] Malcolm MacDonald, *Titans and Others* (London, 1972), p. 224. MacDonald was at this time British High Commissioner in Delhi.

[93] Pethick-Lawrence to Nehru, 5 November 1956.

[94] 'In these difficult days through which we are passing, India has never been far from my mind.' St Laurent to Nehru, 7 November 1956.

26   Nehru, Bertrand Russell and Pethick-Lawrence, London, February 1955

27   With Bulganin and Khrushchev, Delhi, December 1955

28   Nasser, Nehru and Tito at Brioni, July 1956

29   With Lord and Lady Attlee, Delhi, October 1956

in bringing about a speedy settlement.'[95] The Egyptian Government were willing to accept an international force consisting of troops from India, Greece and Colombia only.[96] Krishna Menon advised the addition of Canada and, if Colombia were to be accepted, of Yugoslavia or Poland or Czechoslovakia as a balance.[97] Pearson announced the offer of a Canadian contingent, and Hammarskjöld said that the advance party would consist of Canada, Colombia and India. But on 12 November Fawzi, the Foreign Minister of Egypt, suddenly objected to India's participation in the international force on the ground that neither close friends nor declared foes of Egypt should be represented. The Indian Ambassador attributed this sudden cooling off towards India to either dislike of the Commonwealth or the objection made by the United States, at the instance of the British, to the inclusion of India and the exclusion of Pakistan, Canada and New Zealand. Later, in the evening, Nasser overruled his Foreign Minister, whose attitude was put down to apprehension that India's presence in what many Egyptians would regard as an occupation force might damage India's popularity.[98]

Egypt now suggested that the international force should be manned by the four Scandinavian countries, Colombia, Yugoslavia, India and Indonesia. Canada was still objected to as seemingly the choice of Britain and France. She was a member of NATO, her troops wore British uniform and she had recently agreed to supply jet aircraft to Israel. Pearson sought Nehru's personal intervention.[99] Although the Indian Ambassador felt that he could not press Nasser on this beyond a certain point, Nehru strongly argued the case for Canada with Nasser. Despite her close links with Britain and France, Canada had opposed their policy from the start of the Suez crisis, and Egyptian insistence on Canada's exclusion would harm Egypt's interests. The argument about membership of NATO had fallen with Egypt's acceptance (to please Hammarskjöld) of Denmark and Norway; and Canada had with courage cancelled the contract for supply of aircraft to Israel.[100] Nasser agreed at first only to a Canadian ambulance corps or air supplies and Hammarskjöld was satisfied with this. But India still insisted that Nasser allow a Canadian contingent that would not wear its own emblems but United Nations helmets, and Nasser agreed on principle.[101]

The Suez crisis was basically now over. The British Government tacitly accepted defeat and were ready to withdraw their forces from Egypt

[95] Lord Home, Commonwealth Secretary, to Indian Deputy High Commissioner in London, reported in telegram to Foreign Secretary, 6 November 1956.
[96] Telegram of Indian chargé d'affaires reporting views of Ali Sabry, 9 November 1956.
[97] Menon's telegram to Nehru, 9 November 1956.
[98] Indian Ambassador's telegrams to Foreign Secretary, 12 November 1956.
[99] Message from Pearson to Nehru transmitted by Canadian High Commissioner in Delhi, 15 November 1956.
[100] Nehru's telegram to Indian Ambassador in Cairo, 15 November 1956.
[101] Indian Ambassador's telegrams to Nehru, 16 and 17 November 1956.

without, as before, demanding any assurance regarding the Canal. 'All they want now appears to be to avoid humiliation.'[102] It was Nasser's Government that Nehru had at this stage to pull up for proposing to deport British and French nationals and persons of Jewish origin even though they had not been guilty of anti-Egyptian activities.

> You have in the recent past shown exemplary patience in the most provocative circumstances. If I may say so, this has impressed the world almost as much as your courage throughout this critical period. I would request you, therefore, not to take steps which would compel a large number of persons to leave Egypt in penurious circumstances . . . Even from the short-term point of view a little patience and tolerance at this stage would help in the discussion of bigger issues concerning Egypt in the United Nations and elsewhere.[103]

But Nasser was unwilling to act on this advice. He argued that British, French and Jewish interests had dominated the Egyptian economy for decades and, in recent months, had tried to paralyse the country's economic life. He could not ignore these interests, particularly in the context of British and French radio propaganda aimed at his overthrow: and he was therefore attempting to rid Egypt of them.[104]

Nehru was disappointed, for he had hoped that Nasser would not spoil his success on all the major issues by pettiness on minor ones. 'True wisdom consists in knowing how far we can go, to profit by the circumstances and to create a feeling of generosity which again results in a change in one's own favour.'[105] Egypt would be well advised to consolidate her triumph step by step and to utilize it to reduce the perennial crisis in Arab-Israel relations.

The Suez crisis had brought out the best in Nehru. He had at no time compromised on principles and had been unshaken in his evaluation of the rights and wrongs of the basic issues. But he had combined such firmness with a genuine desire to protect British interests and, as the crisis developed, to rescue Britain from the mistaken decisions of her Prime Minister. His position in the other crisis which erupted during the same months was not so patently faultless.

---

[102] Nehru to Tito, 2 December 1956.
[103] Nehru to Nasser, 5 December 1956.
[104] Report of Indian chargé d'affaires of interview with Nasser, 5 December 1956.
[105] Nehru to Indian Ambassador in Cairo, 26 December 1956.

14

Hungary

When, at the end of October, Soviet troops quickly moved in to crush the revolt in Hungary, Nehru came round to the view, despite diverse and confusing reports, that a powerful and widespread national uprising was being suppressed with large-scale slaughter on both sides. Yet he declined to associate himself with the move of the United States to raise the matter in the United Nations.[1] This refusal to place Hungary tactically on a par with Suez exposed Nehru to severe criticism both in India and abroad. Even senior officials in his Ministry of External Affairs warned him against an application of double standards.

> If it is true that Soviet troops are trying to occupy Budapest and other areas in Hungary, whatever the ostensible reason, and if it is true also that this is being opposed by the Hungarian Government and that they have appealed to the United Nations, we cannot afford to appear to be indifferent in regard to these developments. I am not suggesting that we should raise our voice in the same way as certain others are doing; but I think the time has come for us to give further thought to the Hungarian situation with a view to deciding our attitude in the light of the principles we have been advocating.'[2]

But it was not easy to determine what those principles demanded. In the Suez crisis, the issues were clear; but on Hungary the main source of information was the Western press agencies, who were perhaps exaggerating the 'continuing intervention' made possible by the Warsaw treaty. Besides, a public condemnation of Soviet action might be self-defeating, having the reverse effect of what was intended. It could well be argued that, in the circumstances, the best way of assisting nationalist forces in Hungary was to bring pressure on the Soviet Government in private. But there was probably also a tendency, in Nehru's thinking, for policy to follow

[1] Telegram from External Affairs Ministry to Indian Embassy in Washington, 30 October 1956.
[2] Note of Secretary-General to Prime Minister, 2 November 1956.

inclination. 'In the Foreign Office at New Delhi,' the then Foreign Secretary wrote years later, 'events in Hungary took a second place to those in Egypt.'[3]

So all that Nehru did at the start was direct his Ambassador in Moscow to let the Soviet authorities know informally the reaction in India and to point out that sympathy naturally went to those who represented the national desire for freedom. The next day he cabled again, seeking full information from the Soviet Government. 'Any further conflict between Russians and Hungarians would be most unfortunate and will be used to divert attention from the Middle East situation.'[4] Till such information was obtained, he decided to move softly and instructed the Indian delegation at the United Nations to avoid condemnation of the Soviet Government, while making clear that fighting should stop and the people of Hungary should be free to decide their own future without external intervention or pressure.[5]

Censure of Nehru's reluctance to make an open reference to the Soviet action in Hungary was widespread. 'If you do not speak out,' wrote Jayaprakash Narayan, 'you will be held guilty of abetting enslavement of a brave people by a new imperialism more dangerous than the old because it masquerades as revolutionary.'[6] In an attempt to stem such accusations, Nehru, on 5 November, for the first time publicly expressed his sympathy with national forces in Hungary and condemned Soviet conduct.[7] This was not regarded as adequate by his critics, especially as Krishna Menon stated in New York that events in Hungary were a domestic affair. Nehru did not go as far, but it does seem that until the cease-fire was secured in Egypt, his mind, like Hammarskjöld's,[8] was more engrossed in the aggression there than in the intervention in Hungary.

> I have no doubt that the action of the Soviet Government is deplorable. But we do not yet have full information as to how and why these changes occurred. The case of Egypt is absolutely clear and there is no doubt about it. Because of this and because of our own intimate contacts both with Egypt and with the Suez Canal issue, we had to express our opinion immediately and forcibly.[9]

He wrote to Eisenhower on 7 November that there was nothing to choose

[3] S. Dutt, *With Nehru in the Foreign Office* (Calcutta, 1977), p. 177.
[4] Nehru's telegrams to K. P. S. Menon, 2 and 3 November 1956.
[5] Nehru's telegram to Permanent Mission at United Nations, 4 November 1956.
[6] 5 November 1956.
[7] Speech at UNESCO General Conference in New Delhi, 5 November. *The Hindu*, 6 November 1956.
[8] 'If you disregard all other aspects and look at the time sequence, I think it is perfectly clear to you that Suez had a time priority on the thinking and on the policy-making of the main body in the United Nations. That was not their choice. It was history itself, so to say, which arranged it that way.' Hummarskjöld, quoted in H. P. Van Dusen, *Dag Hammarskjöld* (New York, 1964), pp. 141-2.
[9] Telegram to K. P. S. Menon, 5 November 1956.

between Suez and Hungary. 'I entirely agree with you that armed intervention of any country in another is highly objectionable and that people in every country must be free to choose their own governments without interference of others.' But it was in Suez that he pressed for American action. What had happened in Egypt had revived fears of colonialism and created an atmosphere of ill-will which it might take a long time to remove; but the United States could do much to remove these fears and apply the healing touch to the deep wounds that had been inflicted.

After the cease-fire in Egypt, Nehru, still awaiting fuller information, moved with caution on Hungary but did not feel that he had in any way compromised his general principles. But his position became more awkward when Krishna Menon, acting on his own, abstained from voting on a resolution condemning the Soviet Union for the use of force, justifying his action with some abrasive speeches. Nehru stood by Menon in public, but privately expressed his unhappiness.

> There is much feeling in AICC circles that our attitude in regard to Hungary has not been as clear as it might have been. There is naturally great sympathy for the Hungarian people and resentment at the use of the Russian army in strength to suppress them. It is recognized that the position in Hungary has been different from that in Egypt; but nevertheless it is felt that we have not been quite clear in our declarations. From the legal point of view and because of lack of full information, our statements can be justified. But the fact remains that large bodies of Soviet forces have suppressed a nationalist uprising in Hungary involving terrible killing and misery for the people. Events move fast and it is not possible to have consultations. Generally speaking, it appears better to abstain from voting on resolutions containing some objectionable features and moving amendments, rather than voting against it.[10]

So clearly it was not Menon's abstention but his speeches in the debate that worried Nehru. Any criticism of the Soviet Government by Menon had been not direct but only by implication and immediately balanced by references to the conduct of other powers elsewhere or by vague statements which could be regarded as criticism of anti-Soviet elements in Hungary. Even the representatives of Yugoslavia and Poland had been more vigorous and forthright in their criticisms of the Soviet action than Menon had been. Menon's defence was that he had left no doubt that India desired and expected the withdrawal of foreign troops, and he had supported continuing consideration of the item. But no judgment was possible till the report, which the Secretary-General had been asked to make on the situation in Hungary, had been received. Counter-revolution was active in

[10] Nehru's telegram to Krishna Menon, 11 November 1956.

Hungary and the issue was being used at the United Nations as part of the cold war, to restore Western unity, to rehabilitate Britain and France and to slow down progress with regard to Egypt. There was no deliberation on Hungary but only invective, and silent abstention by India would have been denounced as silent support of the Soviet Government. The Soviet Union had the right by treaty to prevent the return of fascism to Hungary. Apart from legalities, the Yugoslav delegation reported that there was no immediate alternative to the existing government in Hungary, and any abrupt Soviet withdrawal would cause anarchy and retard the liberalizing movements in Poland and Rumania. But Menon claimed that he had not argued a legal or a political case, as he should have if he had been fully free and honest; so it was wrong to insinuate that he had been influenced by any fear of the Soviet Union or desire to accommodate it. However, contrary to the facts and perhaps against his better judgment, he had spoken strongly about violence and India's grave concern at events. 'To do more would be to put ourselves in a sheer opportunist and somewhat dishonest position even though we might, but only might, gain some temporary applause. I feel unable to do this and don't feel you would approve either.'[11]

This long effort at justification did not convince Nehru and, to counter the impression of deliberate bias created by Menon's speeches, he decided that India would help to implement the resolution and serve, if invited, on the investigation and observation groups.[12] But Menon was rescued from his personal predicament by Pakistan, which introduced a resolution calling for a police force and elections supervised by the United Nations. Menon, while abstaining on the rest of the resolution, voted against such elections as contrary to the Charter and a truncation of Hungarian sovereignty. He told his Prime Minister that India should help towards a settlement and, while making clear her anxiety about the situation and her dislike of violence and foreign intervention, should not get drawn into vilification or the power politics of the two blocs.

> What we have done and should continue to do is to refuse to be made an instrument of power politics of either side and as things are here become part of Western propaganda and action to bring about a régime of their choice by using the United Nations.[13]

Menon now had Nehru's full support. The Prime Minister agreed that elections under the auspices of the United Nations were not only contrary to the provisions of the Charter but also likely to come in the way of the very thing desired, which was the withdrawal of Soviet troops.[14] But

---

[11] Krishna Menon's telegram to Nehru, 11 November 1956. A more elaborate justification by Menon of his attitude can be found in M. Brecher, *India and World Politics* (London, 1968), pp. 85-96.

[12] Foreign Secretary's telegram to Krishna Menon, 11 November 1956.

[13] Krishna Menon's telegram to Nehru, 12 November 1956.

[14] Nehru to R. Sorensen M.P., 16 November 1956.

obviously both Nehru and Menon, whatever the general principles enunciated, had in mind the possibility of elections in Hungary supervised by the United Nations serving as a precedent in discussions on Kashmir. 'A government', as Nehru commented, 'may follow a broad line of policy, but usually its policy is the resultant of various pulls and urges. Sometimes one pull is greater than the other.'[15]

That Nehru had not changed his mind on the basic issue was made clear once again in a joint communiqué issued by the Prime Ministers of India, Burma, Ceylon and Indonesia, then meeting in Delhi. They reiterated that Soviet troops should be withdrawn speedily from Hungary and the people of that country left free to decide their future and make whatever democratic changes they desired in their political system.[16] But this could not justify any proposal for elections under the supervision of the United Nations or even the dispatch of observers by the United Nations, and Nehru directed Krishna Menon to abstain on this latter issue. It seemed to him that it was rather in Port Said, where atrocities were alleged to have been committed, that observers were required, and he advised Nasser to propose this.[17] But in the case of Hungary he was willing to do no more than inquire of the Indian Ambassador in Moscow whether he had any information on the reported deportation of Hungarian youth to the Soviet Union.[18]

In fact, Nehru's long-standing soreness at the partisanship and dilatoriness customarily shown by the United Nations was leading him to react more sharply than was justified. Krishna Menon surprisingly adopted a more flexible attitude on this issue and advised the Soviet delegation that it was in the Soviet interest to permit observers to go into Hungary, if only because it would allow them time for things to settle down.[19] Nehru came round to this position, but his mind was again centred on Egypt; and he believed that if the situation there worsened the chances of withdrawal of Soviet troops from Hungary would greatly diminish. So his advice to the Hungarian nationalists was to maintain peace, as any violence would not only bring fresh misery but delay Soviet withdrawal.[20] Such advocacy of timidity was not in character.

But within hours the real Nehru, casting off the shadow of old prejudices, the hesitations of *realpolitik* and the influence of other issues, gave full utterance to his feelings. That the rising was popular and widespread and had the backing of the army and even the communists now seemed to Nehru established beyond doubt, and he stated his viewpoint in

[15] Nehru's note to Siquerios, the Mexican mural artist, 14 November 1956.
[16] 14 November 1956.
[17] Nehru's telegrams to Krishna Menon, 15 November, and to Indian Ambassador in Cairo, 16 November 1956.
[18] Nehru's note to Foreign Secretary, 16 November 1956.
[19] Krishna Menon's telegram to Nehru, 17 November 1956.
[20] Nehru's note to Foreign Secretary, 18 November 1956.

public and without qualification. The major fact stood out that the majority of the people of Hungary wanted a change, political, economic or whatever else, and demonstrated and actually rose in insurrection to achieve it but ultimately they were suppressed. There had then followed an extraordinary demonstration of passive resistance, more significant of the wishes of the Hungarian people than an armed revolt. This uprising had coincided with the Suez invasion and the guilty party in each case was attempting to lay stress on what had happened in the other place so as to hide its own misdemeanour. He himself was confident that the Hungarian people would ultimately triumph and felt that the immediate setback had powerfully affected the prestige of the Soviet Government, not only among the uncommitted countries but more among countries and governments which were on the side of that country, 'including, if I may say so, the people of the Soviet Union itself'.[21] He was now, reported the B.B.C. correspondent, as deeply involved emotionally in the fate of Hungary as he had always been in that of Egypt.

Now this speech was tremendously significant. It was delivered without text or notes, not a calculated speech but one straight from the heart. Never before has Mr Nehru spoken out so positively against Russian imperialism and for the oppressed peoples behind the iron curtain. And it seems, from India's latest resolution before the United Nations, that she means to follow this up. What the Soviet reaction will be to this open defiance is something India awaits with the very keenest interest.[22]

This resolution requesting the Hungarian Government to receive observers marked an emphatic change in Nehru's attitude on the subject and was carried by a large majority against Soviet opposition. Nehru then sent strongly worded messages to Bulganin, Kadar and Tito urging acceptance of the resolution and an invitation at least to Hammarskjöld to visit Hungary. The consequences of rejection could be disastrous and might even lead to war, while to deny Hammarskjöld this courtesy would create serious misgivings in the minds even of those friendly to the Kadar régime, and virtually confirm reports about deportations.[23] The Soviet Government were clearly piqued that India should have gone ahead with this resolution even after being informed of Soviet objections and the Soviet Ambassador called on Nehru to discuss, of all things, Kashmir.[24] This was not then an immediate problem, and that the Soviet Government should raise this matter when the world was on the verge of war over Suez

[21] Speech in the Lok Sabha, 19 November 1956. Lok Sabha Debates 1956, Vol. IX, Part II, Cols. 371-89.

[22] Gerald Priestland, 20 November 1956.

[23] Nehru's telegrams to Bulganin, Kadar and Tito, 22 November 1956.

[24] Nehru's note, 23 November 1956.

and Hungary was obviously an effort at gentle blackmail — a reminder of Soviet support to India on this issue as well as a hint of possible withdrawal of such support. But no such pressure could be expected to make Nehru shift his position. Indeed, he now felt so strongly about Hungary that Krishna Menon thought it necessary to caution him against intervention. 'The best we can do at the moment is to press the visit of the Secretary-General and also hope that our Ambassador will get there quickly. I do not think we shall make any progress by our telling the Soviet Government in public what to do.'[25] There was, replied Nehru, no question of intervention; but he had little doubt that it was the Soviet military commander and not the Kadar Government who ruled Hungary. The only solution was a phased withdrawal of Soviet troops, and as there seemed no way of bringing this about, Nehru approved of Krishna Menon's offer to lapse into silence.

> None of us can control events. All we can do is to try our best and avoid any step which might aggravate the situation. At the same time we do not improve a situation by saying or doing something which we cannot easily justify and we have to adhere to our broad principles. If war comes, it will come in spite of us.[26]

A few days later, the abduction of Nagy in a manner which was a direct affront to the Yugoslav Government greatly annoyed Tito, who had till this time been arguing the Soviet case with Nehru, and he sought Nehru's support in any action he might be forced to take.[27] But both Krushchev and Bulganin again reminded India of Kashmir, and remarked that Hungary was as close to the Soviet Union as Kashmir was to India.[28] Unshaken, Nehru authorized Krishna Menon, 'politely if possible but firmly' to state India's disapproval both of the arrest and deportation of Nagy and of the Hungarian refusal to receive Hammarskjöld. 'We cannot put ourselves in the wrong and do something which is against our own convictions. But we should try to avoid giving needless offence or aggravating a situation that is bad enough.'[29] He directed general support to a resolution on Hungary which was being tabled by the United States, and Menon inquired if this indicated a change in India's policy towards the great powers in view of recent Soviet actions and Nehru's impending visit to Washington.[30] This was presumptuous rhetoric, but Nehru answered patiently. The Soviet

[25] Krishna Menon's telegram to Nehru, 22 November 1956. India was represented only by a chargé d'affaires in Budapest, the Ambassador being resident in Moscow.
[26] Nehru's personal telegrams to Krishna Menon, 23 November 1956.
[27] Tito to Nehru, 28 November 1956.
[28] Telegrams of minister, Indian Embassy, reporting conversation with Khrushchev, 28 November, and of Indian Ambassador reporting an interview with Bulganin, 29 November 1956.
[29] Nehru's telegram to Krishna Menon, 2 December 1956.
[30] Nehru's telegram to Krishna Menon, and Menon's reply, 2 December 1956.

Union should not be condemned for defiance of the United Nations Charter, nor need any withdrawal of Soviet troops be required to be carried out under observation by the United Nations. Any such attempt at humiliation would prove self-defeating. But in her desire to do nothing which might lead to war, India could not defer support for right action so long that she appeared to be opposing it and thus compromising her principles.

> While we do not wish to condemn and make the situation more difficult for us and others, we cannot remain silent when silence itself becomes acquiescence in patent wrong. We have always said that our policy is independent and we judge each situation from the point of view of our general principles. We have to follow that policy . . . I am very much concerned with maintaining the peace of the world, but I am equally concerned with our acting rightly and in conformity with the principles we have proclaimed.[31]

The most that he was prepared to concede was to agree to abstention on the resolution of the United States, but not to non-participation.[32] He also turned down a request from the Kadar Government that he use his influence with the Austrian authorities to secure permission for an official Hungarian delegation to visit refugee camps in Austria in order to give assurances and provide clarifications.[33]

In the years that followed, there was no change in Nehru's expression of censure of developments in Hungary. On 8 January 1957, the United States sought an immediate plenary session and brought forward a resolution to which the Soviet Union objected strongly. Krishna Menon offered to remain silent and sought instructions on voting.

> Even if we make a reasonable speech, unless it at the same time supports them it will irritate the Americans which it is our desire to avoid. It is wholly difficult to maintain any sense of integrity in any statement we can make without causing offence to both sides which latter is not our purpose.

Ignoring the sarcasm, Nehru approved of Menon not speaking and ordered abstention on the vote;[34] and Moscow's reply to this was to abstain later in the month in the Security Council on a resolution on Kashmir

[31] Nehru's personal telegram to Krishna Menon, 9 December 1956.
[32] Krishna Menon's telegram, 9 December, and replies of Foreign Secretary and Nehru, 10 December 1956.
[33] Foreign Secretary's telegram to Nehru in Washington, 17 December, and reply of Secretary-General, N. R. Pillai, 19 December 1956.
[34] Krishna Menon's telegrams to Nehru and to Foreign Secretary, 8 January, and Nehru's reply, 9 January 1957.

which was unacceptable to India.[35] Repeated requests from Kadar that the diplomatic representation between the two countries be raised to embassy level were turned down by Nehru as a mark of disapproval, and he only agreed in December 1959 to the appointment of a resident ambassador in Budapest.

On the revolt in Hungary in 1956, therefore, Nehru's attitude requires no unqualified apology. He was a little late off the mark and was too concerned with Egypt to take in at the start the full measure of the Hungarian crisis. It was also, in the nature of things, difficult to obtain an unprejudiced account of events. But once he had grasped what was happening Nehru spoke out unflinchingly, regardless of veiled pressure from the Soviet Union. He repeatedly proclaimed that, making all allowance for foreign incitement and reactionary activity, what had taken place in Hungary was basically a nationalist uprising which had been brutally suppressed. No government could call itself free so long as a few thousand foreign tanks were stationed in its capital and the neighbourhood; and his policy was shaped in accordance with this evaluation. The restoration of normal conditions would be most easily achieved, it seemed to him, if the Soviet Union were not roundly condemned in formal resolutions, but this should not, need not, and did not involve a compromise on primary principles. He had picked his own path through the crisis and it was, on the whole, an honourable one.

---

[35] The Soviet Government probably believed that the lesson had been learnt, for a few days later they vetoed another resolution on Kashmir.

15

Mid-Term Assessment

By the end of 1956 Nehru was recognized as one of the few living men who made an impression on the world — 'the man who,' in the words of *Harper's Magazine*, 'since the end of the Churchill-Stalin-Roosevelt era, is the most arresting figure on the world political stage.' A writer in the *New York Post* described him as 'one of the most incandescent figures of contemporary history';[1] and the *Chicago Daily Tribune* warned its readers that 'he will lead India as long as he wishes — for better or for worse — and his voice will be heard as long as he lives in world councils — again for better or for worse.'[2] The *New York Times* recognized in him one of the world's most important politicians, and of the unchallenged rulers of the world perhaps the only one who ruled by love and not fear.[3] This acceptance of Nehru was, of course, primarily because of the impact which the central strength and sanity of his foreign policy had achieved. He had, on assuming office, made clear that India would participate actively in the world not merely because of his own international interests and his understanding of the role which India had assumed and could not shirk; foreign policy was also to him a way of safeguarding India's newly won freedom.

> What does independence consist of? It consists fundamentally and basically of foreign relations. That is the test of independence. All else is local autonomy. Once foreign relations go out of your hands into the charge of somebody else, to that extent and in that measure you are not independent.[4]

National security did not imply defence of the borders alone; it also involved resistance to political and economic domination. He saw no

[1] 30 September 1956.
[2] 30 September 1956.
[3] Book review, 7 October 1956.
[4] Speech in the Constituent Assembly, 8 March 1949. J. Nehru, *India's Foreign Policy* (Delhi, 1961), p. 240.

reason why India should take over the traditional quarrels between the established powers or have policies framed for her; and in adopting this attitude he spoke for all the countries of Asia and Africa that were attaining independence. Despite the differences between themselves and the variations in their immediate situations, what they found in common in non-alignment was, beyond its political and economic connotations, an attitude of mind. It was a common way of looking at the world and its problems, the obvious expression of peoples who, after centuries of suppression, could again make their voices heard.

Beyond the concerns of these 'new' continents, Nehru gave articulation to the widespread longing for reason and honest intelligence in world politics. To a considerable extent, he even made reason prevail. By the right mixture of principle and finesse, he helped to secure settlements in Korea and Indochina, enabled Britain and France, almost despite themselves, to redress their mistakes in Suez, and, adopting what was then an unpopular approach, did his best in the circumstances for the people of Hungary. He established India as a beacon in the cold war by never tiring of the assertion that such a confrontation, at its worst brings the world close to destruction and, even in more favourable circumstances, clogs, paralyses and coarsens the future. This brought him squarely into conflict with Dulles, who found Nehru's policy repellent. Both were crusaders, but in these years it was Nehru's efforts which were, fortunately for mankind, more effective. They were not wholly successful. He could not secure an agreement with Pakistan on Kashmir and he could not convince the world that India had adopted a fair policy on this issue. It was a general and oft-repeated criticism that, while India presented a kindly and pacifist face to the world, she showed a much less pleasing one to her neighbours.[5] Even her non-alignment did not always appear to be rigidly equidistant, and the motto 'friendly with all' was thought to have gradually changed to 'friendlier with some'.[6] As relations with the Soviet Union grew firmer, this tendency was believed to have grown, and even before Suez, *The Economist*, generally friendly to India, was outspoken on this point: 'If India seeks to be helpfully neutral, she has to guard against one very neutral tendency, a tendency to nag people with whom she is basically sympathetic more sharply than she nags those whom she does not understand or from whom she expects little understanding.'[7]

This particular criticism was unfair. On issues such as racialism and colonialism, and on the willingness to contemplate a general war, Nehru genuinely felt that the Western Powers were more to blame than the communist states; but such conviction did not disguise his aversion to totalitarian methods and his awareness of the possibilities of the deliberate

[5] See, for example, 'India's Two Faces', editorial in *The Times*, 2 June 1956.
[6] Editorial in the *Manchester Guardian*, 29 April 1953.
[7] 'No room for freedom', article in *The Economist*, 10 March 1956.

spread of communism. But the warm, comfortable feeling of gratuitous virtue that underlay many of his speeches was irritating. It is also true that, though he was clear-eyed about Chinese communist leadership and the innate potential for a clash between India and China, he did not expect it in the immediate future. Certainly he believed that the mountainous terrain of the border areas, China's interest in domestic development and the configuration of world forces ruled out any military conflict. 'So far as the external danger to India is concerned, the only possible danger is from Pakistan. There is no other danger — not even the remotest danger.'[8] As the context of world affairs gradually changed, this was revealed as a grave deficiency of judgment.

As the writer in the *New York Times* recognized, Nehru's advantage was that he spoke to the world from within a framework of assurance — the enthusiastic support of a very large majority of his people. Unlike Gandhi, who was a strong man imparting strength to others, Nehru drew sustenance from popular idolatry. His immense influence over his countrymen fortified his belief both in them and in himself. He could not get close to others, either as individuals or in a crowd; but the people of India became a mystique with him. He had unqualified faith in them and they, in turn, until the end, saw neither any flaw in him nor any major fault in his actions. Their romantic image of him outlived his death.

Such strength of mutual attachment assisted the introduction in India of a democratic system. It would have seemed natural, considering the legacy of viceregal rule as well as his own personal standing, to develop a plebiscitary monarchy. Instead, Nehru preferred to strengthen libertarian traditions. This was to him worthwhile in itself as well as the proper setting for other objectives. The organizer of the civil liberties union was not lost in the Prime Minister. He ensured the precise elaboration in the Constitution of the rights of the individual, and the vesting of the courts with full authority to protect those rights. He was reconciled to keeping in preventive detention those whom he regarded as enemies, not so much of the state as of society, especially those spreading communal animosity; but even in such cases he insisted that detention should be for short periods, and never longer than necessary. Uneasy that India was dominated by one party and that party by one man, he shied away from any action that suggested wanton weakening of opposing elements. He insisted that advertisements be withdrawn from journals and newspapers only for scurrilous writing and not for criticizing, however severely, himself or the government.[9] His ultimate responsibility for the detention of Sheikh Abdullah gnawed persistently at his whole sense of public values. He virtually apologized to the jailed comrade of former days for his helplessness.

[8] Nehru's address to senior police officers, 13 March 1956.
[9] See Nehru's note to principal private secretary, 10 September 1956.

We, who are in charge of heavy responsibilities, have to deal with all kinds of forces at work and often they take their own shape. We see in the world today great statesmen, who imagine they are controlling the destinies of a nation, being pushed hither and thither by forces beyond their control. The most that one can do is to endeavour to function according to one's judgment in the allotted sphere.[10]

While unwilling to interfere with the policy of the state government, he continuously pressed on them to consider the release of Abdullah. 'So far as I am concerned my whole mind rebels against the long detention of any person without trial. I have objected to this so often in the past that naturally I do not like it.' Circumstances sometimes compelled action that was normally undesirable; but the balance of advantage in imprisoning Abdullah appeared to have been passed, and a man could not be kept indefinitely in detention. 'That very detention will become an increasing factor for instability and for reactions against us in India and abroad, apart from the effect on Kashmir itself.'[11]

Nehru gave as much importance to the institutional aspects of the democratic system. At the highest executive level, this was basically a personal problem. He had to curb his inclination to take all the decisions and make out that they were the results of innumerable discussions. He had to disown the eagerness of his colleagues to leave all making of policy to him and insist on the Cabinet seeming to function as a reality. The advice he gave to his Chief Ministers on this subject was faultless.

The main thing is teamwork of those in the Government and the organization; secondly, division of responsibility and at the same time close coordination of all activities; thirdly, the building up of cadres of workers with responsibility; fourthly, creating good reactions in the public about the work of Government and the organization. Above all, there must be the strengthening of your position, not some kind of a rival of others, but as the undisputed head of responsible colleagues who work as a team supporting each other and frankly discussing every important matter.[12]

But he himself found it no easy matter to function as merely the leader of a team and, particularly after the death of Patel, the Cabinet was gradually reduced to a collection of tame subordinates. Ambedkar had not really fitted into what was, once Syama Prasad Mookerjee had resigned, primarily a Congress government and he seized the first opportunity to depart. Then Deshmukh remained as an odd man out till he finally broke

[10] Nehru to Sheikh Abdullah, 8 April 1955.
[11] Nehru to Karan Singh, 11 January 1956.
[12] To Bakshi Ghulam Mahomed, Chief Minister of Kashmir, 15 August 1956.

loose in 1956. But from the end of 1950 the Government of India was basically a one-man show. Even Pant, the Home Minister, although he enjoyed prestige and standing in the Party, was willing to be no more than Nehru's anchor-man and sought to anticipate Nehru's wishes rather than to participate in the making of joint decisions. In the framework of democratic institutions that Nehru strove to install in India, the weakest link was Cabinet government. He insisted that all important matters should at some stage be brought up in Cabinet; there were numerous Cabinet committees and consultation was frequent; the deficiency was in spirit and animation. But at least the procedures of collective policymaking were established, for life to be later instilled in them. This was the work of Nehru, achieved against the drive of his own personality and despite the eager subservience of mouldering mediocrities who claimed to be his colleagues.

This frail machinery of Cabinet government had to be set in the wider context of parliamentary authority. Building on the familiarization with politics brought about by the national movement, Nehru defied conventional wisdom and introduced adult suffrage. Much as he disliked the sordid rivalry implicit in elections to legislative assemblies, Nehru gave life and zest to the campaigns; and, between elections, he nurtured the prestige and vitality of Parliament. He took seriously his duties as leader of the Lok Sabha and of the Congress Party in Parliament, sat regularly through the question hour and all important debates, treated the presiding officers of the two houses with extreme deference, sustained the excitement of debate with a skilful use of irony and repartee, and built up parliamentary activity as an important sector in the public life of the country. The tone of his own speeches in Parliament was very different from that which he adopted while addressing public meetings. There was no suggestion of loose-lipped demagoguery. He still sometimes rambled, but sought to argue rather than teach, to deal with the points raised by critics, to associate the highest legislature in the country with deliberation on policy and to destroy any tendency to reduce it, in Max Weber's phrase, to 'routinized impotence'. By transferring some of his personal command to the institution of Parliament, he helped the parliamentary system take root. This ensured that no one else would be able to dominate Indian politics as he had done. One of his greatest achievements was the preclusion of a successor in any real sense.

Whereas in the West liberal democracy had developed gradually, leading even to the maintenance of the theory that it could endure in its purest form only in a setting of capitalist industrialization, Nehru was making the superhuman, anti-historical effort to impose it on a society whose central fact was backwardness. Today, mainly because of the Indian example, few hold the patronizing view that the poor are only interested in economic issues. But it is true that if democracy in such a society is not to be wholly 'premature', it has to be intertwined with considerable economic and social advance. And this socialism again has to be fundamentally different from that known in the West, a rapid movement towards industrialization rather than the liberation of an industrial proletariat from bureaucratic organization. It was Nehru who initiated the effort of adaptation of established ideologies to a new context, for which they were generally thought to be unfitted. He was not so much a profound as a pioneering thinker. Looking back today at the theoretical formulations of Asian and African independence, with the integrated drive of Mao and the clear-cut ideas of Fanon before us, Nehru's efforts appear weak and fumbling. His attempts to build a coherent body of thought and practice seem halting, incomplete, and perhaps circumscribed by his class background. Gandhi, however lacking in some respects, and though he borrowed much from the West, had the advantage of internalizing all his ideas and activities in the Indian experience, whereas Nehru was always, in a way, the outsider. But he took up the burden of constructing a framework of democratic socialism for an under-developed and underprivileged country and, denying himself the easy because complete answer of Marxism, strove to work out what was necessarily a more untidy and complex programme of action. It was an unprecedented experiment in world history. It has not yet succeeded; but it has also not yet failed, and the question is still very much with us, 'How is it possible to devise a form of government which ensures domestic peace, invites popular participation in conditions of freedom, and also creates conditions for an assault on intolerable poverty?'[13]

By the end of 1956, certainly, the experiment seemed well set to succeed. Internal developments in Kashmir formed the only major and startling exception to the adequate functioning of democracy in all its aspects. Not only was an ideal being realized; parliamentary administration appeared to be the only practical mode of government for a country of India's size, diversity and immensity of problems. Planning for socialism was also pushing ahead. The lack of definition in Nehru's economic thinking, and in the two resolutions on industrial policy, was more than offset by the success of the first Plan and the widening of horizons characteristic of the second Plan, which was being drafted. Ideology may not have been discussed in the Cabinet or in the planning commission;[14] but the socialist objective was not lost to sight. A wise and experienced, if committed, observer wrote that the second Plan papers and estimates possibly constituted one of the most important documents in the world at that time.

Even if one is pessimistic, and allows a 15 per cent chance of failure through interference by the United States (via Pakistan or otherwise), a 10 per cent chance of interference by the Soviet Union and China, a

---

[13] First article in the *New Statesman*, 8 July 1977.
[14] C. D. Deshmukh, *The Course of My Life* (Delhi, 1974), p. 209.

20 per cent chance of interference by civil service traditionalism and political obstruction, and a 5 per cent chance of interference by Hindu traditionalism, that leaves a 50 per cent chance for a success which will alter the whole history of the world for the better.[15]

This fair chance of raising a rational, educated and forward-looking society based on modernization, industrialization and a scientific temper was made possible by a government that accepted the task, planned for it, and informed the people that they had been sentenced to hard labour striving for it. 'We have to work with our hands and march forward on our feet. No stars will come to our help. We have to use our brains and our strength to solve all our problems.'[16] Though India was a labour-intensive society, progress could be accelerated with the help of science and technology, which the British had done little to promote. Even in the years before 1947, when political issues demanded priority, Nehru had not failed to emphasize the indispensability of scientific development and to draw attention to the immense possibilities which the proper use of technology would open up. But at that time he could do little more. As Bernal pointed out even then, perhaps not the dedicated scientists but the political workers, struggling for the freedom that would enable the unrestricted development of the Indian people, were rendering the best service to science in India.[17] Yet within ten days of assuming office as Prime Minister, in the midst of communal orgy, Nehru found time to attend a meeting of the Council of Scientific and Industrial Research. He established the tradition of the Prime Minister presiding over that council and attending the annual sessions of the Indian Science Congress. He periodically multiplied the funds allotted to scientific research by the government and stressed to scientists the contribution they should make to industrial development. The Tata Institute of Fundamental Research, set up in 1944, received official support; the first of the five institutes of technology, based on considerable assistance from various foreign countries, was established in 1951; and a large number of national laboratories, specializing in different fields of scientific endeavour, were strung out across India.

One of the biggest things that we have done since independence is the development of our magnificent national laboratories all over India, which are already showing important results and which are likely to be the very basis of India's progress in the future. If we had done nothing else during the last five years but the development of these laboratories, we would have had some reason to take credit for our achievements.[18]

[15] J. B. S. Haldane to P. C. Mahalanobis, 16 May 1955. Nehru Papers.
[16] Speech from the Red Fort at Delhi, 15 August, *National Herald*, 17 August 1954.
[17] J. D. Bernal, *The Social Function of Science* (London, 1940), p. 204.
[18] Nehru to Mahavir Tyagi, 9 August 1952.

As a further step, Nehru constituted the atomic energy commission, convened a meeting of eminent Indian scientists and gave public support to the proposal of Homi Bhabha, India's leading nuclear physicist, for setting up an atomic reactor in Bombay.[19] The attainment of criticality by this reactor, the first in Asia, in August 1956, was the spectacular climax of nearly ten years of sponsorship by Nehru's government of science and scientists.

At one end of the scale, planning was 'science in action';[20] at the other it was the forward movement of a whole people building their own future. A British journalist described the basic attempt in India as 'Nehruism: India's Revolution without Fear';[21] and, though Nehru disliked the word Nehruism, the article as a whole seemed to him a fair assessment. For it pointed out that a socialist revolution by consent was under way in India and, if it continued to be as successful as it already had been, it would make communism look both old-fashioned and barbarian by comparison. It was a revolution without class wars, heretics or victims, and its weapon was a series of tedious legal acts. But, in fact, it was more than a revolution by mere consent. Nehru was not content to impose legislation. He envisaged a more positive role for the people. He was anxious to explain his policies to the masses and give them a sense of participation in economic and social development as well as in political activity. The meaning of democracy was the chance being given to people to decide for themselves on all basic issues rather than merely the securing of acquiescence in decisions taken by others. Modernization can, of course, be imposed from above. Kemal Ataturk achieved it in this manner in Turkey. Even in our own times, political democracy is not always regarded as a necessary element in the ideals of modernization.[22] But Nehru's attitude was entirely different. To him participation was an integral part of modernization and that which vested it with endurance. Even in technical matters like planning, progress would be more certain, even if less swift, if the people were taken into confidence and there was as little suggestion as possible of imposition.

> In this matter, if I may say so, I am a good judge. Nothing is so helpful as the public knowing that you want their advice and you rely upon them. In fact, of course, the actual help coming, in so far as planning is concerned, will be very limited. But the mere approach makes a good atmosphere.[23]

The community development programme evoked in him a crusader's zeal

---

[19] R. Ramanna, 'Development of Nuclear Energy in India, 1947-73' in B. R. Nanda (ed.), *Science and Technology in India* (New Delhi, 1977), pp. 100-101.

[20] Nehru's speech at the Indian Institute of Public Administration, 6 April 1957.

[21] Taya Zinkin, 'Nehruism: India's Revolution without Fear', *Pacific Affairs*, September 1955.

[22] G. Myrdal, *Asian Drama*, Vol. 1, (New York 1968), p. 65 and fn.

[23] To V. T. Krishnamachari, 4 April 1955.

because it involved the masses directly and gave them considerable initiative and responsibility. By 1956 it covered over a quarter of rural India and was spreading fast. The organization was still well-knit, and Nehru thought the scheme could be extended from the development of amenities like roads, schools and wells to intensive agricultural production.

This programme, therefore, had not crumbled, and Nehru regarded it as the main avenue leading to his vision of India's future — an opinion, particularly as regards the National Extension Service, which was widely shared among expert observers.[24] But this programme, in itself, would not be adequate. If the Indian peasantry were to be rescued from its servitudes, it was necessary immediately to effect extensive land reforms and, as a long-term measure, to take steps to control the growth of population. Nehru was aware of the importance of giving the peasants a sense of ownership of the land and it was his constant goading of the chief ministers which led to the abolition, soon after independence, of the *zamindari* system. But this did not mean the abolition of landlordism and its replacement, as Nehru desired, by rural cooperatives. There being no limits to the extent of land which any individual could own, the rich tenants became more powerful and secured more land, and the middle and lower peasantry obtained no more than some forms of relief. While the ideology of Indian land reform was in the interests of the peasantry as a whole, in practice it served primarily the richer peasants rather than the rural poor.[25] This dispropor-tionate improvement by the higher class of tenants of both their power and their resources also affected electoral politics for the worse. The well-to-do peasantry built up considerable local influence, compelling political parties to seek their support; and this enabled them to determine the choice of candidates and to strengthen all those factors against which Nehru incessantly inveighed — caste, linguistic considerations and narrow pro-vincialism. Nehru's efforts at revolution by participation and consent were being converted by influential sectors of Indian society into a revolution by revisionist methods, thereby reducing it into virtually no revolution at all.

Nehru, moreover, did not wake up quickly enough to the arrest of planning and the decline in economic growth which the rapid increase in population was causing. While a family planning programme was initiated in 1950, there was little seriousness or enthusiasm in implementing it. Nehru failed to give priority to this programme because he felt that increase in food production and exploitation of natural resources would be more than adequate to meet the pressure of growing numbers. Indeed, in the early years he went as far as to contend that India was under-populated because large tracts of the country were unpopulated.[26] He later fell back

[24] John Strachey, 'The Indian Alternative', *Encounter*, October 1956.

[25] P. C. Joshi, 'Land Reform and Agrarian Change in India and Pakistan since 1947', *Journal of Peasant Studies*, January and April 1974.

[26] Speech at Ootacamund, 1 June, *Hindustan Times*, 2 June 1948.

from this extreme position and acknowledged that family planning was no longer a fad of some individuals but had become one of the important issues before the country.[27] Even so, there was as yet no feeling of urgency about the need to curb the rise in population. He considered the rate of increase to be by no means abnormal, and in fact less than in most countries of Europe; and he was willing to rely on long-term forces, such as the spread of education, the development of a health service and industrial progress, to mitigate the problem.[28]

Although Nehru preferred to exercise his pre-eminent personal authority through democratic machinery, the fact that his was the primary impetus in both the Party and the administration lends significance to his style of functioning. The differences between him and Patel derived from an impersonal conflict between two different systems of thinking and feeling; and what enabled an avoidance of open rupture was mutual regard and Patel's stoic decency. But even with Patel Nehru played the game of politics with professional skill; and after Patel's death, beneath the veil of idealist language which he cast over the disagreeable features of party struggle, one can discern formidable talents at work, far superior to those of obvious manipulators like Kidwai. He had no base in faction, nor did he need it, for he knew that his standing with the people made him indispensable to the Party; and when necessary he was willing to draw on this asset. On the only occasion in these years when he felt that his position was seriously challenged and he had to play to win — to defeat the challenge of Tandon — he showed acute tactical insight, an ability to let matters slide until the most advantageous moment of confrontation, and a sureness of touch in facing the Party with the fact that this time he was not prepared to compromise. Nehru was a subtle aesthete of power. But his methods of confirming his dominance of the Party were not equally well suited to control of the administration of a country like India. Every branch of policy was supervised and often determined by him, and he inspired a great flow of action. These were the years when the Prime Minister was working at full stretch, putting in a twenty-hour day with hardly even breakfast as a private meal. A probing interest in every aspect of the central administration was combined with full acceptance of his obligations in Parliament and general surveillance of developments in the country as a whole. Nothing that was happening in India was of indifference to him. He would have agreed with Sir Harold Wilson's definition of the job: 'A prime minister governs by curiosity and range of interest.'[29] He gave orders for a sunshade to be provided for the policeman on traffic duty at Great Place in New Delhi, chided the Chief Minister of Bombay for the arrest of a man and wife found kissing in

---

[27] Nehru's report to AICC, 6 July 1951. AICC Papers, File G-49/1951, N.M.M.L.
[28] To Julian Huxley, 14 January 1955.
[29] *Observer* magazine, 24 October 1965.

public, and was concerned that parts of the film of *Hamlet* had been censored. He took time off from Indian and world problems to send to the planning commission details of the standards of physical fitness to be expected of young men and women.[30] During the weeks when his whole Kashmir policy was crumbling, he had the time and interest to suggest to the Health Minister that an official investigation be undertaken into the case of a girl in south India who claimed to live on air.[31]

However, along with such limitless attention to even trivial matters, there was a deficiency in some major aspects of administration. His recognition of the value of pluralist trends led to a slackness of central supervision and guidance and even, as in the case of the reorganization of States, to a measure of drift. He allowed the provincial Congress parties, which were in office in all the States, to choose their own leaders and was content to do no more than advise those Chief Ministers on how they should function. The result was that men like Bidhan Roy of Bengal and R. S. Shukla of Madhya Pradesh functioned as they pleased. Roy's partiality for the private sector and prejudice against left-wing parties led to actions discordant with Nehru's general line, while Shukla was aggressively anti-Christian. Even on prohibition, which Nehru did not favour, his respect for provincial autonomy meant that he would go no further than warn those governments which introduced prohibition of the financial disadvantages of their policy. The reluctance to utilize his firmly established leadership of the Congress Party to check and guide his old political colleagues led to an unnecessary loosening of his authority and slackening of relations between the central government and the States.

Similar personal commitments weakened Nehru's authority in Delhi as well. In 1956, when Krishna Menon was in one of his moods of sepulchral despair, Nehru finally overcame Azad's resistance by citing the report of the parliamentary public accounts committee that Menon had been guilty of only bad judgment and carelessness. But it was not certain that the appointment of Menon as Minister without Portfolio, however much Nehru might have desired it, would strengthen his hand. An effective High Commissioner in London because of his dedication to both Britain and India, and a resourceful negotiator at the United Nations, Menon's abilities were ill-suited in the Indian setting. Histrionic and self-regarding, ostentatiously standing apart, while he operated with clandestine deviousness, he was not fitted to the administrative position which Nehru clearly had in mind for him. But the full impact of Menon's presence in Delhi was still to come. At this time, the more dangerous influence tarnishing Nehru's image was that of his special assistant, M. O. Mathai. A stenographer with no education, he had joined Nehru's staff in February 1946, when Nehru had not yet assumed office. As Prime Minister, Nehru,

[30] 28 July 1952, P.M. Secretariat File 40(81)/49-PMS.
[31] Nehru to Amrit Kaur, 13 July 1953.

although he functioned as overlord of the whole administration, managed with a small personal secretariat — a private secretary who was a civil servant of middle rank, the special assistant and six to eight typists. As a measure of economy this was advisable, and set an example to his colleagues and Chief Ministers, who regarded large offices as symbols of high personal standing. From the point of view of work too, a small office was no drawback. Nehru worked long hours and was very much his own draftsman. Receiving, throughout the years of his prime ministership, about 2,000 letters every day — not all concerning official matters — Nehru spent four to five hours every night dictating replies. All he needed was a flotilla of typists who worked round the clock. Nehru's paperwork was never in arrears. Even the most inconsequential letter was answered within twenty-four hours.

So the private secretary, whoever he was — and many officials held that post during Nehru's term — had little work to do. In fact, Mathai, who soon usurped the position of head of the secretariat, saw to it that men of no great competence, men who were willing to let things be, were appointed to the post. But Mathai's own position very rapidly became of nodal significance, because all important papers had to pass through the Prime Minister's secretariat, and Mathai could decide which papers Nehru saw and on which papers he could himself decide or give an opinion in the Prime Minister's name, without the latter's knowledge. He also attached advisory notes to papers going up to the Prime Minister, sent memoranda to Nehru giving his own views on various subjects and even fed his master with ill-founded gossip which frequently prejudiced Nehru against those whom Mathai disliked.

Prime ministers, by the very nature of their office, are lonely figures. They are obliged to maintain a certain distance from their colleagues, are on guard against the many who may seek to profit from their acquaintance and are cut off from ordinary society. For seventeen years Nehru did not step into a bookshop in India, hail a taxi or catch a bus. In his case, there was even further isolation, caused by personality and circumstances. He sustained close personal relationships with his sister, Vijayalakshmi, and his daughter, but did not, in these years, consult them seriously in public affairs. The long association with Kidwai, broken only by his death in 1954, gave Nehru unsteady assistance rather than solid support. Kidwai's devotion to Nehru was unquestioning and beyond question; but in consequence he rarely gave advice, being content to follow his hero. His ways of functioning too were solitary and conspiratorial. Nehru accepted this and only complained on the rare occasions when Kidwai's actions embarrassed him. For Nehru had been confirmed in his loneliness. The disorientation he had experienced after Gandhi's death had been surmounted by the achievement of a new inner balance; but he became all the more dependent on his own resources. In the 1950s, with Patel gone, he did not have a full exchange of ideas with anyone — not even Krishna Menon, Mountbatten or Radhakrishnan. He was a man firmly enclosed within himself.

This was Mathai's opportunity. He was not Nehru's confidant; but Nehru, placing faith in his devotion, integrity and ability, relied on him for information, for saving him from minor routine, for sheltering him from importunate friends and for warning him against intriguing colleagues. Mathai, not the faithful retainer as Nehru thought but disloyal, avaricious and opportunistic, exploited the access to the Prime Minister, which he was quickly known to have, to build up an independent position of his own. In the flunkey atmosphere of the capital, senior ministers were not above seeking his good offices, officials called on him and carried out his behests and a small coterie grew up around him exercising considerable authority. Unknown to Nehru, Mathai's irregular activities were generally accepted and his influence either sought or feared. Indira Gandhi encouraged him beyond normal limits, Vijayalakshmi addressed him as Deputy Prime Minister, Rajagopalachari told Mathai that he looked on him as a son, Padmaja Naidu regularly sent him affectionate birthday greetings and even the Mountbattens, who should have known better, fussed over him. Thus an illiterate upstart had succeeded in making Nehru the victim of his own isolation and had revived in Delhi the atmosphere of a decadent court.

Perhaps this failure to keep the vital central machine of control completely in his own hands was made easier by the fact that Nehru was not merely a political leader. In these early years of independence, he was the presiding genius in all aspects of Indian public life; and if he delegated administrative authority without knowing it, one major cause may be found in the varied demands on his attention. He occupied a larger area of the national consciousness than the mere office of prime minister warranted. To a large number of Indians he was the measure of all things. He never shed his earlier role as a hero of youth and the guide of intellectuals; and, especially after Gandhi's death, he became also the father-confessor to whom many came with their personal problems. Nehru did not encourage this. 'I do not function as a *guru* for anyone and my life is such that I cannot give personal guidance to anyone in the manner you suggest.'[32] But he was not successful in rejecting this new dimension of his popular appeal, and when pressed to help in solving a marriage problem or restoring harmony in a family he was too kind-hearted to decline advice. When he set out, as he did almost every month, to visit some part of India to gain first-hand information and keep in tune with the people, the crowds gathered not merely to hear him and be educated but to see him and be blessed. A Brahmin who was Gandhi's chosen heir, with a long record of

[32] Nehru to P. C. Agrawal, 26 May 1954.

national service and now Prime Minister — all helped to make him a thaumaturgic personality.

Though Nehru disliked being dragged into personal problems, acting as arbiter in matters outside normal administration came to him naturally. He had not a total commitment to politics and was never swallowed up, even as Prime Minister, in the outer events of his life. He retained to the end his wide range of sympathy and interest, his sensibility and dislike of vulgarity in all its forms. The year 1947 had witnessed a political act, a transfer of governmental authority; it was now the task of his generation to bring about the more fundamental transformations of the structure of Indian society. For this, mere economic development, however essential, was not sufficient. There was need too for modernization of society if India were to be a civilized nation and Indians integrated persons. Towards the end of his life, asked what he regarded as the greatest real advance achieved under his leadership, he had no hesitation in referring to the enactment of measures for the improvement of the condition of Hindu women.[33] Nothing could be done for Muslim women because that might alarm the Muslim community. Even as regards Hindu women, faced with the inertia of orthodoxy, he could not secure the acceptance of the Hindu Code as a whole. But traditional authority was slowly but sufficiently undermined to enforce monogamy on Hindu men and obtain for Hindu women the rights of divorce and inheritance to ancestral property.[34] He had not tired of asserting, even during the years of British rule in India, that the test of a country's progress was the status of its women;[35] and after 1947, when he had the opportunity, he led the assault on the barriers of ages and cleared the way for the majority of Indian women to have full social as well as political equality. Perhaps, as Ambedkar bitterly complained when he resigned the law ministership in 1951, Nehru could have moved faster rather than proceeding gradually, introducing piecemeal measures. But the opposition was not to be lightly dismissed; and the results, however belatedly achieved, were firm.

In that sense, the passage of this legislation marks an epoch in India. It indicates that we have not only striven for and achieved a political revolution, not only are we striving hard for an economic revolution, but that we are equally intent on social revolution. Only by way of advance on these three separate lines and their integration into one great whole, will the people of India progress.[36]

[33] Aubrey Menen's account of his interview with Nehru in Roloff Beny, *India* (London, 1969), p. 189.

[34] Lotika Sarkar, 'Jawaharlal Nehru and the Hindu Code Bill' in B. R. Nanda (ed.), *Indian Women from Purdah to Modernity* (Delhi, 1976), pp. 87-98.

[35] E.g., speech at Mahila Vidyapith, Allahabad, 31 March 1928. *Selected Works of Jawaharlal Nehru*, Vol. 3 (Delhi, 1972), p. 361.

[36] Nehru to Chief Ministers, 10 May 1956.

5/5/55

PRIME MINISTER'S HOUSE
NEW DELHI

Long waiting

historic occasion. moved –

Minor faults. may be corrected later – Better

further delay –

Criticism = sacrament – religious ceremony.

Samskāra –

Manu – Yajnavalkya   mighty men & shapers of India's destiny

Hindu Law variety in India.

Kinsey report –   Damaging Stress –

Ashoka Edict.   mote & beam –

Women of India   beauty, grace & charm –

intelligent – shy & modest.

gay & sorrowful –

infinite variety =

South – East West North

beauty unmistakable stamp of India

Indian women abroad – Refinement spirit of

India more than men –

Sītā – Sāvitrī

Kumarasambhava – P. [illegible]

Notes for a speech in Parliament on the rights of Hindu women, 5 May 1955

This was not all. Beyond these three avenues of prosaic endeavour lay the need to give India again a living culture. Himself responsive to all manifestations of art and beauty and moving with the ease of birthright in the world of style and elegance, Nehru was keen to share with others his pleasure in the grace of living. 'A man of culture does not speak of culture but acts culture and, in fact, lives culture.'[37] He demanded a toning up of the environment such as could give play to sensibility in normal day-to-day activities even of those who were not rich. Seeing no reason why all Indians should not, like him, possess energy, gaiety and imaginative curiosity, he sought to enlarge their values till they matched his own vision and conceptions. He urged the introduction of fresh vitality into the creative arts. Much of what went for culture in India was merely, to use the phrase of H. G. Wells, 'the ownership of stale piddle'.[38] It was this which Nehru wanted to replace. He planned the establishment in Delhi of a national theatre (a project still in the blueprint stage), and brought folk dancers from all parts of India to the capital every year on Republic Day. He directed the unimaginative Works and Housing Ministry to encourage the painting of modern murals on the walls of official buildings which would break the decorative tradition with new motifs and forceful themes. 'Murals have not been developed adequately in India yet. They are a popular form of art. Our art in the past was very fine, but it is of the past. Our paintings are definitely small and precise and not popular in that sense.'[39]

This portrait of a personality of many colours is incomplete without a reference to the whole man who held together such a variety of talents, sympathies and attitudes. Nehru was not an easy person to know. He was adored by the crowds but held in awe by individuals. It was not only high office and the carefully calculated reserve but an inner core of aloofness which kept his personal sanctuary inviolate. His company manners were normally bad. On most social occasions he would be sunk within himself, with a seemingly sadistic indifference to his guests or neighbours. Polite table chatter demanded an effort of which he was not normally capable. But when in the mood, he could be an entrancing companion with a lively sense of fun, neither coarsened by politics nor mesmerized by the circumstance of power. There was mobility in his mind and he could create any atmosphere he wanted. A natural spontaneity made him particularly good with children, and the country virtually drifted to celebrating his birthday as Children's Day. He was not a compulsive worrier and had the gift of throwing off care. During the turmoil in the first months of independence, there was anger and misery on his face as he toured the riot-afflicted areas and gazed on long trains of refugees; but he could also, in the

[37] Speech at Calcutta, 24 March, *National Herald*, 25 March 1952.
[38] H. G. Wells to Bernard Shaw, 22 April 1941. See N. and J. Mackenzie, *The Time Traveller* (London, 1973), p. 431.
[39] To Swaran Singh, Minister for Works, Housing and Supply, 11 June 1956.

course of the same tours, take his mind off the suffering by reading the translation of an old Sanskrit play.[40]

Nehru enjoyed the almost endless scope, diversity and responsibility of his work. 'It's such an exciting job to lead the Indian people today!'[41] Hearing that the ministers in Kashmir were finding the task of governing too heavy, he wrote back, 'I just wondered how you would feel if you had to shoulder about twenty different burdens, each as important as the Kashmir issue. However, I survive and refuse to get distressed.'[42] What helped him to maintain his equanimity was a firm sense of detachment, born of temperament and character as well as of his general attitude to life. For all his boundless energy and high spirits, he was one of nature's anchorites, an onlooker by disposition and a participant only by necessity. He was aware of his ultimate responsibility as Prime Minister for all that happened in India and accepted this burden with faith and dedication. 'But under this tricolour I have pledged to serve India with my last breath and the same pledge I gave to Mahatmaji.'[43] But he could always stand a little apart from the immediate problems in hand and set them in perspective. The fortnightly letters to Chief Ministers, in which he knit together his thoughts and comments on urgent issues as well as long-term purposes, were discursive monologues of an ardent and yet philosophic mind. Nehru was not capable of deep or original thought, and he knew it. He once disarmingly said to Deshmukh in the early days when their relations were harmonious, 'I wish, C. D., that I was cleverer.'[44] His was, in fact, a commonplace mind, nourished by idealism and passion and strengthened by reflection. The result was ceaseless, even if sometimes shapeless, thought, striving to carry forward an innovative, many-sided crusade which was rooted in liberal principle and specifically suited to India. He had no doubt that this was the right approach, the effort was going well, and he had enough of both courage and stamina to give the lead in this long haul.

Nehru was not a religious person, as the word is generally understood. He had no spiritual beliefs or consolations and was always a mild agnostic. He prided himself on his pagan outlook on life and approved of the ancient practice of an altar to the unknown god. But the training under Gandhi, the attraction which the teachings of the Buddha had for him, and the influence of the *Gita* all blended to strengthen the attitudes of his mind and personality — uninvolved in the immediate end but wholly committed to the larger purpose. 'It is true that there is no end to problems, but

[40] See articles by A. Moore and H. V. R. Iengar in R. Zakaria (ed.), *A Study of Nehru* (Bombay, 1959).

[41] Nehru to John Strachey in 1956, cited in J. Strachey, 'Interview with Nehru', *New Statesman*, 23 June 1956.

[42] To Bakshi Ghulam Mahomed, 23 February 1953.

[43] Speech at Kurukshetra refugee camp, 9 April, *National Herald*, 10 April 1948.

[44] C. D. Deshmukh to the author, 9 April 1969.

ultimately perhaps one learns the lesson that one must do the day's work with as much strength as one possesses, and not worry too much about consequences.'[45] And beneath such unruffled endeavour was the strong foundation of confidence in India and in her people.

> I try to do my best in the circumstances and am worried sometimes about the solution of some problem. But in the final analysis I am not worried about the future of India, about the things that I care for. Having done my best I have a good sound sleep and I get up refreshed in the morning whatever may happen. And if I speak to the great people of the earth, leaders of other nations, who probably are much cleverer than I am, may be more experienced than I am, I am not bowled over by their greatness or by their cleverness. Because my mind is fairly clear and frank and I say what I have to say and I want to be friends with them, but anyhow I am not afraid of what they might do or say.[46]

By the end of 1956, Nehru's long-term objectives did not appear beyond attainment. Unbroken growth at home was linked with increasing prestige abroad. After watching the military and civil parade at Delhi on Republic Day in 1955, the Prime Minister glowed with satisfaction. 'My heart was filled with pride and joy at the sight of our nation on the march, realizing its goals one by one. There was a sense of fulfilment in the air and of confidence in our future destiny.'[47] Individual freedom, social justice, popular participation, planned development, national self-reliance, a posture of self-respect in international affairs — all high and noble goals, yet all being steadily achieved under the guidance of the Prime Minister, himself brimming with confidence. 'There is the breath of the dawn, the feeling of the beginning of a new era in the long and chequered history of India. I feel so and in this matter at least I think I represent innumerable others in our country.'[48] When power came to him in 1947, he knew that he had great needs to meet and great hopes to fulfil; and he had not been found wanting. He had set himself against political and communal reaction and social conservatism; he had set out to add to political independence economic sovereignty and the rudiments of socialism — land to the people, adult literacy, equality, employment, better health facilities. He was the national appeaser, enclosing various conflicting elements in a broad pattern of agreement. Once the communist attempt at revolt had been beaten back, this was a period of undemanding politics, when the general habit of

---

[45] To Sir Archibald Nye, 26 January 1952.
[46] Address to Congress Parliamentary Party, 29 May 1956. Tape M-17/C. N.M.M.L.
[47] Nehru to Chief Ministers, 26 January 1955.
[48] Nehru to Chief Ministers, 5 June 1955.

success permitted the occasional, reparable mistake. The handling of the demand for linguistic provinces had left behind an atmosphere of stale hysteria; but this by itself did not endanger the general effectiveness and recognition of Nehru's command. The axis of his leadership still held. The year 1956 was the summer solstice of the prime ministership.

Biographical Notes

Abdullah, Sheikh Mahomed (b. 1905). Organized the National Conference in Kashmir State in 1938; president of the All-India States Peoples Conference 1946; Prime Minister of Kashmir from 1948 to 1953, when he was dismissed and arrested; thereafter served long terms in prison; assumed office again as Chief Minister of Kashmir in 1975.

Acheson, Dean (1893-1971). American lawyer and politician; Secretary of State 1949-53.

Ali, Mahomed (1909-1963). Member of Muslim League in Bengal 1937-47; ambassador of Pakistan in various countries 1948-53; Prime Minister of Pakistan 1953-55.

Ambedkar, B. R. (1891-1956). Harijan leader; member of the Viceroy's council 1942-6; Law Minister 1947-51 and one of the principal draftsmen of the Indian Constitution.

Amrit Kaur (1889-1964). A Christian disciple of Mahatma Gandhi; Minister for Health 1947-57.

Attlee, C. R., first earl (1883-1967). Labour M.P. 1922-55; member of the Indian Statutory (Simon) Commission 1927-30; Deputy Prime Minister 1942-5; Prime Minister 1945-51.

Auchinleck, Sir C. (b. 1884). Field-Marshal; joined Indian army 1903; Commander-in-Chief India 1941 and 1943-7; Commander-in-Chief Middle East 1941-2; Supreme Commander in India and Pakistan 1947.

Bajpai, Sir G. S. (1891-1954). Entered Indian Civil Service 1914; member of Viceroy's council 1940-41; agent-general for India in Washington 1941-7; Secretary-General in Ministry of External Affairs 1947-52; Governor of Bombay from 1952 till his death.

Bakshi, Ghulam Mahomed (1907-72). Leading member of National Conference in Kashmir; Deputy Prime Minister 1947-53 and Prime Minister of Kashmir 1953-63.

Baldev Singh (1902-61). Sikh leader; Minister in the Punjab 1942-6; member of the Interim Government 1946-7; Minister for Defence 1947-52.

Bevin, Ernest (1881-1951). General Secretary of Transport and General Workers Union in Britain 1921-40; Minister of Labour 1940-45; Foreign Secretary 1945-51.

Bhabha, Homi (1909-66). Fellow of the Royal Society; Chairman of the Indian Atomic Energy Commission; Chairman of the international conference for peaceful uses of atomic energy 1955.

Bulganin, N. A. (1889-1975). Chairman of Moscow Soviet 1931-7; given rank of marshal 1947; Deputy Chairman of Council of Ministers 1949-55; Prime Minister of the Soviet Union 1955-8.

Casey, R. G., Baron (1890-1976). Governor of Bengal 1944-6; Foreign Minister of Australia 1951-60; Governor-General of Australia 1965-9.

Chou En-lai (1898-1976). Founded Chinese communist youth group in Paris 1922; chief negotiator for communists 1946; Prime Minister of People's China from 1949 till his death.

Churchill, Sir Winston (1874-1965). Served in army in India 1895; Chancellor of the Exchequer 1924-9; Prime Minister 1940-45 and 1951-5.

Cripps, Sir S. (1889-1952). Visited India after the outbreak of war 1939; member of War Cabinet and deputed by it to India 1942; President of the Board of Trade 1945-7; member of Cabinet Mission to India 1946; Chancellor of the Exchequer 1947-50.

Daulatram, J. (b. 1892). Congressman of Sind; member of Working Committee 1928-41; Governor of Bihar 1947; Minister for Food and Agriculture 1948-50; Governor of Assam 1950-56.

Deo, Shankarrao (1894-1974). Congressman of Maharashtra; member of Working Committee 1938-50.

Desai, Morarji (b. 1896). Resigned from Bombay provincial service and joined civil disobedience movement 1930; minister in Bombay Government 1937-9 and 1946-52; Chief Minister of Bombay 1952-6; Minister of Commerce 1956-8 and of Finance 1958-63; Deputy Prime Minister 1967-9 and Prime Minister from 1977.

Deshmukh, C. D. (b. 1896). Joined Indian Civil Service 1918; Governor of Reserve Bank 1943-9; Minister of Finance 1950-56.

Dixon, Sir O. (1886-1972). Judge of High Court of Australia 1929-52 and

Chief Justice 1952-64; United Nations mediator in Kashmir dispute 1950.

Dulles, J. F. (1888-1959). American lawyer; consultant to Secretary of State 1950; Special Representative 1950-51; Secretary of State 1953-9.

Dutt, S. (b. 1905). Joined Indian Civil Service 1928; Ambassador in West Germany 1952-4; Foreign Secretary in Ministry of External Affairs 1954-61.

Eden, Sir A., 1st earl of Avon (1897-1977). Foreign Secretary 1935-8, 1940-45 and 1951-5; Prime Minister 1955-7.

Eisenhower, D. D. (1890-1969). Supreme Allied Commander in Europe 1943-5; President of Columbia University when Nehru received a degree 1949; President of the United States 1953-61.

Elwin, V. (1902-64). Missionary who worked for many years among the tribes in central and north-eastern India; adviser to the Governor of Assam on tribal affairs from 1954.

Fraser, Peter (1884-1950). Joined Labour Party in New Zealand 1912; Minister for Health 1935-9 and Prime Minister 1939-49.

Gandhi, Mahatma (M.K.) (1869-1948). A barrister of Gujarat who trained Indians in South Africa to resist injustice by non-violent passive resistance; on return to India in 1915 adopted same methods to resist British rule; assassinated by a Hindu fanatic.

Ghulam Mahomed (1893-1956). In official service from 1923 to 1947; Finance Minister of Pakistan 1947-51; Governor-General of Pakistan 1951-55.

Gopalan, A. K. (1904-1977). Member of Congress from 1927 to 1939, when he joined the Communist Party; member of Lok Sabha 1952-77; member of politbureau of C.P.I. (Marxist) from 1964 till his death.

Gopalaswami Ayyangar, N. (1882-1953). Served in Madras provincial service; Dewan (prime minister) of Kashmir 1937-43; Minister without Portfolio 1947-50, for States 1950-52 and of Defence 1952-3.

Gordon Walker, P. C., Baron (b. 1907). Labour member of Parliament 1945-64 and 1966-74; Parliamentary under-secretary for Commonwealth Relations 1947-50; Secretary of State for Commonwealth Relations 1950-51; Foreign Secretary 1964-5.

Graham, Frank (1886-1972). Professor of history at North Carolina University; United Nations mediator in Kashmir dispute 1951.

Hammarskjöld, D. (1905-61). Swedish official and economist; Secretary-General of the United Nations 1953-61; killed in an air accident in central Africa.

Henderson, L. (b. 1892). Member of United States foreign service; Ambassador to India 1948-51; member of United States delegation to London conference on Suez 1956.

Home, 14th earl (b. 1903). Disclaimed peerage 1963, created life peer 1974; Secretary of State for Commonwealth Relations 1955-60; Foreign Secretary 1960-63; Prime Minister 1963-4; Foreign Secretary 1970-74.

Ismay, 1st baron (1887-1965). Commissioned in British Army 1905; Military Secretary to Viceroy 1931-3; Chief of Staff to Winston Churchill 1940-45; Chief of Staff to Lord Mountbatten in India March-November 1947; Secretary of State for Commonwealth Relations 1951-2; Secretary-General of NATO 1952-7.

Jain, A. P. (1902-1977). Congressman from Saharanpur in U.P.; Union Minister for Rehabilitation 1950-54, and for Food and Agriculture 1954-9; associate of R. A. Kidwai.

Jayaprakash Narayan (b. 1902). One of the founders of the Congress Socialist Party 1934; member of Working Committee of Congress 1936; after 1947 was for some time a leading member of the Socialist Party; in detention 1975.

Jinnah, M. A. (1876-1948). A barrister of Bombay and President of the Muslim League 1916, 1920 and from 1934 till his death; a nationalist who later campaigned for the creation of Pakistan, of which he was Governor-General 1947-8.

Joshi, P. C. (b. 1907). General Secretary of the Communist Party of India 1935-48.

Jowitt, 1st earl (1885-1957). Labour M.P. 1929-31 and 1939-45; Attorney-General 1929-32; Lord Chancellor 1945-51.

Kadar, J. (b. 1912). Member of Communist Party of Hungary from 1931; in prison 1951-4; formed government after suppression of national uprising in 1956.

Kamaraj, K. (1903-75). Congressman from Madras; President Tamil Nad Congress Committee 1940-54; Chief Minister of Madras 1954-63; President of Indian National Congress 1963-7.

Karan Singh, (b. 1931). Son of Maharaja Hari Singh of Kashmir; acted as ruler of Kashmir 1949-52 and served as elected head of state 1952-65;

Governor of Kashmir 1965-7; Union Minister for Civil Aviation 1967-73 and for Health 1973-77.

Kashmir, Maharaja Hari Singh of (1895-1961). Succeeded as Maharaja 1925; withdrew in favour of son 1949.

Katju, K. N. (1887-1968). Lawyer and Congressman of Allahabad; Minister in U.P. 1937-39 and 1946-7; Governor of Orissa 1947-8 and of West Bengal 1948-51; Union Minister for Law 1951-2, for Home Affairs 1952-5 and for Defence 1955-7.

Khan, Liaqat Ali (1895-1951). General Secretary of the Muslim League from 1936; member of Interim Government 1946-7; Prime Minister of Pakistan from 1947 till his assassination in 1951.

Khan Sahib (1882-1958). Elder brother of Ghaffar Khan and personal friend of Nehru; Chief Minister of Congress ministries in North-West Frontier Province 1937-9 and 1945-7; in prison in Pakistan 1947-53; Chief Minister of West Pakistan 1955-7; assassinated in 1958.

Kher, B. G. (1888-1957). Solicitor and Congressman of Bombay; Chief Minister of Bombay 1937-9 and 1946-52; Indian High Commissioner in London 1952-4; Chairman, Official Language Commission 1955-6.

Khrushchev, N. S. (1894-1971). Elected to Central Committee of Communist Party of Soviet Union 1934; member of the Presidium 1949; First Secretary of Central Committee 1953-64 and Chairman of Council of Ministers of Soviet Union 1958-64.

Kidwai, R. A. (1894-1954). A Congressman of the U.P. and a close associate of Nehru; Minister in the U.P. 1937-9 and 1946-7; Minister in the central government (with short intervals) from 1947 till his death.

Koirala, B. P. (b. 1914). Educated in India; Prime Minister of Nepal 1959-60; thereafter served long terms in prison and spent many years in exile.

Kripalani, J. B. (b. 1888). General Secretary of the Congress 1934-46 and President in 1946; later resigned from the Congress.

Krishnamachari, T. T. (1899-1974). Businessman of Madras; joined Congress in 1942; Union Minister for Commerce and Industry 1952-6, for Finance 1956-8, without Portfolio 1962, for Economic and Defence Coordination 1962-3 and for Finance 1963-5.

Krishnamachari, V. T. (1881-1964). Entered Madras civil service 1908; Dewan (prime minister) of Baroda 1927-44 and of Jaipur 1946-9; deputy chairman of planning commission 1953-60.

Lloyd, Selwyn, created baron Selwyn-Lloyd (1904-78). Conservative M.P. 1945-70; Foreign Secretary 1955-60, Chancellor of the Exchequer

1960-62 and Lord Privy Seal 1963-4; Speaker of the House of Commons 1971-6.

MacDonald, M. (b. 1901). Son of Ramsay MacDonald; Secretary of State for Dominions 1935-8 and for Colonies 1938-40; British Commissioner-General in South East Asia 1948-55; High Commissioner in India 1955-60.

Macmillan, H. (b. 1894). Conservative M.P. 1924-9 and 1931-45; minister at Allied Headquarters in North-West Africa 1942-5; Minister for Housing 1951-4, for Defence 1954-5 and for Foreign Affairs 1955; Chancellor of the Exchequer 1955-7; Prime Minister 1957-63.

Malan, D. F. (1874-1959). Prime Minister of South Africa 1948-54.

Matthai, J. (1886-1959). Professor of economics at Madras 1920-25; chairman of tariff board 1931-4; joined the firm of Tata's 1940; Union Minister for Railways 1947-8 and for Finance 1948-50.

Mehta, G. L. (1900-74). Businessman at Calcutta 1928-47; chairman of tariff board 1947-50; member of planning commission 1950-52; Ambassador to the United States 1952-8.

Menon, V. K. Krishna (1896-1974). Secretary of India League in London 1929-47; Indian High Commissioner in London 1947-52; member of Indian delegation to United Nations from 1952; Minister without Portfolio 1956-7; Minister for Defence 1957-62.

Menon, K. P. S. (b. 1898). Joined Indian Civil Service 1921; later seconded to Indian Political Service; Ambassador to China 1947; Foreign Secretary in Ministry of External Affairs 1948-52; Ambassador to the Soviet Union 1952-61.

Menon, V. P. (1894-1966). Reforms Commissioner in Government of India 1942-7; secretary in States Ministry 1947-8 and 1949-51; Acting Governor of Orissa 1951.

Mikoyan, A. I. (1895-1978). Member of Central Committee of Communist Party of Soviet Union from 1923 and of Politbureau from 1935; Minister for Trade 1953-5; first deputy chairman of council of ministers 1955-64; President of the Presidium of Supreme Soviet 1964-5.

Mirza, I. (1899-1969). Joined Indian army 1921 and selected for political service 1926; Defence Secretary in Pakistan 1947; Minister for Home Affairs 1954; Governor-General 1955 and President of Pakistan 1956-8.

Mookerjee, S. P. (1901-53). Vice-Chancellor of Calcutta University 1934-8; joined Hindu Mahasabha 1939; minister in Bengal 1941-2; Union Minister for Industry and Supply 1947-50; founder of Jan Sangh 1952; died in detention in Kashmir.

Mountbatten of Burma, 1st earl (b. 1900). Chief of Combined Operations 1942-3; Supreme Allied Commander South East Asia 1943-6; Viceroy of India March-August 1947; Governor-General of India August 1947 - June 1948.

Mountbatten of Burma, Edwina, Countess (1901-1960). Married Lord Louis Mountbatten in 1922.

Munshi, K. M. (1891-1971). Minister in Bombay 1937-9; Union Minister of Food and Agriculture 1950-52; Governor of Uttar Pradesh 1952-7; later joined the conservative Swatantra Party.

Nasser, G. A. (1918-70). Deputy Premier of Egypt 1953; Prime Minister 1954-6 and President 1956-70.

Neogy, K. C. (1888-1977). Member of Central Assembly 1921-34 and 1942-7; Union Minister for Commerce 1948-50.

Nizam, Asaf Jah of Hyderabad (1886-1967). Became ruler in 1911; retired from public life in 1956.

Noel-Baker, P. J. (b. 1889). Labour M.P. 1929-31 and 1936-70; Secretary of State for Commonwealth Relations 1947-50.

Nu, U (b. 1907). Joined nationalist party in Burma 1938; Prime Minister 1947-58 and 1960-62; a devout Buddhist.

Nye, Sir A. (1895-1967). Vice-Chief of Imperial General Staff 1941-6; Governor of Madras 1946-8; British High Commissioner in India 1948-52.

Panikkar, K. M. (1895-1963). Historian; served in the Princely States; after 1947 Ambassador to China, Egypt and France; member of the States reorganization commission.

Pant, G. B. (1887-1961). Leading Congressman of U.P.; Chief Minister of U.P. 1937-9 and 1946-55; Union Home Minister 1955-61.

Patel, V. (1875-1950). Organizer of no-rent campaign in Bardoli 1928; President of the Congress in 1931; member of the Interim Government 1946-7; Deputy Prime Minister and Minister for Home, States, Information and Broadcasting 1947-50.

Pearson, L. (1897-1972). Served in Canadian diplomatic service 1928-46; Foreign Minister 1948-57; Prime Minister 1963-8; President of U.N. General Assembly 1952-3.

Pethick-Lawrence, 1st baron (1871-1961). Secretary of State for India 1945-7; member of Cabinet Mission to India 1946.

Pillai, N. R. (b.1898). Joined Indian Civil Service 1921; Secretary-General in Ministry of External Affairs 1952-60.

Pineau, C. (b. 1904). French Minister for Foreign Affairs 1956-7.

Prakasam, T. (1869-1957). Barrister in Madras and leader of Congress in Andhra; minister in Madras 1937-9 and Chief Minister 1946-7; left Congress in 1950 and returned in 1953; Chief Minister of Andhra 1953-4.

Prasad, Rajendra (1884-1963). President of the Congress 1934, 1939 and 1947-8; President of the Constituent Assembly 1946-50; President of India 1950-62.

Radhakrishnan, S. (1888-1975). Professor of philosophy at Calcutta 1921-41 and of eastern religions at Oxford 1936-52; Ambassador to Soviet Union 1949-52; Vice-President of India 1952-62; President of India 1962-7.

Raghavan, N. (1900-77). Educated in Madras; set up legal practice in Malaya 1928; joined Subhas Bose during the war; Ambassador to China 1952-5, Argentina 1956-9 and France 1959-60.

Rajagopalachari, C. (1878-1972). Leading Congressman of Madras; Chief Minister of Madras 1937-9; Governor of West Bengal 1947-8; Governor-General of India 1948-50; Union Minister without Portfolio and then for Home Affairs 1950-51; Chief Minister of Madras 1952-4; founder of the conservative Swatantra Party.

Ranadive, B. N. (b. 1904). Member of Politbureau of Communist Party of India 1947-8 and general-secretary 1948-50; in prison 1962-6; member of Politbureau of Communist Party of India (Marxist) since 1964.

Rau, B. N. (1887-1953). Joined Indian Indian Civil Service 1910; adviser to Constituent Assembly 1947-9; Indian permanent representative at United Nations 1949-52; judge of the International Court 1952-3.

Roy, B. C. (1882-1962). Physician and Congressman of Calcutta; Chief Minister of West Bengal from 1948 till his death.

St Laurent, L. (1882-1973). Lawyer of Quebec; Minister of External Affairs of Canada 1946-8; Prime Minister 1948-57.

Saxena, M. (1896-1965). Secretary of U.P. Provincial Congress Committee 1928-35; Union Minister for Rehabilitation 1948-50.

Shukla, R. S. (1877-1956). Minister in Central Provinces 1937-8 and Chief Minister 1938-9 and from 1946 till his death.

Sri Prakasa (1890-1971). Contemporary of Nehru at Cambridge; secretary of U.P. Provincial Congress Committee 1928-34; after 1947 served as High Commissioner in Pakistan, Union Minister and Governor of Assam, of Madras and of Maharashtra.

Stevenson, A. (1900-65). Governor of Illinois 1949-53; Democratic candidate for presidentship of United States 1952 and 1956; visited India 1953; United States Ambassador at United Nations 1961-3.

Sukarno, A. (1901-70). Leader of Indonesian nationalist movement; President of Indonesia 1949-67.

Tandon, Purushottam Das (1882-1962). Congressman of Allahabad; Speaker, U.P. Assembly 1937-9 and 1946-50; elected President of the Congress 1950 but resigned in 1951 because of differences with Nehru.

Tara Singh (1885-1967). Prominent Sikh leader; agitated for division of East Punjab to provide a separate province for Sikhs.

Thimayya, General K. S. (1906-65). Soldier with distinguished service in Second World War and in Kashmir operations 1947-8; chairman of neutral nations repatriation commission in Korea 1953; Chief of Army Staff in India 1957-61.

Tito, Marshal (b. 1892). Leader of guerilla forces in Yugoslavia during Second World War; Prime Minister of Yugoslavia since 1945 and President since 1953.

Truman, H. S. (1884-1972). Elected Vice-President of United States 1945 and President 1945-53.

Vijayalakshmi Pandit (b. 1900). Sister of Nehru; married R. S. Pandit in 1921 (he died 1944); minister in U.P. 1937-9 and 1946; Ambassador in Moscow 1947-9, and to United States 1949-51; president of United Nations General Assembly 1953-4; High Commissioner in London 1954-61; Governor of Maharashtra 1962-4.

Vyshinsky, A. (1883-1954). Public Prosecutor in Soviet Union 1931-8; Foreign Minister 1949-53; Soviet permanent delegate at United Nations 1953-4.

Zafrulla Khan, M. (b. 1893). Member of Viceroy's Council 1935-41; Judge of the Federal Court 1941-7; Foreign Minister of Pakistan 1947-54; permanent representative of Pakistan at United Nations 1961-4; Judge of the International Court 1954-61 and 1964-70; President of the Court 1970-73.

Glossary

Akali Dal: semi-military organization of the Sikhs
Anna: one-sixteenth of a rupee
'Azad Kashmir': the portion of Kashmir occupied by Pakistan

Bapu: father; Mahatma Gandhi was addressed in this way by Nehru and many others
Bhai: brother

Crore: ten millions or one hundred lakhs

Darshan: sight of a person which is believed to be auspicious

Guru: teacher

Jan Sangh: Hindu communal party

Karma: fate; belief in past actions influencing one's destiny

Lakh (lac): one hundred thousand
Lok Sabha: House of the People; lower house of Parliament

Pie: one-twelfth of an anna

Rajya Sabha: House of States; upper house of Parliament
Rashtriya Svayamsevak Sangh: militant wing of the Hindu communal party

Swadeshi: produced in one's own country

Yuvaraj: crown prince

Zamindari: landowner's estate

Bibliography

Manuscript Sources

Jawaharlal Nehru Papers

Nehru kept copies of all personal and private letters and of most official letters drafted by him. Only copies of official correspondence drafted by others and merely signed by him are not to be found in his papers. These papers are still in the custody of Shrimati Indira Gandhi. They are kept in large files, one for each month, except for correspondence with some leading personalities, which has been kept in separate files.

Nehru Memorial Museum and Library

The files of the All-India Congress Committee

These are of particular importance for the years from 1951, when Nehru was president of the Indian National Congress.

Tape-recordings of the proceedings of the Congress Parliamentary Party

National Archives of India

Purushottam Das Tandon Papers
Rajendra Prasad Papers

University College Library, Oxford

Attlee Papers (some only have been transferred)

Kingsley Martin Papers

At the time of consultation in the possession of Miss Dorothy Woodman

Official records

Some files of the Prime Minister's secretariat.

Published Sources

Constituent Assembly Debates 1947-1950
Constituent Assembly (Legislative) Debates 1947-1952
First Five Year Plan (Delhi 1952)
Second Five Year Plan (Delhi 1956)
Parliamentary (Lok Sabha and Rajya Sabha) Debates 1952-1956

Brecher, M., *The New States of Asia* (London, 1963). It contains the
   transcript of interviews with Nehru in 1956.
Cousins, N., *Talks with Nehru* (London, 1951).
Foreign Relations of the United States 1947, Vol. 3, and 1948, Vol. 5 Part I
   (published by the State Department, Washington).
Mende, T. *Conversations with Mr Nehru* (London, 1956).
Nehru, J., *A Bunch of Old Letters* (Bombay, 1958).
Jawaharlal Nehru on Community Development, Panchayati Raj and Cooperation
   (Delhi, 1965).
Nehru, J., *Speeches* Vol. I, 1946-1949 (Delhi, 1949); Vol. 2, 1949-1953
   (Delhi 1953); Vol. 3, 1953-1957 (Delhi, 1957).
Nehru, J., *India's Foreign Policy* Selected speeches (Delhi, 1961).
Patel, Sardar Vallabhbhai, *Correspondence 1945-1950*, 10 Vols. (Ahmedabad,
   1971-4).

Newspapers and Journals

Only series consulted and not stray issues cited are mentioned here.

The Bombay Chronicle
The Economist (London)
The Hindu (Madras)
The Hindustan Standard (Calcutta)
The Hindustan Times (Delhi)
Manchester Guardian
National Herald (Lucknow)
New York Times
The Statesman (Calcutta)
The Times (London)
The Times of India (Bombay)

Oral Testimony

Nehru Memorial Museum and Library
Kingsley Martin

Names of those who granted interviews to the author have been mentioned in the footnotes.

Secondary Works

Only books and articles involving more than a passing reference are listed.

Acheson, D., *Present at the Creation* (London, 1969).
Austin, G., *The Indian Constitution : Cornerstone of a Nation* (Oxford, 1966).
Lord Birkenhead, *Walter Monckton* (London, 1969).
Brass, P. R., *Language, Religion and Politics in North India* (Cambridge, 1974).
Brecher, M., *Nehru* (London, 1959).
Brecher, M., *The New States of Asia* (London, 1963).
Brecher, M., *India and World Politics* (London, 1968).
Brecher, M., *The Foreign Policy System of Israel* (Oxford, 1972).
Brecher, M., 'India's Decision to Remain in the Commonwealth', *Journal of Commonwealth and Comparative Politics*, (March and July 1974).
Campbell-Johnson, A., *Mission with Mountbatten* (London, 1951).
Cameron, J., *Point of Departure* (London, 1969).
Childs, M., *Witness to Power* (New York, 1975).
Desai, M., *The Story of My Life*, 2 Vols. (Delhi, 1974).
Deshmukh, C. D., *The Course of My Life* (Delhi, 1974).
Dutt, S., *With Nehru in the Foreign Office* (Calcutta, 1977).
Eden, A., *Full Circle* (London, 1961).
Gdo Agung, I. A. G., *Twenty Years of Indonesian Foreign Policy 1945-65* (The Hague, 1973).
Gittings, J., *The World and China 1922-1972* (London, 1974).
Gupta, S., *Kashmir* (Delhi, 1966).
Hanson, A. H., *The Process of Planning* (Oxford, 1966).
Heikal, M. H., *The Cairo Documents* (New York, 1973).
Hodson, H. V., *The Great Divide* (London, 1969).
Lord Home, *The Way the Wind Blows* (London, 1976).
Hughes, R., *Foreign Devil* (London, 1972).
Jain, A. P., 'Kashmir', *Imprint* (June, 1972).
Jeffrey, R., 'The Punjab Boundary Force and the Problem of Order, August 1947', *Modern Asian Studies*, 1974.
Joshi, P. C., 'Land Reform and Agrarian Change in India and Pakistan since 1947', *Journal of Peasant Studies*, January and April 1974.
Kahin, G. Mc., *The Asian-African Conference* (New York, 1956).
Kapur, H., *The Soviet Union and the Emerging Nations* (London, 1972).
Kotelawala, Sir J., *An Asian Prime Minister's Story* (London, 1956).
Laik Ali, *The Tragedy of Hyderabad* (Karachi, 1962).
MacDonald, M., *Titans and Others* (London, 1972).

Madhok, B., *Syama·Prasad Mookerjee* (Delhi, 1955?).

Mahajan, M. C., *Looking Back* (Bombay, 1963).

Menon, K. P. S., *The Flying Troika* (Bombay, 1963).

Miller, J. D. B., *Survey of Commonwealth Affairs: Problems of Expansion and Attrition 1953-1969* (Oxford, 1974).

Millar, T. B. (ed), *Australian Foreign Minister, the Diaries of R. G. Casey 1951-60* (London, 1972).

Nanda, B. R. (ed.), *Indian Women from Purdah to Modernity* (Delhi, 1976).

Nanda, B. R., (ed.), *Science and Technology in India* (New Delhi, 1977).

Narayana Rao, K. V., *The Emergence of Andhra Pradesh* (Bombay, 1973).

Nehru Abhinandan Granth, presented to Nehru on his sixtieth birthday (New Delhi, 1949).

Panikkar, K. M., *In Two Chinas* (London, 1955).

Pearson, L., *Memoirs*, Vol. 2, 1948-57 (London, 1974).

Pyarelal, *Mahatma Gandhi: The Last Phase*, 2 Vols. (Ahmedabad, 1958).

Scarfe, A. and W., *J. P., His Biography* (Delhi, 1975).

Shiva Rao, B., *The Framing of Indian's Constitution*, 5 Vols. (Delhi, 1968).

Stair, D., *The Diplomacy of Constraint* (Toronto, 1974).

Strachey, J., 'Interview with Nehru', *New Statesman* (23 June, 1956).

Strachey, J., 'The Indian Alternative', *Encounter* (October 1956).

Sulzberger, C. L., *The Last of the Giants* (London, 1970).

Tendulkar, D. G., *Mahatma*, 8 Vols. (Bombay, 1963 edition).

Thomson, D. C., *Louis St Laurent: Canadian* (Toronto, 1967).

Tinker, H., *Separate and Unequal* (London, 1976).

Urquhart, B., *Hammarskjöld* (London, 1972).

Zakaria, R. (ed.), *A Study of Nehru* (Bombay, 1959).

Zinkin, T., 'Nehruism: India's Revolution without Fear', *Pacific Affairs*, (September 1955).

Index

Abadan, 167

Abdullah, S. M., 18, 19, 20n, 21, 27, 29, 113, 115; attitude to India, 116-21, 127; agitation against, 122-4; Nehru's appeal to, 124-5, 129, 130-31; arrest and detention of, 132-3, 181; 182, 183, 220, 302-3

Acheson, D.: on meeting with Nehru, 60; on Kashmir, 62; 102, 103n, 110n, 184

Adams, Truslow, 62

Aden, 279

Adenauer, C., 236-7

Addison, first viscount, 85

Afghanistan, 186, 275

Africa, 43, 111, 125, 166; Nehru's attitude to, 167-9, 170-71; 194, 218, 232, 233, 238, 239, 240, 254, 279, 301, 305

Africa, Central, 170

Africa, East, 43; British policy in, 167-9, 170-71

Africa, South, 52, 53, 54, 170, 233

Agarwal, S. N., 245n

Agra, 170n

Agrawal, P. C., 312n

Ahmadnagar, 62, 75n, 260

Ahmedabad, 197n, 271

Akali Dal, 122

Akalis, 66

Algeria, 273, 274, 277

Ali, Aruna Asaf, 85n

Ali, Asaf, 33n, 73n

Ali, Laik, 40 and n, 41

Ali, Mahomed, 128, 129, 132; visits Delhi, 182; 184, 185, 186n, 187, 189, 191, 239, 243

Ali, S. Fazl, 210n, 212n

Allahabad town, 15n, 36, 313n

Allahabad University, 17n, 76n

All-India Congress Committee (AICC), 24n, 86, 149, 152, 155, 205n, 215n, 261n, 268n, 293, 309n

Alvares, P., 216n, 218n

Ambedkar, B. R., 159, 303, 313

Amrit Kaur, 15, 190n, 209n, 310

Amritsar: rioting in, 13; 262-3

Andhra districts, 71, 151, 220, 223

Andhra province, 168, 205, 235; creation of, 256-9; 260, 261

Ankara, 113n

Arabs, 33; Nehru's attitude to, 169-70; 184, 232, 233, 242, 244, 282, 284, 286, 290

Asia, 43, 45, 48, 50, 54, 55, 56, 59, 61, 63, 102, 103, 104, 105, 106, 108, 109, 111, 135, 136, 138, 139, 142, 145, 166, 177, 185, 186, 187, 188, 189, 190, 191, 192, 193, 194, 195, 218, 227, 228, 229, 232, 233, 235, 236, 238, 239, 240, 243, 244, 251, 254, 277, 278, 279, 285, 286, 301, 305, 307

Asia, East, 146, 233, 238, 248

Asia, South, 51, 187, 192

Asia, South East, 65, 97, 194, 238

Asia, West, 114, 183, 187, 232, 238, 277

Asian-African conference (1955), 228, 232-43 (see also Bandung)

Asian prime ministers' conference (1954), 191, 192, 232

Asian Relations Conference (1947), 238

Assam, 72n, 88, 176, 207n, 210, 211n

Assam, Government of, 207, 210, 211, 212

Assembly, Constituent, 15n, 20n, 34n, 44n, 46n, 54n, 70n, 76, 77, 78, 79, 84n, 256, 257, 300n

Associated Press of America, 158n

Aswan Dam, 277, 278, 283

333

DUE